D1556989

ST ANTONY'S/MACMILLAN SERIES

General editors: Archie Brown (1978–85) and Rosemary Thorp (1985–   ), both Fellows of St Antony's College, Oxford

Roy Allison FINLAND'S RELATIONS WITH THE SOVIET UNION, 1944–84

Said Amir Arjomand (*editor*) FROM NATIONALISM TO REVOLUTIONARY ISLAM

Anders Åslund PRIVATE ENTERPRISE IN EASTERN EUROPE

Omer Bartov THE EASTERN FRONT, 1941–45, GERMAN TROOPS AND THE BARBARISATION OF WARFARE

Archie Brown (*editor*) POLITICAL CULTURE AND COMMUNIST STUDIES

Archie Brown (*editor*) POLITICAL LEADERSHIP AND THE SOVIET UNION

Archie Brown and Michael Kaser (*editors*) SOVIET POLICY FOR THE 1980s

S. B. Burman CHIEFDOM POLITICS AND ALIEN LAW

Renfrew Christie ELECTRICITY, INDUSTRY AND CLASS IN SOUTH AFRICA

Robert O. Collins and Francis M. Deng (*editors*) THE BRITISH IN THE SUDAN 1898–1956

Wilhelm Deist THE *WEHRMACHT* AND GERMAN REARMAMENT

Guido di Tella ARGENTINA UNDER PERÓN, 1973–76

Guido di Tella and D. C. M. Platt (*editors*) THE POLITICAL ECONOMY OF ARGENTINA 1880–1946

Simon Duke US DEFENCE BASES IN THE UNITED KINGDOM

Julius A. Elias PLATO'S DEFENCE OF POETRY

Ricardo Ffrench-Davis and Ernesto Tironi (*editors*) LATIN AMERICA AND THE NEW INTERNATIONAL ECONOMIC ORDER

David Footman ANTONIN BESSE OF ADEN

Bohdan Harasymiw POLITICAL ELITE RECRUITMENT IN THE SOVIET UNION

Neil Harding (*editor*) THE STATE IN SOCIALIST SOCIETY

Richard Holt SPORT AND SOCIETY IN MODERN FRANCE

Albert Hourani EUROPE AND THE MIDDLE EAST

Albert Hourani THE EMERGENCE OF THE MODERN MIDDLE EAST

J. R. Jennings GEORGES SOREL

A. Kemp-Welch (*translator*) THE BIRTH OF SOLIDARITY

Paul Kennedy and Anthony Nicholls (*editors*) NATIONALIST AND RACIALIST MOVEMENTS IN BRITAIN AND GERMANY BEFORE 1914

Richard Kindersley (*editor*) IN SEARCH OF EUROCOMMUNISM

Bohdan Krawchenko SOCIAL CHANGE AND NATIONAL CONSCIOUSNESS IN TWENTIETH-CENTURY UKRAINE

Gisela C. Lebzelter POLITICAL ANTI-SEMITISM IN ENGLAND, 1918–1939

Nancy Lubin LABOUR AND NATIONALITY IN SOVIET CENTRAL ASIA

C. A. MacDonald THE UNITED STATES, BRITAIN AND APPEASEMENT, 1936–39

Robert H. McNeal TSAR AND COSSACK, 1855–1914

David Nicholls HAITI IN CARIBBEAN CONTEXT

Patrick O'Brien (*editor*) RAILWAYS AND THE ECONOMIC DEVELOPMENT OF WESTERN EUROPE, 1830–1914

Amii Omara-Otunnu POLITICS AND THE MILITARY IN UGANDA, 1890–1985

Roger Owen (*editor*) STUDIES IN THE ECONOMIC AND SOCIAL HISTORY OF PALESTINE IN THE NINETEENTH AND TWENTIETH CENTURIES

D. C. M. Platt and Guido di Tella (*editors*) ARGENTINA, AUSTRALIA AND CANADA: STUDIES IN COMPARATIVE DEVELOPMENT, 1870–1965

Irena Powell WRITERS AND SOCIETY IN MODERN JAPAN

Alex Pravda (*editor*) HOW RULING COMMUNIST PARTIES ARE GOVERNED

T. H. Rigby and Ferenc Fehér (*editors*) POLITICAL LEGITIMATION IN COMMUNIST STATES

Hans Rogger JEWISH POLICIES AND RIGHT-WING POLITICS IN IMPERIAL RUSSIA

Marilyn Rueschemeyer PROFESSIONAL WORK AND MARRIAGE

A. J. R. Russell-Wood THE BLACK MAN IN SLAVERY AND FREEDOM IN COLONIAL BRAZIL

Nurit Schleifman UNDERCOVER AGENTS IN THE RUSSIAN REVOLUTIONARY MOVEMENT

Amnon Sella and Yael Yishai ISRAEL THE PEACEFUL BELLIGERENT, 1967–79

Aron Shai BRITAIN AND CHINA, 1941–47

Lewis H. Siegelbaum THE POLITICS OF INDUSTRIAL MOBILIZATION IN RUSSIA, 1914–17

David Stafford BRITAIN AND EUROPEAN RESISTANCE, 1940–45

Nancy Stepan THE IDEA OF RACE IN SCIENCE

Marvin Swartz THE POLITICS OF BRITISH FOREIGN POLICY IN THE ERA OF DISRAELI AND GLADSTONE

Rosemary Thorp (*editor*) LATIN AMERICA IN THE 1930s

Rosemary Thorp and Laurence Whitehead (*editors*) INFLATION AND STABILISATION IN LATIN AMERICA

Rosemary Thorp and Laurence Whitehead (*editors*) LATIN AMERICAN DEBT AND THE ADJUSTMENT CRISIS

Rudolf L. Tökés (*editor*) OPPOSITION IN EASTERN EUROPE

Toshio Yokoyama JAPAN IN THE VICTORIAN MIND

Series Standing Order

If you would like to receive future titles in this series as they are published, you can make use of our standing order facility. To place a standing order please contact your bookseller or, in case of difficulty, write to us at the address below with your name and address and the name of the series. Please state with which title you wish to begin your standing order. (If you live outside the UK we may not have the rights for your area, in which case we will forward your order to the publisher concerned.)

Standing Order Service, Macmillan Distribution Ltd, Houndmills, Basingstoke, Hampshire, RG21 2XS, England.

Latin American Debt and the Adjustment Crisis

Edited by

Rosemary Thorp
Fellow of St Antony's College, Oxford,
Lecturer in Latin American Economics,
University of Oxford

and

Laurence Whitehead
Fellow of Nuffield College, Oxford

MACMILLAN
PRESS

in association with
ST ANTONY'S COLLEGE,
OXFORD

© Rosemary Thorp and Laurence Whitehead 1987

All rights reserved. No reproduction, copy or transmission of this publication may be made without written permission.

No paragraph of this publication may be reproduced, copied or transmitted save with written permission or in accordance with the provisions of the Copyright Act 1956 (as amended).

Any person who does any unauthorised act in relation to this publication may be liable to criminal prosecution and civil claims for damages.

First published 1987

Published by
THE MACMILLAN PRESS LTD
Houndmills, Basingstoke, Hampshire RG21 2XS
and London
Companies and representatives
throughout the world

Typeset by Mid-County Press, London SW15

Printed in Hong Kong

British Library Cataloguing in Publication Data
Latin American debt and the adjustment
crisis.—(St Antony's/Macmillan series)
1. Latin America—Economic conditions
I. Thorp, Rosemary   II. Whitehead,
Laurence   III. Series
330.98   HC123
ISBN 0–333–42648–7 (hardcover)
ISBN 0–333–42649–5 (paperback)

To Carlos

Contents

List of Tables

ix

List of Figures

Notes on the Contributors

Victor Bulmer-Thomas is a Lecturer at Queen Mary College, University of London. He has a doctorate from the University of Oxford.

Dionísio Dias Carneiro is Associate Professor of Economics at the Pontifícia Universidade Católica da Rio de Janeiro. He has an MA from Vanderbilt University, USA.

Carlos Díaz Alejandro was Professor of Economics at Columbia University, New York, until his death in July 1985. He had recently moved there from Yale University.

Guido di Tella is Professor of Economics at the Universidad de Buenos Aires and the Universidad Católica Argentina. He is also President of the Instituto Torcuato di Tella and Associate Member of St Antony's College, Oxford.

José Antonio Ocampo is Director of Fedesarrollo, Bogotá. He has a PhD from Yale University.

Jaime Ros is at present working in CEPAL, Mexico City, and was until recently Director and Researcher at CIDE (Centro de Investigación y Docencia Económica) Mexico. His postgraduate studies were in the Universidad Nacional Autónoma de México and the University of Cambridge, England.

Rosemary Thorp is a Fellow of St Antony's College, Oxford, and Lecturer in Latin American Economics at the University of Oxford.

Laurence Whitehead is a Fellow of Nuffield College, Oxford, and for 1985–6 Director of the Center for US–Mexican Studies, Institute of the Americas, University of California at San Diego.

Preface

This book is the result of collaboration between eight researchers variously based in England, the USA and Latin America. Distance notwithstanding, great efforts have been made to ensure an interchange of views as the chapters were rewritten, and each of us feels a considerable debt to the group as a whole. The concluding chapter in particular benefited greatly from our joint discussions. With financial assistance from the Oxford Interfaculty Committee for Latin American Studies, the International Development Research Center of Canada and the Nuffield Foundation, England, various meetings took place in Oxford and at the LASA Conference in Albuquerque, April 1985, while our final working session took place in Fedesarrollo, Bogotá, in July 1985.

Tragically, by the time of that last meeting Carlos Díaz Alejandro was already in hospital, and he died shortly after. He had completed his chapter in draft form and was anticipating the reiterative process we had planned for Bogotá, whereby his general interpretation could be matched against the country studies, to the enrichment of both. It was our great loss that he was not able to be with us. His paper (Chapter 2 of this volume) is obviously briefer than the final version he would have gone on to write.

As his dear friends and *compañeros de trabajo*, we have dedicated this volume to his memory.

Rosemary Thorp
Laurence Whitehead

1 Introduction

Rosemary Thorp and Laurence Whitehead

In August 1982, Mexico, by then the largest oil producer in Latin America, ran out of foreign exchange. Initially the Mexican government announced a ninety-day moratorium on repayment of the principal due on its external public debt. Soon the moratorium was extended into 1983, and Mexico was forced into a series of drastic remedial measures: severe devaluation, unprecedented exchange controls, an 'unthinkable' nationalisation of the private banks and, of course, an emergency agreement with the IMF.

The credit crunch faced by Mexico was certainly the most dramatic event of 1982, but in reality the financial crisis of that year extended far beyond Mexico. Latin America as a whole was severely affected, as was the US banking system (Mexican debt alone accounted for 44 per cent of the capital of the nine largest US banks) and the prosperity of many US exporters.[1] Even before the Mexican crisis, Argentina was already in technical default for reasons which were only partly related to the South Atlantic conflict of April–June 1982. By the end of the year, Brazil was far advanced down a path similar to that of Mexico. Under pressure to tap new sources of foreign exchange, Brazilian private banks had run up heavy liabilities on the interbank market. Thus they suffered side effects from the Mexican nationalisation. In addition, Brazil's exports were hampered by the international recession, and its large external debt implied a heavy balance-of-payments cost when interest rates rose. Venezuela, Chile and Cuba were soon all engaged in comparable negotiations, together with many of the smaller Latin American countries. Indeed, virtually every nation in the region was shortly either openly negotiating or on the brink of such action.

This book considers the repercussions of these events for Latin American economic development. It is the third in this series to consider the topic of international crisis and the Latin American economy. The first, completed in 1978, considered the adjustment forced on Latin America by the first oil shock of 1974 and its repercussions.[2] Its focus of interest was whether the style of adjustment typically attempted in Latin America was of a nature which permitted long-term accumulation, with a viable political model, and it reached generally negative conclusions. The second studied the development of the crisis of 1929 and its effects on

1

Latin America:[3] although the crisis was devastating and costly, the recovery in Latin America documented in the study was remarkably rapid, in advance of the North American economy, and in some cases of the international economy in general. It was thus possible to perceive positive dimensions to the shock, an element totally absent in the analysis of the 1970s.

This volume takes up the theme again with respect to the 1980s. What is fascinating is how much louder are the echoes of the 1930s study than of our work on the 1970s, with the major difference that the escape routes of the 1930s are not easy options today – we refer principally to default and import substitution.

In 1978, although the changed role of the dollar was already in evidence, it was not yet clear that international recovery required more than learning to recycle OPEC surpluses. Since the breakdown of the Bretton Woods system, the USA has increasingly withdrawn from the responsibility of stabilising the international economy, partly because of the weakening of its relative economic power, and partly in response to domestic political pressures to become more inward-looking. In important respects this mirrors the decline in the role of the UK in the first decades of the century.[4] Curiously, however, whereas the heady lending of the 1920s represented the inexperience of the newly dominant creditor country, the USA, the lending of the 1970s again came out of the USA, the banks having forgotten the lessons of fifty years before. But just as in the 1920s, so today: the rapid expansion and the way loans were used has much to do with the nature and the difficulties of the adjustment crisis. In 1976–8 lending never stopped, except to certain countries, as we see in the next chapter. Today the scenario of 1930 appears more appropriate.

In the 1970s' shock, the crisis was not general. Colombia and Central America did not feature in the first volume, although they do here, for the good reason that they experienced no crisis in the previous round, since in the 1970s luck in the 'commodity lottery' was enough to see a country through. Today not only is the depression of commodity prices as general as in 1929, but also commodity prices alone do not comprise the crisis: we concluded in the 1930s volume that the capital account was then as much involved, a factor neglected by the CEPAL analysis. Today all countries – even Cuba – have borrowed heavily, often rationally at the time, up to a point, and the debt service burden following the rise in interest rates and the cessation of new money is a general problem. Curiously, common to both shocks is the outflow of capital from Latin America – *before* the main shock hit. In the 1920s the outflow occurred in

1928, while this time our case studies show a significant increase in capital flight as early as 1981 from several countries. Also in both crises there was a rather precise date – September 1929, August 1982 – when a 'sea-change' occurred: in 1929 a precipitous collapse of the US stock market, in both a sudden reversal of capital flows and attitudes of creditors.

To understand the behaviour of capital movements in this most recent crisis, factors internal to the USA are key elements in the explanation (again there is a parallel with 1929). First, we should note that much of the debt acquired by Latin America was denominated at floating rates and in dollars,[5] making the continent particularly vulnerable as very low real interest rates on dollar debt became sharply positive following the advent of Paul Volcker as Federal Reserve Chairman in 1979. Interest burdens escalated as interest rates rose and the dollar appreciated. While the tightening of US credit was meant to cut off credit demand in the USA by weak domestic borrowers, the end result of the policy hit the weakest borrowers outside the USA – and particularly Latin American nations, whose interest payments were of course not tax deductible, in contrast to those of most domestic debtors.

The crucial role of the USA in the debt crisis is also illustrated by the reaction of US monetary policy to the spectre of a crash of the world financial system after the Mexican debacle of August 1982. An easing of monetary policy followed, as the crisis threatened disaster for the US banking system. As a result, US growth in the 1982–4 period has been instrumental in improving the trade balance of Latin America. Not only has US real growth exceeded that of Europe (see Table 1.1), but the

Table 1.1 Indicators of the international economy, 1977–84

	1977	1978	1979	1980	1981	1982	1983	1984
US GDP growth	5.5	4.9	2.4	−0.3	2.6	−2.0	3.8	6.8
OECD GDP growth	3.9	4.0	3.3	1.3	1.6	−0.2	2.4	3.4
US inflation rate	6.5	7.7	11.3	13.5	10.4	6.1	3.2	4.2
Dollar price of oil (growth rate)	9.4	6.4	46.4	63.0	10.0	−3.9	−12.3	−1.3
US prime rate (nominal) (%)	6.8	9.1	12.7	15.3	18.9	14.9	10.8	12.0
US prime rate (real) (%)	0.4	1.4	1.4	1.8	8.5	8.7	7.6	8.0

Sources: IMF, *International Financial Statistics*; IMF, *World Economic Outlook*; *Economic Report of the President* (1985).

percentage of debtor country exports bound for the USA has increased. (Unfortunately, the US import bonanza is not likely to continue, which will have serious implications – a topic we return to in the concluding chapter.)

One major difference between 1929 and the 1980s is discussed in Chapter 2, and we will not anticipate its very interesting discussion by Diaz Alejandro, except to comment that it remains a moot point which crisis will be easier to resolve. The 'resolution' which he describes is producing at present an outcome unthinkable in the 1930s: the USA is today a net debtor, financed in part by transfers, legal and illegal, *from* Latin America. The 'adjustment' policies which are making possible such a transfer therefore become critically important to study. Are they actually sustainable and efficient policies? Are they compatible with domestic growth? Are they contributing to capital flight itself, by their effect on growth, social discord, etc.? Our earlier analysis would lead us to expect an unfavourable verdict. However, both the policy environment and the structure of the international economy have changed in unforeseen ways since the 1970s, so that previous interpretations require thorough reassessment.

In fact, the *modus operandi* of these very adjustment policies *has* changed with the changes in the international context which we have outlined – in particular with the rise in interest rates, which is shown in Table 1.1. In the space of two years this introduced a whole new element of vulnerability into the region's balance of payments. A rise in international interest rates of one point means for Brazil, for example, that exports must increase by 3 per cent simply to cover the increased interest burden. But what such a rise did was also to weaken still further the effectiveness of conventional adjustment measures. (By these we mean the 'package' which, in more or less similar form, the IMF and the international banking community usually recommend and try to insist on. It typically comprises credit and fiscal restraint, with targets for the reduction of the fiscal deficit and the money supply, and 'correction' of prices including exchange rates.[6]) As is well recognised, these measures depend for their 'bite' on the effect of internal recession on the consumption of imports; in the 1970s this was already an inefficient method of curing a balance of payments problem, since it often required a severe decrease in domestic activity, and especially investment, to cut imports significantly. With the growth in interest payments, a new component has been added to the balance-of-payments disequilibrium which is not affected at all by the key instrument in use.

What the increase in the interest burden has also done, together with the rise in inflation rates, is to confuse greatly the standard analysis of the fiscal aspect of the disequilibrium.[7] This may lead to misdiagnosis and 'overkill'. The point is as follows: if inflation is present, then an 'interest' payment typically includes an element of repayment of principal as well as a true 'income'. If we are looking to analyse the effect on demand of the public sector's activities, then, as a limiting case, on the expenditure side only that part of the interest payment which is over and above repayment of capital comprises an addition to disposable income. If both inflation and interest are non-negligible, this may lead to a substantial distortion if the correction is not made, and in several of our case studies the accounts used by the government and by international agencies do not make it. This can lead to misspecification of policy targets and to 'overkill', as is shown in the Mexican case study.

In a parallel fashion, the fact that most interest payments flow directly out of the economy may distort policy goals. The IMF analysis turns on the causal sequence 'fiscal deficit → excess internal demand → inflation → balance-of-payments disequilibrium'.[8] But fiscal expenditure may flow directly out of the economy, as with public sector imports and now also with interest payments; deflationary measures that affect the *general* level of domestic activity become in this case inappropriate. (This does not of course mean that such expenditure is not inflationary; rather, it is, but via pressure on the exchange rate. See the section below on inertial inflation.)

The new developments we have listed so far have all represented discontinuities, differentiating the 1980s from the previous decade. We must finish with one that is not discontinuous and which is therefore harder to pin down; some may wish to argue that to speak of it as a differentiating characteristic is to exaggerate. But it is of such importance and colours so deeply the analysis of the case studies presented here that we must include it. We refer to the changes brought about by prolonged inflation, and in some cases by prolonged and painful efforts at adjustment.

First, a brief word is needed to clarify the part that inflation plays in 'the adjustment crisis'. The central concern of this book is with adjustment to changes in the international economy and to the resulting burdens of debt: these changes impinge on economies already saddled in varying degrees with problems of internal disequilibrium. Among our case studies the range is from the near price stability of certain countries in Central America to the inflationary conditions of Argentina, where already in the 1970s the rate had once touched 900 per cent. In varying degrees, therefore, depending upon the magnitude of the inflation problem, the priorities of policy-makers and their diagnosis of the interaction between the two sources of disequilibrium, 'adjustment' comes to comprise correction both of the external and internal disequilibrium.

We have argued above that the standard analysis, by the IMF for instance, of the interaction between the two problems is badly flawed. As time passes and inflation becomes an entrenched characteristic of the economy, then a further qualification to the Fund's approach is pertinent. With continuing inflation, a large part of the rise in prices in any one year can usually be explained simply by 'inertia', as the effect of past price rises. In our case studies this is not often or necessarily the result of formal indexation, but of policy responses and private sector expectations revolving around four crucial 'prices': the exchange rate, the interest rate, certain public utility prices and the wage rate. Certain other controlled prices – typically food prices – may also play a strategic role. (Interestingly, the Argentine and Peruvian studies both stress the unimportance of the wage variable, which in the Mexican study emerges as the key in the deceleration of inflation; we return to this in the concluding chapter.)

As inertial inflation becomes entrenched, so inflation becomes less responsive to demand, and therefore to the typical adjustment package used. This, together with the significance of the increased interest burden, explained above, goes far to explaining the diminishing returns to conventional adjustment measures and the growing appeal of so-called 'heterodox shocks' such as the *Plan Austral* adopted in Argentina in mid-1985 and the *Plan Cruzado* in Brazil in early 1986. Inertial inflation has in recent years become so clear-cut that in the Brazilian and Mexican case studies the authors claim very little sensitivity to demand.[9] Others suggest a higher degree of sensitivity, plus asymmetry: a rise in demand may affect inflation where a fall does not. Thus the Peruvian and Argentine studies argue that on occasion pressure of demand may be overlaid on the process of inertial inflation and so accelerate prices. Analytically, what is important is to realise that nominal money supply and nominal public sector borrowing requirements act as very poor indicators of demand pressure; what is needed is a careful isolation of independent real demand pressure.

What may facilitate (if that is the word) the continuance of inertial inflation, apparently independently of declining levels of activity, is the development of 'defence mechanisms'. The various ways that people learn over time to live with inflation and with continued recession, both weaken the political base for an anti-inflation stand and strengthen and perpetuate the cost-price spiral, since businessmen know that certain groups can protect themselves and that therefore their market will continue to exist. This phenomenon is seen in its most pronounced form in countries such as Peru and Bolivia.

One aspect of such defence mechanisms can be observed quite widely, and is an important aspect of the new developments of the 1980s: the changed relationship between the state and the private sector. Faced with lengthy recession, a desperate private sector may in various ways knit itself into the public sector to secure subsidies and guarantees. Chapter 2 takes up the international dimension of this theme. We return in the concluding chapter to an evaluation of the notion that the old-fashioned 'shake-out' simply cannot occur today – just as debts cannot be defaulted on but must be continually rolled over.

In various ways, we are hypothesising, the developments of the 1980s have made short-term adjustment in the conventional manner more difficult and/or less rewarding. Unfortunately, of course, this leads in its turn to more broken agreements, to policy uncertainty and to higher costs in terms of output forgone. All of these elements in their turn aggravate capital flight, and certainly make its reversal unthinkable – this being perhaps the most deadly of the circularities the studies will identify. It is time now to look in some detail at the facts before turning in the conclusion to a further evaluation of some of these points, as well as to a discussion of future options and perspectives.

Notes

1.   'Debt crises were a major factor in reducing US sales in 1983 to at least six Latin American debtor countries. The combined 1982–3 loss in US exports to them totalled nearly $15 billion, equalling over one-half of the total drop in US exports in 1982 and 1983', US Department of Commerce (1984, p. 29).
2.   Thorp and Whitehead (1979).
3.   Thorp (1984).
4.   See Whitehead (1986).
5.   This may seem surprising in the light of the fact that US interest rates were higher at the time than those of other countries. But it is less illogical when one considers that the dollar was thought of as a weak currency for much of the 1970s.
6.   As in the earlier volume, we use the shorthand 'orthodox' or 'conventional' policies, while recognising that very orthodox economists would in fact recommend different measures.
7.   This point is discussed more fully in the concluding chapter.
8.   See the quotations cited by Bulmer-Thomas (p. 296) and by Thorp (p. 226).

9.   Obviously they recognise that at some (theoretical?) point of full
      employment the conventional demand model does comes into operation.

References

INTERNATIONAL MONETARY FUND, *International Financial Statistics*,
    Washington, annual.
INTERNATIONAL MONETARY FUND, *World Economic Outlook*,
    Washington, annual.
Economic Report of the President, Washington, annual.
THORP, R. (ed.), *Latin America in the 1930s: the Role of the Periphery in World
    Crisis* (London: Macmillan, and New York: St. Martin's Press, 1984).
THORP, R. and WHITEHEAD, L. (eds), *Inflation and Stabilisation in Latin
    America* (London: Macmillan, and New York: Holmes & Meier, 1979).
US DEPARTMENT OF COMMERCE, *US Trade Performance in 1983 and
    Outlook* (Washington DC, June 1984).
WHITEHEAD, L., 'Debt, Diversification and Dependency', in K. J.
    Middlebrook and C. Rico, *The United States and Latin America in the 1980s:
    Contending Perspectives on a Decade of Crisis* (University of Pittsburgh Press,
    1986).

2 Some Aspects of the Development Crisis in Latin America

Carlos Díaz Alejandro*[1]

Looking into the future in 1980, few observers would have predicted the magnitude of the development crisis experienced by Latin America since 1982. Now, however, the crisis is often presented as an inevitable consequence of Latin American policy mistakes and even cultural flaws. Some observers focus on foolish macroeconomic policies, others blame long-term policies, such as restrictions on inflowing direct foreign investment.

This chapter will first try to put the crisis of the early 1980s into historical perspective; it will show that several countries managed to achieve reasonable growth rates until 1981, in spite of far from perfect policies. It has become reasonably clear that the interaction of faulty domestic policies with the breakdown of normal international financial markets was the major trigger for the crisis, and that the cartelisation by lenders and their governments of credit supplies has managed to save major international banks, but at the expense of growth in debtor countries. Therefore, the chapter will look in some detail at the origins and growth of Latin American debt, and at the workings of international financial markets since 1982.

Non-financial shocks will also be reviewed, and the performance of different countries will be related to the various shocks, as a step towards isolating the role of more or less effective policies. The chapter will close with a discussion of the prospects for sustained recovery in Latin America.

SOME PERSPECTIVES

In spite of shocks, distortions and mismanagement, ten Latin American republics achieved growth rates in per capita gross domestic product

* *Editors' note*: this chapter was completed as a basis for discussion and comment shortly before the author's death in July 1985. It is obviously shorter and less developed than the version he would have gone on to write. We have included it as he left it, with a few small corrections.

9

(GDP) between 1960/1/2 and 1979/80/81 which exceeded the Alliance for Progress target of 2.5 per cent per annum, a target regarded as ambitious when first promulgated. The ten countries, in descending order of per capita growth, are: Brazil, Ecuador, Mexico, Paraguay, Panama, the Dominican Republic, Costa Rica, Colombia, Guatemala and Bolivia. The list includes not only the three largest countries, but also an interesting assortment of small countries.

The nine relatively slow growers, with per capita GDP annual growth no higher than 1.6 per cent, include, also in descending order of performance: Argentina, Honduras, Uruguay, Venezuela, Chile, El Salvador, Peru, Nicaragua and Haiti. (Venezuela would rank higher if only non-oil GDP were considered.) The list includes the three Southern Cone countries, and three Central American republics. Together with Peru, these seven countries witnessed an unusual degree of political instability, especially during the 1970s. The nine relatively slow growers include the four countries with the highest per capita income in Latin America during the early 1960s (Venezuela, Uruguay, Argentina and Chile), but also two of the poorest (Honduras and Haiti).

A glance at the long-term performance of the two groups of countries suggests caution in making generalisations about the 'Latin model' of development. Vigorous growth was compatible during the 1960s and 1970s with policies and characteristics which during the early 1980s are blamed for poor Latin performance. It would be difficult to argue that the ten relatively good performers suddenly became, during the early 1980s, more corrupt, more hostile to foreign investors and more biased against exports. It is also implausible that countries whose policies could not have been that atrocious for two decades would, in a fit of collective mania, all start blatantly mismanaging their affairs during the early 1980s. It remains to be seen, later in the chapter, whether the pre-1981 relatively good performers have weathered the early 1980s crisis better than the chronic poor growers.

A look at indicators of foreign trade will also stress the region's heterogeneity, and dispel some of the more superficial diagnoses of the crisis. Consider first, in Table 2.1, the growth in the volume of exports between 1971–3 and 1982–4, shown in the first column. Six countries show export volume expansion of at least 6 per cent per annum, not a bad record given the state of the world economy. The six countries, in descending order of performance, are Mexico, Brazil, Chile, Uruguay, Argentina and Paraguay. Excepting Mexico, however, these countries also underwent some of the worst terms of trade losses, as shown in the second column of Table 2.1. One may conjecture that the calculation of

Table 2.1 Foreign trade indicators: average annual growth rates between 1971–3 and 1982–4 (percentages)

	Volume of merchandise exports	Terms of trade	Purchasing power of merchandise exports	Volume of merchandise imports
Argentina	7	−4	2	−1
Bolivia	−2	5	3	0
Brazil	10	−5	4	1
Colombia	1	2	3	8
Costa Rica	2	−2	0	−2
Chile	9	−7	1	−1
Dominican Rep.	1	−2	−1	2
Ecuador	3	7	10	8
El Salvador	0	−2	−2	0
Guatemala	3	−3	1	2
Haiti	4	−1	3	6
Honduras	2	−1	1	3
Mexico	14	2	16	4
Nicaragua	0	−5	−5	0
Panama	0	−6	−5	−2
Paraguay	6	−3	3	8
Peru	2	0	2	3
Uruguay	8	−5	3	3
Venezuela	−6	13	6	6

Sources: United Nations, Economic Commission for Latin America, *Statistical Yearbook for Latin America 1983* (June 1984); Enrique V. Iglesias, 'La Economía Latinoamericana durante 1984: Un Balance Preliminar', *Revista de la CEPAL*, no. 25 (April 1985).

the foreign trade indices could involve a spurious negative correlation between prices and quantities, a conjecture not easily investigated. Or for the highly indebted non-oil countries (Brazil, Chile, Uruguay and Argentina) the data could be signalling a partial transfer problem, e.g. attempts to expand export volume, to service debt, have been partly offset by the induced deterioration in terms of trade.

Oil countries, of course, did much better even when volume suffered. Mexico, Ecuador and Venezuela registered the fastest growth in the region for the purchasing power of exports, shown in the third column of Table 2.1. The Mexican and Venezuelan data clearly indicate that the troubles of the early 1980s could not have been produced solely by negative external shocks in the trade account.

The poor or mediocre trade performance of the rest of the countries shown in Table 2.1, mostly small countries, seems to fit the usual eclectic explanation of weak prices, sluggish external demand and insufficient domestic supply incentives. The terms of trade deterioration for Central American and Caribbean republics, spanning eleven years, is nevertheless remarkable and must be regarded as exogenous.

The last column of Table 2.1 shows growth rates for import volume. For the whole period, most major debtors registered import volume expansion lower than the growth of the purchasing power of exports. It will be seen below that import volume expanded vigorously between 1971–3 and 1979–81, collapsing during 1982–4, far more than the purchasing power of exports. This is a story familiar from the 1930s when, during the early years of the crisis, attempts to maintain debt service squeezed imports beyond depressed exports. Once these efforts were abandoned, import volume recovered at a faster rate than export purchasing power.[2] When the period 1971–3 to 1982–4 is viewed as a whole, it remains striking that few countries were able to raise the growth trend in import volume above that for the purchasing power of exports.

So why did countries such as Brazil and Mexico, which during 1960–2 to 1979–81 grew in per capita terms at rates around 4 per cent per annum, and whose export volume expanded at 10 per cent and more during the 1970s, run into such unprecedented troubles during the early 1980s? And why has the crisis affected, to a greater or lesser degree, all countries in the region? Table 2.2 shows that between 1979–81 and 1982–4 only Panama, Paraguay and the Dominican Republic escaped a fall in per capita GDP. Remarkable declines in per capita GDP were registered in Argentina, Bolivia, Costa Rica, Chile, El Salvador, Guatemala, Honduras, Peru, Uruguay and Venezuela.

I have argued elsewhere[3] that what could have been a serious but manageable recession during the early 1980s in Latin America has turned into a major development crisis mainly because of the breakdown of international financial markets and an abrupt change in conditions and rules for international lending. Unsatisfactory domestic policies during the late 1970s, and a sluggish recognition of the changed international conditions during the early 1980s, left most countries very vulnerable to the *de facto* cartelisation of lending to Latin America. Bargaining power was shifted decisively in favour of creditors, who have taken advantage of the new circumstances 'to improve the quality of their assets' (e.g. forcing countries to guarantee *ex-post* or subsidise private debts) and to maintain, with few concessions, the normal collection of interest and fees.

We now turn to elaborating on these basic themes.

Table 2.2 Average annual growth rates in per capita gross domestic product

	1960–2 to 1971–3	1971–3 to 1979–81	1979–81 to 1982–4
Argentina	2.5	0.3	−3.7
Bolivia	3.4	1.6	−7.3
Brazil	4.1	4.8	−1.8
Colombia	2.6	2.9	−0.3
Costa Rica	3.7	2.2	−4.7
Chile	1.8	0.7	−4.1
Dominican Rep.	3.3	3.2	0.8
Ecuador	3.0	4.9	−1.4
El Salvador	2.1	−0.1	−7.5
Guatemala	2.9	2.5	−4.0
Haiti	−0.9	2.0	−2.5
Honduras	2.0	1.1	−3.3
Mexico	3.7	3.5	−1.2
Nicaragua	2.8	−2.9	−0.4
Panama	4.5	1.9	1.9
Paraguay	2.2	5.5	0
Peru	1.7	0.4	−3.3
Uruguay	0.4	3.3	−4.3
Venezuela	2.0	0.8	−4.2

Sources: as in Table 2.1.

DEBT: ORIGINS AND GROWTH

As late as the end of 1980 only Brazil, Costa Rica and Nicaragua had ratios of total debt, net of international reserves, to exports of goods and services larger than two. (Mexico had also exceeded that ratio in 1979.) Since the end of 1980 that ratio exploded in most countries, as can be seen in Table 2.3. Declining international reserves and exports, the servicing of debt by further debt, and the registration of previously 'hidden' debt all contributed to sharp increases in the ratio of net debt to exports; see especially those for Argentina, Chile and Uruguay.

Current account deficits may be financed by direct foreign investment, the use of reserves, concessional aid or expansions in debt. With the exception of Argentina, Mexico and Venezuela, there is a remarkable coincidence between accumulated current account deficits from 1970 to 1980, and the net debt at the end of 1980. A number of compensating errors may be at work, but the fit between the first two columns of Table 2.4 is nevertheless impressive. Only Argentina, Mexico and Venezuela show a net debt by the end of 1980 substantially higher than the

The Development Crisis in Latin America

Table 2.3 Ratio of total debt, net of reserves, to exports of goods and services

	1978	1979	1980	1981	1982	1983
Argentina	0.84	0.75	1.60	2.59	4.02	4.37
Bolivia	2.05	1.65	1.58	1.96	1.97	2.92
Brazil	2.77	2.73	2.64	2.63	3.56	3.77
Chile	1.76	1.22	1.11	2.08	2.82	3.07
Colombia	0.35	0.02	− 0.03	0.36	0.77	1.62
Costa Rica	1.62	1.95	2.45	2.68	2.84	2.97
Dominican Rep.	1.33	1.09	1.19	1.02	1.53	na
Ecuador	1.29	1.06	1.14	1.69	2.08	na
El Salvador	0.63	0.40	0.63	1.23	1.54	na
Guatemala	− 0.03	− 0.02	0.16	0.69	0.86	1.13
Haiti	0.78	0.85	0.85	1.43	1.46	1.57
Honduras	1.11	1.24	1.40	1.77	2.14	2.42
Mexico	2.78	2.29	1.83	2.20	2.93	3.07
Nicaragua	1.24	1.44	2.95	3.53	5.76	na
Panama	0.93	0.73	0.27	0.22	0.29	0.44
Paraguay	0.45	0.18	0.11	0.18	0.58	1.36
Peru	3.62	1.74	1.40	1.87	2.18	2.74
Uruguay	0.07	− 0.27	− 0.15	0.73	1.68	2.30
Venezuela	0.72	0.61	0.59	0.66	0.95	1.24

Note: na means data are not available.

Sources: total disbursed debt, at the end of the year, obtained from Naciones Unidas, Comisión Económica para America Latina y el Caribe, *Balance Preliminar de la Economía Latinoamericana Durante 1984*, Santiago de Chile, 20 December 1984, Table 13. International Reserves, at the end of the year, and yearly exports of goods and services, obtained from the World Bank, *World Debt Tables; External Debt of Developing Countries, 1984–5*, Washington DC, 1985.

accumulated current account deficits; for Mexico this may involve an already significant net debt in 1970.

The third and fourth columns of Table 2.4 carry out a similar comparison for 1981–4; data only allow examination of *gross* debt and its changes during the period 1981–4. The contrast between Argentina, Mexico and Venezuela and the rest of the region is even more marked than for previous years; for most countries the accumulated current account deficits are higher than the increase in gross debt, while for Argentina, Mexico and Venezuela the opposite is the case, by a large margin. The gap for these three countries is impressive, and suggests very large private capital outflows; the last two columns of Table 2.4 show a gap of US $132 billion between their gross debt at the end of 1984 and current account deficits accumulated from 1970 to 1984. (Venezuela, of course, had an accumulated surplus.)

From 1970 to 1980, only Argentina, Colombia and Venezuela had surpluses in the non-factor payments items of the current account. Even systematic and early borrowers, such as Brazil and Mexico, experienced significant net real resource inflows, as conventionally defined. As shown in Table 2.5, this situation changed drastically in the period 1981 to 1984; during those four years, net factor payments typically exceeded those of the previous eleven years, and net real resource outflows (surpluses in the non-factor payments items) were registered in Argentina, Bolivia, Brazil, Costa Rica, Ecuador, Mexico, Uruguay and Venezuela.

Tables 2.3 to 2.5 indicate that different countries came to their debt problem in a variety of ways. Until the end of 1980 some of the then most heavily indebted countries, relative to their exports, appear to have used debt to finance current account deficits, including substantial real net resource inflows. Brazil and Costa Rica are clear examples of this old-fashioned way of getting into debt (whether the net resource inflows were prudently allocated is difficult to evaluate with available data). Even before 1981–4 other countries, especially Argentina and Venezuela, appear to have had two processes continuing side by side: increasing debt together with substantial accumulation of private assets abroad. Since 1981 this combination expanded dramatically; it can be said (and not just in an accounting sense) that the growth in debt went to finance private asset accumulation abroad. Before 1981 Mexico had elements of the two roads to debt; in 1981–4 it became more like Argentina and Venezuela than Brazil and Costa Rica. Finally, since 1980 the increase in interest rates has fuelled debt expansion everywhere; net factor payments by Brazil and Mexico during 1981–4, for example, represented 44 per cent of their total gross debt at the end of 1984.

The accumulation of private Latin American assets abroad, even as 'national' debts were expanding, is difficult to document precisely. There is, nevertheless, some evidence confirming this phenomenon. Table 2.6 presents changes in the US international investment position *vis-à-vis* the aggregate of 'Latin American Republics and other Western Hemisphere' (LAWH, excluding Canada). The coverage of these data is unclear; it probably includes assets and liabilities of Caribbean islands used as conduits for Middle Eastern and other non-Latin American moneys. Nevertheless, the story told by this table is striking and revealing. It can be seen that in 1976 the outflow from Latin America and into the United States was moderate, and inferior to US investment

Table 2.4 Accumulated current account deficits and debt (billion current US dollars)

	(1) Accumulated current account deficits 1970 to 1980	(2) Net debt, end of 1980	(3) Accumulated current account deficits, 1981 to 1984	(4) Increase in gross debt, end of 1980 to end of 1984	(5) (1) plus (3)	(6) Gross debt at the end of 1984
Argentina	2.93	17.87	11.65	20.84	14.58	48.00
Mexico	33.66	45.17	10.53	46.55	44.19	95.90
Venezuela	−5.32	13.15	−7.18	7.49	−12.50	34.00
Sub total	31.27	76.19	15.00	74.88	46.27	177.90
Bolivia	1.14	1.67	1.04	1.67	2.19	3.20
Brazil	63.00	61.48	35.47	33.45	98.47	101.80
Colombia	0.37	−0.20	9.79	4.52	10.16	10.80
Costa Rica	2.90	2.99	1.36	0.87	4.26	4.05
Chile	6.63	6.96	10.22	7.36	16.85	18.44
Dominican Rep.	2.31	1.56	1.56	1.01	3.87	2.85
Ecuador	3.06	3.40	2.67	2.21	5.73	6.86
El Salvador	0.51	0.79	1.11	1.12	1.63	2.30
Guatemala	0.99	0.30	1.41	0.86	2.39	1.91
Haiti	0.54	0.26	0.86	0.31	1.40	0.60
Honduras	1.35	1.35	1.07	0.74	2.43	2.25
Nicaragua	1.31	1.51	2.13	2.32	3.44	3.90
Panama	2.20	2.09	1.77	1.34	3.97	3.55

Paraguay	0.96	0.08	1.29	0.70	2.25	1.56
Peru	4.49	6.79	5.70	3.91	10.19	13.50
Uruguay	1.86	−0.25	0.82	2.54	2.69	4.70
Sub total	93.62	90.78	78.27	64.93	171.92	182.27

Sources: Current account data obtained from United Nations, Economic Commission for Latin America, *Statistical Yearbook for Latin America, 1983* (June 1984), and *Balance Preliminar De La Economía Latinoamericana Durante 1984* (December 1984). Total disbursed debt also obtained from the *Balance Preliminar*. Net debt obtained by subtracting international reserves from gross disbursed debt; reserves obtained from the World Bank, *World Debt Tables*; *External Debt of Developing Countries, 1984–5* (Washington DC, 1985).

Table 2.5   Composition of current account deficits, 1970–84 (billion current US dollars)

	1970–80		1981–4	
	Net factor payments	*Rest of current account deficit*	*Net factor payments*	*Rest of current account deficit*
Argentina	6.92	−3.99	19.49	−7.84
Bolivia	0.79	0.35	1.67	−0.63
Brazil	29.55	33.45	46.18	−10.72
Colombia	2.48	−2.11	2.68	7.11
Costa Rica	0.86	2.04	1.44	−0.08
Chile	4.08	2.55	7.06	3.16
Dominican Rep.	1.12	1.19	1.18	0.38
Ecuador	2.04	1.03	3.24	−0.57
El Salvador	0.32	0.19	0.62	0.49
Guatemala	0.45	0.53	0.36	1.05
Haiti	0.10	0.44	0.06	0.80
Honduras	0.63	0.72	0.70	0.37
Mexico	22.96	10.70	40.01	−29.48
Nicaragua	0.67	0.64	0.38	1.74
Panama	0.59	1.61	1.01	0.77
Paraguay	0.17	0.79	0.08	1.21
Peru	4.10	0.39	4.51	1.19
Uruguay	0.58	1.28	0.90	−0.08
Venezuela	2.34	−7.66	6.41	−13.60

Sources: as in Table 2.4.

flows into Latin America. After 1976 the outflow of Latin American funds accelerated sharply, reaching high levels. By the end of 1983 the stock of non-official Latin American assets in the USA had reached around $160 billion, not far from the $209 billion owed to US banks. (The returns on these assets are unlikely to be taxed either in Latin America or in the United States.) One may guess that a substantial share of Latin American assets in the USA must be placed in the same banks lending to Latin America. If so, bank officers could have picked up the acceleration in 'capital flight' visible in the late 1970s and deduced that something was amiss, at least in some countries. Apparently, this trend was either unnoticed or ignored. Banks could have reasoned that profits could be earned with some safety by both lending to and borrowing from Latin Americans.

Table 2.6 Changes in international investment position of the United States *vis-à-vis* Latin American republics and other western hemisphere (excluding Canada: LAWH) (average yearly flows, billion current US dollars)

	1971 to 1973	1974 to 1976	1977 to 1979	1980 to 1982	1983	Stock at end of 1983
US official and government assets	0.42	0.79	0.46	1.53	−1.86	14.02
US private assets	2.76	13.83	15.40	40.75	12.13	250.91
US direct investment	(1.17)	(2.48)	(3.76)	(−0.89)	(−3.05)	(29.50)
US bank claims	(1.15)	(10.37)	(10.48)	(41.51)	(13.74)	(208.83)
US other	(0.44)	(0.98)	(1.15)	(0.13)	(1.44)	(12.58)
Total US assets	*3.18*	*14.62*	*15.85*	*42.27*	*10.27*	*264.93*
LAWH official assets	0.29	0.84	0.42	0.03	0.25	6.69
LAWH direct investment	0.60	0.35	0.78	2.41	0.52	13.18
LAWH other assets	0.91	3.50	10.58	22.95	27.05	147.72
Total LAWH assets	*1.81*	*4.68*	*11.78*	*25.39*	*27.81*	*167.59*

Sources: United States Department of Commerce, International Investment Position of the United States by major geographic areas. Data kindly made available by Dr Russell B. Scholl, Chief, Private Capital Branch, Balance of Payments Division, Bureau of Economic Analysis, US Department of Commerce.

A crucial justification for the post-August 1982 creation of an international credit orderly marketing agreement (ICOMA) under the titular leadership of the IMF, was the need to 'bail in' banks which otherwise might try to cut back their lending positions. As can be seen in Table 2.7, the net results of this strategy have been meager; the trend is also discouraging. The 'bailing in' appears to have been concentrated in the two biggest debtors, Brazil and Mexico; even for these two potential threats to the welfare of the biggest international banks, net lending of $4 billion during 1984 appears modest indeed. No 'bailing in' is visible for the smallest countries, most of which have had better debt indicators than Brazil and Mexico.

Table 2.7 New loans from international banks, 1982–4 ($US billion)

	1982	1983	1984	Total
Brazil and Mexico	9.93	5.15	4.06	19.14
Chile, Colombia and Uruguay	1.86	1.09	0.33	3.28
Argentina, Peru and Venezuela	0.52	0.07	−4.01	−3.43
Bolivia, Costa Rica, Dominican Republic, El Salvador, Guatemala, Haiti, Honduras, Nicaragua, Paraguay and Ecuador	−0.73	−0.35	−0.60	−1.69

Source: Bank for International Settlements, *International Banking Developments, Fourth Quarter 1984*, Basle, April 1985, Table 5. New loans have been calculated as changes in bank assets *vis-à-vis* different countries.

One area where international banks have exerted their enhanced bargaining power since 1982, with the tacit support of their governments and of the IMF, has been in the incorporation of previously unguaranteed private debts into the public debt. Rescheduling agreements have been held up until governments agreed to subsidise purely private enterprises indebted to international banks. For some countries, e.g. Chile, this process has sharply increased debt burdens on both the balance of payments and the national budget. No coherent justification for this procedure has been provided; countries have accepted it under threat of a credit and perhaps a commercial embargo. Few features of the post-1982 ICOMA reveal more clearly the abuse of asymmetric power. As a blunt banker in Argentina has stated: 'We foreign bankers are for the free-market system when we are out to make a buck and believe in the state when we're about to lose a buck. This thing will come down to a matter of muscle'.[4]

OTHER SHOCKS AND PERFORMANCE

Shocks received via the trade account during the early 1980s were also quite severe for most countries, and no doubt reinforced the bankers' reluctance to lend. Declines in terms of trade between 1979–81 and 1982–4 were comparable to those registered during the early 1930s for

Table 2.8   Foreign trade indicators: average annual percentage changes between 1979–81 and 1982–4

	Terms of trade	Purchasing power of merchandise exports	Volume of imports
Argentina	−2.5	0.3	−16.3
Bolivia	1.6	−5.1	−15.2
Brazil	−6.4	3.7	−9.9
Colombia	−0.7	−5.9	6.9
Costa Rica	−8.1	−8.6	−14.4
Chile	−8.6	−3.4	−14.8
Dominican Rep.	−7.5	−10.0	−5.9
Ecuador	−5.1	−2.4	−10.6
El Salvador	−6.7	−14.9	−8.2
Guatemala	−10.2	−11.0	−13.1
Haiti	−5.5	−1.8	−1.9
Honduras	−4.9	−7.1	−9.0
Mexico	−5.9	11.1	−18.7
Nicaragua	−8.9	−12.9	−2.1
Panama	−8.0	−10.5	−5.4
Paraguay	−7.1	−5.9	−6.1
Peru	−8.6	−9.1	−3.7
Uruguay	−3.4	2.8	−16.8
Venezuela	0.8	−5.4	−6.8

Source: as in Table 2.1.

several countries (e.g. Brazil and Central American republics). As can be seen in the first column of Table 2.8, only Bolivia and Venezuela escaped worsening terms of trade.

Domestic influence over export volume may be presumed to be greater than that over terms of trade, although various countries are likely to have quite different degrees of influence over their export volume. The second column of Table 2.8 combines terms of trade and export volume; Brazil, Chile, Mexico and Uruguay managed significant gains in volume, while volume losses are noteworthy for Bolivia, Colombia, El Salvador, Nicaragua and Venezuela. The combined terms of trade and volume losses were particularly severe for Central American republics, and for Peru and the Dominican Republic.

The last column of Table 2.8 refers to a variable highly influenced by domestic policy, at least in the short term. The collapse of import volumes during 1982–4 is sharp; only Colombia escaped the import squeeze. For most countries the decline in import volume far exceeds that of the purchasing power of exports, reflecting both the cessation of net capital inflows and the maintenance of hefty interest payments. The negative gap between changes in import volume and export purchasing power has been especially high for Argentina, Bolivia, Brazil, Chile, Mexico and Uruguay.

The weak export performance, the rise in interest rates and the nationalisation of sundry debts meant that registered interest payments soared as a percentage of exports. Between 1979–80 and 1983–4, as shown in Table 2.9, that percentage more than doubled in Argentina, Bolivia, Costa Rica, Chile, El Salvador, Peru, Uruguay and Venezuela. The increase in this indicator was particularly dramatic for Argentina, Chile, Costa Rica, Uruguay and Venezuela. It may also be seen that during 1979–80 interest payments as a percentage of exports did not seem threatening in most countries; Brazil and Mexico showed the largest burdens, which by 1983–4 was no longer the case.

It can be expected that the various shocks, all sharply reducing foreign

Table 2.9 Interest payments as a percentage of exports of goods and services

	1979–80	*1981–2*	*1983–4*
Argentina	17	43	55
Bolivia	21	40	53
Brazil	33	49	40
Colombia	12	23	22
Costa Rica	15	30	37
Chile	18	42	43
Dominican Rep.	15	17	24
Ecuador	16	27	29
El Salvador	6	10	15
Guatemala	4	8	6
Haiti	3	3	5
Honduras	10	19	18
Mexico	24	34	37
Nicaragua	13	24	19
Panama	na	na	na
Paraguay	13	15	22
Peru	15	23	33
Uruguay	10	18	30
Venezuela	8	17	23

Note: na means data not available.

Sources: as in Table 2.1.

Table 2.10   Performance indicators: total percentage changes between 1979–81 and 1982–4

	Real GDP	Manufacturing output	Gross fixed capital formation
Argentina	− 6	− 9	− 36
Bolivia	− 14	− 23	− 25
Brazil	1	− 4	− 20
Colombia	6	3	10
Costa Rica	− 6	− 8	− 36
Chile	− 7	− 13	− 29
Dominican Rep.	10	10	− 13
Ecuador	4	15	− 29
El Salvador	− 13	− 18	− 25
Guatemala	− 4	− 7	− 27
Haiti	0	− 5	− 5
Honduras	0	− 5	− 24
Mexico	4	0	− 21
Nicaragua	9	9	33
Panama	14	0	− 3
Paraguay	7	2	− 16
Peru	− 2	− 10	− 8
Uruguay	− 10	− 23	− 38
Venezuela	− 4	4	− 29

Sources: United Nations Economic Commission for Latin America, as in Table 2.1.

exchange availability for imports, would impact differently depending on country characteristics, such as degree of openness, capacity to transform and the quality of domestic policy-making. Table 2.10 shows three indicators of performance between 1979–81 and 1982–4; no country performs satisfactorily, but there are variations. Foreign exchange scarcity appears to have impacted with particular force on gross fixed capital formation.

The connection between shocks and performance seems loose, but some patterns can be detected. A cluster of Central American countries (El Salvador, Guatemala and Honduras) experienced severe terms of trade deteriorations, which, weighted by their export to GDP ratios,[5] go a long way towards explaining their poor performance. Interestingly, however, these countries did not experience sharp increases in their interest to export ratio, although they suffered from the drying up of international commercial credit.

Two countries, Chile and Costa Rica, one medium-sized and the other small, witnessed both severe terms of trade deteriorations and sharp increases in interest payments (as shown in Table 2.9). Not surprisingly, their performance indicators are especially grim.

Among the worst performers one also finds Argentina, Bolivia and Uruguay, whose pattern is the opposite to the Central American republics discussed above. For these countries the terms of trade deterioration is mild relative to GDP, but they experienced very sharp increases in the ratio of interest to exports. Bolivia and Uruguay are small countries, whose capacity to transform may be presumed to be limited; the Argentine performance should have been helped by size and resource variety. The decline in investment and evidence on capital flight suggests that domestic factors have also played a significant role in the crisis.

Colombia and Paraguay avoided heavy net indebtedness and their terms of trade declines have also been mild; their relatively good performance is no mystery. The performance of the Dominican Republic, Haiti and Ecuador, all fairly small countries, is reasonably good; Haiti and the Dominican Republic had mild increases in interest payments, but experienced significant terms of trade deteriorations. Unlike Central American republics, their domestic circumstances have been relatively tranquil. Ecuadorean oil, and the expectations it creates, probably explains the moderate Ecuadorean performance.

The two largest debtors, Brazil and Mexico, fall between the best and worst performers. Large size and a low export to GDP ratio dampened the impact of worsening terms of trade for Brazil; its capacity to transform allowed significant gains in export volume, even during the crisis years. Its interest payments, while high relative to exports, did not increase much between 1979–81 and 1982–4. Avoidance of capital flight also helped Brazil to weather the crisis. Mexican capital flight has been high, but oil resources appear to have provided substantial strength, as indicated by the relatively strong growth in the purchasing power of exports during the crisis years.

There are puzzling gaps between shocks and performance, which are not easily explained. The Nicaraguan and Panamanian performances are too good relative to trade and debt indicators, especially given the small size of these two countries. On the other hand, the Venezuelan performance is surprisingly poor, given trade and debt indicators; for the Venezuelan case domestic factors, including capital flight, must bear a large share of the blame for the crisis.

IN RETROSPECT AND PROSPECT

Even those who have criticised the way the debt crisis has been handled since August 1982 have agreed that international emergency measures avoided a worse catastrophe. By mid-1985 one begins to doubt this consensus. Imagine a counterfactual where banks and countries had been left alone to work out their differences, with the central banks of industrialised countries and the International Monetary Fund limiting themselves to a strict lender-of-last-resort function. Perhaps some large banks would have gone bust, but with alert central banks maintaining overall liquidity, a generalised financial crash could have been avoided. In retrospect, it appears that the fate and prosperity of a few international banks were much too rigidly linked to the stability of the international financial system.

Under the counterfactual scenario, the bargaining power of most countries would have been stronger; events such as the nationalisation of private debts would have been unlikely, and some debt write-offs could have been negotiated. The countries would have gone through difficult months and even years, as credit dried up. But most countries have received few net credits since August 1982 anyway. As in old-fashioned financial crises, in the counterfactual scenario a sharp restructuring period would have 'cleared up' much of the excess debt burden, with both lenders and borrowers suffering from their bad forecasts.

The *laissez-faire* cum lender-of-last-resort scenario is not the only one imaginable. Another, similar to what actually occurred but accompanied by the provision of public funds and debt restructuring, including the writing-off of hopeless loans, would have been preferable.

The prospects, as of mid-1985, for a resumption of growth at historical rates were not encouraging. The Mexican experience during late 1984 and early 1985 illustrates the difficulties. Mexican growth picked up, but so did imports; the trade surplus declined, generating pressures from alarmed bankers to brake growth. The variables determining growth and balance of payments prospects for most countries remain what they have been: export growth, net new lending and international interest rates. Only the last variable looked better by mid-1985 than it had a year earlier. An expansion and normalisation of net lending continues to be postponed into a misty future. Collectively, bankers remain wedded to expecting trade surpluses from Latin America for many years. Unless unprecedented export booms can be engineered, such an expectation appears highly unrealistic.

26   The Development Crisis in Latin America

Notes

1.   I am grateful to Mr Andres Bianchi, of the United Nations Economic
      Commission for Latin America, for much kind help.
2.   A classic contrast is between Argentina, which maintained service of its
      national debt throughout the 1930s, and Brazil, which by the second half of
      the 1930s had sharply reduced service payments. Merchandise imports,
      expressed as percentages of merchandise exports, evolved as follows:

	1925–9	1930–4	1935–9
Argentina	92	83	75
Brazil	88	70	87

      For more on this see Díaz Alejandro, 1982, pp. 336–8.
3.   See Díaz Alejandro, 1984, pp. 335–405.
4.   See Hatch, 1985. Foreign banks were reported to be angry that the
      Argentine government would not assume unguaranteed loans owed by the
      failed private Banco de Italia y Rio de la Plata. For the Chilean case, it has
      been estimated that debt-relief programmes financed by the Chilean
      taxpayer had a net present value in 1984 of 12 per cent of Chilean GDP. See
      Gallagher, 1985.
5.   This technique for evaluating external shocks has been employed by
      Maddison, 1985.

References

BANK FOR INTERNATIONAL SETTLEMENTS, *International Banking
    Developments*, Basle, quarterly.
DÍAZ ALEJANDRO, C. F., 'Latin America in Depression 1929–39', in Mark
    Gersovitz *et al.* (eds) *The Theory and Experience of Economic Development:
    Essays in Honor of Sir Arthur Lewis* (London: Allen & Unwin, 1982).
DÍAZ ALEJANDRO, C. F., 'Latin American Debt: I Don't Think We Are in
    Kansas Any More', *Brookings Papers on Economic Activity*, 2, 1984.
GALLAGHER, D., 'Chile after the Fall: Free Market Policy Gradually
    Vindicated', *The Wall Street Journal*, 31 May 1985, p. 23.
HATCH, G., 'Argentina's Banking Woes Aren't Likely to Lead to System's
    Collapse, Experts Say', *The Wall Street Journal*, New York, 24 May 1985,
    p. 29.
IGLESIAS, E. V., 'La Economía Latinoamericana durante 1984: un Balance
    Preliminar', *Revista de la CEPAL*, No. 25, April 1985.
INTERNATIONAL BANK FOR RECONSTRUCTION AND
    DEVELOPMENT, *World Debt Tables: External Debt of Developing
    Countries*, Washington, various issues.
MADDISON, A., 'Growth, Crisis and Interdependence: 1929–38 and 1973–83',
    Development Centre Studies (Paris: OECD Development Centre, 1985).
UN ECONOMIC COMMISSION FOR LATIN AMERICA, *Balance
    Preliminar de la Economía Latinoamericana durante 1984*, Santiago,
    20 December, 1984.

UN ECONOMIC COMMISSION FOR LATIN AMERICA, *Statistical Yearbook for Latin America*, New York, annual.
US DEPARTMENT OF COMMERCE, *International Investment Position of the United States by Major Geographic Areas*, Washington.

3 Long-run Adjustment, the Debt Crisis and the Changing Role of Stabilisation Policies in the Recent Brazilian Experience[1]

Dionísio Dias Carneiro

INTRODUCTION

International shocks are not exactly exceptional events in the economic history of Latin America. Whether ultimately they will constitute a hindrance or a help when we evaluate their long-run consequences for economic development depends on the interplay of the conflicting forces of stabilisation policies enacted to correct the balance of payments or control inflationary pressures and the structural policies adopted to adjust the long-run path of economic development. The Brazilian experience in the past ten years, with international indebtedness, three-digit inflation and long-run adjustment of its productive capacity after the two oil shocks, the general rise in interest rates and the 1982 sudden cut-off of voluntary international lending, is an interesting illustration of this interplay.

The aim of this chapter is to describe and evaluate the recent experience of the Brazilian economy over the past five years (1979–84) in the context of the painful adjustment policies to which it has been subjected since the end of the last decade.

Brazil has not suffered from the abundance of oil that lies behind today's problems for Mexico and Venezuela, or from the severe financial entanglements stemming from monetarist experiences that plague Argentina and Chile, or the political stalemates of Chile and Nicaragua. Nevertheless, the Brazilian story of international indebtedness post 1974 has elements that seem to be present to some degree in every Latin American country. We must keep in mind the excessive confidence in the country's potentialities, the political obstacles to achieving radical changes in expenditures, and the fragility of its incipient (albeit swollen) financial sector when we set ourselves the task of drawing a realistic sketch of the factors behind the accumulation of the largest foreign debt of any developing country up to the first half of the 1980s.

The second section of the chapter briefly sketches the major issues involved in the design of development and stabilisation policies in the late 1970s. The third section describes the conflicts of such policies in the first two years of the Figueiredo government (1979–85). The fourth section analyses the policy reactions following the first signs of binding financial constraints, and the fifth covers internal developments after the interest rate shock and the immediate consequences of the failure of international capital markets up to the economic recovery of 1984. The final section presents some conclusions as to the perspectives of the Brazilian economy.

The picture that emerges is blurred: a blend of success with import substitution strategies cum export promotion, side by side with economic blunders in the domain of short-run macroeconomic policy; a relatively peaceful democratic transition, together with a dangerously high rate of inflation, in the 200 per cent range; the maintenance of a growth-prone economy which has its investment potential reined back by a need to transfer annually around 4 per cent of its GDP to international creditors.

The main empirical conclusions of the chapter are: (i) that there has been an important structural adjustment in the Brazilian economy in the past ten years reflected in improved exploitation of its natural resources, a lower dependence on imported oil and on imported industrial inputs, a higher export coefficient, and a viable current account in spite of the high interest payments it has to face in the next years; (ii) that the long-run adjustment to the post-1973 international conditions was not accomplished without deep policy conflicts, whose solution has not always obeyed the canons of economic rationality but rather the narrow limits of political feasibility; (iii) that the particular political bounds which defined the contours of feasible short-run policies in fact ended up favouring long-run structural adjustment; and (iv) that since most of the foreign debt accumulated in the process is held by the public sector, future servicing of the debt will require that real resources be transferred from the private to the public sector. The particular way this transfer is promoted will have an important bearing on future distributive outcomes of the present policy dilemmas.

The main theoretical conclusions are that the demand-led model –

which, it will be seen, inspired all too many of the different policy efforts – is wrongly based: the evidence reveals that restrictive policies were perverse in their effect on inflation, which by contrast is well explained by changes in controlled prices, costs and indexation. Secondly, relative price policies aggravated inflation, but perhaps less than they might have since they were strongly backed by long-run structural adjustment policies.

THE STARTING POINT: THE BRAZILIAN ECONOMY FACING THE 1980s

Brazilian economic growth between the second half of the 1960s and the first years of the 1970s exhibits distinctive features when compared with previous experiences. The average growth rate of industrial output was 13.7 per cent between 1967 and 1973. The composition of industrial growth showed an imbalance in favour of durable consumption goods, which had grown at 22 per cent per annum, whereas capital and intermediate inputs had more moderate rates (respectively 15 per cent and 13.4 per cent per annum) and non-durable consumption goods, which encompass the traditional industries, grew at the relatively modest average rate of 8.6 per cent. Tables 3.1 and 3.2 exhibit the structure of production and employment of manufacturing industry at the end of the so-called 'miracle' years, when it tended to be closer to that of modern industrialised countries than to that of underdeveloped economies.

The structural fragility of the pattern of growth followed by the Brazilian economy up to the mid-1970s has been abundantly analysed in the literature.[2] It then seemed necessary to maintain a highly unequal income distribution in order to generate the structure of consumption demand in line with the continuous expansion of the durable goods sector, as well as to provide savings compatible with the increasing share of investment in income. The role of the state, which had surpassed any expectations that could be justified by the dominant ideological content of public discourse, was to keep an increasing share of the state in the process of investment–savings intermediation so that it could channel the necessary savings into infrastructure investments and the provision of basic inputs, as well as mobilise cheap capital for private projects. The control of the process of financial intermediation was thus crucial in harnessing private initiative to long-run priorities. The option for an outward-looking strategy had a double goal: to avoid the worst

Table 3.1 Brazil: growth of manufacturing industry and structure of production (%)

Sectors	Average annual growth			Structure of production		
	1976/80	1981/3	1984	1975	1980	1984
Non-metallic minerals	18.1	−9.0	1.0	3.9	4.1	3.5
Foundry/metal processing	8.4	−6.9	13.3	13.1	13.8	14.3
Engineering	5.0	−15.3	14.5	8.7	7.8	6.2
Electrical goods/ communications	10.8	−9.2	3.5	4.5	5.3	4.7
Transportation	5.9	−13.2	8.4	8.2	7.7	6.2
Paper/cardboard	11.6	0.4	6.4	2.3	2.8	3.4
Rubber	6.5	−7.0	12.6	1.6	1.5	1.5
Chemical	8.6	−1.2	8.7	17.9	19.1	22.8
Pharmaceutical	2.4	−1.7	8.8	1.4	1.1	1.3
Perfumery	9.3	0.4	−0.7	0.7	0.8	0.9
Plastic goods	10.0	−8.9	1.3	1.8	2.1	1.8
Textile	5.7	−7.0	−8.8	7.4	6.9	6.1
Clothing/footwear	6.6	−2.5	3.1	3.6	3.5	3.8
Food	5.2	2.5	−0.9	15.1	13.8	16.7
Beverages	8.0	−7.5	0.1	0.9	1.0	0.9
Tobacco	5.3	0.8	0.6	0.7	0.6	0.7
Others	–	–	–	8.2	8.0	5.2
Total	7.2	−5.0	5.9	100.0	100.0	100.0

Sources: CNI, *Política Industrial*, background paper for the 'Encontro Nacional de Indústria', September 1984. Updated by the author from Fundação Instituto Brasileiro de Geografia e Estatística (FIBGE), *Indicadores Conjunturais da Indústria*, Rio de Janeiro, July 1985.

distortions of import-substitution industrialisation and to maintain a steadily rising import capacity to prevent foreign exchange scarcity from checking the continuity of a pattern of industrial growth increasingly dependent on imports of intermediate and capital goods.[3]

At least two of these three factors of fragility were under strain when the new government took over in 1974. First, the US $6.5 billion increase in import outlays in 1974 caused by the quadrupling in the price of imported oil and the rising costs of machinery and other intermediate goods, accompanied by a fall of about 20 per cent in the import capacity, provoked a fourfold increase in the current account gap to a dramatic 6 per cent of GDP. In spite of the abundance of international finance –

Table 3.2 Brazil: employment in manufacturing industry (%) and structure of employment

Sectors	Average annual growth			Structure of employment		
	1976/80	1981/3	1984	1975	1980	1984
Non-metallic minerals	6.4	− 8.9	− 8.8	7.6	8.0	6.9
Foundry/metal processing	4.1	− 9.8	3.6	11.9	11.3	11.0
Engineering	5.9	− 13.8	3.3	10.7	11.1	9.4
Electrical goods/ communications	6.7	− 11.3	− 8.3	4.9	5.2	4.3
Transportation	4.0	− 9.1	− 2.0	6.0	5.7	5.4
Paper/cardboard	4.8	− 6.4	− 3.3	− 2.4	2.3	2.4
Rubber	4.1	− 9.0	10.2	1.3	1.2	1.2
Chemical	5.8	− 5.7	1.2	3.5	3.5	3.8
Pharmaceutical	0.6	− 8.7	− 8.7	0.9	0.7	0.7
Perfumery	2.9	− 8.3	− 9.5	0.6	0.5	0.6
Plastic goods	8.3	− 8.2	− 0.9	2.2	2.5	2.4
Textile	3.7	− 9.4	− 8.0	9.1	8.5	7.4
Clothing/footwear	7.9	− 1.7	− 2.2	8.1	9.2	11.0
Food	5.4	− 0.5	− 2.6	12.1	12.2	14.9
Beverages	1.4	− 4.2	− 6.5	1.4	1.2	1.2
Tobacco	− 2.6	− 5.3	− 5.1	0.6	0.4	0.4
Others	–	–	–	16.8	16.4	17.0
Total	5.2	− 7.2	− 2.1	100.0	100.0	100.0

Sources: as Table 3.1.

which, in the previous years, had led the government to impose restrictions on foreign borrowing – a loss of reserves of almost $1 billion occurred for the first time since 1967. The impact of the change in the external environment was crucial for the design of the economic policy of the new government and had important implications for the strategy of growth for the next ten years.

Second, the income-concentrating nature of the previous experience was severely criticised; this found echo within the military establishment and narrowed the scope of policy actions required to deal with both the loss of wealth implicit in the change in relative prices and the inflationary pressures from abroad and from a clearly overheated economy.[4] A wage policy that resulted in real wage compression seemed to be a course of action no longer available, if a period of gradual transition towards democracy was to be a reality. Claims for correction in the wage formula could no longer be postponed, and resulted in slight but meaningful increases in government-imposed wage adjustment indices above past rises in the cost of living.[5] On the other hand, political pressures for more relaxed social policies implied higher claims on the fiscal budget for social expenditures. A reduction in government consumption or subsidies found no political support, especially if the political strength of the government were to be tested in the polls as a means to counterbalance the loss of confidence on the part of that portion of the military establishment whom President Geisel referred to as 'sincere but radical revolutionaries'.

The above remarks help us to understand why the availability of international finance was so important in the determination of the long-run strategy adopted by the Geisel government following the first oil shock. If it was virtually impossible to obtain higher domestic savings from either the public or the private sector, owing to income distribution constraints and other political considerations, resort to external funding was the route of least resistance to finance an investment programme designed to redirect the economic structure in line with the new prospects for import capacity. The new investment programme announced in 1975 as part of the second development plan (II PND) was directed at removing the constraints imposed by the fall in import capacity, through the creation of new incentives to the domestic production of intermediate inputs and capital goods, by resorting to an increase in protection through tariff increases and direct import controls. In parallel, a new wave of incentives to manufactured exports was designed.

Finally, another element of fragility was added to the picture, generated essentially by the interplay of anti-inflationary policies in 1974 and stagnationist expectations that followed the slump of world trade in mid-1975. The sudden deceleration of export revenues in the last four months of 1975 brought their rate of growth down from the annual equivalent of 29 per cent (achieved up to August) to 9 per cent at the end of the year, making export growth insufficient to compensate for the increase in service expenditures. The perspective of a permanent current account deficit between US $6 billion and $7 billion and the pressures of a growing debt/export ratio led the economic authorities to adopt a policy of rigid import rationing, whereby priority projects were granted special privileges based upon their contribution either to the reduction of the import coefficient or to the growth of export capacity. In 1976, investments in the production of capital goods and basic inputs (especially metallurgic and chemical) absorbed around 98 per cent of fixed capital outlays approved by the Industrial Development Council (CDI).[6] The so-called 'Programme of Basic Inputs' aimed at reducing external dependence represented by items like paper and pulp, non-ferrous minerals, fertilisers, petrochemicals and steel. By 1979, four years before most projects were scheduled to reach full maturity, such investments allowed a reduction of imports of around US $1.2 billion.[7]

Between 1974 and 1977, the trade deficit had been reduced practically to zero, and nominal imports were kept virtually constant in current dollars, while export revenues were growing at an average of 13.9 per cent per annum. In 1978, due to bad crops which led to a fall of 1.7 per cent in agricultural output, the exports of soybeans, sugar and corn were reduced, and the need to import grains resulted in a trade deficit of $1 billion. Net imports of goods and services went down from $6.1 billion in 1974 to $1.5 billion in 1977, and up again to $2.8 billion in 1978. The story of external indebtedness in the same period can be completed by saying that in spite of the fall in the need for real transfer of resources from abroad, the combined effect of rising nominal interest rates and of the accumulation of debt was to decrease the current account deficit from $7.1 billion in 1974 to $6.0 billion in 1978.

With the increase in the inflation plateau from around 20 per cent per annum in the first half of the decade to 40 per cent in the second half, one may say that the conflict between short-run stabilisation efforts and the need to provide an appropriate environment for long-run structural adjustments and thus a guarantee that economic performance could not be a hindrance to political opening, was solved essentially in favour of the latter.

Following the attempt at monetary control in 1974, and with the help of price controls, inflation rates fell between mid-1974 and mid-1975 from 33 per cent to 24 per cent in annual equivalents. However, signs of recession were detected as the rate of growth of industrial output decreased from 10 per cent to minus 6 per cent. The gains obtained by the opposition party in the November 1974 elections for Congress were thus partly attributed to the recessive measures. They turned out to be an important element in strengthening the role of those in government who favoured long-run adjustment through higher investments and more expansionary fiscal policies.

At the end of President Geisel's term, however, long-run adjustment was still only half-way, since the list of on-going large projects that had to be finished under the next government required an estimated investment expenditure of more than $100 billion.[8]

1979–80: THE GOVERNMENT DEFINES ITS ECONOMIC STRATEGY. OR DOES IT?

In March 1979, President Figueiredo took office with a well-defined political project: the promotion of the transition from military rule to a democratic civilian government. As the last year of his predecessor's government had shown, the feasibility of such a project hinged on his ability to manage both civilian and military forces within the often too-narrow path defined by the need to keep the military establishment bound together by legalism.

On the economic front, several obstacles would have to be faced by the new economic team under the command of Mario Simonsen. In his new capacity as Minister of Planning, Simonsen would have under his control not only the fiscal budget, but also the investment spending of state enterprises and the so-called 'monetary budget'. Contrary to what had been the rule thus far, he would retain the presidency of the all-powerful National Monetary Council (CMN), where most decisions on monetary policy were taken, including the concession of subsidised credit and the size of the financial resources of the National Development Bank.

The likelihood of implementing a stabilisation programme of orthodox inspiration designed to bring inflation back to pre-1974 figures and control external indebtedness was made increasingly remote at the very beginning of the new government's term, by external as well as domestic developments.

The second oil shock was already under way, accompanied this time by a risk of supply shortage because of the deteriorating situation in the Middle East. Interest rates were rising in the USA, and the price of Brazilian exports showed no sign of significant recovery. The prospect of crop failures in several export products, especially soybeans, added up to a dim outlook for the current account.

On the domestic scene, inflationary expectations were rising following a two percentage point rise in the March inflation rate to 5.8 per cent if compared to 3.7 per cent in the first two months of the year, and of three points if compared with the average monthly rate of the previous year. In annual figures, the March rate represented a more than doubling of the rate of inflation relative to that of the previous year. The increase in strike pressure for higher wages in the state of São Paulo, the announced exchange-rate devaluation exceeding current inflation, and finally the intention to promote a bumper crop in the following year by raising minimum guaranteed prices for agricultural products by an average of

70 per cent, eroded any remaining public confidence in the orthodox control of demand as intended by the new government. In fact, following a diagnosis of excessive monetary expansion in the previous year due to a balance-of-payments surplus of $3.9 billion, the new government had promoted an emergency plan according to which a fiscal surplus of Cr$40 billion (around 1 per cent of expected GDP) was to be achieved in 1979, by cutting public enterprises' permits to borrow; it also tried to control private spending via credit controls and restrictions on short-term lending by commercial banks.[9]

By the end of the first six months, facing increasing difficulties in finding political support from the President himself and under harsh criticism from government supporters in Congress, Mario Simonsen resigned and was replaced by the Minister of Agriculture. Delfim Netto took office following a wave of protest, including politicians and industrialists, against the menace that soaring interest rates represented to the level of economic activity. In his inaugural address as the all-powerful Minister of Planning, Delfim was hailed by entrepreneurs as a sign of a return to the bonanza period of the so-called 'economic miracle'. He promoted an immediate cut of 10 per cent in nominal interest rates, ruled out recession as a solution to the problems of the Brazilian economy, and opted for a vigorous stimulus to agriculture as the key means to control inflation. A draft of the six-year development plan that had been prepared under Simonsen was purged of any reference to smaller growth rates and was used to express the faith of the new economic team in economic growth as a means to deal with inflation and solve balance-of-payments deficits. Since the new plan presented no figures concerning quantitative targets or assumptions about the external constraints, nothing could be said about the official evaluation of the additional pressure that the new priorities for public investment would exert on domestic savings or the need for more international borrowing.

At this point, total investment as a proportion of GDP had declined from a record high of almost 30 per cent in 1975 to 24.4 per cent in 1978, comparable to its level in the first years of the 1970s. Total domestic sources of funds for investment (defined as personal plus entrepreneurial plus government current account surpluses) had declined from 27 per cent of GDP in 1975 to 22 per cent in 1978 (see Table 3.3). This reduction in domestic sources for capital accumulation reflected not only the slight increase observed in private consumption, but also a progressive decline in government disposable income (Table 3.3). Roughly, tax revenues minus transfers and subsidies from central government decreased by

Table 3.3 Brazil: selected economic indicators 1970–84 (as a percentage of GDP[a])

Year	GDP real growth	Investment[b] (1)	Investment[b] (2)	Domestic sources for investment	Import of goods and services	Private consumption	Government disposable income	Net factor income paid abroad
1970	9.5	23.8	23.8	24.2	7.4	63.7	16.6	0.8
1971	12.0	24.7	24.7	23.3	8.1	64.7	16.8	0.8
1972	11.1	24.9	25.2	23.5	8.9	64.7	16.6	0.9
1973	13.6	25.8	25.6	25.3	9.5	63.2	16.8	0.8
1974	9.7	27.3	27.9	23.7	14.0	65.6	14.3	0.8
1975	5.4	29.2	29.6	26.7	11.4	61.3	14.4	1.3
1976	9.7	29.0	26.7	23.4	9.5	64.5	14.9	1.4
1977	5.7	26.8	25.1	23.5	7.9	65.3	13.4	1.4
1978	5.0	27.0	24.4	21.7	7.5	66.7	11.5	1.5
1979	6.4	26.4	22.3	17.5	8.8	70.5	11.6	2.0
1980	7.2	26.3	21.8	17.3	10.6	70.8	10.0	2.6
1981	−1.6	23.5	21.2	17.0	9.4	70.2	10.0	3.4
1982	0.9	22.3	21.2	15.6	8.2	69.5	10.3	4.2
1983	−3.2	19.0	17.0	13.6	8.8	71.2	8.7	4.9
1984	4.5	na	na	na	7.4	na	na	5.1

Notes:
[a] except first column; na means data are not available.
[b] Col (1) At 1970 constant prices.
   Col (2) At current prices.

Sources: Boletim do Banco Central do Brasil and Fundação Getulio Vargas, Contas Nacionais do Brasil, Rio de Janeiro, 1984.

one-third as a proportion of GDP from the first half of the 1970s to 1978. Since the new plan contained no quantitative estimates of the effects of the new strategy on the pattern of transfers of income between the private and the public sector, its announcement could be welcomed by the private sector as positive, in the sense that no additional pressure would be forthcoming. Perhaps in no other instance of Brazilian discussions of policy-making in recent times has wishful thinking so clearly predominated over a realistic appraisal of the constraints limiting the continuation of economic growth without more inflation or higher external deficits. It is hard to overemphasise how far the peculiarity of the political situation at the time set limits to the possibilities of finding support for a programme of fiscal reforms to provide funding for new or ongoing projects, but there are no records of a realistic diagnosis either, and there is some evidence of systematic underestimation of the strain that the financial requirements of ongoing projects would impose on government finances in the following years. The pragmatic style of the new team proved to be a good way to unite Brazilian capitalists and the military establishment around the new government, but, of course, it stopped short of providing a way out of the crucial policy dilemmas.

The accommodating stance of the new economic team had further consequences for the behaviour of the economy in the following years. It became clear, for example, that inflationary pressures would not be a sufficient reason for the adoption of contractionary domestic policies, and that the government would tolerate increasing deficits in the current account of the balance of payments as long as international finance could be made available. In practical terms, there was a belief that private financial markets would provide funds for payments imbalances, given that the country could exhibit a reasonable growth performance and signs of structural adjustment compatible with long-run adaptation to the relative price configuration prevailing in international markets. This meant, of course, accelerating investment in the activities that led to substitution of imported oil and to more export capacity. Apparently, the belief in the role of agricultural prices in bringing inflation back to tolerable levels implied setting incentives to agriculture high on the list of priorities. Finally, the need to put a stop to the labour strikes, seen as a threat to the peaceful transition to civilian rule, led the Congress to approve a government-sponsored law modifying wage adjustments. This law, voted at the end of October and signed by the President at the beginning of November 1979, reduced the interval between wage adjustments from one year to six months, thereby increasing the degree of wage indexation just as the economy was being exposed to successive inflationary shocks stemming from the rise in prices of agricultural products, petrol, fuel oil and other oil derivatives, public tariffs, and wage increases in excess of past inflation following the strikes of the first ten months of the year.

In the second half of 1979, prices were rising at an annual rate of 101.3 per cent, as against 56 per cent per annum in the first six months. The increase in wage indexation implied by the new wage law played an important role in defining this rate as the new plateau around which inflation rates would fluctuate for the next three years.[10] A curious type of argument that related inflation to calendar years led the government, at the end of the year, to decree a sharp devaluation of 22 per cent.[11] In order to prevent speculation over another maxi-devaluation, and to control financial indexation, exchange-rate correction and indexation were pre-announced at target levels of 40 per cent and 45 per cent respectively for the coming year, in an effort to 'bring down expected inflation' and promote a real devaluation without further raising the inflation plateau. Needless to say, the effects of corrective inflation and of the new rhythm of cost increases defined in the wage formula led to the abandoning of the prior fixing of monetary and exchange-rate correction in the middle of the following year, at least three months *after* it was totally discredited.

Attempts to deal with expectations absorbed most of the new team's efforts during 1980, while it became progressively clearer at home and abroad that the whole macroeconomic policy programme had turned into a tragic blunder.[12] By the end of the year, the effects of devaluation had disappeared, and the average exchange rate of 1980 in fact appreciated by about 3 per cent in relation to the previous year, when deflated by the general price index. The discrediting at home of economic policy was minor in its consequences compared with the consequences of discredit in the eyes of international lenders. On the domestic scene, the economic policy meant cheap credit for consumption expenditures and working capital, negative real rates of return on personal savings, and a windfall subsidy granted to mortgages, the Development Bank's debtors and other debtors. The net result was a sharp increase in the sale of durable consumption goods, a fall in financial assets (in real terms) by 13.2 per cent following a drop by the same amount in non-monetary assets, and a fall in government disposable income of about 1 per cent of GDP.

Turning to the balance of payments, there was an increase in non-oil imports of over $2 billion (see Table 3.4). Added to the increase of almost $3 billion in expenditures on imported oil, this figure leads to a total rise

Table 3.4 Brazilian imports (US $ millions)

	Consumer goods		Intermediate goods[a]		Oil		Capital goods		Total
	$ mil	%	$ mil	%	$ mil	%	$ mil	%	$ mil
1979	1786	9.9	12 311	68.1	6 264	34.7	3975	22.0	18 072
1980	1887	6.1	16 937	73.8	9 372	40.9	4619	20.1	22 943
1981	1106	4.9	16 698	75.8	10 604	48.1	4257	19.3	22 061
1982	1014	5.3	14 862	76.6	9 566	49.3	3519	18.1	19 395
1983	793	5.2	12 130	78.6	7 822	50.1	2505	16.2	15 428
1984	695	5.0	11 063	79.4	6 736	48.4	2169	15.6	13 927

Note:
[a] excluding oil.

Sources: Banco do Brasil, Carteira de Comercio Exterior, *Relatorio CACEX*, 1984; Fundação Centro de Estudos do Comercio Exterior, *Balança Comercial e Outros Indicadores Conjunturais*, Rio de Janeiro, several issues.

in import outlays of almost $5 billion, rising from 7.6 per cent to 9.2 per cent of GDP between 1979 and 1980. In spite of a gain of 6 per cent in export prices and an increase in the quantum of exports by 22.6 per cent in the same year, the trade deficit remained practically the same (see Tables 3.5 and 3.6).

By this time, rates of interest in the US economy had already risen by more than six points above 1978 levels, and Brazilian net interest

Table 3.5 Current account deficit and its main components (US $ millions)

	Trade balance	Resource balance[a]	Net interest payments	Current account deficit
1979	− 2 827	5 205	4 185	10 742
1980	− 2 810	5 931	6 311	12 807
1981	1 232	1 631	9 161	11 734
1982	780	2 808	11 353	16 310
1983	6 470	− 4 063	9 555	6 837
1984	13 078	− 11 364	10 076	− 166

Note:
[a] excess of absorption over GDP.

Source: Boletim do Banco Central do Brasil.

Table 3.6   Brazil: foreign trade indices[a] (1977 = 100)

	Exports		Imports		Oil imports		Terms of trade[b]	
	(P)	(Q)	(P)	(Q)	(P)	(Q)	(1)	(2)
1979	101	124	128	115	135	124	79	81
1980	107	152	164	115	226	107	65	78
1981	101	183	182	99	270	104	55	71
1982	95	167	176	91	260	98	54	69
1983	89	191	167	76	235	90	53	54
1984	94	229	160	72	230	79	59	73

Notes:
[a] P = price, Q = quantity.
[b] The first column includes oil, the second excludes it.

Source: Boletim do Banco Central do Brasil.

payments had climbed from $2.7 billion in 1978 to over $6.3 billion in 1980, absorbing more than 30 per cent of export revenues. As a result, the current account deficit was $12.8 billion in 1980 (Table 3.5). Mounting disbelief on the part of international bankers with respect to macroeconomic policy led to increasing difficulties in raising finance to meet balance-of-payments needs. With the benefit of hindsight, we might say that Delfim Netto tried to play a stronger hand than was credible with foreign bankers, and before the end of the year had to announce a complete turnaround of short-run policies. An increase in domestic interest rates was enacted so as to induce voluntary borrowing abroad on the part of the private sector, as well as to display a political will to control the need for external finance in the following years. The lack of confidence on the part of international banks, however, made it impossible to raise sufficient foreign exchange, and by the end of 1980 foreign reserves had dropped by about $3 billion.

The observed growth of 7.2 per cent in real terms in GDP in 1980 could not, alas, be hailed as a sign of the success of the strategy announced by Delfim Netto eighteen months earlier. Instead, it was foreseen at home and abroad that a painful and perhaps long adjustment could no longer be postponed. Inevitably, orthodox discipline was now to be called upon to deal with inflation and to bring the current account deficit on to a more acceptable course. Needless to say, the acceleration of inflation from 40 per cent to 100 per cent between 1978 and 1980 had little to do with monetary policy, as the experience of the following years would witness.[13]

1981–2: RESTRICTIVE DEMAND POLICIES WITHOUT IMF SURVEILLANCE

As we saw in the previous section, the first serious sign of shortage of international finance came when the lenders' willingness to comply with adjustment without heavy short-run internal costs was put to the test in 1980. From the end of 1980 on, one may say that the main lines of macroeconomic policy were dictated by the availability of foreign finance.

Economic space for manoeuvre provided by the availability of finance in 1979 and 1980 was partly wasted by the policies of 1980, but time was an important factor for the success of structural adjustment, and the most important elements of the long-run strategy of the late 1970s had still not matured. Investments in oil-drilling facilities, energy-substitution in industry and transportation, import-substitution in basic inputs and export-orientated activities proceeded in spite of repeated announcements of budget cuts, and were singled out in the list of priorities in the third development plan.

Perhaps the most important consequence of the 1979–80 failures in dealing with inflation and current account deficits was an impending lack of confidence in the short-run management of the economy. As a result, the following years were plagued by the need for a continuous display, in the official discourse, of orthodox faith in demand controls as a means of dealing with inflation. Old-fashioned monetary policy, aided by ceilings on credit growth, was considered as the effective instrument to control inflationary pressures, and in spite of the known resistance of indexed economies to respond in the desired fashion to monetary controls, a continuous preoccupation with the size of the monetary base, side by side with a belief that maintaining a high level of interest rates was crucial to keeping the private sector borrowing abroad, led to a disastrous policy of financing government needs by selling more and more government bonds to the private sector.[14]

The new prescription that inspired macroeconomic management had the following ingredients: (i) state enterprise capital expenditures were to be cut in order to control the broadly defined government deficit as well as to adjust public sector imports to a predetermined budget;[15] (ii) loans to the private sector were subjected to a ceiling of 50 per cent over the nominal values of December 1980; (iii) lending interest rates were freed from controls except for loans to the agricultural sector and special credit lines to exporters; (iv) the nominal growth of means of payments and the monetary base were limited to 50 per cent; (v) tax incentives to manufactured exports that had been removed since the exchange devaluation of December 1979 were reinstated.

The macroeconomic strategy that prevailed in 1981 and 1982 was basically directed towards reducing foreign exchange needs by controlling domestic absorption. The fall in capacity utilisation for domestic needs was to render export activities more attractive at the same time as it contributed to reducing intermediate imports. The degree of success of such a strategy in effectively reducing the real resource gap depends, of course, on the effects of the resulting recession. The smaller the fall in GDP for a given reduction in domestic absorption, the less the need for a real transfer of resources from abroad. Expenditure-switching policies may lead to more efficient short-run adjustments, that is to say, smaller output losses. In the Brazilian case, raising the domestic price of oil derivatives was valuable in enhancing direct substitution efforts, but the bulk of the expenditure-switching effect in favour of tradables depended on government investment and on the availability of finance intermediated by government agencies such as the National Development Bank (BNDE). On the other hand, substantial real devaluations were ruled out not only because of recent memories of the frustrated attempt in December 1979, but also because of the prevailing belief at that time that exports were limited not by capacity but by world recession.

The effect of the years of restrictive policies on the rate of inflation was practically zero. Both general and industrial prices accelerated steadily up to mid-1981, reaching a local peak of about 120 per cent when we consider twelve-month rates and declining back to the 100 per cent plateau by the end of the year due to the deceleration of agricultural prices (see Figures 3.1 and 3.2 on p. 52), following a larger crop in key foodstuffs and a decline in international prices of exported agricultural products.[16] The effect of this substantial decline on the average price index in 1982, however, was dampened not only by the downward resistance of industrial inflation, but also by the countervailing pressure exerted by the correction of relative prices in favour of oil derivatives and other public prices.

In spite of a further deterioration in the terms of trade (Table 3.6), a significant reversal in the trade balance was obtained, resulting in an improvement of about $4 billion in the real resource balance in 1981 in comparison with 1980 (Table 3.7). Exports as a proportion of GDP were

Table 3.7 Current account deficit and its main components as a percentage of GDP

	Trade balance	Resource balance[a]	Net interest payments	Current account deficit
1979	1.2	2.2	1.8	4.5
1980	1.1	2.4	2.5	5.1
1981	0.4	0.6	3.3	4.3
1982	0.3	1.0	4.0	5.8
1983	3.1	1.9	4.5	3.3
1984	5.9	5.2	4.6	0.1

Notes:
[a] Excess of absorption over GDP.

Source: *Boletim do Banco Central do Brasil.*

up by 0.5 per cent and a gain of 1 per cent was made in the import coefficient. The increase of international lending rates by almost four points in 1981, however, led to an addition of $3 billion in interest payments which now absorbed almost 40 per cent of export revenues (Table 3.9).

At this point the Brazilian economy suffered a deep recession as industrial output fell by 5.4 per cent in 1981, and a decline in real GDP (Table 3.10) was observed for the first time in postwar years. Doubts as to the usefulness of the recession were raised even in conservative minds, as capital inflows became scarcer and only a modest increase in foreign reserves (Table 3.11) was obtained at the end of the year, thanks to a sharp increase in short-term financing that foreshadowed the deterioration of debt maturities in the following years.

The deepening of world recession in 1982 was enhanced by the defensive behaviour of policy-makers in central economies and by the declining import capacity of some of Brazil's newer customers for manufactures. This led to a loss of almost $3 billion in export revenues in that year, the result of a 6 per cent fall in export prices and of almost 9 per cent in quantum (Table 3.6). Continuing substitution in intermediate goods (both oil and non-oil) and a recession-induced decline in capital goods allowed a fall in total import expenditures of over $2.6 billion, and therefore a relatively small loss in the trade balance (Tables 3.4 and 3.7). However, the increase of over $3 billion in interest payments (Table 3.5) made the current account deficit virtually independent of domestic absorption. The stage was set for a new round of foreign exchange restrictions to economic growth, starting with the Mexican moratorium of August 1982.

On 25 October 1982 the government formally announced that the macroeconomic performance of the Brazilian economy in the following year would be further restricted. International bankers and official lenders, who had acted in unison since August, had put a ceiling of $10.6 billion to Brazilian borrowing in the coming year. The rules of the game of external finance had been suspended since the Mexican moratorium, and for the foreseeable future the country would have its creditworthiness formally evaluated by a committee of bankers.

Although it should have been evident by then that IMF supervision would be a necessary condition for the new scheme to work out and that a thorough rescheduling of payments would have to be forthcoming, the proximity of general elections (scheduled for 15 November) made government officials dismiss any intention of going to the Fund for help until late November. Needless to say, the deterioration of economic

Table 3.8 Brazil: GDP, selected financial assets and credit aggregates, 1970–84 (real growth rates, %)

	GDP	Monetary base	Money supply	Financial assets	Non-monetary financial assets	Financial system loans	Monetary authorities' loans
1971	12.0	5.6	8.4	18.4	32.0	24.5	17.0
1972	11.1	10.3	11.7	28.1	46.4	30.2	19.3
1973	13.6	16.7	27.9	37.0	44.3	36.3	31.8
1974	9.7	9.4	7.5	7.6	7.8	20.5	46.8
1975	5.4	-3.9	4.0	14.4	21.8	22.4	40.2
1976	9.7	2.6	-0.3	9.5	14.8	12.7	13.2
1977	5.7	13.0	-3.5	3.6	7.4	7.6	7.4
1978	5.0	5.2	1.2	7.5	10.8	8.3	2.8
1979	6.4	2.9	-0.8	1.9	3.4	2.1	-4.6
1980	7.2	-15.0	-12.2	-13.2	-13.8	-12.5	-11.8
1981	-1.6	-22.9	-21.0	-2.2	6.3	-11.3	-24.9
1982	0.9	-5.4	-6.5	24.8	34.6	7.7	-15.3
1983	-3.2	-23.0	-27.7	0.1	6.5	-6.5	-26.9
1984	4.5	-20.4	-24.4	1.3	5.2	-12.8	-37.4

Sources: *Boletim do Banco Central do Brasil* and Fundação Getulio Vargas, *Contas Nacionais do Brasil*, Rio de Janeiro, 1984.

Table 3.9 External sector: main indicators (%)

	1979	1980	1981	1982	1983	1984
Exports/GDP	6.4	8.0	8.5	7.1	10.4	12.3
Imports/GDP	7.6	9.2	8.0	6.8	7.3	6.3
Net debt/exports	264.0	233.0	231.0	325.0	351.0	304.0
Debt service/ exports[a]	70.0	65.0	72.0	97.0	91.0	71.0
Interest/exports	27.5	31.3	39.3	56.3	43.6	37.3
Reserves/imports	53.6	30.1	34.0	20.6	29.6	86.1

Note:
[a] (amortisation + interest)/exports.

Sources: Tables 3.3, 3.5, 3.6, 3.10, 3.11.

Table 3.10 Gross domestic product (billion cruzeiros)[a]

	GDP (1)	GDP (2)	GDP (3)	GDP (4)
1979	6 312	416	237	91
1980	13 164	446	250	98
1981	25 632	439	276	96
1982	50 815	443	283	97
1983	121 055	429	210	94
1984[b]	405 594	448	220	96

Notes:
[a] Col. (1) = Current cruzeiros.
   Col. (2) = Constant cruzeiros of 1970.
   Col. (3) = GDP (1) divided by the average exchange rate, millions of dollars.
   Col. (4) = GDP (2) divided by the average exchange rate (1970), millions of dollars.
[b] Estimated by the author (real growth of 4.5%).

Sources: Fundação Getulio Vargas, *Conjuntura Económica* and *Contas Nacionais do Brasil*, Rio de Janeiro, 1984.

conditions and the mounting signs of uncertainty as to future prospects played an important role in the severe loss inflicted on the government party in the November elections, in spite of the government's relative success in keeping the controversial issue of IMF supervision out of the campaign. Renegotiation of the external debt was a favourite campaign issue for the opposition parties and remained a question for the coming presidential election two years ahead.

Table 3.11 Brazilian foreign debt and international reserves (US $ million)

	Gross foreign debt[a]	International reserves[b]	Net foreign debt[c]	Non-registered debt
1979	49 904	9 689	40 216	na
1980	53 848	6 913	46 935	na
1981	61 411	7 506	53 904	na
1982	69 654	3 994	65 659	13 635
1983	81 319	4 563	76 756	10 319
1984	93 960	11 995	81 955	8 920

Notes:
[a] Medium and long-term debt.
[b] Gross.
[c] Gross debt minus gross international reserves.

Sources: Banco Central do Brasil, *Boletim Mensal*, Brasilia DF, several issues.

1983–4: MUDDLING THROUGH TO RECOVERY

From the first half of 1982, when export revenues began to decline, the road was open for a political rescheduling of financial commitments related to external debt. As several authors observed (Simonsen, 1984; Díaz Alejandro, 1984), there is simply no way out of the debt crisis without a growing demand for exports. As time became too short for a market solution, it became clear that any solution would have to come through negotiation. The episode of the Mexican moratorium and the failure of the Toronto meeting of September 1982 to provide more financial resources to international lending agencies signalled that the deadlock would require a painstaking effort in order to avoid concerted behaviour on the part of debtors and prevent aggravation of the position of both borrowers *and* lenders through the withdrawal of marginal lenders.

The participation of Brazil, the largest LDC debtor, in the so-called muddling-through strategy aimed at preventing general repudiation, required the supervision of macroeconomic management by the IMF. An agreement between the Brazilian government and international banks was reached by December. At the same time, after three months of formal denials, for already-mentioned political reasons, the Minister of Finance announced that a letter of intent was being presented to the

IMF. In the next twenty-four months the Brazilian government would have seven letters of intent examined by the IMF board.[17]

This painful exchange between Brazilian government officials and the IMF illustrates the difficulties involved in adapting orthodox IMF recipes to a highly indexed developing economy in which the public sector has not only been directly responsible for something between one-third and one-half of total investment, but also intermediates a high proportion of private investment through the administration of important compulsory savings funds.

The story of IMF supervision of macroeconomic policies in the past two years begins with the targets of the first letter of intent concerning the performance criteria for 1983. A ceiling for the current account deficit of $6.9 billion was defined and required the generation of a trade surplus of $6 billion and a target for net exports of goods and services of about $4 billion in comparison with the negative figure of $2.8 billion of the previous year. The trade surplus was to be obtained through an expected increase of 12 per cent in exports and a cut of imports by $2.4 billion over the previous year. With respect to domestic targets, a rate of inflation of 78 per cent was projected, to be achieved by cuts in domestic spending brought about by a contraction in government expenditures in order to reduce nominal public sector borrowing requirements as a proportion of GDP, and net domestic credit of the monetary authorities to one-half its estimated value in the previous year. In order to induce expenditure-switching, the monthly devaluation of the exchange rate would exceed monthly inflation by one percentage point, and drastic cuts in state enterprises' outlays were programmed so that import restrictions would affect the public sector more intensively than the private sector.

On 18 February, following a wave of speculation in the black market, the exchange rate was devalued by 30 per cent and new policies were announced which required that Brazilian authorities send a second letter of intent before the IMF board had a chance to approve the first one. The new package of policies included new credit allocation programmes to encourage exports and to facilitate import substitution as well as the announcement that for the next twelve months monetary correction applying to government-indexed bonds would be equal to the exchange-rate correction and both would be defined by the monthly behaviour of the general price index.

The combination of domestic recession, price incentives provided by the exchange-rate devaluation and favourable developments in exogenous variables like the international price of oil and interest rates, as well as the signs of recovery in the US economy, especially strong during the second half-year, helped the fulfilment of practically all commitments concerning the external accounts. At the year's end, a trade surplus of $6.47 billion was announced. A current account deficit of $6.2 billion (Table 3.5), or 2.7 per cent of GDP, was the most important sign of successful adjustment towards the control of the snowballing indebtedness.

The figures behind these results, however, were an increase of only 7.3 per cent in exports (instead of the projected 12 per cent – but a significant figure when we consider that export prices fell by 6.4 per cent for the third consecutive year!) and a drop in import expenditures of 21.5 per cent relative to the 1982 figures (Tables 3.4 and 3.12). This reduction in imports to 6.8 per cent of GDP was obtained due to the combined effect of a 4.7 per cent reduction in the international price of oil, direct import controls, a recession-induced fall in import demand, as well as long-run import substitution due to the operation of several of the new projects that had been developed in the post-1975 investment programme. The latter would contribute to a possible permanent reduction in the import coefficient (Table 3.4). Lower prices, high domestic production of oil and substitution of petrol and fuel oil contributed to a decrease in expenditure on imported oil of 9.7 per cent. Income effects and higher domestic production were the dominant factors behind the 20 per cent decrease in imports of consumer goods (especially wheat) and the 32 per cent fall in the remaining items (see Table 3.4).

This success story of external adjustment was accompanied, however, by very complicated negotiations concerning domestic targets, occupying the greater part of the time and effort both of the Brazilian authorities and of IMF officials during the year. The dominant factor behind the difficulties lay in the behaviour of inflation rates, illustrated by Figures 3.1 and 3.3. By the end of the first quarter, it was clear to most economists who understood the effects of indexation that the promised reduction in the rate of inflation would not be fulfilled. Two causes conspired against monetarists' faith in the ability of budget cuts and recessive monetary policies to reduce inflation in 1983: the induced effects of the maxi-devaluation through indexation and the upward trend of agricultural prices, which gave downward rigidity to inflation rates. The former rendered the reduction of nominal borrowing requirements of the public sector virtually impossible, due to the effect of indexation on the service of the public debt. The latter represented an additional supply shock to the rate of inflation, comparable in intensity to that provoked by the maxi-devaluation. Econometric evidence available for the Brazilian economy today indicates that from a starting

Table 3.12 Brazilian exports (US $ million)

	Primary		Semi-manufactured		Manufactured		Others		Total
	$ mil	%	$ mil	%	$ mil	%	$ mil	%	$ mil
1979	7078	46.4	1864	12.2	6143	40.3	160	1.1	15 245
1980	9438	46.9	2031	10.1	8395	41.7	268	1.3	20 132
1981	9647	41.4	2029	8.7	11 244	48.3	373	1.6	23 293
1982	8238	40.8	1433	7.2	10 253	50.8	251	1.2	20 175
1983	8535	39.0	1781	8.1	11 275	51.4	307	1.5	21 398
1984	8978	33.2	2824	10.5	14 894	55.2	309	1.1	27 005

Sources: Banco Central do Brasil, *Boletim Mensal*, Brasilia, DF, several issues.

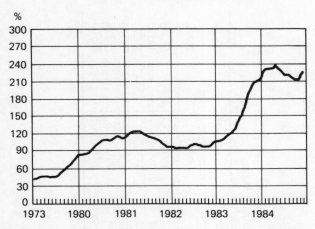

Figure 3.1   General price index (% change in 12 months)

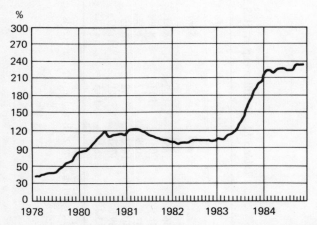

Figure 3.2   Industrial wholesale price index (% change in 12 months)

point of a relatively stabilised inflation of around 100 per cent, a real devaluation of 30 per cent plus a 30 per cent increase in real agricultural prices are sufficient to explain the resulting rate of about 230 per cent observed at the end of 1983[18] (Table 3.13).

The progressive acceleration of inflation since the beginning of the year was sufficient to discredit the projected annual rate upon which nominal values for the public sector and for monetary targets were based. In fact, three months after formal approval of the stabilisation

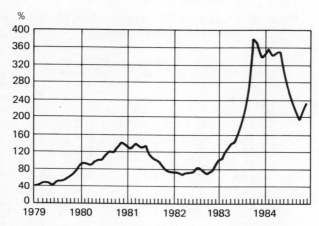

Figure 3.3   Agricultural wholesale price index (% change in 12 months)

programme, the IMF suspended the drawing of $2 billion because of the failure of the Brazilian government to accomplish the projected reduction in nominal deficits. A number of factors led to a postponement of discussion of the fundamental issues that lay behind the difficulties. First, the IMF money was essential to the realisation of other parts of the programme agreed with the private banks in December. Second, political support for an economic team who had at least moderate goodwill towards the IMF could be impaired by an excessive delay in finding a new way out of the impasse. At that point it looked as though none of the parties involved in the agreement – Brazilian authorities, bankers or the IMF – would take the risk of a potentially dangerous change in the economic team. Third, informal pledges were made on changes in the indexation rules, so as to make the new targets more plausible for the following months. Some of these measures could be taken by the executive alone, such as those pertaining to financial indexation;[19] others, like the modification of wage laws in order to act directly upon wage costs affecting both the private sector and public expenditures, required congressional approval. Since the Constitution allowed the President to sign decrees with immediate effect concerning loosely defined 'economic matters' and submit them to Congress for review within forty-five days, between March and October[20] a total of four decrees were signed in an effort to change indexation rules as a whole and wage adjustments in particular. Uncertainty as to the net effects of the prolonged negotiation with the IMF over the appropriate measurement of budget deficits and the resulting substantive

Table 3.13   Brazil: price and industrial output indices, 1979–84 (quarterly figures, real growth rates, %)

	General price index	Agricultural wholesale price index	Industrial wholesale price index	Industrial output
1979.2	12.0	16.1	11.2	7.1
1979.3	14.6	15.2	15.8	5.7
1979.4	19.6	19.9	20.2	− 0.2
1980.1	19.0	19.3	19.0	− 2.8
1980.2	18.8	20.4	20.1	5.6
1980.3	22.3	35.0	23.5	9.2
1980.4	21.9	30.1	20.4	− 4.5
1981.1	22.7	18.3	21.9	− 11.0
1981.2	19.9	19.6	19.7	− 3.3
1981.3	17.2	9.4	18.2	3.6
1981.4	15.5	14.2	17.0	− 6.1
1982.1	18.7	13.9	18.9	− 5.1
1982.2	20.4	21.7	20.3	10.0
1982.3	19.6	11.9	21.2	8.2
1982.4	15.3	14.8	15.8	− 9.4
1983.1	24.3	34.8	20.5	− 11.6
1983.2	29.1	43.5	27.8	6.2
1983.3	39.0	55.7	38.0	7.8
1983.4	36.8	52.9	35.4	− 2.4
1984.1	32.3	30.6	32.2	− 7.0
1984.2	31.3	39.4	29.8	8.1
1984.3	33.2	21.7	38.8	9.0
1984.4	37.0	41.3	39.0	− 0.2

Sources: FGV, *Conjuntura Económica*, and FIBGE, *Indicadores Conjunturais da Indústria*, Rio de Janeiro.

macroeconomic impact of fiscal restraint on ongoing projects, together with the general understanding that the economy was being run with negative reserves (Table 3.11), played an important role in the strong demand for dollar-denominated assets during the year.

Thanks to strict exchange controls, capital flight was prevented or at least reduced to insignificant levels when compared with other Latin American countries[21]. Another important element that offered a hedge against exchange risk without putting pressure on the country's capital account was the existence of exchange-rate-indexed government bonds. Excess demand for dollars due to expected devaluation spilled over to domestic assets, driving up the prices of government bonds with exchange-rate correction clauses, and contributed to the control of the premium of black market rates over official rates during the period of worst uncertainty. At the peak of speculation in the middle of 1983 the difference between black market rates and official rates was around 40 per cent, when the risk of another maxi-devaluation was thought to be at its height.

At least three factors contributed to reducing the margin between black market and official exchange rates between the second half of 1983 and the first quarter of 1984. First, gradual improvement of the trade balance helped to foster the hope that the expectations concerning the trade surplus and the current account would be fulfilled by the end of the year. In August the accumulated trade surplus during the year was already above $4 billion and in October it exceeded $5 billion and continued at a monthly rate of over $500 million. Second, as successive rounds of negotiations were held between the government and IMF officials, the real rules of the game were seen to be less strict than anticipated, as two providential 'waivers' were approved by the IMF board. Finally, domestic financial intermediaries carried substantial losses in their accounts as their position in dollar-denominated assets was financed at a level of interest rates above the monthly rate of exchange correction. Their progressive fragility *increased* as the threat of new disasters in Brazilian external accounts diminished during the latter part of the year, so that the level of confidence in the maintenance of exchange-rate policy correspondingly reduced the demand for dollar-denominated assets. In the first quarter of 1984, as massive speculation against the cruzeiro virtually came to a stop, the monetary authorities rescued the financial system by purchasing the greater part of dollar-indexed bonds in exchange for cruzeiro-indexed bonds, thus absorbing some of the losses derived from unsuccessful speculation.

Recession during 1983 hit the industrial sector in its most traditionally dynamic sectors (machinery, durable consumer goods and metallurgy) although the less dynamic ones like textiles, food and beverages were also badly affected by falling real wages and employment. The heaviest losses seem to have been suffered in the third quarter, and a moderate but steady recovery could be felt in some sectors, benefited by the vigorous picking up of export demand, especially in the US market. Increases in oil production and the first effects of changes in relative prices in favour of agriculture on the derived demand for intermediate and capital goods helped to avoid a still worse loss of output. The total loss in per capita income between the peak of 1980 and the trough in 1983 was almost 12 per cent in constant cruzeiros. Between 1981 and 1983, manufacturing industry declined at a 6 per cent annual rate, in comparison with a 7.2 per cent average rate between 1976 and 1980. The behaviour of particular sectors of manufacturing industry can be seen in Table 3.1. Employment in manufacturing decreased by an estimated 7.2 per cent per year in the worst recession experienced in the Brazilian industrial sector in its recorded history (Table 3.2). Talk about the need to scrap industrial equipment became commonplace among conservative economists: based on crude estimates of effective protection, they offered a curious argument that industrialisation during the late 1970s had been artificially promoted by the Brazilian technocracy with no regard for relative prices or international comparative advantage. Therefore, once the IMF-sponsored policies prevented the government pumping demand into the system, the Brazilian economy in fact faced not a depression but a healthy purging of its industrial inefficiency brought about by market forces. Needless to say, the argument lost credibility when, under the continuous pull of export demand, the most 'artificial' sectors of Brazilian industry showed a vigorous recovery in the first two quarters of the following year.

The firmness of US recovery in the first two quarters of 1984 was of fundamental importance for the performance of the Brazilian economy in 1984. In the first quarter alone, steel exports rose by 40 per cent, taking advantage of the import outburst that led US imports from Latin America to increase at a rate above 50 per cent in the first five months of 1984 in comparison to the same period in the previous year. On the other hand, the violent rise in agricultural prices (Figure 3.3) had provided a significant stimulus to higher purchases of intermediate inputs and machinery from industry. The import-substitution strategy implemented after 1975 was being put to a test with the progressive coming to maturity of a whole vintage of projects (such as steel, non-ferrous metallurgy, petrochemicals, and the replacement of imported oil by electricity in the production of industrial heat and by alcohol for transport fuel, to name but a few). These projects were called to play an important role in allowing macroeconomic recovery with a sustained high export coefficient and an all-time low import coefficient in spite of the unfavourable behaviour of terms of trade since the late 1970s (Table 3.6). In 1984, the improvement in non-oil terms of trade was barely sufficient to recover the level of 1981, around 30 per cent below its level of 1977 – see Table 3.6. In the first quarter of 1984 there were unequivocal signs of recovery in the industrial sector as the level of output rose 4 per cent relative to the first quarter of 1983 (Table 3.11).

As the positive signs coming from the behaviour of the trade balance indicated that industrial recovery would neither interfere with the external balance during 1984 nor necessarily mean a further increase in inflation rates, it became progressively clearer to economic agents that the domestic recession as experienced in the previous years was not necessary for the improvement of the external accounts. These signs were important in restoring confidence in the economic prospects of the country and in reducing the role that the precarious agreements with the IMF had played in destabilising expectations in the exchange market, with disturbing effects on the economic plans both of investors and consumers. Industrial recovery that was initially led by metallurgy (+ 13.3 per cent), chemicals (+ 8.7 per cent) and engineering (+ 14.2 per cent) (Table 3.1) turned into steady growth as consumers' expenditures picked up in the second half, induced by an improvement in real wages. The latter improvement was brought about by the recovery of rural income thanks to the performance of agricultural exports and to wage adjustments granted by São Paulo industry above the level prescribed by the wage laws, especially in those sectors which were favourably affected by strong export demand. Finally, from the third quarter onwards, an upsurge of inflationary expectations provoked by higher wage claims, local monetarists' hysteria over allegedly loose monetary policy *and* an increase in the frequency of adjustments of public tariffs, led to an anticipation of purchases of durable goods and helped to spread the recovery to other sections of manufacturing industry. With the exception of food, perfumery and textiles, the remaining segments exhibited positive rates of growth in 1984 (Table 3.1). At the year's end, GDP had increased by 4.5 per cent, with agriculture growing by 4.3 per cent and industry 5.8 per cent.

Thanks to the growth of exports and a fall in total imports (Tables 3.4 and 3.12), the trade surplus in 1984 was $3.5 billion above the target of $9.5 billion agreed with the IMF, and larger (by almost $2 billion) than the net interest bill for the first time since the first oil shock. A positive resource balance above $11 billion (Table 3.5) was achieved and the current account was virtually brought into equilibrium. The resulting figures for the Brazilian balance of payments in 1984 illustrate first of all the importance of the behaviour of demand for exports in achieving non-recessive adjustment in the external debt situation. Secondly, we can see where the costs involved in curbing the explosive indebtedness under normal conditions of international trade lie: namely, in the adjusting of existing productive capacity and at the same time the transfer abroad of 4 per cent of the domestic product. The results also show that the long-run strategy followed after the first oil shock was basically sound: a substantial growth of GDP was finally achieved with a drop in the import coefficient from 7.7 to 6.3 per cent of GDP and a rise in the export coefficient from 10.4 to 12.3 per cent of GDP (Table 3.9), once most of the projects associated with long-run structural adjustment began to work.

A thorough evaluation of the possibilities of continued improvement in debt-related ratios in the medium and long term requires a deeper understanding of the contradictory effects of orthodox attempts at stabilisation and the requirements imposed by the need to promote a continuous change in the structure of productive capacity.

The highest costs associated with the 1981–3 recession, besides the losses in per capita income and industrial employment, can be identified as the high rate of inflation (in the neighbourhood of 200 per cent) that resulted from relative price changes during the period (in favour of tradables in general, and of agricultural and oil derivatives in particular), and the resulting disorder in the government's finances, both of the narrowly defined central government and of broadly defined government inclusive of state-owned enterprises. These two consequences have important implications for the design of future policies, as both appear to lend support to continuous orthodox claims for more austerity, meaning higher interest rates, a reduction in public investment and more liberal market-oriented trade policies. The most visible benefits were quite obvious: the continuity of structural change was maintained as investment projects managed to hobble along through the repeated attempts at paralysing the public sector and the private sector capital accumulation activities in the name of short-run stabilisation efforts, with or without the supervision of the IMF.

FINAL REMARKS AND CONCLUSIONS

In this final section we face the hard question of the prospects for a lasting recovery after 1984. Our answer to this question will require an appraisal of two issues that will be addressed below under the headings of external and domestic constraints, for lack of better labels.

External Constraints

As discussed in the previous section, one remarkable aspect of the 1984 recovery was that it was achieved without interrupting either the rise in the export coefficient or the decline in the import coefficient, both important signs of the long-run structural adjustments that have been carried out in the Brazilian economy over the past ten years. An evaluation of the prospects for external constraints on economic growth has to start by asking how permanent these favourable changes in coefficients are likely to be.

One crucial point has to do with imports. Oil imports have been reduced both due to a decrease in consumption per unit of GDP – thanks to conservation and to substitution of electricity, alcohol and natural gas for oil in the past ten years, with the help of credit and price incentives – and to an increase in domestic production. Today Brazil is able to produce around 60 per cent of its consumption, compared with only 20 per cent ten years ago. If investment in drilling and incentive policies are not suspended, a situation close to self-sufficiency before the end of the next decade cannot be ruled out. As to non-oil imports, there is sufficient econometric evidence to indicate that the cyclical behaviour of the import coefficient may be prolonged both through appropriate price-related policy measures and through careful government control of incentives for import substitution.[22]

Adopting rather conservative, albeit non-tragic, assumptions about the behaviour of the international economy, such as constant terms of trade, rates of growth of real world imports of around 2 to 3 per cent, and, of course, international lending rates compatible with resulting growth of export revenues (in the 10 to 12 per cent range), I and my colleagues Eduardo Modiano and Francisco Lopes have obtained simulations with an econometric model for the Brazilian economy according to which an average growth rate close to historical trends (around 7 per cent) for the second half of the 1980s is consistent with declining debt/export ratios and capital inflow requirements compatible with a moderate trend of voluntary risk capital.[23]

With respect to balance-of-payments constraints, the foregoing remarks are, unfortunately, too similar to what John Wells described as the official Brazilian view in 1977.[24] Fortunately, they are not far from what Carlos Díaz Alejandro (1983) called the 'prudent planner's' forecasts in his counterfactual analysis of the Brazilian balance-of-payments crisis of 1982–3. Today's prudent planners, however, are not entitled to be optimistic but must make the necessary provisions for financial disarray.

We are thus led to qualify any favourable prospect for external equilibrium based upon the assumption of tranquillity in external financial markets. Even without a lengthy discussion, it appears extremely probable that the current muddling-through process of debt rescheduling will not survive the present sluggishness of world trade. Moderately recessive policies in the US economy could do the job of destabilising world financial markets, since imports by the remaining OECD countries are unlikely to compensate for the negative impact of a significant slowdown in US imports from Latin America on the foreign debt indicators of Mexico and Brazil.

Domestic Constraints

Suppose that neither the demand for exports nor international interest rates will obstruct the recovery path of external indicators for the next few years. Existing unused capacity may allow for some demand-pulled growth with rather small increases in capacity, but as growth resumes, the need to transfer 4 to 5 per cent of GDP abroad to service the debt means that domestic policies will have to face the need to reverse the falling trend of domestically financed investment as a proportion of GDP. As shown in Table 3.3, this fall has two important components up to 1982, the last for which national accounts statistics are available in Brazil. The first component is the decrease in the investment ratio (I/Y) from its peak of 30 per cent in 1975 to 21 per cent in 1982. The second is the decrease in domestic sources of funds (defined roughly as private plus public sector current account surpluses) as a proportion of total capital expenditures from 93 per cent in 1975 to 73 per cent in 1982. Behind these figures lies an important phenomenon, namely the fall in government disposable income as a proportion of GDP (Table 3.3), mainly caused by the increase in government transfers to the private sector. Transfers increased from 32 per cent of total revenue to 48 per cent between 1975 and 1982, while subsidies declined from 11 per cent of government receipts in 1975 to 6 per cent in 1976 and 1977 and increased again to 15 per cent in 1980.

The nature of the domestic constraints on GDP growth may be classified as follows.

The first, of course, is the fact that resort to current account deficits will no longer be possible as a permanent source of savings. Therefore, domestic savings will have to be mobilised not only to finance investment but to transfer abroad around 4 per cent of GDP in the second half of the decade. This means that from the 73 per cent figure for 1982, domestic savings will have to be raised to 104 per cent of total investment. This will require a reversal of the flows between the public and the private sector, since most of the external debt is in the public domain.

The second point is related to investment requirements once the existing productive capacity is used up. Investment lags will require an increase in investment expenditures well before actual signs of capacity constraints show up and a careful anticipation of bottlenecks is needed in order to prevent shortages or increases in import coefficients. If the increase in capital/output ratios observed by Díaz Alejandro (1984) proves to be a long-lasting phenomenon and not just the effect of the unusually long maturity of most projects associated with the 1975 programme, an additional difficulty will have to be faced, namely that of investment productivity.

Finally, the question of the appropriate demand policies needed to maintain a high level of investment will require a fiscal reform to prevent the government budget becoming an obstacle to continued growth. Fiscal reform here means an increase in net public receipts which have been falling, at least up to 1983, according to available estimates. This will probably require both an increase in gross tax rates, which are rather low in Brazil when compared to most industrialised countries, as well as a reduction in subsidy and transfers.[25] Since an important portion of governmental transfers to the public sector is determined by the service of the public debt, domestic interest policy will have to be totally reversed.

As noted before, the increase in the extent of government intermediation of the savings/investment process, together with an old-fashioned monetarist belief in the perils of monetary financing of public deficits, led to an increase in public sector domestic borrowing.[26] With the shift from passive monetary policy directed towards 'the needs of trade' of the late 1960s and early 1970s, to post-1974 concern with the size of the money supply and to direct controls of credit aggregates of the early 1980s, an important shift has also occurred in the factors determining domestic interest rates. From 1977 onwards the cost of the public debt becomes more of a burden, since domestic interest rates have been kept high in order to induce private sector external borrowing. An increase in the cost of domestic credit was required to counterbalance the effects of increasing foreign exchange risk on desired private borrowing. This was particularly true in 1981, when ceilings were imposed on the supply of domestic credit (Table 3.8) and as a consequence, rationed banks were willing to purchase public bonds, making the monetary authorities happy that they could control the money supply. Since 1981, domestic interest rates have been intolerably high in both the private and the public sectors, reaching incredible levels of 30 per cent above inflation. Such rates are, of course, not compatible with any economic calculation of the prospective yield on investment. The role of the state in financial intermediation was thus crucial to prevent the collapse of capital expenditures. Finishing the 1975 vintage of investment projects required a massive transfer of real resources to the private sector, both through borrowing at high cost and lending at low cost.

The resulting situation is, of course, that a relevant portion of the public debt, both foreign and domestic, has as its counterpart private assets, as has happened in other Latin American indebted countries. One fortunate aspect of the Brazilian experience is that most private assets are held *inside* the country, and therefore the income they will yield may be taxed and provide resources to be transferred abroad. The fiscal reform makes economic sense, as does the need to lower domestic interest rates.

As in so many instances of recent Brazilian history, however, the option in favour of orthodox demand policies is what most endangers the process of removing domestic constraints. Since existing capital has to be put to use so that resulting income may be taxed, the level of economic activity has to be maintained at a high level. An orthodox interpretation of high interest rates, however, leads to a cut in public spending so as to diminish 'crowding-out' of private investment. This will lead to further recession and a fall in taxable income, aggravating the burden of accumulated public debt. For non-orthodox adjustment, the financial mix of the public sector borrowing requirements has to be reversed in favour of more base money and less debt so as to lower interest rates and prevent recession from increasing the public deficit. The mid-1985 debate concerning the ways to lower domestic interest rates, and the resulting policies, are crucial in determining the role of domestic constraints in the future growth prospects of the Brazilian economy.

Notes

1.   The author is grateful to Rosemary Thorp, Marcelo de Paiva Abreu, Rogério Werneck, Jaime Ros and the participants of the Latin American Seminar at Oxford University for valuable comments on previous drafts. He wishes to thank Rosemary Thorp for providing a most hospitable environment at St Antony's College, where most of the chapter was written, Rodrigo Fiães and Sonia Olinto for assistance in the preparation of statistical tables, and Luis Chrysostomo for having prepared the figures.
2.   See, for example, Bacha (1977), Malan and Bonelli (1976), Fishlow (1972) and Wells (1977, 1978) and Bacha and Taylor (1978).

3.   A brief discussion of the basic characteristics of the Brazilian growth model and a view of the main issues of macroeconomic policy following the first oil shock are provided in Carneiro (1977, 1978). In the 1978 paper a more detailed account of the role of stabilisation policies after 1974 is given.

4.   The average price of petrol increased 111 per cent above the general price index in 1974. Modiano (1982) rightly observes that this was far below what was needed in order to correct the internal price, in view of the rise in the dollar price of oil. It illustrates, nevertheless, the relevance of imported inflation, especially when one notes that import prices as a whole increased by 54 per cent in 1974.

5.   Data on the official wage adjustment indices for the period are given in Carneiro (1977). In fact, wage increases above past increases in the cost of living resulted from the wage formula adopted in 1974. Much of the pre-1974 discussion about wage repression in the mid-1960s stabilisation efforts centred around the fact that in the old formula, part of the adjustment was determined by officially defined expected inflation. Whenever this expected inflation was underestimated, a new wage squeeze occurred. Mario Simonsen, the author of the post-1964 wage formula and then Minister of Finance, proposed in 1974 a compensation for previously underestimaed inflation, and this element was adopted in the new wage rule. For a detailed discussion of wage policy after 1964, see Carvalho (1982).

6.   For a detailed description of industrial policy in the period, see Baumgarten and Cunha (1977).

7.   Velloso (1982) evaluates the import-substitution programme for basic inputs, and presents estimates of the effects of the programme upon Brazilian imports up to 1981.

8.   The figure of $101 billion is obtained by adding official estimates of investment expenditures necessary to finish the largest projects in the period 1980–4, namely the Alcohol Programme, oil-drilling by Petrobrás, coal production facilities, the steel and non-ferrous programme, the Carajás mining complex, the so-called Polonoroeste projects to extend the agricultural frontier, and the hydroelectricity projects, including the Tucuruí and Itaipú dams and their respective transmission lines.

9.   According to preliminary estimates (reproduced in Table 5.1 in Carneiro, 1985), the PSBR went up in 1979 as a proportion of GDP both in nominal terms and when adjusted for the effect of inflation on the outstanding federal government's debt.

10. For an analysis of the effects of the role of indexation in the multiplication of such shocks, see Modiano (1985), where a detailed system of price equations for the Brazilian economy is analysed and estimated.

11. Government officials tried to convince economic agents that the inflationary effects of the price corrections of 1979 would be confined to that year, minimising the linkages between past and future inflation brought about by indexation rules.

12. Tragic because it helped to strengthen the position of those who favoured a recession as a means to curb inflation and stop snowballing external indebtedness.

13.   On this issue, see the exchange of views between Lara-Resende and Lopes (1981, 1982) and Contador (1982), as well as the interesting findings of Camargo and Landau (1983).

14.   In fact, in spite of monetary contraction partly evidenced by the fall in all (monetary and non-monetary) financial aggregates in real terms, the estimated public deficit went up both in nominal terms (from 5.1 to 9.1 per cent of GDP) and when adjusted for inflation (from 0.9 to 5.2 per cent of GDP). One can see in Table 3.8 that the monetary base dropped by 22.9 per cent, conventional M1 by 21 per cent, total financial assets by 2.2 per cent, and total loans to the private sector fell by 11.3 per cent. As pointed out elsewhere (Carneiro, 1985), it was one of the rare instances in recent Brazilian history when all indicators of monetary policy exhibited an unequivocal sign of contraction.

15.   Maintenance of the investment capacity of state enterprises after 1980 required substantial transfers from the fiscal budget in order to make up for the weight that the service on past foreign debt exerted on state companies' financial statements. Such companies had been used as absorbers of foreign finance needed for balance of payments reasons in the previous period and were induced to borrow far beyond their individual needs. Attempts at controlling their 'deficits' or borrowing requirements in the following years constituted a repeated menace to the continuation of investment programmes that were badly needed for the adjustment of Brazilian productive capacity. On this issue see the evidence presented by Werneck (1983 and 1985).

16.   The annualised rate of change of agricultural prices as of mid-1982 fell by almost 50 per cent compared to the record high of 138 per cent in March 1981.

17.   The story of the details of the Brazilian negotiation with the IMF and the international banks is told by Fritsch (1985), Marques (1985) and Carneiro (1985).

18.   Modiano (1985) presents an econometric evaluation of reduced form multipliers for the different supply shocks which affected Brazilian inflation in 1983.

19.   For an analytical evaluation of the effects of indexation on the feasible fiscal policies when PSBR is limited as a proportion of GDP, see Carneiro and Modiano (1983), where a simulation model was used in order to evaluate the effects of partial deindexation of government bonds for the Brazilian economy.

20.   For a quantitative evaluation of the effects of different indexation schemes implied by the several wage formulae, see Lopes (1983).

21.   Available estimates of total capital flight tend to be very low when Brazil is compared with other Latin American countries. Sachs (1984) presents a figure of $1 billion. Informal estimates indicate figures below $2.5 billion.

22.   See the interesting analysis by Pombal-Dib (1984) of the behaviour of imports and the effects of different industrial policies in the period 1947–52.

23.   See Modiano, Carneiro and Lopes (1984), for further explanation of the assumptions. The formal structure of the model is essentially described in Modiano (1983b).

24. Wells (1978, p. 261) described the official view in 1977 as: 'following a period of adjustment similar to the mid-1960's, domestic capacity will grow and the balance of payments strengthen so that, by 1990, the economy will be able to resume rapid growth, based on a high elasticity of supply and the absence of foreign exchange constraints'.

25. See Longo (1984) and Costa (1984) for an analysis of the behaviour of governmental revenues in the past years. As both authors observe, there has been an important decrease in net taxation due to obsolete taxation schemes and to an increase in government transfers and subsidies.

26. For *new* monetarists, of course, it should make no difference whether fiscal deficits are financed by issue of money or debt, since the rational behaviour of consumers should lead to appropriate discounting of future taxes.

References

BACHA, E., 'Issues and Evidence in Recent Brazilian Economic Growth, *World Development*, vol. 5, no. 5, 1977.

BACHA, E., 'Vicissitudes of Recent Stabilization Attempts in Brazil and the IMF Alternative, Texto para Discussão no. 27, Departamento de Economia, PUC-RJ, June 1982.

BACHA, E. and TAYLOR, L., 'Brazilian Income Distribution in the 1960s: Facts, Model Results and the Controversy, *Journal of Developing Countries*, vol. 14, no. 3, April 1978.

BAUMGARTEN, A. L. and CUNHA, L. R. A., 'Política Industrial: Da Recuperação a Recessão?', in Carneiro, D. D. (ed.) *Brasil: Dilemas da Política Econômica* (Rio: Editora Campus, 1977).

CAMARGO, J. M. and LANDAU, E., 'Variações de Demanda, Estrutura de Custo e Margem Bruta de Lucro no Brasil – 1974–1981', *Pesquisa e Planejamento Econômico*, December 1983.

CARNEIRO, D. D., 'Introdução', in D. D. Carneiro (ed.) *Brasil: Dilemas da Política Econômica* (Rio: Editora Campus, 1977).

CARNEIRO, D. D., 'O Terceiro Choque: É Possível Evitar-se a Depressão?', in P. Arida (ed.) *Dívida Pública Externa, Recessão e Ajuste Estrutural* (Rio: Paz e Terra, 1982).

CARNEIRO, D. D., 'Brazilian Economic Policy in the Mid Seventies', *Brazilian Economic Studies*, no. 4, 1978.

CARNEIRO, D. D., 'Estimativas da Equação Orçamentária do Governo, 1979–84', mimeo, February 1985.

CARNEIRO, D. D. and MODIANO, E., 'Inflação e Controle do Déficit Público: Análise Teórica e Algumas Simulações para a Economia Brasileira', *Revista Brasileira de Economia*, no. 4, December 1983.

CARVALHO, L. W., 'Políticas Salariais Brasileiras no Período 1964–81', *Revista Brasileira de Economia*, vol. 36, no. 1, January–March 1982, pp. 51–84.

CONTADOR, C. R., 'Sobre as Causas da Recente Aceleração Inflacionária: Comentários', *Pesquisa e Planejamento Econômico*, vol. 12, no. 2, August 1982.

COSTA, M. H., 'O Setor Privado e a Carga Tributária', mimeo (Rio: FGV, 1984).

DÍAZ ALEJANDRO, C. F., 'Some Aspects of the 1982–1983 Brazilian Payments Crisis', *Brookings Papers in Economic Activity*, 1, 1983, pp. 515–52.

66   *Recent Brazilian Experience*

DÍAZ ALEJANDRO, C. F., 'Latin American Debt: I Don't Think We Are in Kansas Any More', *Brookings Papers in Economic Activity*, 2, 1984, pp. 335–403.

FISHLOW, A., 'Some Reflections in Post-1964 Economic Policy', in A. Stepan, *Authoritarian Brazil* (New Haven: Yale University Press, 1972).

FRITSCH, W., 'A Crise Cambial de 1982–83 no Brasil: Origens e Respostas', in C. A. Plastino and R. Bouzas (eds) *A América Latina e a Crise Internacional* (Rio de Janeiro: Instituto de Relações Internacionais, PUC-RJ, 1985).

LARA-RESENDE, A. and LOPES, F., 'Sobre as Causas da Recente Aceleração Inflacionária', *Pesquisa e Planejamento Econômico*, vol. 11, no. 4, December 1981.

LARA-RESENDE, A. and LOPES, F., 'Sobre as Causas da Recente Aceleração Inflacionária: Réplica', *Pesquisa e Planejamento Econômico*, vol. 12, no. 2, August 1982.

LONGO, C. A., 'Imposto de Renda', ANPEC, XII Encontro Nacional de Economia, Anais, Dec. 1984.

LOPES, F., 'Inflação e Nível de Atividade no Brasil: Um Estudo Econométrico', *Pesquisa e Planejamento Econômico*, vol. 12, no. 3, December 1983.

LOPES, F. and MODIANO, E. M., 'Indexação, Choque Externo e Nível de Atividade: Notas Sobre o Caso Brasileiro', in *Pesquisa e Planejamento Econômico*, vol. 13, no. 1, April 1983, pp. 69–90.

MALAN, P. and BONELLI, R., 'Os Limites do Possível: Notas Sobre o Balanço de Pagamentos e Indústria no Limiar da Segunda Metade dos Anos 70', *Pesquisa e Planejamento Econômico*, vol. 6, no. 2, August 1976.

MARQUES, M. S. B., 'FMI: a Experiência Brasileira Recente', mimeo (Rio: FGV, 1985).

MODIANO, E. M., 'A Dinâmica de Salários e Preços na Economia Brasileira 1966/81', *Pesquisa e Planejamento Econômico*, vol. 13, no. 1, April 1983a.

MODIANO, E. M., 'Choques Externos e Preços Internos: Dificuldade da Prática de Ajuste', in P. Arida (ed.) *Dívida Externa, Recessão e Ajuste Estrutural: o Brasil Diante da Crise* (Rio: Ed. Paz e Terra, 1982).

MODIANO, E. M., 'Salários, Preços e Câmbios: os Multiplicadores dos Choques Numa Economia Indexada', *Pesquisa e Planejamento Econômico*, vol. 15, no. 1, April 1985.

MODIANO, E., 'Consequências Macroeconômicas da Restrição Externa em 1983: Simulações com um Modelo Econométrico da Economia Brasileira', *Revista Brasileira de Economia*, vol. 37, no. 3, July–September 1983b, pp. 323–36.

MODIANO, E., CARNEIRO, D. and LOPES, F., 'Projeções Macroeconômicas para a Economia Brasileira', acompanhamento trimestral 84/3, mimeo, PUC-RJ, 1984.

POMBAL DIB, M. F. S., *Importações Brasileiras: Políticas de Controle e Determinantes da Demanda 1947–1981* (Rio: BNDE, 1984).

SACHS, J., 'Comment', in *Brookings Papers in Economic Activity*, 2, 1984.

SIMONSEN, M. H., 'The Developing Countries' Debt Problem', mimeo, Washington, 1984.

VELLOSO, R., 'O Setor Externo e o Desenvolvimento Econômico Recente do Brasil', mimeo, August 1982.

WELLS, J., 'Brazil and the post-1973 Crisis in the International Economy',

Chapter 7, in R. Thorp and L. Whitehead (eds) *Inflation and Stabilization in Latin America* (London: Macmillan, and New York: Holmes & Meier, 1978), pp. 227–63.

WELLS, J., 'Growth and Fluctuation in the Brazilian Manufacturing Sector During the 60's', unpublished thesis (Cambridge University, 1977).

WERNECK, R. L., 'Uma Análise do Financiamento e dos Investimentos das Empresas Estatais Federais no Brasil 1980–83', *Revista Brasileira de Economia*, vol. 39, no. 1 (Rio: FGV, January–March, 1985).

WERNECK, R. L., 'Estrangulamento Externo e Investimento Público', in *Dívida Externa, Recessão e Ajuste Estrutural – o Brasil Diante da Crise* (Rio de Janeiro: Paz e Terra, 1983).

4 Mexico from the Oil Boom to the Debt Crisis: an Analysis of Policy Responses to External Shocks, 1978–85[1]

Jaime Ros

Mexico has a very special place in the present international debt crisis. It was the country where, in August 1982, the crisis started, and also, from 1983 onwards, the country whose adjustment to it was increasingly seen, by international organisations and banks (more than by the Mexican government itself) as a demonstration of how to get out of the crisis. This chapter is very critical of these optimistic views on Mexico's adjustment process. Indeed, it argues that the Mexican experience is an example of the limitations of orthodox policies. Although the conditions for their application were comparatively favourable, the fragility and internal contradictions of this policy approach progressively eroded the room for manoeuvre that had been obtained through a large short-term external adjustment. Consequently, after three years of depression and large relative price adjustments, the country was left in continuous economic and financial troubles with no significant long-term, structural adjustment having taken place.

The chapter is wider in scope, however. The first section reviews the performance of the Mexican economy during the oil boom (1978–81), with particular attention being paid to the increasing economic vulnerability and financial fragility which prepared the ground for the 1982 crisis. The second section examines the management of policy instruments and the behaviour of the economy during the adjustment programme from 1983 to mid-1985. Finally, a third section brings together a general appraisal of the short- and long-term economic strategies followed up to now, and outlines some alternative policy proposals to deal more effectively with the present problems of stagflation.

THE ORIGINS OF THE CRISIS AND THE ROLE OF
INTERNAL AND EXTERNAL FACTORS

Table 4.1 shows the performance of the Mexican economy during the oil boom from 1978 to 1981 and the subsequent debt crisis from 1982 onwards. It also includes, for comparative purposes, the period of sustained but increasingly unstable growth (1963–75) and the recession of 1976–7 under the previous IMF stabilisation programme.

As can be seen from the table, the economic slowdown of 1976–7 was mild and short-lived. The discovery and massive exploitation of Mexico's oil reserves relaxed the balance-of-payments constraints on growth, leading to a period of economic expansion, from 1978 to 1981, at rates well above the historical norm. Led by oil production (19.4 per cent annual growth) and oil exports (52.7 per cent annual growth), gross domestic product expanded at 8–9 per cent per year, and real national income (benefiting from the favourable shift in the terms of trade given by the oil price rise of 1979–80) grew even faster (9–10 per cent).

This rapid expansion, however, was associated with increasing real and financial vulnerability and so contributed to the 1982 crisis. Two aspects of this increasing vulnerability require emphasis: the pattern of growth and trade, and increased financial fragility.

In spite of the ambitious industrial and development plans established by the López Portillo government from 1977 onwards,[2] the oil boom was very far from creating conditions in which the industrial and agricultural sectors could take a leading role once oil revenues had ended an expansion which, from the beginning of the López Portillo regime, had been seen as temporary.[3] Although investment was very dynamic, its sectoral pattern, as shown in Table 4.2, was strongly biased in favour of the oil industry and the commerce and service sectors. With the exception of a moderate shift towards agriculture – which produced high returns in terms of agricultural output growth (see Table 4.1) – public investment was strongly reorientated towards the oil industry, which absorbed nearly one-half of all public enterprise investment (compared with one-third in the period 1970–7). Private investment, on the other hand, shifted radically towards services and distribution, and against manufacturing: the latter's share declined from one-half in 1970–7 to one-third in 1978–80. It is not surprising, then, that for the first time in a boom period, the growth of manufacturing output slowed down below the overall rate of growth, declining from 10 per cent in 1979 to 7 per cent in 1980 and 1981.[4]

This sluggishness of strategic sectors of the non-oil economy was

Table 4.1 Performance of the Mexican economy, 1963–84

	1963–75	1976–7	1978	1979	1980	1981	1982	1983	1984
Real national income (annual growth)	7.1	3.0	8.0	10.3	12.1	7.7	-1.6	-7.6	1.7
Ratio of investment to GDP (%)	18.9	19.9	20.1	22.1	23.4	24.9	21.1	16.0	16.3
Unemployment rate (%)	7.2[a]	7.7[b]	6.8	5.7	4.6	4.2	4.2	6.7	6.0
Real public sector surplus (% GDP)	na	-1.0	-2.5	-2.0	-0.6	-5.6	3.7	9.6	5.9
External current account (billion $)	-1.2	-2.7	-2.7	-4.9	-6.8	-11.7	-4.9	5.5	4.0
Foreign debt (billion $) (public and private)	20.2[a]	29.0[b]	33.2	38.9	50.6	75.0	84.8	88.6	95.9
GDP by sectors (annual growth rates) (1970 prices)									
Agriculture	4.5	4.2	5.2	-1.3	7.1	6.1	-0.6	2.9	2.4
Oil industry	5.1	9.2	16.9	18.2	23.6	16.5	8.8	-1.6	2.7
Non-oil industry	9.0	3.6	9.7	11.0	7.9	7.8	-2.8	-9.3	4.5
Commerce and services	7.7	3.7	7.6	9.9	8.1	7.9	0.2	-4.6	3.2
Total GDP	7.6	3.8	8.1	9.3	8.3	8.0	-0.5	-5.3	3.5
Domestic expenditure, exports and imports (1970 prices, annual growth)									
Private consumption	6.6	3.3	6.9	10.1	7.5	7.4	1.1	-7.5	2.8
Public consumption	9.0	2.6	9.7	9.8	9.5	10.1	2.4	-1.3	6.9
Private investment in dwellings	na	5.1	-4.6	8.6	6.5	6.6	0.2	-10.2	5.8
Other private investment	8.9[c]	-6.5	16.2	38.1	19.5	19.2	-28.5	-36.9	12.7
Public investment	11.7	-7.1	33.0	15.9	16.7	15.8	-14.2	-32.5	0.7
Exports (goods and services)	4.7	15.6	17.4	6.6	6.1	6.2	13.7	11.5	10.8
Oil and natural gas	na	40.1	77.4	49.7	74.4	36.4	19.4	15.3	-3.3
Other exports (goods)	na	7.4	28.2	-0.6	-4.9	-6.9	15.3	16.7	18.7
Imports (goods and services)	8.0	-4.8	18.7	33.4	31.9	20.3	-37.1	-41.7	21.0

71

Prices and wages

Consumer prices (annual growth)	6.8	21.1	17.5	18.2	26.3	28.0	58.9	101.9	65.5
Average real wages (annual growth)	na	4.1	1.0	5.5	−0.8	4.2	−2.4	−26.5	−5.7
(Free) real exchange rate (1970 = 100)	127.4[a]	92.9[b]	101.1	107.2	118.3	128.0	87.6	61.5	78.6
(Controlled) real exchange rate (1970 = 100)							80.0	75.7	86.4

Notes:
[a] 1975.
[b] 1977.
[c] Total private investment.

Sources: Banco de México, *Producto Interno y Gasto* (1960–77); **SPP**, *Sistema de Cuentas Nacionales* (1970–8, 1979–81, 1981–3, 1984); Banco de México, *Estadísticas de Balanza de Pagos* and *Informes Anuales*; Economía Aplicada SC, *Cuentas de los Sectores Institucionales* (1985).

Table 4.2   Composition of total public and private investment in 1970–7 and during the oil boom (1978–81)

	Total investment (*excluding dwellings and central government*)				
	1970–77	*1978*	*1979*	*1980*	*1981*
Agriculture	7.3	8.4	7.5	7.2	na
Mining	2.2	1.6	2.9	3.1	na
Oil	11.2	20.7	18.4	19.0	na
Manufacturing	38.0	20.7	24.7	25.6	na
Electricity	8.1	10.1	9.5	9.8	na
Commerce and services	33.3	38.4	36.9	35.3	na
Total	100.0	100.0	100.0	100.0	
Public investment (excluding central government)					
Agriculture	1.8	1.7	2.2	2.5	3.5
Mining	0.7	0.7	1.0	1.1	1.0
Oil	32.0	44.6	41.9	44.2	44.7
Manufacturing	14.2	9.8	14.3	11.6	15.2
Electricity	23.1	21.8	21.8	22.8	19.4
Commerce and services	28.2	21.4	18.8	17.8	16.2
Total	100.0	100.0	100.0	100.0	100.0
Private non-residential investment					
Agriculture	10.2	14.2	11.7	10.7	na
Mining	3.0	2.3	4.4	4.6	na
Oil	0.0	0.0	0.0	0.0	na
Manufacturing	50.8	30.3	32.8	36.1	na
Electricity	0.0	0.0	0.0	0.0	na
Commerce and services	36.0	53.0	51.1	48.6	na
Total	100.0	100.0	100.0	100.0	

Source: Santamaría (1985).

related (as cause or as effect?) to a striking deterioration in non-oil foreign trade: from mid-1979 non-oil exports started falling while imports of goods grew, from mid-1978 to mid-1981, at the unprecedented rate of more than 30 per cent per year, attaining absolute increases in current dollars larger than the increase in oil export revenue. This explosive growth in imports and the sluggishness of the manufacturing sector are in turn the result of three possibly interrelated phenomena: the import liberalisation policies started under the 1976–8 stabilisation programme, the progressive revaluation of the real exchange rate from 1978 to 1981 (see Table 4.1) and the insufficient growth of non-oil industrial capacity (relative to the rapid expansion of domestic demand) associated with the above-mentioned pattern of private investment. There was much controversy over the relative weight of each of these three factors, particularly with respect to the role of import liberalisation.[5]

In any case, the following trade pattern emerged: exports became concentrated on only one commodity, oil, which was to become very vulnerable to changes in international markets, while imports involved intermediate and capital goods that tend to grow, as domestic production increases, independently of the composition of final demand. Economic growth thus became increasingly dependent on the export of a single commodity, which, given the nature of this specialisation, was increasingly vulnerable to external demand constraints. The balance-of-payments constraint was bound to re-emerge with renewed force.

Oil exports increased from US \$0.6 billion in 1976 to \$14 billion in 1981, but even so there was a progressive imbalance in the balance of payments (see Table 4.3). The current account deficit increased from \$2.7 billion in 1978 to \$12.5 billion in 1981, due in substantial measure to rising interest payments on accumulated foreign debt. Thus, as can be seen in Table 4.3, income paid abroad represented 64 per cent of the overall current account deficit over the period 1978–81, compared with 42 per cent over the previous period (1972–7).

These increasing payments imbalances were financed through foreign debt, mainly public, which rose from \$29 billion in 1977 to \$75 billion in 1981. The debt structure, on the other hand, became increasingly vulnerable towards the end of the period. By 1981, short-term loans accounted for more than half of net external indebtedness. The ratio of foreign debt interest payments to total exports rose from 27 per cent in 1977–8 to 37 per cent in 1981–2. However, it is worth pointing out that this increase was fully explained by rising interest rates since the debt/export ratio shows a moderate decline over the same period from 3.1 to 2.8.

The financial fragility that developed over the period also affected the private sector. The boom in domestic demand and investment triggered a rapid growth of private indebtedness: the debt/capital ratio of large private firms rose from 0.9 in 1978 to 1.2 in 1981. More important, however, was the changed composition of this debt: the share of dollar-denominated debt in the overall debt of large private firms rose from 30 per cent in 1978 to 63 per cent in 1981.[6] The upsurge of long-term foreign indebtedness by private firms in 1978–80 can be explained by the optimistic expectations prevailing as to the exchange rate at a time when the rule of monetary policy was to set domestic nominal interest rates

Table 4.3 Use of foreign debt, 1972–84[a] (billion dollars)

	1972–7[b]	1978	1979	1980	1981	1982	1983	1984
1. Increase in public and private external debt less change in reserves[c]	3.7	3.3	5.8	9.6	23.4	14.4	−1.1 (7.3)	−1.5 (10.7)
2. Trade balance	−1.5 (40.0)	−0.5 (15.2)	−1.8 (30.8)	−2.1 (21.7)	−5.3 (22.5)	5.4	14.4	13.8
3. Factor income from abroad	−1.1 (30.3)	−2.2 (66.6)	−3.1 (53.7)	−4.7 (48.8)	−7.3 (31.0)	−10.3 (71.6)	−8.9 (61.6)	−9.6 (69.7)
4. Gross acquisition of foreign assets by the private sector[d]	−1.1 (29.7)	−0.6 (18.2)	−0.9 (15.5)	−2.8 (29.5)	−10.9 (46.5)	−9.5 (66.1)	−4.5 (31.1)	−2.7 (19.6)

Notes: (1) + (2) + (3) + (4) = 0.

[a] Negative items (outflow of foreign exchange) are expressed in parentheses as percentage of the sum of positive items (inflow of foreign exchange).

[b] Yearly average for the period.

[c] Includes direct foreign investment.

[d] A negative figure refers to a positive acquisition of foreign assets.

Sources: Banco de México, Informe Anual, several issues.

equal to foreign interest rates plus the 'expected' devaluation of the peso implied by the gap between spot and forward exchange rates in the Chicago futures market.[7] Since, however, the actual mini-devaluations engineered by the Central Bank were not consistent with the (expected) devaluation implicit in its interest rate policy – the latter being much greater than the former – domestic interest rates remained for several years well above *ex post* interest rates abroad (expressed in a common currency).

The First External Shock: 1979–80

It is against this background of increasing financial fragility and dependence on oil, which reached 72 per cent of total exports of goods in 1981, that international developments played their destabilising role. After 1979 the Mexican economy experienced two successive external shocks (see Table 4.4). The first of these was the doubling of the international oil price and the rise in foreign interest rates in 1979–80, which had, on balance, a favourable short-term effect. Not only was oil export income twice what was originally projected[8] but, for the same reason, the rise in interest rates (which were still low in real terms) was accompanied by an almost unlimited availability of foreign loans. The oil bonanza turned Mexico into a preferred customer of the international banks, and foreign loans were conceded in amounts and on conditions notably more favourable than for the rest of the developing countries. Thus, from 1978 to 1981, while international bank loans to developing countries as a whole increased by 76 per cent, in the case of Mexico (already a very large debtor in 1978) they rose by 146 per cent.[9]

With hindsight, the nature of this first external shock was dramatically misinterpreted by the Mexican government (as well as by many other economic agents). High and increasing real oil prices were taken to be a permanent feature of the international economy, while the increase in interest rates was interpreted as a temporary phenomenon. These views therefore reinforced the policies of import liberalisation, real exchange-rate appreciation and fiscal expansion, although only after heated debates, especially with respect to import liberalisation and Mexico's proposed entry into GATT. Paradoxically, however, the government decision in 1980 not to become a member of GATT was accompanied by a further and accentuated relaxation of import controls.

Table 4.4 Indicators of the international economy, 1977–84

	1977	1978	1979	1980	1981	1982	1983	1984
US GDP growth	5.5	4.9	2.4	−0.3	2.6	−2.0	3.8	6.8
OECD GDP growth	3.9	4.0	3.3	1.3	1.6	−0.2	2.4	3.4
US inflation rate	6.5	7.7	11.3	13.5	10.4	6.1	3.2	4.2
Dollar price of oil (growth rate)	9.4	6.4	46.4	63.0	10.0	−3.8	−12.3	−1.3
US prime rate (nominal) (%)	6.8	9.1	12.7	15.3	18.9	14.9	10.8	12.0
US prime rate (real) (%)	0.4	1.4	1.4	1.8	8.5	8.7	7.6	8.0

Sources: IMF, International Financial Statistics (1984); IMF, World Economic Outlook (1984); Economic Report of the President (1985).

1981: Falling Oil Prices, Fiscal Expansion and Private Capital Flight

An optimistic outlook continued to prevail during the first half of 1981, even though the US recession had started weakening the international oil market and foreign interest rates had continued to rise, the US prime rate reaching a peak of 19 per cent for 1981 as a whole (see Table 4.4). Accordingly, fiscal expansion was reinforced in 1981, stimulated also by ready access to foreign finance and by the particular phase in Mexico's political cycle. This was the fifth year of a six-year presidential term when, as in 1963, 1969 and particularly 1975, a rush set in to carry through the government's plans, and control over public expenditure was relaxed as the country entered a political period centred on the nomination of the next PRI candidate for the presidential elections to be held a year later. The inflation-corrected public sector deficit[10] (5.6 per cent of GDP) reached its historical peak in 1981, as did the real exchange rate (around 30 per cent appreciation above its historical level by the end of the year).

The government's optimistic expectations were shared by international banks, which redoubled their lending to Mexico during 1981[11] in response to the government's increased demand for foreign loans as the current account deficit widened.[12] But official expectations were not shared by everybody else: after borrowing heavily from abroad in 1979–80, the Mexican private sector started an unprecedented speculative attack on the peso in the first half of 1981, and more than 20 billion dollars fled out of the country in a period of about eighteen months. The magnitude of the capital flight is such that it absorbed as much as 54 per cent of the increase in Mexico's total foreign debt (net of international reserves) in 1981 and 1982 (see Table 4.3), generating growing political tension between the López Portillo government and the large private financial conglomerates.

As can be seen from Table 4.5 (which shows the flow of funds between the public, private and external sectors), a major shift in the composition of the private sector's portfolio was beginning. As the table shows, in normal years (1979 and 1980) the (nominal) financial deficit of the public sector had as its counterpart a current account deficit (equal to about half the public sector deficit) and a (nominal) private sector financial surplus (corresponding to the remainder of the public sector deficit). The financial surplus of the external sector was used to finance the public sector's borrowing abroad and the net indebtedness of the private sector. In 1981 the expansion of the public sector financial deficit was accompanied by a larger current account deficit and a very substantial

Table 4.5   The flow of funds identity, 1978–84 (percentage of GDP)

	1978	1979	1980	1981	1982	1983	1984
1. Public sector financial deficit	6.4	6.2	6.1	14.6	17.1	8.8	6.5
2. External sector financial surplus (= current account deficit)	2.9	3.6	3.9	5.3	−0.2	−3.7	−2.2
3. Private sector financial surplus (= private sector net acquisition of financial assets) of which:	2.9	3.2	1.7	8.5	17.2	13.0	8.5
4. Net acquisition of public sector debt	3.5	4.6	4.0	6.6	13.0	8.6	6.2
5. Net acquisition of foreign assets	−0.6	−1.4	−2.3	1.9	4.2	4.4	2.3
6. Public sector borrowing abroad (= 2 + 5)	2.3	2.2	1.6	7.2	4.1	0.7	0.1
7. Statistical discrepancy	0.6	−0.5	0.5	0.8	0.1	−0.6	0.3

Source: Banco de México, *Informe Anual*, several issues.

increase in the private sector financial surplus. But now the net acquisition of foreign assets by the private sector turned from negative to a large positive figure. The financial surplus of the external sector financed only a fraction of public sector borrowing abroad, the remainder being financed by the domestic private sector *through the intermediation of foreign banks*, which were in a sense relending to the Mexican government funds obtained from the acquisition of foreign deposits by Mexican residents.

The Events of 1982

At the beginning of 1982 the international price of oil was still falling, capital flight was at its peak, and nearly half the country's foreign debt was due for repayment or refinancing over the following twelve months. Although import controls were reimposed in mid-1981 and a 4 per cent cut in the 1981 budget was introduced, a more radical shift in economic policies was now unavoidable.

In February the government decided on a fiscal contraction plus a devaluation package, maintaining the free convertibility of the peso. The fiscal package included cuts in real public expenditure, particularly investment (-14.2 per cent over the year, see Table 4.1), an increase in public energy prices, and reductions in subsidies on basic foodstuffs. At the same time the Bank of Mexico announced an end to its intervention in the foreign exchange market, leading to an 80 per cent depreciation of the peso during February. In April the Director of the Central Bank publicly opposed the adoption of an exchange control regime in Mexico. The large peso devaluation was followed some time later by 'emergency increases' of 30 per cent in the minimum wage and 20 per cent and 10 per cent for higher wage levels.

This was the starting point of the recession, and of a rapid acceleration of inflation. The fall in real aggregate demand was led by private investment (-28.5 per cent in 1982) affected by the stagflation effects of devaluation and by the fiscal and public investment contraction, as well as other factors. First, the sudden and radical shift in exchange-rate expectations, which continued to be pessimistic despite the size of the February devaluation, led to a large increase in the expected profitability of financial investment in foreign assets relative to the profitability of domestic productive investment. Second, the present and expected future profitability of domestic investment was reduced by the sharp increase in the price of imported capital goods, and in the real value of firms' foreign debt resulting from devaluation, together with the depression of the real market value of physical assets, determined to a large extent by the massive capital flight. The financial breakdown of Grupo Alfa, the country's largest industrial conglomerate, is the most representative and best known example of the financial difficulties affecting, in early 1982, several large private firms with substantial dollar-denominated debts.[13]

Although the trade balance became positive by the second quarter of 1982, the policy package was ineffective in stopping post-devaluation capital flight and the financial speculation which flourished in the absence of any kind of restriction on capital flows. Capital flight became by far the most important source of payment imbalances (see Table 4.3) and, with foreign loans increasingly rationed, of the resulting fall of foreign reserves at the Central Bank.

In August 1982, when the official reserves were almost completely exhausted, the flow of international lending to Mexico was suddenly interrupted. Dramatic new devaluations followed, together with the adoption of a dual exchange-rate regime, and the government suspended payments on its foreign debt, signalling the beginning of the international debt crisis. The domestic political context was centred on the recent (July) election of the PRI's candidate for President, Miguel de La Madrid – formerly Budget and Planning Minister – and on the mounting political conflict between the government and the large financial conglomerates.

These are the economic and political circumstances in which, in his last annual presidential address to the nation (1 September 1982), López Portillo dramatically announced the nationalisation of the private banking system and the adoption of full exchange controls on capital flows. This brought to a head a major crisis between the government and the large private banks, a crisis which was to modify drastically the relations between the state and the private sector. But it was too late for the adoption of an exchange control regime: foreign reserves were exhausted and the international debt crisis had arrived. In spite of an attempt at a heterodox monetary policy under very adverse conditions (see Tello, 1984), the last few months of the López Portillo administration was marked by the appearance of the IMF and the negotiation and preparation of the adjustment programme to be applied by a new government.

Before turning to an analysis of the 1983–5 period, it may be worth speculating on policy making during 1981 and 1982, and on the issue of a possible alternative course of events. Since mid-1981, two main alternatives to the prevailing inertia were put forward from different sides of the economic cabinet. The Ministry of Finance under David Ibarra (who remained in office until February 1982, when he was replaced by Jesus Silva Herzog) pressed for rapid measures to correct the exchange rate and reduce the growth of public expenditure. On this view, the increasing trouble with the balance of payments, both in the current and in the capital accounts, was mainly attributable to the continuous real appreciation of the exchange rate and to the huge expansion of public spending. A second and different view, put forward at the Ministry of Industry and by other close collaborators of López Portillo, favoured the adoption of direct controls on imports (as was done in June 1981) and on capital flows as the only effective policy response to the capital flight and to the external shocks coming from an increasingly unstable international economy. This view recognised the need for fiscal moderation – less emphatically than the former position – but for most of the period it opposed a maxi-devaluation on the grounds that it would simply exacerbate inflation and could even accelerate capital flight.

The policy debates of the period focused increasingly on these two options, but no major shifts in policies occurred during 1981 to head off the worst of all possible worlds: free capital mobility plus huge fiscal expansion plus real exchange rate appreciation. Given the extreme vulnerability of the Mexican economy at the time and, in particular, its almost absolute external dependence on increasingly unstable oil and financial markets, we tend to view the absence of any restrictions on capital flows as the major policy error of the period. However, with hindsight, two additional points should be made. First, the 1981 fiscal expansion was also a major policy error. It was based, as we have seen, on a misinterpretation of international developments, and it generated some of the incentives and the means for the massive capital flight. The second point refers to the exchange rate issue. The real appreciation in the period 1978–81 is probably not to be seen, at least for most of the period, as a policy error but rather as the unavoidable by-product of the oil boom and the 1981 fiscal expansion. However, when the growth of oil export revenues stopped, the real exchange rate became incompatible overnight with medium-term growth and a viable balance of payments. In other words, the sustainable real exchange rate in the medium term was suddenly and radically altered by the new prospects of stagnating or falling oil revenues.[14] A gradual correction of the exchange rate, with a temporary increase in foreign finance during the transition, would probably have been an economically less costly and socially more efficient way to deal with the problem. But this would have required that foreign finance to Mexico behaved countercyclically (with respect to the oil market), i.e. exactly the contrary of its actual behaviour. In practice the pattern of external financing aggravated still more the extent of the real exchange-rate adjustment.

THE NATURE AND EFFECTS OF THE ADJUSTMENT PROCESS: 1983–5

On 1 December 1982, de la Madrid took office, committed to a three-year IMF stabilisation plan, just as López Portillo had been six years before. The new government's room for political manoeuvre was relatively large: first, because the presidential figure is so strong in Mexico that despite the fact that de la Madrid had been the ruling party candidate and the former Budget and Planning Minister, the new government was able to shift the responsibility for economic chaos on to López Portillo; second, compared to the previous administration, de la Madrid's economic team was relatively homogeneous, with no heterodox economists in ministerial positions.[15]

On the other hand, the economic constraints were very tight: inflation was running at more than a 100 per cent annual rate in the last quarter of 1982, and the flow of external finance was suspended. However, these economic constraints soon began to ease. First, the real exchange rate had already been adjusted, and as recession deepened the trade surplus rapidly grew: by the fourth quarter of 1982 there was a current balance of $1.4 billion. Second, a large fiscal adjustment had already taken place during 1982 (see Table 4.6), although this was not at all evident from the conventional measure of the public sector deficit (non-corrected for inflation) which reached a peak of 17.9 per cent of GDP as a result of enlarged nominal interest payments on public debt and the exchange rate adjustments. Third, new instruments of economic policy, such as exchange controls and a nationalised banking system, were now available to the new government.

The Short- and Long-term Targets of the Adjustment Programme

Table 4.7 shows the main targets for the three-year programme – including both the original IMF macroeconomic projections and the revisions made in the light of yearly results – as well as the actual performance of the target variables. The short-term goals focused on an ambitious reduction of the inflation rate and a gradual adjustment in the current account of the balance of payments (which, incidentally, had almost been achieved in 1982). An additional and drastic fiscal adjustment – cutting by half the nominal public sector deficit as a percentage of GDP in 1983 – was assumed to affect only marginally GDP growth, which was to be 0 per cent in 1983, and recover its historical rates by 1985.

On the other hand, a long-term model of 'structural change' was proposed, aimed at efficient and sustained economic growth – at rates somewhat lower than historical ones (5–6 per cent according to the National Development Plan) – from 1985 onwards. The main aspects of the structural change were: (i) a radical alteration of the structure of relative prices, to be achieved during the stabilisation phase; and (ii) the progressive elimination of inefficient state intervention in production

Table 4.6 Public sector accounts (% of GDP), 1980–4[a]

	1980	1981	1982	1983	1984
1. *Revenues*	19.4	18.6	20.9	24.3	23.0
Net indirect taxes	8.3	8.1	8.6	11.6	11.0
Direct taxes	6.0	6.0	5.2	4.5	4.6
Social security and other central govt.[b]	2.7	3.1	3.5	2.9	2.5
Gross surplus of public enterprises[c]	2.4	1.4	3.7	5.3	5.0
2. *Expenditures* (*excluding interest*)	23.6	27.8	29.7	20.6	19.5
Current consumption	10.8	11.7	11.4	9.3	9.4
General government investment	4.4	4.6	4.5	3.5	3.6
Public enterprise investment	6.4	7.2	5.9	4.0	4.1
Other expenditures[d]	1.9	4.4	7.9	3.8	2.4
(1) − (2) = 3. *Nominal surplus excluding interest*	−4.1	−9.2	−8.8	3.7	3.5
4. *Interest payments*	3.5	5.3	9.1	12.5	10.6
Internal	1.9	3.3	5.6	7.9	6.1
External	1.6	2.0	3.5	4.6	4.5
(3) − (4) = 5. *Nominal financial surplus*	−7.6	−14.5	−17.9	−8.8	−7.1
6. *Inflation correction*	7.0	8.9	21.6	18.4	13.0
(5) + (6) = 7. *Real financial surplus*	−0.6	−5.6	3.7	9.6	5.9

Notes:
[a] The public sector includes here the federal government, public enterprises (subject or not to budgetary control) and the Federal District.
[b] Net of transfers to the private sector.
[c] Gross of interest payments on public enterprise debt.
[d] Residual including the deficit of public enterprises not subject to budgetary control, the deficit for financial intermediation and the deficit on 'other accounts'.

Sources: Economía Aplicada SC, *Cuentas de los Sectores Institucionales* (1985); Banco de México, *Informe Anual*, several issues.

and foreign trade. Both aspects implied a larger economic role for market signals and the private sector, and were expected to induce an export-led pattern of growth.

'Getting the prices right' involved, first, a radical shift in the price of tradables relative to non-tradables, in order to stimulate non-oil exports. Second, it involved correcting public enterprise prices, real interest rates and taxes, and reducing subsidies. Given the present and future scarcity of foreign savings, pricing policies were needed which would generate the domestic savings necessary to 'finance' economic growth. Third, a new structure of factor prices was required which, together with export-led

Mexico from the Oil Boom to the Debt Crisis

Table 4.7 Main targets of the adjustment programme, 1983–5

	1982	1983	1984	1985
Inflation (Dec.–Dec. consumer prices) (%)				
Original IMF projection[a]		55.0	30.0	18.0
Revised targets (government)[b]			40.0	35.0
Actual performance	98.9	80.8	59.2	63.7
PSBR (% *of GDP*)				
Original IMF projections[a]		8.5	5.5	3.5
Revised target (government)[b]		8.5	5.5	5.1
			6.5	5.6[c]
Actual performance	17.9	8.8	7.1	9.9
Current account balance				
Original IMF projections (% of GDP)		−2.2	−1.8	−1.2
Actual performance (% of GDP)	−2.7	5.7	3.4	0.4
Revised targets (government) (billion dollars)[b]			0.0	1.0
			0.5	2.0
Actual performance (billion dollars)	−4.9	5.5	4.2	0.5
Real GDP growth (%)				
Original IMF projections[a]		0.0	3.0	6.0
Revised targets (government)[b]			0.0	3.0
			1.0	4.0
Actual performance	−0.5	−5.3	3.5	2.7

Notes:
[a] Original macroeconomic projections by the IMF (late 1982).
[b] Annual targets, which are revised in the light of the results obtained, contained in the document: Presidencia de la República, 'Criterios Generales de Política Económica'. This document is sent to Congress in November–December of each year and presents the main objectives of economic policy for the coming year.
[c] In the letter of intent to the IMF (March 1985) this target was modified to 4.7 per cent of GDP. However, none of the other targets was revised to ensure internal consistency.

Sources: see notes for projections. For actual performance, see the other tables in this chapter.

growth, would promote a more efficient use of domestic factor endowments.

The elimination of public sector inefficiencies included the 'rationalisation' of public enterprises, which includes the sale or liquidation of 236 small and medium-size enterprises in 1985, and steps towards a progressive import liberalisation, especially from July 1985.

In the government's view, the short- and the long-term goals were closely complementary. However, over the last two and a half years increasing tensions have emerged between three conflicting aspects of the adjustment programme: (i) the achievement of the inflation targets: (ii) the radical alteration of the relative price structure: and (iii) the need to avoid social and political disruption.

The Management of Policy Instruments

Fiscal policy

Fiscal adjustment was considered the main policy instrument to eliminate the excess demand which is supposedly the cause of high inflation and external imbalance. The adjustment was to be concentrated on 1983, when the nominal deficit (PSBR) was to be slashed by half as a percentage of GDP from 17.9 per cent in 1982 to 8.5 per cent in 1983. The actual reduction was close to target (8.8 per cent) and came about from two sources, as shown in Table 4.6: first, a reduction by 9 percentage points (of GDP) in public expenditures (excluding interest payments) through a fall by 32.5 per cent in public investment (mainly public enterprise investment) and a sharp reduction in the real wages and salaries of public sector employees;[16] and second, a 3 percentage point increase in indirect taxes (net of subsidies) and an upward adjustment of public sector relative prices. The latter, together with the revaluation of PEMEX oil export revenues, due to the exchange rate adjustment, led to an increase of 1.6 percentage points in the gross surplus of public enterprises (and almost 4 points above its 1981 levels). Direct taxes, on the other hand, declined as a percentage of GDP – as they had also done in 1982 – probably as a result of the joint effects of the acceleration of inflation and fiscal lags in tax collection.

In 1984, fiscal adjustment was relaxed, leaving the nominal fiscal surplus (excluding interest) unaffected as a percentage of GDP (see Table 4.6), while the PSBR declined only because of a 2 percentage fall in the nominal interest payments on public debt as nominal interest rates declined in line with the deceleration of inflation from 1983 to 1984. However, since inflation was well above the 40 per cent target, higher-than-planned interest payments covered an overshoot of the PSBR target by about one percentage point of GDP. Public investment in real terms once again suffered from the attempt to achieve the PSBR target, and grew less than originally planned (0.7 per cent growth instead of the original figure of 5.0 per cent).

As is pointed out in the introduction to this book, the definition of fiscal targets on the basis of the conventional measure of the public sector financial deficit (PSBR unadjusted for inflation) has been discussed increasingly in the literature. Criticisms of this approach can be made on two grounds.[17] The first is that the nominal interest rate includes, in real terms, a proportion of capital repayment on public debt. This makes the conventional or nominal deficit a bad indicator of the fiscal stance under inflationary conditions, and one that is itself highly sensitive to the rate of inflation – since the nominal interest rate rises and falls with it. Thus, alternative measures of the fiscal deficit, corrected for inflation, should at least be considered in the definition of fiscal policy. Corrections for inflation may be applied only to the interest-bearing component of public debt or to the whole of public sector liabilities (including, therefore, also a correction for the inflation tax on monetary public debt).[18] The latter would yield a measure of the real fiscal deficit as the change in the real value of public sector liabilities. Estimates of the corresponding real fiscal surplus in Mexico are shown in Table 4.6.

A second criticism is that when fiscal targets are set for the PSBR as a percentage of GDP, the fiscal stance becomes geared exclusively to the achievement of inflation targets, regardless of any other economic objective (economic activity or the balance of payments). For by including in the fiscal target the capital repayments on public debt, which are highly sensitive to inflation, the real fiscal stance automatically becomes more restrictive than planned, whenever actual inflation overshoots the inflation forecast on which the budget was prepared, while it is automatically relaxed when actual inflation is below the level planned.[19] We are, indeed, a long way from Keynesian management of fiscal policy!

The efficiency of the whole approach, however, depends crucially on inflation being highly sensitive to demand pressures, i.e. on fiscal policy being an effective policy instrument to deal with inflation. The evidence for Mexico suggests quite the contrary. Between 1979 and 1984 there was a clear positive relationship between the real fiscal surplus[20] as a percentage of GDP and the rate of inflation, which strongly suggests that the large increases in net indirect taxes and public rates have more than offset the demand-induced effects on inflation of a contractionary fiscal policy. This view is supported by much research on price formation and on the determinants of inflation in Mexico.[21]

If inflation is less responsive to a fall in demand than is implicitly assumed in the IMF approach to fiscal policy, the inflation performance will typically overshoot the inflation forecast on which the budget was prepared. In this case, as several authors have pointed out,[22] either the PSBR targets become unattainable (in spite of an increasingly restrictive fiscal stance) – as has been the case in Brazil over the recent period (see, in this volume, the chapter by Dias Carneiro) – or, if achieved, the result is to devastate the economy. An automatic stabiliser for inflation becomes an automatic destabiliser of the level of economic activity. What happened in Mexico in 1983 approximates to the latter case.

Indeed, as can be seen in Table 4.6, the fulfilment of the 1983 target for the nominal deficit, together with the overshooting by 25 percentage points of the inflation forecast, implied that the fiscal adjustment indicated a surplus of 3.7 per cent of GDP in the fiscal balance, excluding interest payments, and of 9.6 per cent of GDP when the fiscal surplus is fully corrected for the effects of inflation on public debt. In face of the failure to consider the real fiscal stance implications of the 1983 PSBR target, it is not surprising that recession was much deeper than expected (a 5.3 per cent fall in GDP instead of 0 per cent) and that the adjustment in the current account balance was overdone by 7 percentage points of GDP.

Monetary policy

The adjustment programme included monetary ceilings on domestic credit expansion. However, the latter do not seem to have played a major role in the adjustment process largely because excess reserves in the banking system increased continuously during 1983 and 1984 as the private sector's demand for bank loans collapsed with the decline in investment and economic activity. Additionally, the Central Bank became increasingly concerned with the unexpectedly large increase in its foreign reserves resulting from the adjustment in the current account of the balance of payments.

During 1983 and 1984, interest rate policy involved setting deposit nominal rates so as to yield a high premium over foreign interest rates plus the announced rate of mini-devaluations (related to the government's inflation targets) in an effort to deter capital flight. Since, however, the rate of mini-devaluations remained below actual inflation performance, *ex post* real rates on deposits stayed at relatively low levels. The structure of interest rates followed from government forecasts of a

Table 4.8   Composition of the gross acquisition of domestic financial assets by the (non-bank) private sector (percentages of the change in M5)

	1978–81	1982	1983	1984
Cash	12.7	14.0	7.6	11.0
Cheque accounts	16.6	8.5	10.6	11.3
Liquid deposits[a]	16.0	27.1	19.7	66.4
Term deposits[b]	49.7	36.9	49.2	0.0
Non-bank financial assets[c]	5.0	13.5	13.0	11.3
Total (change in M5)	100.0	100.0	100.0	100.0

Notes:
[a]   Less than three months.
[b]   More than three months.
[c]   CETES, petrobonos, papel comercial, aceptaciones bancarias, bonos de indemnización bancaria and obligaciones quirografarias.

Source: Banco de México, *Informe Anual* (1984).

continuous decline in the rate of inflation, yielding higher nominal rates for liquid deposits than for term deposits. The spread between the two was increased at the beginning of 1984: as inflation ran well above government's forecasts, this led to a sudden shift in the composition of the private sector's financial savings from term deposits to liquid deposits from March 1984 onwards. The actual nominal acquisition of term deposits was in fact nil in 1984, as can be seen in Table 4.8. The highly liquid structure of private domestic financial assets by the beginning of 1985 may well be related to subsequent troubles and pressures on the exchange rate, as inflation continued to run above target, and exchange-rate expectations became increasingly pessimistic.

In spite of low real deposit rates, real lending rates have remained very high for most of the recent period. The explanation centres on two factors. The first concerns the shift, discussed above, in the private sector's financial savings. For, given the structure of real *ex post* interest rates, the shift towards liquid deposits tended to increase the average real cost of bank funds. The lower share of cheque accounts in financial savings, associated with high inflation from 1982 onwards, had similar effects.

A second set of circumstances may explain the high spread between lending rates and the average cost of funds. This has to do with the possibility of a perverse response on the part of lending rates to the collapse of private sector demands for bank loans, in an inflationary context. Thus, as excess bank reserves accumulated and inflation remained at high levels during 1983 and 1984, the inflation tax on bank reserves increased in spite of the Bank of Mexico's auctions of interest-bearing reserve assets.

This increased 'tax burden' on bank reserves may have been shifted on to the remaining borrowers through a rise in real lending rates. In support of this explanation we may refer to the high correlation of the spread (between lending rates and the average cost of bank funds) with the rate of inflation, and also to the fact that the decline of the spread accelerated with the recovery of the demand for loans during 1984, although causality may have run both ways.

Exchange-rate policy

In September 1982, a two-tier peso-dollar rate was established, pegged at 50 pesos for foreign trade transactions, and at 70 pesos for other transactions (which were subject to rationing). A black market, later legalised, sprang up on both sides of the US–Mexico border, with foreign exchange houses dealing at a flexible rate of about 130 to 140 pesos in October and November of 1982. In December 1982 one of the first steps of the new government was to 'catch up' with the black market rate through establishing a 'free rate' at 150 pesos and setting up a 'controlled rate' at 95 pesos, with daily mini-devaluations of 13 cents (implying, therefore, a declining percentage rate of mini-devaluations starting from an annualised rate of around 60 per cent). The 13 cent daily devaluation was also applied, from September 1983, to the free rate, and daily mini-devaluations increased, for both exchange rates, to 17 cents in December 1984 and to 21 cents in March 1985. The history of these adjustments, together with the behaviour of real exchange rates, is presented in Table 4.9. Taking into account all the adjustments carried out during 1982, the nominal devaluation from February to December had been approximately 450 per cent for the free rate and 250 per cent for the controlled rate. Real exchange rates reached record lows, with the controlled real rate in mid-1983 still almost half its January 1982 level and about 30 per cent below its mid-1978 level, which is also, more or less, the historical average of the good old 1960s.

After the large initial adjustments of December 1982, the rate of mini-devaluations was set so as to contribute to the deceleration of inflation and yet, at the same time, to maintain an undervalued (by historical standards) real exchange rate in order to promote (non-oil) export-led

Table 4.9 Exchange rates, quarterly behaviour, 1982–5

		Controlled[a] (nominal, pesos per dollar)	Free[b] (nominal, pesos per dollar)	Spot (nominal, pesos per dollar)	Spot/free (%)	Controlled[c] real (index 1978 = 100)	Free real (index 1978 = 100)[b,c]
1982	I		39.5	na	na		92.9
	II		46.9	na	na		88.2
	III	49.7[d]	68.1	na	na	102.8[d]	72.6
	IV	65.2	96.2	na	na	92.0	62.6
1983	I	104.2	147.9	151.0[e]	2.1	71.8	50.5
	II	116.0	147.9	na	na	74.1	58.1
	III	127.9	148.0	154.0[f]	4.1	75.1	64.9
	IV	139.9	156.6	163.0	4.1	76.6	68.4
1984	I	151.8	168.5	167.8	-0.4	81.6	73.5
	II	163.6	180.3	189.5	5.1	84.5	76.7
	III	175.6	192.3	196.2	2.0	85.7	78.2
	IV	187.8	204.5	208.7	2.1	87.8	80.6
1985	I	203.0	219.8	233.7	6.3	93.8	86.7
	II	221.5	238.3	261.9	9.9	93.9	87.2
	III	275.3	336.2	na	na	83.5	68.3

Notes:
[a] From August to November 1982 corresponds to the preferential rate.
[b] From August to November 1982 corresponds to the general or ordinary rate.
[c] Real exchange rates were obtained using the dollar per peso rate and US and Mexican consumer price indices.
[d] Average of August and September.
[e] Average of August and September.
[f] Average of January and February.

Source: Banco de México, Indicadores Económicos, several issues; Excelsior, several issues.

growth. The appropriate real exchange parity was, initially, considered to be the mid-1983 level of the controlled rate. This approach required that from then onwards actual inflation followed, approximately, the percentage rate of announced mini-devaluations, i.e. that it followed the government's inflation targets.

What happened next exemplifies the increasing tensions in policy management resulting from the latent conflict between the short-term (inflation) objectives of the programme and the maintenance of a structure of relative prices considered appropriate to the achievement of the long-term (structural change) objectives. These tensions expressed themselves in different and changing views on the criteria for exchange-rate management. In the government's main economic policy document (*Plan Nacional de Desarrollo*) published in mid-1983, the exchange rate was considered a major policy instrument in the 'structural change' strategy, and 'realism', in a long-term perspective, was considered essential in its management.[23] Subsequently, however, a second view – popular at the Bank of Mexico – was put forward. The large and unexpected increase in foreign reserves, resulting from the external adjustment of 1983 and 1984, and a growing concern about its monetary implications, led these analysts to consider the short-term overall performance of the balance of payments as the best criterion for exchange-rate management. Apparently a simple neoclassical small open economy model also led to the conclusion, among some Central Bank economists, that exchange-rate policy was incapable of affecting the real exchange rate and moreover that the attempt to do so risked generating explosive inflation. A favourable balance-of-payments position, an improved performance of non-oil exports, and increasing difficulties in regulating other key prices contributed to the prevalence of short-term criteria and objectives. The room for manoeuvre given by the external adjustment was therefore used to decelerate inflation, and from mid-1983 to December 1984 real exchange rates appreciated by about 20 per cent (controlled rate) and 30 per cent (free rate).

As export performance weakened substantially, from the last quarter of 1984, and as speculation about the peso intensified, from the beginning of 1985, the government increased the rate of daily devaluations moderately in December 1984 and again in March 1985. These steps, however, appeared to be insufficient in the face of increasing troubles,[24] aggravated by the prospect of a large overshoot of both the inflation target (60 per cent *vis-à-vis* 35 per cent) and the current account target, and by speculation stimulated by falls in the oil price. Thus in July–August 1985 a new collapse of the exchange market followed, with new devaluations of the controlled and free rate, while a new exchange-rate system was introduced. The controlled rate was devalued by about 20 per cent and then allowed to crawl down, while a completely 'free' rate was legalised which proved highly unstable.

Trade policy

Direct import controls were fully re-established in mid-1981, and this policy stance prevailed throughout 1982 and most of 1983. The agreement with the IMF allowed for the maintenance of 'temporary' non-tariff controls. 1984 saw the beginnings of a moderate import liberalisation through the relaxation of controls and the replacement of import licences by tariffs in respect of 15 to 20 per cent of the value of total imports of goods.

Additional steps were announced in early 1985. First, in the context of the medium-term plan prepared at the Ministry of Industry and Trade, a programme was launched for the gradual (but reversible) elimination of import licences between 1985 and 1989, together with a 'rationalisation' of the tariff structure, mainly a series of steps towards the establishment of uniform effective protection rates. Second, a US–Mexico bilateral agreement was signed, re-affirming the commitment to liberalisation and pledging elimination of export subsidies. In exchange, Mexico obtained from the USA some of the advantages normally reserved for members of GATT.

Trade policy has also been affected by conflicting views within the government concerning the speed and methods of import liberalisation. An example was the heated debate in the first half of 1985 on a policy instrument for export promotion: DIMEX. In its original form, DIMEX was to provide exporting firms with unrestricted import licences free of tariffs and freely negotiable – equal in value to 40 per cent of the firm's exports. A substantially modified version later emerged whereby the percentage export value was reduced to 30 per cent and import licences were restricted to inputs required by the exporting firm.

A second example refers to the criteria for the management of trade policy. An increasingly influential view attributes failure to achieve inflation targets to the sluggishness of trade liberalisation. On this view the absence of foreign competition explains the downward rigidity, during a recession, of profit mark-ups in manufacturing, which, in turn, accounts for the relatively slow deceleration of inflation. Import controls should, therefore, be eliminated as fast as possible in order to force down inflation, improve industrial efficiency, and reverse the anti-export bias of present trade policies. This approach met with some resistance, notably at the Ministry of Trade and Industry, which took a more gradualist and long-term view. However, in July 1985 a substantial acceleration of the liberalisation programme was decided on anti-inflationary grounds (as part of a devaluation and fiscal correction package). The percentage of imports subject to import licences was then abruptly reduced from around 80 per cent to only 35 per cent.

From our point of view, the main problem with using trade policy as an anti-inflationary weapon is that if import liberalisation does in fact reduce inflation, it will do so through its effects on the rate of growth of tradable goods prices. Thus, for a given rate of mini-devaluations, the mechanism will work through the deterioration of the tradables–non-tradables price ratio. This in turn, according to very conventional first principles, will shift resources away from the tradable goods sectors, while at the same time shifting the consumption pattern towards tradables; therefore, the (constant-employment or long-term) trade balance will deteriorate as a result of import liberalisation. As Chilean and Argentine experiments show, the damage thus done may not only have devastating consequences on industrial growth and the dynamic efficiency of the whole economy, but may subsequently lead to exchange-rate adjustments which once again accelerate the rate of inflation.

Wage policy

Table 4.10 shows the minimum wage settlements, since January 1981, which have been negotiated periodically in a tripartite commission by representatives of the government, large unions and business confederations. The table also shows the change in consumer prices since the last wage settlement and the ratio between the former and the latter, i.e. the extent to which wages were adjusted to past inflation, an indicator of what may be called the 'wage policy stance'.

Wage policy has been the unconfessed centrepiece of the strategy for reconciling the goal of decelerating inflation with the desired modification of the structure of relative prices, which involved a fall in real wages. An *ex post* alteration of the structure of relative prices against real wages – starting from a situation of constant inflation and unchanged wage indexation mechanisms – will normally be accompanied by an acceleration of the inflation rate towards a new plateau, accelerating inflation being the mechanism by

Table 4.10   Minimum wage settlements, inflation and the wage policy stance, 1981–5

	(1)	(2)	(3)
		Consumer price inflation since	
	Minimum wage settlement	last wage settlement	(1)/(2)
January 1981	30.9	29.8	1.04
January 1982	34.0	28.7	1.18
July 1982[a]	30.0	32.0	0.94
January 1983	25.0	50.7	0.49
June 1983	15.4	35.9	0.43
January 1984	30.4	33.0	0.92
June 1984	20.2	25.8	0.78
January 1985	30.0	26.5	1.13
June 1985	18.0	22.6	0.80

Note:
[a] This wage increase was 'recommended' by the Minimum Wages Commission in February 1982 but became fully legal on 1 November 1982. We assume it to have been awarded in July. By July, inflation, after the February devaluation, had more or less completely eroded the previous (January) wage increase.

Source: SPP, *Boletín Mensual de Información Económica*, several issues.

which *ex post* real wages are eroded and other relative prices are shifted upwards. This is the case, however, unless the reduction in real wages is imposed *ex ante* on wage-earners by the alteration of the indexation or adjustment mechanisms of wages to past inflation.

As can be seen in Table 4.10, a sharp alteration of indexation mechanisms is exactly what happened in the wage negotiations from January 1983 to June 1984, especially during 1983, when the wage adjustment coefficient was brought down from a normal level of around 1 to an unprecedented level (since the Second World War) of less than 0.5. Nevertheless, the acceleration of inflation in 1982 made it unavoidable to offer a 'compensating' increase in the frequency of wage settlements – yearly to half-yearly – whose effects on inflation and real wages run in a contrary direction to the reduction of the wage adjustment coefficient. Here lies the secret of Mexico's relative success in avoiding an explosive acceleration of the inflation rate which, in other Latin American countries, has often accompanied the sharp relative price shifts required since 1982. It also helps to explain Mexico's relative success in the achievement of its initial PSBR targets.

The comparatively large room for manoeuvre of wage policy has been for decades a remarkable feature of the Mexican social and political system. As pointed out thirty years ago by Juan Noyola, it has to do with

the history of the Mexican working class movement, the composition of some of its leaders and its *sui generis* relations with the state since the twenties ... [thus] Mexican trade unions have been weak at their base; their general orientation has been influenced to a large or lesser degree by official paternalism and, among their leaders, cases of corruption have not been absent.[25]

The result of wage policy in Mexico, however – as also discussed by Noyola – is that a comparatively low level of inflation has a larger negative effect on real wages, compared with other Latin American countries. The large fall in real wages explains why, since January 1984, a relaxation of the 'wage policy stance' has been progressively introduced, in spite of the government's insistence on settling wage adjustments in relation to 'expected inflation' rather than past inflation. The 'rational expectations behaviour' of Mexican union leaders and the patience of the rank and file have their limits.

The Performance of the Economy in a Comparative Perspective

In 1984 Mexico was presented by the IMF as an example of successful orthodox adjustment to the debt crisis. On this view, the necessary fiscal adjustment has been painful but rewarding in terms of an outstanding balance-of-payments performance, a decelerating inflation rate since mid-1983, and the beginnings of an economic recovery in 1984. In our review of the management of policy instruments we have raised some doubts about this simplistic approach. A more detailed analysis of the performance of the economy in 1983–5, and some comparisons with 'badly-behaved' Brazil, may also lead to very different conclusions.

Economic activity and the balance of payments

Tables 4.11 and 4.12 show the half-yearly behaviour from the second half of 1981 onwards of a number of indicators of economic activity, trade and the balance of payments. Table 4.11 includes the official figures on urban open unemployment, together with our estimates, which correct

Table 4.11 Industrial output, investment and employment, 1981–5 (half-yearly performance)

	1981	1982		1983		1984		1985
	II	I	II	I	II	I	II	I
Growth rates[a]								
Oil production	−10.5	32.8	25.2	−7.8	10.6	−0.9	3.1	−10.4
Manufacturing production	6.5	−1.5	−18.1	−3.4	−6.3	12.7	3.7	12.0
Consumer non-durables	5.6	5.0	−11.4	0.3	−3.6	7.8	−1.9	11.0
Consumer durables	3.7	−8.7	−29.8	−15.8	−21.4	13.0	13.5	18.5
Intermediate goods	8.0	−3.0	−17.1	−2.0	−4.6	14.7	5.2	10.5
Capital goods	3.1	−9.4	−40.6	−20.0	−18.8	24.3	12.6	25.8
Gross fixed investment	2.5	−16.7	−32.8	−32.6	−5.5	1.4	27.8	2.1
Manufacturing employment	3.8	−0.9	−10.7	−11.5	−4.8	−1.0	3.0	2.6
Percentage rates								
Urban unemployment	4.1	4.0	4.5	6.6	6.9	5.7	6.4	na
Adjusted urban unemployment	6.4	5.8	6.4	9.1	9.3	9.1	10.0	na

Note:
[a] Annualised growth rates with respect to previous six months (not seasonally adjusted); na means data are not available.

Sources: SPP, *Boletín Mensual de Información Económica*; Banco de México, *Informe Anual*, several issues; Banco de México, *Indicadores Económicos*, several issues.

Table 4.12 Trade and the balance of payments, 1981–5 (half-yearly performance) (billion dollars)

	1981	1982		1983		1984		1985
	II	I	II	I	II	I	II	I
Exports (goods and services)	13.8	11.3	15.3	13.0	13.9	15.4	14.5	13.9
Goods	9.1	9.5	12.5	10.3	11.1	12.3	11.6	10.7
Services	4.7	1.8	2.8	2.7	2.8	3.1	2.9	3.2
Imports (goods and services)	17.0	13.5	8.3	5.8	6.8	7.2	9.0	9.3
Goods	11.5	9.2	5.2	3.5	4.2	4.9	6.3	6.7
Services	5.5	4.3	3.1	2.3	2.6	2.3	2.7	2.6
Trade balance (goods and services)	-3.2	-2.2	7.0	7.2	7.1	8.2	5.5	4.6
Income from abroad	-4.2	-3.9	-5.7	-4.9	-3.9	-4.8	-4.9	-4.6
Current account balance	-7.4	-6.1	1.3	2.3	3.2	3.4	0.6	0.0
Long-term capital (balance)	11.8	5.5	4.8	0.9	3.3	0.9	1.6	0.1
Short-term capital (balance)	0.9	-0.2	-1.6	-0.6	-4.4	-2.8	-1.4	-1.2
Errors and omissions	-4.0	-2.4	-6.0	-0.9	-0.5	0.1	-0.1	-0.5
Bank of Mexico	1.3	-3.2	-1.5	1.7	1.5	1.6	0.7	-1.6

Source: Banco de México, *Indicadores Económicos*, several issues.

the official figures for changes in activity rates and 'disguised unemployment' (people willing to work but not actively seeking jobs).

After a combination of demand and supply shocks (scarcity of foreign exchange) had produced a sharp decline in manufacturing activity in the second half of 1982, the recession deepened, albeit at a slower pace, during the first half of 1983. However, the continuous collapse of public and private investment (at rates over 30 per cent) and the income distribution effects of the fiscal and exchange-rate adjustments, which led to a fall of 7.5 per cent in private consumption over the year, produced an additional demand shock to economic activity. In the second half of 1983, manufacturing output and employment started falling again at annual rates above 6 per cent for the former and 4 per cent for the latter. The consumer durables (highly elastic to real income changes) and the capital goods industries showed the largest falls in output. Urban unemployment (adjusted) reached a level of more than 9 per cent.

Sharp declines in public and private investment and the collapse of the consumer durable industries, which have relatively high import requirements, led to a fall of total imports by 41.7 per cent in 1983, on top of the 37.1 per cent decline already achieved during 1982. Imports of capital goods made a substantial contribution through a fall of 62.2 per cent (42 per cent in 1982). Non-oil exports also began to respond to the real exchange-rate adjustments and to the fall in domestic demand. During 1983 they grew at a rate of 16.7 per cent. Their contribution to the external adjustment is, however, very minor compared with the fall in imports.

The trade balance (goods and non-factor services), already showing a substantial surplus in the second half of 1982, climbed dramatically to $14.2 billion in 1983, converting the current account deficit into a surplus of $5.5 billion.

The 1983 external adjustment is outstanding when compared with other Latin American countries, even when correcting for differences in output falls. In 1983, for example, Brazil, with similar interest payments on its foreign debt to Mexico and after a 16.3 per cent fall in its industrial output since the previous peak in 1980, was struggling to achieve a $6 billion deficit in its current account, at a time when Mexico's current account was showing a large surplus. A more detailed comparison shows, however, that this difference is mainly attributable to two main factors with worrying long-term implications for Mexico. The first factor is oil. In order to balance its current account, the Brazilian economy must generate a $20 billion surplus in its non-oil trade balance in order to pay for interest on debt and a $9 billion bill for oil imports. The Mexican economy can count on $16 billion of oil export revenues so that, in order to balance the current account, it can accept a $5 billion to $6 billion deficit in the non-oil trade balance, i.e. after deducting interest payments.

The second factor is related to the well-known fact that the capital goods industry is much less developed in Mexico than in Brazil, both relative to the overall demand for capital goods and to its relative importance in the industrial sector. Given the high elasticity of investment with respect to output growth, this feature is a comparative disadvantage for Mexico, in conditions of economic growth, but becomes a short-term advantage during a recession. For since investment is the element of aggregate demand which falls most drastically during the recession, the presence of a developed capital goods industry amplifies the multiplier effect on domestic output and employment while reducing the impact (for a given fall in output) on imports and the trade balance. Vice-versa, the decline of investment has a lower impact on output and employment and allows for a larger trade balance adjustment (for a given fall in output), when the domestic capital goods industry is less developed. This contrast can be illustrated by the fact that in Brazil, from 1980 to 1983, a 16.3 per cent fall in industrial output was accompanied by a 43 per cent fall in capital goods imports,[26] while in Mexico, from 1981 to 1983, only a 10 per cent fall in manufacturing output was needed to achieve a 78 per cent reduction in capital goods imports.

The important implication of these comparisons is that Mexico's large external adjustment in 1983 was not only based on the total collapse of domestic investment and capital goods imports, but was supported, paradoxically, by what are long-term weaknesses of Mexico's economic structure: its dependence on oil revenues and the underdevelopment of its capital goods industry. The comparatively short-term nature of the adjustment will become still clearer below when we discuss the 1984 developments and some contrasts are again made with the Brazilian experience.

After a sharp decline in industrial activity in the second half of 1983, manufacturing output recovered sharply at the beginning of 1984, with, however, a declining rate thereafter. Urban unemployment started rising again. For the whole of 1984, GDP grew at a 3.5 per cent rate and manufacturing output at a 5.4 per cent rate. Two general factors, besides the US import boom, account for this moderate economic recovery.[27] First was the relaxation of the fiscal stance (in spite of the reduction of the

PSBR as a percentage of GDP) as measured by the real fiscal surplus. This came about as a result of a 6 per cent growth in general government employment, a reduction in the inflation tax induced by the deceleration of inflation, and the granting of generous fiscal incentives to private investment (to be discussed below). Second, the *medium-term* expansionary effects of the real exchange rate devaluation of 1982 and 1983 combined with the also favourable *short-term* impact of the 1984 real appreciation. The joint consequences of these two factors can explain the moderate recovery of private consumption (related to public sector employment growth and to the reduction of the inflation tax) at a rate of 2.8 per cent. The 9 per cent expansion of private investment was induced by fiscal incentives. For most of the year non-oil exports continued to grow rapidly (18.4 per cent in current dollars), stimulated by the acceleration in 1984 of the US economic recovery and import boom. It is worth observing, nevertheless, that the net contribution of the external sector to Mexico's GDP growth was substantially reduced by the resumption of import growth at a high rate of 31.6 per cent (current dollars).

Superficially, the 1984 economic recovery looked like the beginnings of a much expected export-led plus private investment-led process of economic growth. A closer look, however, reveals several worrying aspects. The first concerns the interrelated patterns of industrial production and private investment. As can be seen in Table 4.13, besides a slow and demographically determined growth of traditional food industries and an export-related recovery of some industries with large underutilisation of capacity (cement, steel), the industrial recovery was largely concentrated in the automobile industry. Almost everything else continued to decline or stagnate. This strange picture of a booming automobile industry (26.6 per cent growth) in the midst of stagnation or decline is related to another strange feature of the 1984 recovery: a boom of corporate vehicle purchases in the context of stagnating or declining productive investment in plant and machinery (especially in most public enterprises). The fiscal initiatives presented and approved in late 1983 in Congress included incentives to private investment in the form of accelerated depreciation allowances at rates of 75 per cent in 1984, 50 per cent in 1985 and 25 per cent in 1986. Given the depression of economic activity in 1983 and the low levels of capacity utilisation prevailing in the industrial sector, these fiscal incentives were used by private firms mainly to replace the stock of automobiles, taking the opportunity of a high depreciation allowance in 1984. The boom of vehicle sales to private firms which followed (33.4 per cent growth) led the recovery of the

Table 4.13 The 1984 economic recovery, annual growth rates (%)

GDP growth by sector, and investment		Manufacturing industries	
Agriculture	2.4	Traditional foodstuffs	2.8
Oil and mining	1.6	Other foodstuffs	− 1.0
Manufacturing	5.4	Drink	− 0.2
Construction	3.7	Clothing	− 1.8
Electricity	7.0	Electrodomestic goods	20.9
Commerce and services	3.2	Chemicals, plastic and rubber	7.2
		Cement, glass and	
Investment in machinery and		non-metal products	8.9
equipment	8.9	Steel	13.0
Vehicle purchases	33.4	Automobiles	26.6
Imports of capital goods	5.9	Car parts	19.4
Purchase of domestic		Capital goods	2.2
capital goods	2.2		
Investment excluding vehicle			
purchases	3.2		

Sources: SPP, *Cuentas Nacionales* (*Información Preliminar*); Banco de México, *Informe Anual* (1984).

automobile industry and explains most of the increase in 'private investment' which took place over 1984. Indeed, as can be seen in Table 4.13, domestic production of capital goods stagnated in 1984 (2.2 per cent growth) and when private investment is corrected for vehicle purchases, it only increases by 3.2 per cent (due mainly to imports of capital goods stimulated also by the fiscal incentives which offered an effective exchange rate for capital goods imports much lower than its ordinary level). The least to be said about all this is that keeping public investment at extremely low levels while giving subsidies to private firms' purchases of executive vehicles seems a rather dubious way of allocating public resources, and an unfortunate waste of the increased room for manoeuvre provided by the 1983 adjustments.

The second worrying aspect of developments in 1984 is the speed at which the trade surplus was declining towards the end of the year, as non-oil exports started falling while imports continued to grow at very high rates (see Table 4.12). These trends continued in the first half of 1985 and the trade surplus was therefore 44 per cent lower than in the first half of 1984.

Besides the fact that imports were increasing from abnormally low levels and that the first consequences of real appreciation (plus the beginnings of import liberalisation?) may already have been coming through, the rapid growth of imports appears to be strongly related to the pattern of industrial growth during 1984. Indeed, the import-intensive nature of the Mexican automobile industry and the fact that the pattern of import growth is strongly biased towards intermediate goods, tends to support this hypothesis, suggesting that the economy has entered a traditional growth path, only less vigorous than in the past, that will end in a balance-of-payments crisis.

The end of export growth, in late 1984 and early 1985, is equally worrying. The fact that it coincides with the deceleration of the US economy and a continuing real appreciation of the peso exchange rate, suggests that the 1983/4 manufacturing export boom was the result of three exceptional conditions which will hardly reappear simultaneously: first, the fact that the US economy grew at its fastest since 1970; second, the effects of an unprecedented internal depression which yielded high exportable surpluses; third, a real exchange rate which was exceptionally favourable for exports.

The traditional character of the 1984 Mexican recovery, induced by fiscal means and strongly biased towards import-intensive industries, tends to confirm the short-term nature of the 1983 external adjustment and contrasts strongly with the *net* export-led economic recovery of Brazil in 1984. Indeed, the latter is a rare case of external adjustment with growth, induced by long-run structural changes and led by both a strong expansion of manufacturing exports (33 per cent in current dollars) and the import-substitution effects of past investments (a 10 per cent fall in imports in current dollars). The long-run adjustments – described in this volume by Dias Carneiro – which have been going on in the Brazilian economy since 1974, and Brazil's persistence in maintaining the pace of productive capacity creation, seem to be at the roots of the differences in the recent Mexican and Brazilian experiences.

Inflation, relative prices and the distribution of income

It is possible to derive from accounting identities (Ros, 1984) a formula in which the rate of inflation in a given period is governed by the following variables: (i) the rate of inflation over the previous period; (ii) the extent to which wages, the exchange rate and public prices are adjusted to past inflation; (iii) the rate of growth of the price–cost relationship (and, therefore, the behaviour of interest rates to the extent that they affect gross profit mark-ups); (iv) the rate of growth of the market price–factor cost relationship (dependent on the behaviour of indirect tax and subsidy rates); (v) the current rate of inflation abroad; (vi) the rate of productivity growth. In addition, inflation over a number of adjustment periods (a year, for example) is also related to the frequency of adjustment.

Let us now use this framework for the analysis of the dynamics of inflation over the last three years. Table 4.14 shows half-yearly behaviour of the inflation rate, the growth of 'key prices' and their adjustment coefficients to past inflation, and the evolution of relative prices over the period 1981 (*II*) to 1985 (*I*). In 1980 and 1981, inflation was running at a relatively stable rate, with no major changes in relative prices occurring, except for the gradual appreciation of the real exchange rate. From the beginning of 1982 onwards, three main phases may be distinguished in the dynamics of the inflation rate and the structure of relative prices. In the first phase, from early 1982 to mid-1983, inflation accelerated continuously, as a consequence of the large adjustments in the exchange rate, public prices and net indirect taxes (in 1983, *I*). During 1982, wages tried to keep in line with past inflation through the 'emergency' increases of April 1982 and the *de facto* transition to half-yearly settlements. Thus, for most of 1982, all key price adjustments were above past inflation – especially the exchange-rate and public price adjustments – and the alteration of the *ex post* structure of relative prices was, therefore, brought about by a dramatic acceleration of the inflation rate. In 1983 (*I*), wage adjustments were substantially repressed, but as a result of continuing *ex ante* increases in the exchange rate, public prices and net indirect taxes, inflation continued to accelerate, although at a slower pace. For this first phase as a whole, a radical alteration of relative prices took place – with real wages 20 per cent and the real exchange rate 40 per cent below, and public prices 90 per cent above their levels in 1981 (*II*) – through a substantial acceleration of the inflation rate, up from an annual rate of 25–30 per cent in 1981 to an annualised rate of 100–120 per cent during the first half of 1983.

During a second phase, from mid-1983 to late 1984, the inflation rate showed a continuous downward trend from its peak of 100–120 per cent to a level of 55–60 per cent during most of 1984. As can be seen from the table, this substantial deceleration was related to the unprecedented repression of wage adjustments during 1983 and to the setting of the rate of mini-devaluations according to 'expected' inflation which led to a substantial fall in exchange-rate adjustments to past inflation. The adjustment of public rates was also substantially relaxed, and net

Table 4.14 Inflation and relative prices, 1981–5 (half-yearly behaviour)

	1981 II	1982 I	1982 II	1983 I	1983 II	1984 I	1984 II	1985 I
Growth rates over previous six months								
Consumer prices	11.9	24.0	42.7	49.8	29.1	31.8	22.7	29.0
Nominal wages[a]	8.7	22.3	37.0	28.2	16.8	28.2	21.6	28.6
Adjustment to past inflation		1.9	1.5	0.7	0.3	1.0	0.7	1.3
Foreign prices in domestic currency[b]	6.1	84.6	54.8	60.3	23.9	20.5	17.6	18.7
Adjustment to past inflation		7.1	2.3	1.4	0.5	0.7	0.6	0.8
Public rates[c]	10.7	52.8	80.8	83.8	46.1	45.7	26.2	na
Adjustment to past inflation		4.4	3.4	2.0	0.9	1.6	0.8	na
Relative prices (index 1981 (II) = 100.0)								
Real wages	100.0	98.6	94.7	81.0	73.3	71.2	70.6	70.3
Real exchange rates	100.0	67.2	62.0	57.8	60.3	66.1	69.0	75.0
Real public rates	100.0	123.3	156.1	191.6	216.8	239.7	246.6	na

Notes:

[a] Wage increases are assumed to follow minimum wage settlements according to the following pattern: a third of the labour force (minimum wage-earners) receive the increase at the time of the minimum wage settlement, another third receives it during the first quarter after the settlement, and the remaining third receives it during the second quarter. The high coefficients of wage adjustments in 1982 (*I*) and (*II*) are partly illusory. They are due to the fact that we are comparing 1982 (*I*) with the inflation rate of 1981 (*II*), when minimum wage settlements were still annual, to the bunching of settlements in the first half of 1982 (*I*), and to the transition in 1982 from annual to half-yearly settlements.

[b] US prices multiplied by the nominal controlled exchange rate.

[c] Fuel and energy prices.

Sources: SPP, *Boletín Mensual de Información Económica*, several issues; Banco de México, *Indicadores Económicos*, several issues.

indirect taxes made no further contributions to the inflation rate. The structure of relative prices continued to be modified over the period against those key prices that were relatively more repressed. Thus, from 1983 (*I*) to 1984 (*II*), real wages fell by an additional 13 per cent, the real exchange rate appreciated by 16–19 per cent, while real public prices continued to increase by a further 30 per cent.

In early 1985, the dynamics of inflation entered a third phase, characterised by the fact that the underlying rate of inflation departed from its downward trend and indexation mechanisms became progressively entrenched. First, wage adjustments to past inflation continued their return to normal levels after a period of extreme wage repression. Second, exchange-rate policy was adjusted upwards in December 1984 and March 1985, and again in July–August 1985 as the previous attempts proved insufficient to avert a continuing real appreciation during the first half of 1985 (see Table 4.14). Third, public price adjustments are unlikely to be repressed in future given the importance of PSBR targets in policy making.

The implication of these trends is that inflation is likely to remain relatively stable, with no major changes occurring in the *ex post* structure of relative prices. The fact that inflation is running in 1985 (*I*) at a similar rate to that in the same period one year earlier, and that real wages are stabilising at 30 percent below their level in 1981 (*II*), tends to support this view.

Whether these trends can continue for a long time is another issue which depends on the overall performance of the economy and, mainly, on when and with what intensity the latent disequilibria in the balance of payments may lead to additional major adjustments in the exchange rate, and also on how wages and wage policy will behave in the future.

A final remark is that although Mexico, due to its wage policy and, more generally, its relative lack of indexation and defence mechanisms, has avoided the wild accelerations of the inflation rate in highly indexed economies like Argentina and Brazil, the shift in the structure of relative prices has nevertheless been achieved through an acceleration of inflation towards a new, higher plateau. Compare 1985 (*I*) and 1981 (*II*): real wages were 30 per cent below, the real exchange rate was 25 per cent below, and real public prices were about 2.5 times the levels of 1981 (*II*). Inflation, however, was steady at a 60–65 per cent annual rate compared with 25–30 per cent in 1981. Moreover, the higher rate of inflation has brought with it an increased degree of formal or informal indexation which is implicit, for example, in the mechanisms of mini-devaluations or in the increased frequency of wages and public prices adjustments. The important implication of this phenomenon is that in the future further changes in the structure of relative prices will be more difficult to achieve and may be accompanied by larger accelerations of the inflation rate than in the past.

The burden of capital flight

We cannot finish our review of recent developments without commenting on a feature of the Mexican economy which has acquired unprecedented dimensions. This is the substantial increase in the 'propensity to save abroad' on the part of the Mexican private sector. As illustrated in Table 4.5 the domestic private sector's increased desire for foreign financial assets was not counteracted by the large exchange-rate adjustments of 1982 and 1983. In fact, the proportion of the private sector financial surplus invested abroad has actually *increased* during the recession from 1983 onwards, although large adjustments in the real exchange rate have substantially reduced the dollar value of the financial savings that are flowing out of the country. It is worth noting that inflation-corrected financial deficits and surpluses and their composition would look still more dramatic since, from 1983 onwards, the change in the real value of the private sector holding of Mexican public debt has actually been negative, and thus the whole of its *net* real savings has been invested abroad. At present (1985), the private sector is financing the current account deficit of the rest of the world (with respect to Mexico) and also – through the intermediation of foreign banks – the (nominal) borrowing abroad by the Mexican public sector. This borrowing is therefore a consequence of the need to balance the external accounts in the face of a major alteration in the asset composition of the private sector's net financial savings.

The burden that capital flight puts on the balance of payments and economic activity is actually greater than is suggested by official figures on the balance of payments or on the flow of funds. Indeed, the official balance-of-payments statistics do not include the returns on foreign assets held abroad by Mexican residents as an entry in the current account (income from abroad) or its reinvestment abroad as an outflow in the capital account, as proper accounting would suggest. In Table 4.15

we present some calculations, based on rather conservative assumptions (see the note to the table) of the corrected current account, the capital flight and the stock of foreign assets held by Mexican residents. As can be seen from the table, the reinvestment of interest abroad is imposing on the economy, in 1983 and 1984, the need to generate a current account surplus $4 to 5 billion larger than would otherwise be required. The total burden of capital flight implies the generation of a current account surplus (and therefore a trade surplus) which is more than $8 billion greater than it would be in the absence of capital flight. This is close to the total nominal interest payments on the country's foreign debt.

The increased propensity to save abroad on the part of the Mexican private sector is partly the result of the present crisis in the relations between the state and the private sector, and partly the response of an outward-oriented bourgeoisie to the external financial troubles of its country. To this extent, therefore, capital flight is a consequence of the international debt crisis. But, in fact, capital flight and debt crisis interact with each other in a vicious circle, since the burden that capital flight puts on Mexico's balance of payments tightens the constraints on economic activity and makes it more painful and difficult to service the foreign debt.

As can be seen in Table 4.15, as a result of past asset accumulation and the high foreign interest rates in recent years, the stock of foreign assets held abroad by Mexican residents stood at the end of 1984 at around $64 billion – almost the same as the total stock of the Mexican public sector's foreign debt. This situation implies that the latter has as its counterpart private assets held abroad by Mexicans, the rate of interest paid by the Mexican public sector on its foreign debt being higher than the rate of interest that the Mexican private sector is receiving on its assets held abroad, while the margin is being appropriated by foreign banks which intermediate between the Mexican private and public sectors. It would seem, therefore, that there is room for a deal whereby the Mexican public debt is held directly by the Mexican private sector. But such a deal would require a reversal of the vicious circle mentioned above, putting an end to the flight from Mexican public debt and opening a period of growth and stability. (We should like to draw attention here to the highly pro-cyclical behaviour of private capital flows, including direct foreign investment which has collapsed in recent years. Thus the creation of conditions favourable to economic growth may contribute substantially

Table 4.15 Adjusted and non-adjusted figures for the current account, capital flight and the stock of foreign assets held by Mexican residents, 1973–84[a]

	Current account balance		Private capital flight		Stock of foreign assets held by Mexicans (end of period)	
	Uncorrected	Corrected	Uncorrected	Corrected	Uncorrected	Corrected
1973	−1.5	−1.4	0.9	1.0	2.9	3.0
1974	−3.2	−2.9	1.0	1.3	3.9	4.0
1975	−4.4	−4.2	1.1	1.3	5.0	5.2
1976	−3.7	−3.4	3.1	3.4	8.1	8.6
1977	−1.6	−1.3	1.0	1.3	9.1	9.8
1978	−2.7	−2.0	0.6	1.3	10.4	11.2
1979	−4.9	−3.7	0.9	2.1	11.3	13.2
1980	−6.8	−4.8	2.8	4.8	14.1	18.0
1981	−12.5	−8.4	10.9	15.0	25.0	33.0
1982	−4.9	0.0	9.5	14.4	34.5	47.4
1983	5.5	9.5	4.5	8.5	39.0	55.9
1984	4.2	9.6	2.7	8.1	41.7	64.0

Note:
[a] The corrections are based on the following three assumptions: (i) the stock of foreign assets held abroad by Mexican residents was $2 billion at the end of 1972; (ii) the average rate of return on this stock was over the period 3 percentage points below the US prime rate; (iii) the returns earned on the stock were fully reinvested in the acquisition of foreign assets.

Source: Banco de México, *Informe Anual*, several issues.

to the reversal of capital outflows.) It is to the problems of overcoming inflation and economic stagnation that we now turn.

GENERAL APPRAISAL AND ALTERNATIVE POLICY PROPOSALS

By mid-1985 the fragility of the economic recovery and of the adjustment programme became highly evident. The rapid deterioration of the trade surplus, the difficulties in controlling inflation and (as a consequence) in achieving the fiscal target, together with expectations of falling international oil prices and strong speculation against the peso led in July to the collapse of the exchange market and the adoption of the new policy package mentioned above. However, except for the fact that the new expenditure cuts fall on current expenditures, and there is some recognition that the adjustment in public prices may have been overdone, the revision of the policies seems, in fact, to reinforce the previous policy stance.

In contrast, the analysis presented in the previous section suggests that it is in fact that approach to adjustment that is at the root of present troubles, and therefore that, under present policies, the prospects for the Mexican economy will continue to be very poor, especially if foreign finance remains unavailable for the rest of the 1980s. Since no major long-term adjustment has taken place, the continuation of present policies may lead to a 'structural change' whose nature is very different from what is required, i.e. to the persistence of high inflation rates with economic stagnation, deindustrialisation and rising unemployment. It is worth remembering that in the 1980s Mexico faces the period of highest growth in its labour force due to the demographic boom of the 1960s and early 1970s.

The rest of this concluding section will argue for the need for a different approach to deal with the present problems of stagflation, making explicit some policy proposals which can be derived from the analysis presented above.

Inflation: the Need for a Heterodox Shock[28]

A high rate of inflation would be the source of tensions and conflicts between short- and long-term objectives in any economic strategy. For this as well as for equity and efficiency reasons, its eradication should have a high priority. However, as described in the last section, the present methods for dealing with inflation have been shown to be highly inequitable and increasingly ineffective. The government's gradualist approach to the deceleration of inflation consisted in setting key prices in relation to 'expected inflation' and of manipulating fiscal policy as an automatic stabiliser of inflation. It seems to be flawed by two unrealistic and interrelated assumptions: first, the confidence that 'co-operative behaviour' can be induced among economic agents for a long period of time during which agents are not treated equally (for example, the 'discipline of demand' used as a substitute for price controls but not for wage controls); and second, the assumption that inflation is highly sensitive to demand pressures and therefore that fiscal policy is an effective policy instrument to deal with it (see the previous section).

For similar reasons, substituting the present gradualist approach with an orthodox demand shock would be highly inefficient. The best alternative policy would seem to be a 'heterodox shock', where the inflation target is set at its final desired level (be it zero or the relevant international rate) and where 'co-operative behaviour' is required only once and for all. Such a shock would involve a freeze of 'key prices' (exchange rate, public prices and wages), the sharp reduction of nominal interest rates, the introduction of a regime of price controls and, possibly, for reasons discussed below, a monetary reform.

There are two circumstances favourable to the success of such a policy in Mexico at present. First, as argued in the last section, inflation in 1984–5 has entered an 'inertial phase' where the structure of relative key prices has become more accepted, in the sense that the major alterations of this structure have already occurred. Second, the zero or low inflation fiscal balance is at present in a substantial surplus. Such a fiscal surplus would become visible during the price freeze, as nominal interest rates were substantially reduced. This would imply not only that the policy would meet no obstacles arising from excessive demand pressures (a fiscal deficit being non-existent) but also, and perhaps more important, that a large fiscal surplus would give considerable room for manoeuvre to use taxes and public sector prices in order to increase acceptability and the effectiveness of the price freeze.

This is not to deny that a price freeze would encounter severe obstacles. There are at least three difficulties to deal with. First, although the relative price structure has been tacitly accepted, it has not been fully accepted (otherwise there would be no inflation). This heterodox shock implies freezing a structure of relative prices and a distribution of income which are neither accepted nor desirable. On the other hand, this distribution may be no worse than that resulting from continuous inflation. A central element of the policy must therefore be a 'social pact' which is respected by the main public and private economic agents. The period when the freeze is introduced therefore becomes a crucial issue. The 'best period', from the point of view of the chances for the social pact being respected, is when, given the timing and frequency of price and wage adjustments, the structure of relative key prices is closest to its average or long-term pattern.

A second problem arises, paradoxically, from the fact that the present Mexican inflation is not a hyperinflation but a medium-high inflation. Thus, in contrast to a hyperinflationary process where most prices become fully and almost instantaneously indexed to the exchange rate (so that the central problem becomes the stabilisation of the exchange rate), there are in the present inflation relatively large lags between cost and price changes as well as leads and lags in price and wage relativities. These circumstances necessitate a regime of price controls but they also create a conflict of aims: between the wish to take into account the leads and lags in prices and wages, and the wish to 'de-index' present price changes from past inflation. It is here that a monetary reform, in particular the introduction of a new money somehow indexed or pegged to a foreign currency, may facilitate the task of 'de-indexation', i.e. of cutting the links between present price changes and past inflation and reducing the frequency of price and wage adjustments.

A third problem is related to the lack of confidence and credibility of such a programme and the associated difficulties in defending the exchange rate. It is paradoxical that this obstacle is generally magnified by orthodox economists, for if the private sector had 'monetarist expectations', the appearance of a large and visible fiscal surplus during the price freeze should be enough to ensure the confidence and the credibility of the programme. If the difficulty exists, its true implications are not, therefore, that the proposal is impossible (because of the presence of a nominal fiscal deficit) but rather that it may require external financial support, a tightening of exchange controls and temporarily higher than desirable interest rates. A monetary reform can also make a contribution to the defence of the exchange rate.

We do not wish to minimise the real difficulties facing the present policy proposal. A central point, however, is that all the obstacles mentioned are also present in the gradualist policy that has been followed (and which suffers from other disadvantages). From this point of view, the latter is therefore no better than a more radical approach. A final remark is that either a gradualist approach or a heterodox shock can only be a temporary solution for the present inflationary process unless a permanent solution is achieved to the long-term balance of payments disequilibrium which lies at the root of the present Mexican inflation. This leads us to the problem of economic growth.

Growth: the Need for an Alternative Approach to Industrial Development

The present government's approach to economic growth and structural change has been described in a previous section. It relies for its success on the fulfilment of the following assumptions: (i) economic growth is mainly limited by a savings constraint; (ii) a 'correct' real exchange rate and trade liberalisation are sufficient conditions to promote high export-led growth; (iii) export growth and the 'correction' of factor prices should allow for a significant increase in employment absorption. A detailed discussion and critique of the realism and limitations of these assumptions can be found in work done elsewhere.[29] We shall not repeat that analysis here but rather derive some constructive implications from the critique.

An alternative policy for the resumption of growth and industrial development should, in our view, start from a quite different approach. First, the central role of the balance-of-payments constraint in Mexico's economic growth should be recognised. This is particularly necessary at present and in the near future, given the unavailability of foreign finance. The present ratio of domestic savings to GDP and the present capital–output ratio (given normal capacity utilisation) allow for an overall rate of economic growth of no less than 7 per cent per year. The central problem then is how to ensure a sufficiently high rate of export growth and/or a sufficiently low import elasticity so that the desired rate of growth is consistent with sustainable levels in the balance of payments. In this respect, it is worth pointing out that the task is far from impossible: with an import elasticity of the order of one (which is larger than in the 1960s) and a growth of manufacturing exports of 8–10 per cent (which is much less than the rates achieved in the second half of the 1960s and the early 1970s), an overall growth of 6–7 per cent could be achieved without implying a deterioration of the trade and current account balances.

Another reason for taking seriously this optimistic-sounding outlook, given the present external debt burden, is the presence of $16 billion of oil revenues which cancel out, in the external accounts, the interest payments on foreign debt. Thus, in a certain sense, Mexico is no worse off than at the beginning of the 1970s, when there was not such a large external debt but neither was there a huge amount of oil export revenues. Who would have argued, at the beginning of the 1970s, that it was impossible for the Mexican economy to continue growing at its historical rate of 6–7 per cent, even in the absence of foreign finance? An additional point is that, although the pattern of investment during the oil boom was far from optimal, it did leave Mexico with productive capacity in several strategic industries such as steel, petrochemicals and capital goods. In many cases, these investment projects have not yet matured, but their termination could make a substantial contribution to a future process of import substitution and improve the perspectives of Mexico's economic development.

Notes

1.   This paper was written before the 1986 oil shock. The author is grateful to Rosemary Thorp, Laurence Whitehead and Dionísio Dias Carneiro for comments and suggestions, as well as to the participants of the seminars on Latin American debt organised by the Latin American Centre of the University of Oxford. The group's discussions in Albuquerque and Bogotá were particularly useful. The author is grateful to Susana Marván for her help in the preparation of the tables.
2. See: *Plan Nacional de Desarrollo Industrial 1979–1982*; *Plan Global de Desarrollo 1980–1982*; *Sistema Alimentario Mexicano*.
3. Thus, a ceiling of 1.5 million barrels per day was put on oil exports. This level was reached in 1981.
4. Manufacturing growth in 1980 and 1981 was relatively low compared with the growth of internal demand during the period (10–11 per cent) and also by historical standards. In the 1960s, manufacturing grew at 9.3 per cent per year, with GDP growth at 7.2 per cent and demand at 7.5 per cent.
5. See the papers by Bazdresch, Brailovsky and Singh in Barker and Brailovsky (1982), and Eatwell and Singh (1981); also Schatán (1981). Import liberalisation included the progressive abandonment of import licences and its replacement by tariffs – uncontrolled imports reached 40 per cent of the total import bill by the first half of 1981 – and a general relaxation of controls over import licences, whose quantitative impact is harder to assess. The balance of the evidence, which includes econometric estimates of import functions and disaggregated analysis of the growth of controlled and uncontrolled imports, seems to us to favour the view that liberalisation policies played an important role in the import explosion, particularly when one acknowledges the fact that the re-establishment of direct import controls in mid-1981 radically curtailed the growth of imports. But this evidence, taking as given the boom of internal demand over the period, may not by itself solve completely the policy issue.
6. See on this point López (1985) and the 1981 survey of large private firms by

the Oficina de Asesores del Presidente based on a sample of 2200 firms.
7.   See on this subject Banco de México, *Informe Anual* (1979, 1980 and 1981) and Vázquez (1982).
8.   Barker and Brailovsky (1983) have estimated that the rise in oil prices added \$7 billion to the 1981 exports originally projected in the National Industrial Plan. These \$7 billion represented 31 per cent of total exports of goods in 1981.
9.   See, on this subject, Frieden (1984).
10. The inflation-corrected or real public sector deficit is the change in the real value of government liabilities which, as discussed below, is a more appropriate indicator of the fiscal stance than the conventional measure of the fiscal deficit, which refers to public sector borrowing requirements.
11. There was, however, a shortening of the term structure of the new loans.
12. Barker and Brailovsky (1983) compare the originally projected deficit in the current account with the actual outcome for the period 1979–82 and attribute as much as 40 per cent of the difference to the larger interest payments resulting from *purely financial* factors such as higher foreign interest rates, the capital flight and the interaction between these two factors.
13. These financial troubles had started before February, as a consequence of rising interest rates abroad, but they were greatly aggravated by the devaluation.
14. This constitutes an additional reason for the adoption of a regime of exchange controls.
15. This did not require large changes in the previous government's economic team, but only the removal of Carlos Tello, the director of the Central Bank after the nationalisation of the banks, and of José Andrés de Oteyza's economic team at the Ministry of Industry.
16. Public sector employment actually fell by less than GDP.
17. Besides the well-known argument concerning the adjustment of the public sector deficit for cyclical variations in the level of economic activity.
18. See Buiter (1983).
19. See Miller (1982).
20. Corrected only for the interest-bearing component of public debt. In this comparison we did not correct for the inflation tax, since a positive relationship between the real surplus and the inflation rate would follow naturally from the effects of inflation on the real surplus and not vice-versa. See also on this subject, Economía Aplicada SC (1985).
21. See Ize and Salas (1984), Ros (1980) and the price equations of the main econometric models of the Mexican economy.
22. See, among others, Dornbusch (1983).
23. See SPP, *Plan Nacional de Desarrollo* (1983).
24. In the second quarter of 1985, as can be seen in Table 4.10, the gap between the free rate and the black market rate increased substantially and reached a two-year peak.
25. Noyola (1956). In this remarkable short essay – an early and major contribution to structuralist thinking on inflation – Noyola compares the inflation processes in Mexico and Chile and deals with the apparent

paradox of a milder level of inflation in Mexico combined with a greater impact of inflation on income distribution shares.
26. See the chapter in this volume by Dias Carneiro.
27. Actually, a 3.5 per cent GDP growth is, by Mexican standards, a recession. At least this is the way the 1971 (4.2 per cent growth) and 1977 (3.4 per cent growth) periods used to be described.
28. Some of the analysis and proposals presented here have in fact been more widely developed and discussed by Brazilian economists in the context of their analysis of 'inertial inflation'. See on this subject Lopes (1984a) and the references mentioned there. I am grateful to Dias Carneiro for introducing me to this literature.
29. See Casar, Kurczyn and Márquez (1984) and Casar, Rodríguez and Ros (1985). See also Boatler (1974) on the relatively high capital intensity of Mexico's manufacturing exports.

References

BANCO DE MÉXICO, *Estadísticas de Balanza de Pagos*, Mexico.
BANCO DE MÉXICO, *Indicadores Económicos*, Mexico.
BANCO DE MÉXICO, *Informe Anual*, Mexico.
BANCO DE MÉXICO, *Producto Interno y Gasto*, Mexico, 1960–77.
BARKER, T. and BRAILOVSKY, V., *Oil or Industry?* (New York: Academic Press, 1982).
BARKER, T. and BRAILOVSKY, V., 'La Política Económica 1976–1982 y el Plan Nacional de Desarrollo Industrial', *Investigación Económica*, no. 166 (Mexico: UNAM, 1982).
BOATLER, R. W., 'Las Predicciones de la Teoría del Comercio Internacional y el Crecimiento de las Exportaciones Manufactureras de México, *Trimestre Económico*, no. 164 (Mexico: FCE, 1974).
BUITER, W. H., 'Measurement of the Public Sector Deficit and its Implications for Policy Evaluation and Design', *IMF Staff Papers*, vol. 30, no. 2, June, Washington DC, 1983.
CASAR, J., KURCZYN, S. and MÁRQUEZ, C., 'La Capacidad de Absorción de Empleo en el Sector Manufacturero y los Determinantes del Crecimiento de la Productividad', *Economía Mexicana*, no. 6 (Mexico: CIDE, 1984).
CASAR, J., RODRÍGUEZ, G. and ROS, J., 'Ahorro y Balanza de Pagos. Un análisis de las Restricciones del Crecimiento Económico en México', mimeo (Mexico: CIDE, 1965).
DORNBUSCH, R., 'Discussion on Bacha', in J. Williamson (ed.) *Prospects for Adjustment in Argentina, Brazil and Mexico* (Washington DC: Institute for International Economics, June 1983).
EATWELL, J. and SINGH, A., '¿Está Sobrecalentada la Economía Mexicana?', *Economía Mexicana*, no. 3 (Mexico: CIDE, 1981).
ECONOMÍA APLICADA SC, *Cuentas de los Sectores Institucionales*, Mexico, 1985a.
ECONOMÍA APLICADA SC, *La Opción de Crecimiento Cero. Proyecciones a 1990 de la Economía Mexicana a partir de Galileo*, Mexico, 1985b.

Economic Report of the President, Washington DC, 1985.

FRIEDEN, J., 'Endeudamiento y Fuga de Capital. Los Flujos Financieros Internacionales en la Crisis de México, 1981–83', *Investigación Económica*, no. 170 (Mexico: UNAM, 1984).

INTERNATIONAL MONETARY FUND, *International Financial Statistics* (Washington DC: IMF, 1984).

INTERNATIONAL MONETARY FUND, *World Economic Outlook* (Washington DC: IMF, 1984).

IZE, A. and SALAS, J., 'El Comportamiento Macroeconómico de la Economía Mexicana entre 1961 y 1981: Especificaciones Alternativas y Pruebas de Hipótesis', in A. Ize and G. Vera (eds) *La Inflación en México* (Mexico City: El Colegio de México, 1984).

KALDOR, N., *The Scourge of Monetarism* (Oxford: Oxford University Press, 1982).

LOPES, F., 'Inflação Inercial, Hiperinflação e Desinflação. Notas e Conjecturas', *Revista da Anpec*, año VII, no. 8, November 1984a.

LOPES, F., 'So um Choque Heterodoxo Pode Derrubar a Inflação', *Economia en Perspectiva* (Mexico City: Correcon, August 1984b).

LÓPEZ, J., 'Balance de la Economía Mexicana', mimeo (Mexico: UNAM, 1985).

MILLER, M., 'Inflation Adjusting the Public Sector Financial Deficit: Measurement and Implications for Policy', in T. Kay (ed.) *The 1982 Budget*, (Oxford: Basil Blackwell, 1982).

NOYOLA, J. F., 'El Desarrollo Económico y la Inflación en México y Otros Países Latinoamericanos', reprinted in Solis, L. (1973) *La Economía Mexicana*, vol. II: *Lecturas de El Trimestre Económico*, no. 4 (Mexico: FCE); first published 1956.

ROS, J., 'Pricing in the Mexican Manufacturing Sector', *Cambridge Journal of Economics*, vol. 4, no. 3, September 1980.

ROS, J., 'Propiedades Analíticas del Modelo', *Economia Mexicana*, Serie Temática no. 2 (Mexico: CIDE, 1984).

ROS, J., 'Growth, Trade and the Pattern of Specialisation', mimeo (Mexico City: CIDE, 1985).

SANTAMARÍA, H., 'La Evolución de la Inversión en México', a paper presented to the seminar on the investment process in Mexico and the USA, Stanford University, 1985.

SCHATÁN, C., 'Los Efectos de la Liberalización de Importaciones', *Economia Mexicana*, no. 3 (Mexico City: CIDE, 1981).

SPFI, *Plan Nacional de Desarrollo Industrial, 1979–1982* (Mexico: SPFI, 1979).

SPP, *Plan Global de Desarrollo, 1980–1982* (Mexico: SPP, 1980).

SPP, *Boletín Mensual de Información Económica*, Mexico.

SPP, *Sistema Cuentas Nacionales (Información Preliminar)*, Mexico.

TELLO, C., *La Nacionalización de la Banca* (Siglo XXI) (Mexico, 1984).

VÁZQUEZ, A., 'La Política Monetaria: 1973–1981', *Economia Mexicana*, no. 4 (Mexico: CIDE, 1982).

5 The Adjustment Process in Chile: a Comparative Perspective

Laurence Whitehead

THE DISTINCTIVENESS OF PINOCHET'S CHILE

However widespread and forceful its impact, the Latin American debt crisis of the early 1980s was not supposed to happen in Chile. According to the authorities in Santiago, to predominant opinion in the international financial community, and to that of most free market economists, the fundamental long-term changes of economic philosophy and policy adopted after the military coup of September 1973 set Chile apart from the rest of Latin America (with the possible exception of Uruguay). Even post-1976 Argentina, sometimes grouped with Chile on questions of economic philosophy, was in practice less wholehearted and long-term in its commitment to what Foxley (1984) has termed these 'experiments with neo-conservative economics'. The Chileans started sooner and persisted for longer than the Argentines. They set in place a more solid and permanent set of structures for translating their economic philosophy into practice. Their understanding of, and commitment to, the neo-conservative approach was more thorough. Above all, the Chilean regime was intended to last, to press ahead with irreversible changes, and to overcome internal resistance, to an extent unknown elsewhere in Latin America (except perhaps with very different ends in view in Cuba). General Pinochet and the armed forces had 'saved' Chile from Marxism, at least according to the dominant interpretation. Therefore his regime possessed a degree of unity and determination lacking elsewhere, and all his various opponents laboured under a more absolute disqualification. Moreover these distinctive political circumstances only reinforced what has for more than a century been the most distinctive feature of Chilean history, namely the state's capacity both to design and to implement effectively far-reaching projects intended to reshape society as a whole.

During the 1970s President Pinochet and his economic advisers (the close-knit and ideologically rigid group popularly known as the

117

'Chicago Boys') had indeed designed and implemented a wide range of ambitious policy measures rooted in a 'free-market' outlook and justified in terms of neo-conservative doctrine. Supposedly these measures would guarantee the permanence of liberal capitalism in Chile (blocking forever the possibility of another 'socialist experiment' like that of 1970–3). They were also intended to improve the flexibility and adaptiveness of the Chilean economy, and to create indissoluble links with the major sources of capital and innovation in the advanced capitalist world. The rewards for this would be greatly increased security and freedom for the individual (a claim embodying a particularly narrow view of economic freedom, characteristic of neo-conservative thought); and also accelerated economic growth, prosperity and indeed a rebirth of Chilean national pride and achievement (justifications appealing to the economic and military elites respectively). These results might take a long time to achieve. Indeed, after the experiences of the late 1960s and early 1970s, an entire generation or more might have to pass before the new system and its values were fully implanted and the bad old ways of thinking and acting had been completely forgotten or stamped out. But by 1980 admirers of the Pinochet regime were increasingly confident that the essential transformation had been wrought.

Elsewhere in Latin America (and throughout the capitalist world) public expenditure was still taking an ever-rising share of national product. In Chile, however, fiscal outlay in 1980 was brought down to a percentage of GNP not seen since the initiation of the Alliance for Progress in 1961 (23.1 per cent in 1980, compared with 26.4 per cent in 1970 and a peak of 44.9 per cent in 1973). Elsewhere in Latin America most governments were both enlarging the public sector and relying more heavily on deficit financing. In Chile in 1980 the public sector generated a perhaps unprecedented fiscal *surplus* equal to 3.1 per cent of national income (public expenditure was 23.1 per cent of GNP, public revenues were 26.2 per cent).

Elsewhere in Latin America and the capitalist world in general inflation seemed increasingly out of control. In Chile, in 1981 (for the first time in twenty years, and for only the fourth time in forty years) the consumer price index rose at a single digit rate (see Table 5.1). This 9.5 per cent inflation rate in 1981 was of particular note, since only five years earlier the rate had been near 200 per cent, after a peak in 1973 that had briefly approached 1000 per cent. Elsewhere in Latin America, interest rates were still frequently held below the level of inflation (i.e. real interest rates were negative *ex post*), thus penalising savers and subsidising lucky borrowers. In Chile, *ex post* real interest rates had risen to extraordinary

Table 5.1 Disinflation, fiscal control, but no sustained growth (percentages)

	1974	1975	1976	1977	1978	1979	1980	1981	1982	1983	1984
Consumer prices (Dec./Dec.)	375.9	340.7	174.3	63.5	30.3	38.9	31.2	9.5	20.7	23.1	23.0
Fiscal deficit/GDP	10.5	2.6	2.3	1.8	0.8	(1.7)	(3.1)	(1.7)	2.3	3.8	4.8
GDP growth	+1.0	−12.9	+3.5	+9.9	+8.2	+8.3	+7.8	+5.7	−14.3	−0.8	5.9

Sources: except where otherwise stated, this and the following tables have been compiled from: Banco Central de Chile, *Boletín Mensual*; UN, *Yearbook of National Accounts*; IMF, *International Financial Statistics*.

Table 5.2   Real interest rates (*ex post*) for Chilean debtors (percentages)

	1979	1980	1981	1982	1983
Peso debtors	17.9	13.2	39.7	38.0	16.7
Dollar debtors	0.2	−9.8	10.5	35.5	12.1
All debtors	15.4	10.7	32.6	37.5	15.6

Source: Boletín Mensual de Banco de Chile, Sept. 1984.

levels during the disinflation of the late 1970s (see Table 5.2). By 1980 they were still positive, but down to what the Western world has subsequently learnt to view as a fairly 'normal' rate – around 10 per cent per year.

Elsewhere in Latin America, 'sovereign lending' was proceeding at a frantic and, as it soon transpired, an unsustainable pace. Not so in Chile, or at least not so much, and not so early. During the first four years the Pinochet regime had only very limited access to international credit markets, and the external public debt (which had reached a dangerously high level before the September 1973 coup) grew only slowly. After 1978, it is true, the publicly guaranteed external debt began to rise much faster than before, but so did official exchange reserves. At least until 1979 the Chilean state was still viewed as 'under-borrowed' in sovereign lending terms. The conventional 'debt-service' ratio was on a steady downward path from 1975 to 1982 (see Table 5.3). Since public finances were in surplus and the state was withdrawing from economic interventionism, there was less scope for official lending than in other Latin American countries. From 1979 onwards there was, of course, a huge – and, as it turned out, disastrous – influx of commercial bank credit into the Chilean economy, but in contrast to the rest of Latin America there was relatively little sovereign lending (see Table 5.6 below). Approximately two-thirds of this credit inflow went to the renascent private sector (especially to Chile's recently privatised banking industry). These foreign loans carried no official guarantee. Ostensibly, the only collateral held by these international bankers was their rights as unsecured creditors to various private Chilean corporations. In contrast to the rest of Latin America, Chilean firms were borrowing on world markets without requiring official intermediation and without subjecting themselves to government control.

All these characteristics set Chile apart from the rest of Latin America. Free marketeers could cite them all as reasons why, whatever financial

Table 5.3 Some conventional Latin American debt-service ratios

	1975	1980	1981
Ex ante			
Uruguay	41.2	12.1	13.4
Chile	27.2	21.9	18.7
Argentina	22.0	17.7	24.5
Mexico	25.0	31.9	29.5
Peru	25.6	30.9	36.7
Brazil	17.0	34.5	42.2
Ex post			
Chile	31.2	36.0	63.5

Note: interest and repayments on external public debt (over one year to maturity) as a percentage of exports. The *ex post* figures reflect the contingent liabilities accumulated by the public sector as a consequence of the financial liberalisation. These private liabilities were assumed by the state in 1983. (*Source*: Banco Central de Chile, *Boletin Mensual*, September 1984, p. 2310.) Using a broader definition and a different methodology, Ffrench-Davis arrives at yet another series: 1975, 55.6; 1980, 47.7; 1982, 88.5. See *Estudios CIEPLAN*, no. 11, p. 120.

problems might arise elsewhere in the early 1980s, there should be no comparable debt crisis in Chile. In the event, however, since 1981 Chile has experienced a series of external and economic disequilibria, both in the financial sector and in the 'real' economy, which certainly bears comparison with the debt crisis afflicting the rest of the subcontinent. Although the problem of inflation has been less acute than average, and public sector finances have been relatively well controlled, Chile has experienced difficulties in the financial sector and with the balance of payments that are quite as serious as those affecting most other countries, and its record on output and employment and investment is worse than most. Its record on unemployment is exceptionally bad (see Table 5.9 below). The 'neo-conservative experiment' proved a poor defence against these problems.

This chapter provides a description of Pinochet's economic record; an account of the recent debt crisis and the ensuing adjustment process (1981/5); followed by a review of the various interpretations of what went wrong or could have been done better. I then put forward my own assessment, which involves placing the recent episode in its longer-term context, and contrasting the economic philosophy of Pinochet's Chile with that of other Latin American countries. In conclusion, some implications are drawn about the prospects for successful adjustment in Chile in the next few years.

PINOCHET'S ECONOMIC RECORD[1]

The economic history of Chile is punctuated by severe exogenous shocks coming from a variety of sources. In the early 1970s the economy was acutely affected by the political struggle between Allende's Marxist-led coalition government and its enemies. At a moment of crisis in 1975 it was subjected to a rather different kind of 'shock', this time deliberately administered in order to enthrone the new economic philosophy. Some distinguished analysts regard June 1979 as an equally decisive moment of choice, when the economic team shifted its stance and pegged the Chilean currency at a fixed rate of exchange to the dollar (a measure without parallel in living memory or at least since Chile was forced off the gold standard in 1931). The next major shock came in 1982, and was forced on the authorities rather than chosen by them. It contained several distinct elements, to be disentangled below: world recession, domestic financial crisis, devaluation and a reversal of international capital flows. Finally, in early 1985 the Chilean economy was subjected to yet another type of shock, also of periodic significance in the nation's history. Losses attributable to the March 1985 earthquake are provisionally estimated at about US $1.8 billion (a sum equivalent to six months' export earnings).

Behind this succession of exogenous shocks one can discern some underlying secular trends. Real income per head grew only slowly after the Second World War, and indeed after the 1929 depression. Admirers of the Pinochet regime claimed that its policies would set Chile on an accelerated growth path, perhaps replicating the 'economic miracle' of post-1964 Brazil, or more ambitiously the cumulative export-led growth of the East Asian newly industrialising countries. Between 1974 and 1984, however, GNP grew by only 20 per cent, barely ahead of population growth (Table 5.1), and it will be argued below that accelerated growth is still not yet in prospect.

For more than a generation before 1970, foreign-owned copper mines provided the greater part of Chilean foreign exchange and helped finance a relatively large public sector, a quite extensive and highly politicised welfare system, and some highly protected and inward-looking industries. The 1971 nationalisation of the copper mines has not been subsequently revoked (although new mining legislation has

Table 5.4 The structure of public enterprise

Sector	Public enterprise % of gross value sector's output		
	1965	*1973*	*1981*
Mining	13.0	85.0	83.0
Industry	3.0	40.0	12.0
Electricity, gas and water	25.0	100.0	75.0
Transport	24.3	70.0	21.0
Communications	11.1	70.0	96.3
Finance	–	85.0	28.0

Source: Cristian Larroulet, 'El Estado Empresario en Chile', *Estudios Públicos* (Santiago), no. 14, Autumn 1984, p. 148.

radically altered the terms available to foreign investors), and in general 'privatisation' still leaves a larger proportion of the economy in the public sector than in the 1960s (see Table 5.4), but the welfare system has been drastically reshaped and 'depoliticised' and industrial protection has been dismantled. Public enterprises are for the most part run according to the same business principles as privately owned firms. According to free-market theory, the Chilean state would no longer serve as an agency for distributing the surplus generated by the copper sector.

Trade liberalisation was from the outset a cornerstone of the regime's strategy for creating a 'non-interventionist' state. In 1974 the whole complex and discriminatory system of Chilean tariffs was drastically simplified. Nominal tariffs were progressively reduced, from a maximum level of 140 per cent in 1974 to 60 per cent in 1977 and 10 per cent in 1979 (an extraordinarily low level by Chilean, or indeed Latin American, standards). This very low level was made 'permanent' – at least until the 1982 crisis (after which the tariff was 'temporarily' hoisted for revenue purposes, briefly reaching 35 per cent). Now under the trade liberalisation plan all sectors of the economy would perform according to their 'comparative advantage' in world markets. The copper sector would become no different from any other; indeed, it would no longer be appropriate to make policy on the basis of 'sectors' of the economy. All would respond to the same market incentives, and in practice this would means that other previously subordinated or stifled branches of economic activity would flourish, reducing the country's dependence on the vagaries of a single unstable commodity market. For a few years after 1974 there *was* a substantial diversification of exports, but ten years later copper still accounts for about half of the country's foreign exchange earnings, and the state copper company Codelco is still by far the largest contributor to fiscal revenues. This remains so even though – partly as a result of Chilean production increases – the international copper price has fallen to its lowest level (in real terms) since the great depression (see Table 5.10 below) and, if anything, dependence on the copper industry could increase again in future years if the metal price were to recover. Reflecting this reality, after the 1982 crisis official spokesmen began to relax their earlier practice of disregarding the structural characteristics of the economy, and reverted to interpretations of their country's predicament that emphasised the peculiarities of the copper market. In the next section we will assess the validity of this type of interpretation.

According to the Pinochet government, the past ten years have witnessed some striking advances in social well-being, even though the old system of welfare provision has been dismantled and market forces have been allowed to operate without restraint. Thus it is claimed that the infant mortality rate has fallen from 82 per 1000 in 1970 to 22 per 1000 in 1983, and that life expectancy has risen, over the same period, from 64.2 years to 67.8 years. It is also asserted that 'social expenditure' (on health, education, etc.) has risen from 40 per cent of fiscal outlay in 1970 to 60 per cent in 1983. On the other hand, it would be hard to deny that the underlying trend of unemployment has been sharply rising over the period,[2] or that the distribution of income and wealth has become much more unequal than before. Land reform has been reversed, privately owned enterprises (including those sold off by the state) have become more highly concentrated, and trade unions and similar organisations have been deprived of most of their capacity to resist increasing social inequalities. According to free-market ideologists, there were not supposed to be secular trends away from social equality but only the elimination of artificial distortions. A freer and more individualistic economy would, they supposed, attain its own equilibrium, paving the way for a healthy and indeed democratic form of capitalist expansion and social incorporation. But so far the main secular trend has been towards inequality and exclusion.

There is one more secular shift that requires consideration before we turn to the economic policy record of the past few years. The financial sector underwent a transformation in the mid-1970s, and the Pinochet regime still seems committed to promoting this new model of financial intermediation, despite the severe and unexpected setbacks of the early 1980s.

From the early 1930s until the early 1970s, Chilean banks operated under a highly regulated regime. Even before they were nationalised, under the Allende government, the banks and financial institutions were subject to a great deal of official direction, both in the way they allocated resources and in the interest rates they could pay to depositors or charge to borrowers. Under this 'subordinated' financial system, real interest rates were normally negative (i.e. depositors effectively subsidised borrowers) and access to domestic credit was a highly desirable privilege. Political favouritism affected the allocation of credit, and the government found it relatively easy to finance its deficit through the banking system. A coalition of powerful interests developed, with a vested interest in the continuation of the deficit and unperturbed by relatively high rates of inflation.

Given these antecedents, it is hardly surprising that the Pinochet regime made financial liberalisation one of the highest priorities of its economic strategy. In 1975, about 86 per cent of the equity in the commercial banking system was sold off to private buyers, with generous facilities for payment offered to those bold enough to bid. At the same time banks and financial institutions were granted the freedom to pay and charge whatever interest rates the market would bear. From 1976 onwards the Central Bank began paying interest on commercial bank reserves obligatorily deposited with it, and by 1978 the reserve requirement was drastically reduced. Whereas private banks had been required to deposit more than half their reserves with the Central Bank before 1975, after 1980 they were required to deposit less than one-tenth. Moreover, domestic banks that, in the 1970s, had been sharply restricted in their recourse to foreign borrowing (only allowed to use the proceeds to finance foreign commerce) were permitted, from 1980 onwards, to borrow whatever amounts they judged appropriate from foreign sources, and to lend on such funds to domestic users in any way they considered prudent.

As a result of this financial liberalisation there was a major shift in the locus of economic power in Chile. This shift was also reflected in the size of the financial sector, as a proportion of national income. Between 1976 and 1982 the financial sector's share of GNP rose from 6.1 per cent to 11.3 per cent, with an average annual growth rate of over 21 per cent.[3] However, as is well known, this apparent source of economic dynamism proved unsustainable. For reasons that will be considered below, the private banking system entered into a deep crisis in the early 1980s. In December 1981, the authorities were obliged to intervene in the management of eight banks, holding between them 8.4 per cent of all the nation's bank deposits. In January 1983, a further ten banks experienced some form of official takeover. These ten held 45 per cent of the capital and reserves of the entire financial system (64 per cent if one leaves aside the Banco del Estado).

THE RECENT DEBT CRISIS AND ADJUSTMENT PROCESS

This brief sketch of the main economic trends since 1970 sets the scene for an account of the 1981–3 debt crisis and the ensuing adjustment process. The financial sector is the right place to start, followed by the exchange rate and the external account, and then public finances.

When financial liberalisation began, in 1974–5, the demand for Chilean monetary instruments was at an exceptional low. Extremely high inflation, massive capital flight and a drastic real devaluation of the currency made economic agents extremely reluctant to hold money balances if they could possibly avoid it. Whereas the real money supply had risen very rapidly in 1971 and 1972 (real M1 up 65 per cent), after 1973 it fell precipitously. The low point was reached in 1976, when M1 fell to only 4.8 per cent of GNP, barely half the ratio that had been 'normal' before Popular Unity. Although it gradually rose thereafter, it has not as yet returned to pre-1970 levels – at the peak of the cycle, in 1981, almost half the broadly defined money supply was in interest-bearing deposits of under 90 days maturity (compared with only 3 per cent in 1973). Perhaps the most impressive testimony to the confidence generated by the financial liberalisation (and to the lure of very high real interest rates) was the proportion of deposits with over one year's maturity. These reached a quarter of the total in 1982, compared with a norm of under 5 per cent before the liberalisation.

Taking all those forms of money and 'quasi money' together, the financial liberalisation transformed Chilean willingness to hold peso-denominated financial instruments. Up to 1976 the 'normal' level of such holdings was under 20 per cent of GNP (falling as low as 15 per cent in the crisis year 1973). By the end of the decade this had risen to 30 per cent, and by the time the debt crisis broke it was near 50 per cent. As José Pablo Arellano notes, such a figure is not unusual in countries with well-developed financial markets: 'What is abnormal about the Chilean case is the speed of growth of these resources. The question that arises is where did the funds come from to support real growth in deposits at 18–40 per cent per year?"[4] The kernel of this question is who, within the Chilean productive apparatus, could securely and profitably invest the money paid in by these depositors and thus validate the extraordinarily high real interest rates that all debtors were continually being charged. According to Arellano's calculations, during their six years of financial freedom Chile's newly privatised banks *charged* on average 32.7 per cent per year *real* interest for their short-term loans.[5] Naturally, at these rates the banks were willing lenders (although not of *long-term* money) and found themselves in an exceptionally strong position to attract deposits, even after pocketing a net spread in the area of 10 per cent per annum. But it was the abundance of willing borrowers even at these ruinous rates that both made the financial liberalisation a temporary success and which ultimately guaranteed its collapse. How was it possible for the Chicago Boys to tap such a vast reserve of imprudence and improvidence in the 'bankable' sector of Chilean society? (I set aside here the far-from-negligible portion of the debt that was incurred – quite prudently and appropriately – by the favoured few who could thus buy up state assets at bargain prices.)

The ostensible rationale for the financial liberalisation was to stimulate national savings and investment, as well as to extend market freedoms to individual economic agents. In fact gross savings fell from a norm of about 16 per cent of GNP in the 1960s to an average of 12.4 per cent per year in the period 1975–81, and the investment ratio also fell. What the financial liberalisation actually stimulated was a catch-up in long-postponed middle-class consumption appetites – consumer durables (with a high import content), foreign travel and other manifestations of affluence unsupported by the productive capacity of the real economy. One aspect of the liberalisation measures worthy of note in this context was the abolition of all the credit controls that had formerly existed for the purpose of directing financial resources into production rather than consumption. From the standpoint of the agents concerned this may have been a 'rational' response to the opportunities provided by the Pinochet regime, particularly for those who judged that the good times of 1980 were too good to last (just as 1973 had been too bad to last). Such individual rationality is, of course, 'bounded' by the social conditions within which the individual choices are constrained. In this case the constraining social context was an inegalitarian and authoritarian regime catering to a middle class still traumatised by the nearly successful imposition of radical socialism. Such a context was hardly conducive to accelerated long-term savings or investment in slowly gestating fixed capital projects, least of all when the Chilean state, the traditional sponsor of the long-term view, had largely withdrawn from such 'economic interventionism'. With individual time horizons accordingly foreshortened, concern about the ultimate repayability of imprudent debts proved less than binding. In the short run, credit was plentiful (if dear), so there was no compulsion for debtors to face up to the losses implied by the level of interest rates. The less immediately painful alternative was to borrow more. In fact, the simple accumulation of peso interest from 1977 to 1982 accounts for 72 per cent of the peso debt outstanding at the end of 1982. In the longer run, therefore, individual debtors could see that their difficulties were part of a collective problem, and this realisation weakened their incentives to take corrective action. Experience no doubt suggested to many Chilean debtors that there was strength in numbers. In the end, either their real obligations might be eroded by a new burst of inflation and negative real interest rates, or the banks would be afraid to call in their debts for lack of adequate collateral. 'This second view must have been the perception of the major debtors – in particular the so-called *grupos* – over most of the period, and it has certainly been the expectation of the immense majority of debtors from 1982 onwards.'[6] (There are obvious analogies with the situation that has arisen for many dollar debtors – both within and outside the USA – since 1981, but in Chile the process was much more rapid and extreme.)

Here we encounter an analytical puzzle that underscores the unusual circumstances prevailing in Chile at this time. In most financial systems debtors, creditors and intermediaries are reasonably well informed about the expectations and assumptions governing each other's behaviour. For a short while debtors might still retain access to credit after the realisation had dawned on them that they were no longer creditworthy, but normally this lag in perception would not last long. There is reasonably high 'transparency' between debtors and creditors. However, this was less apparent in Chile. One reason was simply that the liberalised financial system was so new, had expanded so fast and had been subjected to so little supervision. A deeper reason was that such 'transparency' was alien to the Pinochet regime itself. In political matters the citizens do not have the 'right to know' what the authorities wish to conceal, and the courts assume the impunity of the most powerful, so why should it be any different in the realm of finance? In any case the government had apparently staked its entire reputation on the continance of this credit expansion, thus paradoxically reducing the sense of individual responsibility. A further reason may also be adduced, which brings us to the external sector. The *takers* of peso funds were Chilean enterprises and individuals operating in the bizarre and to outsiders almost incomprehensible conditions of post-Allende Chile. However much confidence they *seemed* to express in the ideology of the Pinochet regime, their private agendas reflected continuing hesitancy and insecurity about the future of their country. The *givers* of funds, to a significant extent, were foreign bankers with only the haziest understanding of these attitudes. The official ideology of the Chicago Boys was tailored to appeal to them, and they were far more likely than Chilean nationals to take it at face value, as 'the truth, the whole truth, and nothing but the truth'. The terms on which credits were extended provide confirmation that foreign creditors had greater confidence or were more completely taken in than their domestic counterparts. Private international bankers were willing to lend *in dollars*, for a minimum term of *two years* and without a state guarantee. Chilean domestic banks lent in pesos for much shorter periods, charging much higher spreads for their services even though they were operating from a position of great apparent political strength. Given this radical separation between the mental universes of the domestic takers of funds and the foreign givers, and given the strength of the structures erected to keep these two groups apart, the normal defences against cumulatively more imprudent lending were absent. Apparently many foreign suppliers of credit remained blissfully unaware of the objective and subjective uncreditworthiness of most Chilean debtors until the banking system was in unmistakable collapse. (Foreign suppliers of direct investment may have been more alert. At any rate, as Table 5.7 below shows, the response to the regime's foreign investment incentives was meagre.) Domestic suppliers of credit also went on lending despite their growing awareness that the whole structure was ultimately unsustainable, because the scale of the foreign inflows seemed to offer powerful short-term reassurance.

Associated with the policy of financial liberalisation was that of 'opening' the domestic financial market to international influences. Both of these moves took place very rapidly, and both were allowed to proceed without any restraint until they ended in the financial crash of 1982–3.

Compared with similar developments in other Latin American countries, what stands out about the Chilean case is above all (i) the timing, and (ii) the lack of official guarantees. The net external debt of the public sector peaked at around $4 billion in 1975. By 1981 it had been reduced below $2 billion, partly through amortisation, partly because, with sweeping privatisation and a fiscal surplus, there was little public sector demand for credit, and partly because the Central Bank was accumulating foreign exchange reserves. Over the same period the net external debt of the private sector rose from under $1 billion to almost $10 billion. The great bulk of this increase came in just two years (rising from $3.05 billion in 1979 to $5.99 billion in 1980 and $9.76 billion in 1981). By the time the banking crisis came to a head in January 1983, the net external debt of the private sector (essentially the private banks) had surpassed $10 billion *without state guarantee.*[7]

Table 5.5 shows the evolution of the trade balance and its relationship to the accumulation of external debt. From 1977 to 1980 there was a gradual deterioration in the trading performance, masked, however, by the buoyancy of copper prices in 1979 and 1980. In 1981 export revenue fell by almost US $1 billion and imports surged by over $1 billion, bringing the trade crisis to a head, and requiring depletion of the nation's foreign exchange reserves and urgent recourse to additional foreign financing. Table 5.6 shows how the gross capital inflow accelerated between 1978 and 1981, and how abruptly the gross flow fell back in 1982. It also indicates the unimportance of public sector borrowing, and of direct foreign investment, as compared with private bank finance. Table 5.7 shows the very rapid build-up of interest (most borrowing was at variable rates) and repayments due (most borrowing was quite short-term). It shows that by the end of 1981, even though the *gross* inflow was at an unprecedented and unsustainable level, the *net* resource transfer achieved through foreign borrowing was on the turn. A $2 billion increase in gross inflow produced only a $600 million rise in net resources. Thereafter quite large *negative* net resource transfers were in prospect, and even so the external debt would certainly continue to grow. Although for Latin America as a whole Carlos Díaz Alejandro may be right to argue that on the information available to bankers in 1980 and 1981 increased sovereign lending was not self-evidently imprudent ('not a Ponzi scheme'), an exception should be made for commercial bank lending to Chile in those two years.

The imprudence of domestic debtors and foreign lenders must be seen in the context of the Pinochet regime's economic strategy as a whole, and not just its financial liberalisation aspect. This interacted with the trade liberalisation and exchange-rate policies, which in turn interacted with the chosen balance of fiscal and monetary policies, each of which will now be briefly considered.

The effective rate of protection is determined, of course, by the effective exchange rate as well as by the nominal tariff regime. Between 1975 and 1981 Chile not only reduced nominal tariffs from one of the highest to

Table 5.5 Sluggish exports, soaring foreign debt (US $m)

	1974	1975	1976	1977	1978	1979	1980	1981	1982	1983	1984
Merchandise exports f.o.b.	2151	1590	2116	1185	2460	3835	4705	3836	3706	3851	3700
Imports f.o.b.	1794	1520	1473	2151	2886	4190	5469	6513	3643	2837	3400
Medium- and long-term external debt (end year)	4026	4267	4274	4510	5923	7507	9413	12553	13815	16016	17500

Table 5.6 Sources of capital inflow (US $m)

	1975	1976	1977	1978	1979	1980	1981	1982	1983
Direct foreign investment	−4	−1	+16	+177	+233	+170	+362	+384	+152
Commercial banks	−46	−35	+146	+349	+630	+1907	+2748	+396	−419
Other private capital	+281	+320	+430	+862	+1046	+1003	+1324	−537	−421
Public sector	+9	−85	−20	+558	+338	+85	+264	+972	+1197
Total	+240	+199	+572	+1946	+2247	+3165	+4698	+1215	+509
Note: peso/$ exchange rate (end year)	8.3	17.0	27.6	33.8	39.0	39.0	39.0	72.4	87.1

Table 5.7   External debt servicing and the net resource transfer from abroad
(US $m)

	Foreign borrow-ing	less	Debt amortisa-tion	less	Interest	equals	Net resource transfer
1979	1245		323		174		+ 748
1980	2504		694		384		+ 1426
1981	4517		1591		830		+ 2096
1982	1771		911		1110		− 250
1983	258		413		762		− 917
1984	250		500		770		− 1020

almost certainly the lowest in Latin America; it also shifted from a
severely undervalued exchange rate to an equally severely overvalued
rate (see Table 5.8 for two CIEPLAN estimates).[8] The combination of
these two violent shifts was to expose Chilean industry to the most severe
and destructive external competition, allowing no chance for orderly
restructuring or even for a minimally rational reallocation of resources.
There is an elaborate literature on what the policy makers thought they
were doing, as they presided over this remarkable shift from effective
protection to effective *dis*protection of the Chilean production of
tradable goods. We shall return to the part played by ideological
dogmatism and authoritarian insensitivity in explaining Pinochet's
economic policies. What requires attention here is the relationship
between the capital inflows of 1977–81 and the real exchange rate
appreciation of those years.

Although the Chilean economic model is often referred to as an
unrestrained application of 'free-market' principles, there are some key
prices that have always been determined by administrative diktat. The
dollar exchange rate is a crucial example. Certainly the Pinochet regime
was quick to unify the exchange rate and to lift most restrictions on
currency convertibility, but it never allowed the price of foreign
exchange to be directly market-determined. On the contrary, for the first
five years the Central Bank carried out exchange transactions in
accordance with a pre-determined 'crawling-peg' system that was geared
to the competing aims of improving the foreign balance (which required
undervaluation) and slowing the domestic inflation rate (implying
overvaluation). The authorities used discretionary power quite actively.
Until June 1976 they devalued the currency two or three times a month,
then they abruptly revalued it by 11 per cent, after which they switched

Table 5.8 The CIEPLAN perspective

	1973	1974	1975	1976	1977	1978	1979	1980	1981	1982	1983
Consumer price index (Dec./Dec.) corrected for 'errors'	813.6	369.2	343.3	197.9	84.2	37.2	38.9	31.2	9.5	20.7	23.1
Real wage and salary index (1970 = 100)	77.6	65.0	62.9	64.7	71.4	76.0	82.2	89.3	97.3	97.6	86.9
True unemployment rate (Santiago) (%)	4.3	9.4	16.8	20.1	16.2	16.8	15.5	13.9	12.4	23.8	27.6
Real exchange rate using consumer prices (1977 = 100)	69.7	108.4	148.7	120.2	100.0	111.0	108.5	94.7	80.5	93.5	112.4
Real exchange using earnings index (1977 = 100)	110.0	118.0	168.6	130.8	100.0	104.3	94.2	75.6	59.0	68.7	92.5
External financing of gross fixed investment (%)	24.7	12.0	32.5	−11.4	34.1	50.9	42.2	51.2	108.1	87.2	na

Sources: statistical appendix to *Estudios CIEPLAN*, no. 13, Tables 4, 7, 8 and 14, plus *Estudios CIEPLAN*, no. 11, p. 120. However, Pinochet's penultimate Minister of Hacienda gave the real unemployment rate at 31 per cent in 1982, 28 per cent in 1983 and 25 per cent in 1984 (presumably end-year figures) (*El Mercurio*, 7 April 1985).

to daily devaluations at a pace announced monthly in advance. There was another abrupt revaluation in March 1977, then in 1978 and 1979 daily devaluations took place in accordance with a schedule announced yearly in advance. The most dramatic change of policy took place in mid-1979, when the peso was unexpectedly devalued to the pre-announced end-year level (39 pesos to the dollar), with the promise that it would be permanently held at that level thereafter.

It is important to notice that the authorities pegged the peso to the *dollar*, and not to a trade-weighted basket of foreign currencies, and that they chose to do this at a moment of what proved to be exceptional relative weakness of the US currency. By June 1982, when the peso was forced off this self-appointed dollar parity, the American currency had appreciated by about 25 per cent in real terms against the currencies of other major industrial nations. If, for example, in mid-1979, the Chileans had pegged the peso to the European Currency Unit (ecu), rather than to the dollar, they could have avoided most of the resource misallocation attributable to defence of an inappropriate exchange rate.[9] What in fact happened was that the fixed dollar–peso parity failed to slow domestic inflation sufficiently, even with a very open trading and financial regime. The prices of non-tradables rose far out of line with those obtainable in the increasingly depressed and over-indebted tradable sector. Moreover, the unfulfillable promise of eternal parity with the dollar induced many Chilean enterprises to borrow in dollars even when their prospective revenue was all in pesos. Severe devaluation brought the peso down from 39 to the dollar in June 1982 to 73 six months later, rendering their dollar debts unpayable and precipitating the banking crisis of January 1983. Since then there have been further erratic policy shifts concerning the foreign sector – another period of crawling pegs, interrupted by sharp devaluations in September 1984 and June 1985, while the external tariff has been temporarily jacked up from 10 per cent to a peak of 35 per cent (for revenue purposes) and then brought down again to 20 per cent. The easy exchange convertibility of the late 1970s has, of course, been reversed. This can hardly have been a surprise to seasoned economic agents within Chile, considering all the historical precedents.

How can we explain the fact that the Chilean authorities managed to sustain the fixed dollar parity for three long years, despite all the country's accumulated experience of the overvaluation/devaluation cycle, and all the visible evidence of where this was leading to? The dogmatism of the policy makers, and their seclusion from counteracting pressures in civil society, will be discussed further below. However, they needed not just the will, but also the means, to err. It is here that the unsustainable inflows of foreign capital, between 1979 and 1981, played an essential permissive role. In the three years of dollar parity, gross foreign lending to Chile totalled over $8 billion, more than half of which took place in 1981 alone. Prior to June 1979, gross foreign lending never reached $1 billion per year, and since June 1982 the Chilean external debt has not risen faster than, say, $1 billion per year. The $4 billion lent to Chilean financial institutions ($3 billion) and private firms ($900 million) in 1981 alone financed a current account deficit of equal magnitude (21 per cent of GDP), as compared with an historical level that seldom exceeded 5 per cent of GDP. The conclusion seems inescapable that but for the quite unprecedented and unsustainable foreign lending boom of 1979–81, the attempt to peg the peso to the dollar would have been impossible to finance for so long. Under more normal external financing constraints, no matter how dogmatic the policy makers, the experiment would have been abandoned by early 1981, before really grave misallocation and overindebtedness could take place.

In such matters causality is, of course, two-way. There can be little doubt that foreign willingness to lend on such a massive scale was itself partly prompted by growing external confidence in the stability of the dollar–peso exchange rate. With Chilean banks able to lend in pesos at far higher interest rates than were obtainable on dollar loans, a fixed exchange rate would mean a very high guaranteed rate of profit for those who could borrow in dollars and lend in pesos. If the exchange rate was really to remain fixed, then this interest rate differential, and other divergences between internal and external price levels, could only be transitional. Those who believed in the unshakable resolve of the Chicago Boys and had faith in the 'law of one price' saw an opportunity for exceptional profit that must be seized immediately before it disappeared. Such reasoning seems to have contributed to the frantic rush to lend (without state guarantee) to private Chilean banks and enterprises.

Finally, these financial and exchange-rate considerations also interacted powerfully with the Pinochet regime's domestic monetary and fiscal policies. On the monetary side, it has already been noted that extremely high real interest rates were customarily charged and paid by peso debtors throughout the period 1975–82, during which time the domestic demand for money (and in particular for high interest-bearing quasi-money) grew at a phenomenal pace. The inflow of foreign funds reached such a scale that in 1980–1 they contributed something like 40 per cent of the loans made through the financial system. However, this manifestation of foreign confidence in the Chilean financial system not only added to the supply of credit; it also (and just as powerfully) stimulated credit demand. Part of the demand, as argued above, came from a rather rational wish to purchase imports and to travel abroad while exceptional conditions of overvaluation and exchange-rate liberalism still permitted. Part was also attributable to the wish to purchase domestic assets (houses, enterprises, equities) before foreign-financed demand drove their prices out of the reach of Chilean nationals.

The Central Bank was still, of course, conducting monetary policy with an emphasis on the control of inflation. The influx of foreign capital caused a rise in foreign exchange reserves, and a corresponding expansion of the domestic money supply, which in 1981 caused the Central Bank to reinforce its policy of domestic monetary tightness and reliance on high real interest rates. However, this official restraint in the supply of 'narrow' money proved quite ineffective as a deterrent to domestic borrowing as reflected in the broader aggregates. Much of the explanation both for restraint in the supply of 'narrow' money and for excess in the demand for peso debt comes from the distortion and false expectations created by the foreign lending boom and the associated exchange-rate overvaluation.

In the area of fiscal policy we find a particularly vivid illustration of the distortions and false expectations of the period. Starting in 1975, the Chilean regime was determined to eliminate the fiscal deficits so long associated with democratic government and chronic inflation. Initially, the fiscal deficit fell to a small fraction of GDP, and at the end of the years 1979, 1980 and 1981 Chile recorded a significant fiscal surplus (see Table 5.1 above). Thus as private sector borrowing rose to a speculative peak, borrowing by the public sector fell to an historical low. From a conventional accounting standpoint, Chile's public finances were healthier than for many decades.[10] The inadequacy of a conventional accounting framework was suddenly revealed, however, in January 1983, when 85 per cent of the banking system was 'rescued' by the Central Bank, and when the Chilean state abruptly assumed responsibility for over $11 billion of private foreign debt that it had never previously guaranteed. In retrospect it might have been more realistic to regard all interest on the external debt (including initially unguaranteed debt) as public sector 'expenditure', that could be offset with public sector 'revenue' to the extent that the private debtors were in a position to service their external obligations. Where they are not, the difference constitutes a 'fiscal deficit' in the sense that any permanent gap must be financed either by taxation, borrowing or money creation. The Pinochet regime has sought to disguise this element of fiscal deficit by treating the private sector's debt-servicing problems as a temporary liquidity issue rather than a matter of insolvency. The longer it persists in this approach, the more misleading become the official public sector accounts.

The final section of this chapter contains a brief review of the several approaches to 'adjustment' that have been attempted since January 1983, and a discussion of present prospects and alternatives. Before turning to those questions we need to assess alternative explanations of the nature of the crisis outlined above. First, I consider three interpretations offered by other authors, and then I offer my own synthesis.

ALTERNATIVE INTERPRETATIONS

Bela Balassa's key judgement on the Pinochet regime's economic strategy is that a serious policy error was made in June 1979. He considers that from September 1973 to June 1979 policy was mostly correct, and largely successful. It would be wrong to regard the entire liberalisation strategy of 1973–83 as a failure, simply because 'in the name of an unproven theory, one fundamentally lacking in realism, the liberalisation was perverted and price distortions were increased after 1979'. The Chilean authorities 'did not recognise' that fixing the exchange rate

> would have a high economic cost because of the unfavourable consequences of increasing discrimination against tradable goods. Whilst the inflow of foreign capital led to a rapid expansion in the production of non-tradables this could not continue indefinitely. This increase in the Chilean external debt, together with a substantial decline in the trade balance, led to a decline in solvency. Then when the artificial bonanza in the non-traded sector came to an end both tradable and non-tradable sectors entered into a synchronised downturn. GNP fell in the fourth quarter of 1981, and then continued to fall as the balance of payments situation necessitated the adoption of strong deflationary measures, and abandonment of the fixed exchange rate.

Balassa dismisses the importance of external shocks as an explanation of the unfavourable results of the experiment. With a competitive rate after

1979, external shocks could have been far more successfully absorbed.[11]

Balassa explains the change in policy in June 1979 simply in terms of the adoption of a mistaken economic theory. It falls outside the scope of his analysis to consider why policy makers were so attracted to the new theory, or even why they were in any way dissatisfied with the previous – in his view highly successful – economic strategy. He also leaves aside from his analysis both the political and the economic factors which permitted or even encouraged policy makers to persist for so long with their erroneous prescriptions.

T. G. Congdon, an English monetarist writer, has also written an interpretation of what went wrong that has as its purpose to salvage the reputation of an economic orthodoxy that might otherwise be discredited by the Chilean débâcle. In contrast to Balassa, he plays up the severity of the 'external shock'. He argues that the terms-of-trade loss between 1973 and 1983 reduced Chile's real national income by between 15 to 20 per cent. Rather than adjust to this loss, Chile borrowed abroad to maintain the level of real national expenditures. 'If it had not been for the deterioration in terms of trade, Chile could have enjoyed the same level of real expenditures, but without incurring any debt.'[12] This type of analysis is, of course, very sensitive to the base year chosen as a yardstick for comparison (in 1973 copper was high, oil was low) and presumably, in any case, from a free market perspective terms of trade fluctuations should be absorbed, not used as an excuse. More interesting is Congdon's view of the internal factors contributing to what he calls the 'collapse of the Chilean economic miracle'. Although he thinks that most of the shocks were external, he argues that

they interacted with and exacerbated weaknesses stemming from the financial liberalisation ... the difficult and important question is why Chilean policy makers did not pay more attention at an earlier stage to prudential aspects of the financial liberalisation ... The explanation seems to be that Chilean policy makers were so mesmerised by the virtues of the free market that they did not see anything worrying in the pattern of financial liberalisation. They knew that the high ratios of financial intermediation to national income in advanced economies are sustained by a substantial stock of professional expertise and a variety of regulatory structures and ethical codes. But they were blind to the evidence that Chile, in the course of quintupling private-sector credit in less than four years, was not acquiring the skills and institutions necessary to consolidate an expanded financial system.[13]

According to this view, a major domestic policy error was that the financial liberalisation was simply allowed to proceed too far and too fast (so fast that the term 'monetarist' strikes Congdon as 'oversimplified to the point of misrepresentation'). Chile's financial reforms were aimed in the right direction, and in any case their failures of circumstance or of implementation carry no very ominous implications for the practice of conventional monetarism in more advanced economies.

This line of interpretation raises two significant questions about the Pinochet regime that are not normally admitted on to the agenda for discussion by conventional economic analysts. How long a time horizon is required for an authoritarian regime to consolidate a modern capitalist economic system in a developing country? By January 1983, when Chile's private sector had to be rescued, the financial liberalisation programme had been in operation for over seven years. If in that time these reforms had been pushed through too far and too fast, then how long would be needed to establish them in a more gradual and consolidated manner? The Pinochet administration has had greater stability and a longer life expectancy than most comparable regimes in other countries, yet even in Chilean conditions it would seem overconfident to plan for reforms that require more than a decade of steady application before they take hold. In any case, is it realistic to expect the consolidation of complex ethical codes, or of a sound framework of financial regulation and disinterested professionalism, under the authorship of a regime that depends for stability on censorship, repression and the denial of democratic rights to its citizens? Congdon's interpretation, like that of Balassa, rests on some debatable assumptions about the nature of political order in Pinochet's Chile.

The decision to peg the exchange rate to the dollar comes in for some critical comments from Congdon as well as from Balassa. Congdon likens this system to the 'currency boards' that once operated in British and French colonies, according to which the local monetary authorities were unable to issue liabilities unless backed by foreign currency. This observation also brings certain underlying political issues to the fore. Under colonial conditions this self-denying ordinance was credible so long as the metropolitan government insisted upon it, and the colonial economy could be obliged to accept whatever deflation the system from time to time dictated. In political terms, it was less credible that the Chilean monetary authorities could persist with unlimited deflation, since in the last analysis they were not so completely isolated from Chilean society as the colonial currency boards had been. Thus it was that in mid-1982, faced with the full implications of persisting further with a fixed exchange rate (which would have required domestic cuts in *nominal* wage and price levels, and thus a disastrous increase in the real burden of peso debt), the Chilean monetary authorities abandoned the currency board model. According to Congdon, however, it was not the political obstacles that caused the change of policy, but rather what he calls 'a major conceptual flaw' in the economic model.

> When bank deposits are convertible into dollars, 100 per cent reserve cover for Central Bank liabilities is insufficient to hold the rate of exchange. Instead 100 per cent cover for all bank liabilities is required. Chile did not have that.[14]

However, in reality, as with the decision to abandon the gold standard in 1931, the question policy makers have to judge is not whether further deflation is *technically* still possible (in June 1982 it still was), but whether it is *politically* desirable and/or feasible.

Finally, the Chilean economist, Sebastian Edwards, has also attempted an explanation that requires comment here. He summarises his conclusions as follows:

> The crisis was to a large extent the result of an adverse external setting and of policy errors. In particular the combination of a fixed exchange rate and inflexible real wages constituted an important policy error. Moreover the liberalization of the internal financial market, without providing a clear framework of operational rules and regulations, was a problem that gave rise to a considerable financial crisis. Finally, the government's passive attitude despite certain clear indications of significant economic crisis from mid-1980 onwards (i.e. extraordinarily high real interest rates, great increases in the external debt, a substantial loss of competitivity) was an important error.[15]

The only new point in this summary is the emphasis on the inflexibility of real wages, the importance of which can be seen from the second 'real exchange rate' series in Table 5.8, where real earnings rather than consumer prices are used to deflate the nominal exchange rate. As inflation slowed, real earnings (adjusted periodically in line with past, higher, rates of inflation) proceeded to rise. Rapid expansion in the non-tradable sector kept up the demand for labour despite the profits squeeze in tradables. According to the free-market viewpoint, workers in exposed sectors should have forgone this inflation adjustment or even accepted cuts in nominal wages in order to preserve their jobs. According to a strong version of this view, it was the 'inflexibility' of the labour market (partly a product of the legal provisions governing wage determination) that caused spreading bankruptcy and debt crisis from late 1980 onwards. Edwards, however, backed away from the 'hardline' conclusion of some Chicago Boys that the only error was to flinch from forcing through more downward wage flexibility.

Consequently, in the first version of his paper Edwards came to the same conclusion as Balassa. The greatest error was the fixed exchange-rate policy. However, in a postscript he subsequently revised this judgement as follows:

> I continue to think that the fixed exchange rate of 39 pesos to the dollar was a serious error, but not the worst error. That was to open the capital account of the balance of payments without establishing regulations that would ensure an efficient allocation of resources in the domestic financial market. This mode of financial opening gave rise to the enormous debt which now afflicts us.

> With or without an administratively fixed exchange rate, the massive influx of external finance would have brought about the same overvaluation of the real exchange rate.

> The most probable result of a floating rate is that by mid-1981 the nominal rate would have stood at around 25–27 pesos to the dollar [i.e. even greater overvaluation] ... What was needed was some kind of restriction on the inflow of foreign capital, and the establishment of regulations for its correct allocation.[16]

This perspective puts the June 1979 exchange-rate decision into a very different light. It carries additional conviction when one considers how many Latin American countries, each with very different exchange-rate philosophies, allowed their currencies to become wildly misaligned in 1980–1 as a result of abnormal foreign capital flows. The same occurred in Argentina (under the *tablita* system), Colombia (with a crawling peg) and even Mexico (despite Central Bank protestations that it would never repeat the error of 1975–6, when a fixed and overvalued rate to the dollar was disastrously defended). In view of all this it is difficult to accept Balassa's stress on just one pivotal and voluntarist error, the pegging of the peso in mid-1979.

Edwards concludes his postscript by raising a fundamental issue that I wish to discuss more fully in the next section of this chapter. He vigorously rejects the explanation that the Chicago Boys were simply 'bad economists'.

> I consider that the problem was quite different, and considerably more serious because it demonstrates the persistence of a very unfavourable feature of our national life. The policy errors that were committed are mainly attributable to the dogmatism and sectarianism of the economic team, a deficiency that has systematically characterised preceding economic teams committed to other economic models as well. It was not technical incompetence that was the fault, but an inability to relate to alternative viewpoints ... Even at the level of academic economic discourse there is a manifest lack of communication between those who think differently, so it is hardly surprising that in the area of practical applications of economic policy non-communication should be even more pronounced, with most damaging results for the country. It must be a source of unease that those in the opposition who in the foreseeable future may take up positions of responsibility for managing the economy display the same intransigence and incapability for dialogue as the team which has handled the economy over the past decade.[17]

A POLITICAL ECONOMY INTERPRETATION OF THE CRISIS

The third section of this chapter (pp. 126–37) presented an account of the development of the crisis which drew heavily on the writings of the CIEPLAN school of opposition economists, which Edwards rather uncharitably describes as sectarian and dogmatic in the 'Chicago Boy' style. It must be said that the role of the opposition economist has been far from easy in Chile over the past ten years and that on any reasonable view the government has more responsibility than its academic critics for any lack of dialogue. If the CIEPLAN team does eventually take office it will presumably be as part of a democratic transition, and they will therefore be kept more accountable than their predecessors. In the fourth section of this chapter I tried to set out some of the principal serious explanations for the 1982 débâcle put forward by analysts who are broadly sympathetic to the objectives of the Pinochet regime's economic reforms. The task of this section is to present a political economy interpretation of the Chilean crisis that takes into account the substantive points in the two preceding sections.

The three questions for consideration here are: (i) how Chilean economic policy and economic performance differ from those of the other Latin American countries discussed in this volume; (ii) what the main connections are between these distinctive features of the economic record and the country's authoritarian political regime; and (iii) which interpretation, or combination of interpretations, best accounts for the distinctive trajectory of the Chilean economy.

The answer to (i) is that there has been a greater emphasis on, and success with, the control of inflation in Pinochet's Chile than in the rest of Latin America. On the other side there has been less concern to limit the ravages of unemployment, and less success in promoting growth or preserving the goods-producing sectors of the economy. The answer to (ii) is that the Pinochet regime is dedicated to the maintenance of an internal distribution of power that radically demobilises what used to be called the 'popular classes', and which re-establishes a system of private ownership almost extinguished by September 1973. The long-term improbability of this project, together with the regime's inability to vary it or to find some more feasible goals to aim for, accounts for the dogmatism that characterises its economic management. The answers to questions (i) and (ii) constitute the 'political economy' perspective of this section of the chapter. It can be used to answer question (iii) as well, providing a method for reassessing the interpretations in the two preceding sections.

In the aftermath of the 1982 debt crisis there can be little doubt that Chile is registering the highest rate of open unemployment and the lowest rate of inflation of any of the major countries covered by this study (Tables 5.9 and 10.2). Moreover, it is generally accepted that relatively high unemployment and relatively low inflation are likely to persist for the rest of the decade, especially if we assume that the Pinochet regime remains in power. No matter what weight one attaches to 'external shocks' rather than internal policy choices as explanations for the severity of the Chilean crisis, this particular combination of characteristics must be regarded as distinctive. If the external shock was very powerful, then the 'normal' Latin American response would be a much higher rate of inflation, especially in an economy as highly indexed and as traditionally inflation-prone as that of Chile. If, on the other hand, like Congdon, one points to low inflation as an indication that 'In comparison with other Latin American countries and the situation before 1973, Chile has a relatively good financial system',[18] then the

Table 5.9   Urban unemployment trends (%)

	1970	1980	1981	1982	1983	1984
Greater Santiago (Chile)	4.1	11.7	9.0	20.0	19.0	18.5
Montevideo (Uruguay)	7.5	7.4	6.7	11.9	15.5	14.5
Lima (Peru)	6.9	7.1	6.8	7.0	9.2	10.0
Brazil	6.5	6.2	7.9	6.3	6.7	7.5
Mexico	7.0	4.5	4.2	4.1	6.9	6.3
Greater Buenos Aires	4.9	2.3	4.5	4.7	4.0	3.8

Source: Emilio Klein and José Wurgaft, 'La Creación de Empleo en Períodos de Crisis' (Santiago, Chile: ILE [PREALC], 1985), p. 6. Based on annual household survey data. Chilean data exclude those on 'minimum employment' schemes whose inclusion would add several percentage points (compare Table 5.8).

exceptionally high levels of recorded unemployment require an explanation that must account for Chile's uncharacteristic resignation in the presence of so much joblessness. My own view is that the 'external shocks' afflicting the Chilean economy were rather worse than those discussed elsewhere in this volume, but that on their own they cannot account either for the scale or still less for the composition of the subsequent crisis.

Supposing for a moment that there had been no particularly severe external shock affecting the Chilean economy in the early 1980s, then the Pinochet regime's forceful and far-reaching package of economic measures would be the unambiguous cause of whatever economic developments took place in that period. What would have happened in this case? With the benefit of hindsight most sources seem to accept that there would in any case have been a substantial domestic financial crisis. Opinions may differ on its size and shape. Much would depend on the precise assumptions made about the international environment, and also on the way the authorities would have responded as ripples from the crisis spread through the domestic economy. If one assumes that the authorities would have been extremely slow to recognise the implications of what was happening and very reluctant to modify their pre-existing schemes in order to contain it, then it becomes easy to envisage a major and damaging débâcle, quite comparable in scale to what actually happened.

In the absence of any 'external shocks', the Chicago Boys were most unlikely to vary their prescriptions, no matter how the domestic economy seemed to be behaving. Brecht once remarked that the East German Communist Party, when it encountered massive social rejection of its preconceived theories, 'would like to dissolve the People and elect a new one'. In the same spirit Pinochet's economic managers considered it their responsibility to re-educate a citizenry stubbornly resistant to patterns of behaviour required by free-market theory. That required them to stick to their policies regardless of the short-term results, until economic agents learnt (if necessary from bitter experience) that the laws of market behaviour would no longer be varied in response to mere political lobbying or social protest.

In order to assess how much of the present Chilean economic crisis should be attributed to the domestic financial reform, one has to take a view on the debate about dogmatism and inflexibility. In other words, one has to make an appraisal of the political characteristics of the Pinochet regime, and why it attached so much importance to the implementation of an unrestrained financial liberalisation. The standpoint adopted here is that, over and above the personal characteristics of particular policy makers, or the intellectual merits of one or other position in the theoretical debates that interest the Chicago Boys, what was fundamental for the military junta was to reconstitute a domestic capitalist system that had been almost destroyed by Allende's socialist experiment. The key to reconstituting such a system was to create confidence that there could be no return to the 'bad old ways' and that those who profited from liberalised markets could feel secure in their gains. From this perspective financial freedom was more important than the maximisation of production, low inflation was more important than high employment, and any attempt to regulate or oversee the workings of the financial system was suspect, for it might reopen the way to discriminatory policies, and might undermine the still fragile confidence in the permanence of the liberalisation. For the same fundamentally political reasons it was considered essential to stick to initially decided policies with a minimum of variation (in dogmatism), and to push ahead with financial liberalisation at the *maximum possible* speed. These underlying constraints on economic policy making in the Pinochet regime are different from those operating on most other Latin American policy makers considered in this volume.

The same interpretation applies to Bela Balassa's preferred interpretation of the Chilean crisis – the 1979 choice of exchange-rate regime. Whether or not this was the crucial error of domestic policy that he supposes, it was certainly a drastic and distinctive choice that reveals a great deal about the Pinochet regime's balance of priorities. By pegging the peso indefinitely to the dollar, Pinochet was expressing an inflexible determination to reduce Chile's inflation rate to the level prevailing in the USA. It was not necessary to be highly versed in academic debate about the 'law of one price' in order to understand that. In practice, as it became apparent that Chilean inflation would not swiftly adjust right down to US levels, the decision to persist for three years at any cost with a pegged rate implied a determination to force Chilean inflation *below* US levels, at least for a temporary period. No other Latin American government attached anything like *that* degree of priority to anti-inflation objectives during this period. Moreover, to pursue such strong anti-inflation objectives at any cost clearly involved a willingness to accept very substantial increases in unemployment and losses of output, at least during the transitional period. Whatever the theoretical claims expressed by some of the Chicago Boys, those real power-holders who backed them up must have understood that they had committed themselves to a highly deflationary stance, as a last resort if the hoped-for automatic adjustment failed to materialise. The Chilean military had faced the same problem in 1975, when it had opted for 'shock treatment' with little regard for 'social costs'. As we shall see in the next section, the same regime seems to have made the same choice for the third time, in 1985.

In the previous Thorp and Whitehead volume (1979), I argued that high unemployment might actually have some attractions for the Chilean military regime as a policy objective. It destroyed the social base of the labour movement, just as physical repression and emergency legislation was destroying its organisational base. Moreover, in conditions of severe unemployment, protests and resistance always tend to take an angrier and more dangerous form. Those whose power depended upon the maintenance of a 'national security regime' would not necessarily be averse to economic policies that produced this effect. It is, of course, always extremely difficult to establish how power-holders in a highly authoritarian regime reason about such questions – and more difficult than ever where the Chilean military are concerned. However, what is quite clearly established from the public record is the results of their deliberations. The decision to peg the exchange rate to the dollar is congruent with previous and subsequent decisions that reflect a great determination to curb inflation, and a great indifference to the goals of high employment or the maximisation of immediate growth. Such a balance of priorities and the determination to persist with such policies require a systematic explanation, as outlined in this section.

To sum up on the severity and character of the adjustment crisis in Chile since 1979, we have considered three possible explanations: external shocks, inappropriate financial liberalisation policies, and the severe exchange overvaluation of 1981–2. All three contributed strongly to the outcome observed. It is probably pointless to attach a more precise weight than that to each cause, since they clearly interacted with and reinforced each other. What made the Chilean crisis so distinct and so severe was the way that two 'domestic' policy choices combined with the relatively severe exogenous causes. The domestic choices cannot adequately be explained in terms of 'mistakes' or 'inappropriate theorising' by the economic team viewed in isolation. The essentials of domestic economic policy derive from the very nature of the Pinochet regime itself. Economists in the service of that regime have only very limited freedom to vary their policies, as events since 1982 have made clear. So long as the Chilean junta remains intact, the underlying priorities and style of government will continue, and it is that, more than the technical details of policy making, that will shape the nation's economic performance.

Rather to the surprise of many observers, the Pinochet regime *did* survive the adjustment crisis of 1982–3 intact, and at the time of writing (mid-1985) it seems quite capable of enduring for the balance of the decade. It is on that assumption that the next section turns to the results of the adjustment effort to date, and the medium-term prospects. It does not contain a systematic discussion of alternatives to existing policy, because in keeping with the analysis presented here one would need to specify what kind of regime was involved in order to identify feasible alternatives. For the present there is great uncertainty about what type of regime would emerge if the junta fell, and consequently there is also uncertainty about the economic alternatives. However, it will emerge from the following discussion that whatever the alternative regime might be, economic conditions are likely to be extremely adverse, greatly constraining the scope for economic reconstruction.

THE 'ADJUSTMENT PROCESS' SINCE 1983, AND THE MEDIUM-TERM PROSPECTS

During much of 1983 and early 1984 it seemed as if the economic crisis had not only discredited the 'Chicago Boys' but also shaken the Pinochet regime to its foundations. Many observers noted a loss of coherence in policy making and felt that the initiative had passed into the hands of a resurgent opposition (or more accurately, the oppositions). Serious divisions appeared between various groups that had been regarded as the constitutive elements of the regime. There was open conflict between government and such formerly loyalist groupings as the southern landowners, the truckers, etc. Prominent financial leaders like the former minister Luders and the banker Vial were charged with criminal offences relating to their business practices. In March 1984 the superintendent of the banking system was arrested for complicity with them. It seemed that even senior army officers had lost the will to carry out massive repression at the behest of the President.

However, from early 1984 the political balance began to change. The regime recovered its confidence and effectiveness, and embarked on a new policy of at least apparent conciliation. The oppositions became more visibly divided. The middle classes who had seemed to defect from the regime in 1983 became disaffected from the alternatives in 1984, and a skilful Minister of the Interior succeeded in winning some of them back to the status quo. In economic policy there was a counterpart to this apparent political liberalisation. At the end of 1982 the Central Bank introduced a 'suggested' interest rate for short-term money – effectively a ceiling – and since then the abnormally high real interest rates of 1975–82 have not returned. In March 1983 the minimum tariff was 'temporarily' raised from 10 per cent to 20 per cent, another significant breach with previous orthodoxy. Fiscal deficits of 4 to 5 per cent of GDP are now acceptable. From April 1984 until February 1985 a new Minister of Economics, closely allied with the Minister of the Interior, adopted a rhetoric and even to some extent a series of policies markedly at variance with the philosophy of the previous decade.[19] All this led many commentators to believe that the débâcle of 1982 had led to a definitive eclipse of the 'Chicago Boys' approach to economic policy making. Their theories and their dogmatic style had supposedly been tested to the limit, found wanting and discredited.

However, the Pinochet regime did not founder, and its apparent conversion to political liberalisation/economic reflation proved to be no more than a short-lived tactical device. The regime's attachment to the 'Chicago' approach (and its commitment to repression) was never really shaken, despite contrary appearances. Most of the supposedly unorthodox measures taken since 1982 were explicitly presented as regrettable short-term deviations from an essentially unchanged long-term strategy. Commentators who saw the January 1983 banking measures as an effective abandonment of the privatisation strategy, for example, missed some fundamental differences between this and the Mexican bank nationalisation of September 1982. The Chilean Central Bank took over the non-performing assets of the private banks and guaranteed their foreign debts, and in return these banks deposited long-term adjustable bonds with the monetary authorities. These commercial banks are not allowed to pay dividends to their shareholders until they have paid off their debts to the government, but their management and ownership remain in private hands, and the long-term objective is *still* the creation of a liberalised, privatised financial system. Tariff increases (even the temporary increase to 35 per cent in September 1984) have always been presented as short-term measures to raise revenue in an emergency, rather than any retreat from the basic tenets of trade liberalisation. Even when Minister Escóbar's criticisms of the Chicago approach were at their most acerbic, it was noticeable that he spoke only for himself. Those he was criticising remained entrenched in the power structure, although temporarily out of favour.

None of this can be very surprising, given the 'political economy' characterisation of the regime in the preceding section. Following that interpretation one would expect that since the Chilean junta has reasserted its internal unity and control over society, it will continue with the same basic distribution of power and the same essential mixture of economic policies as before. In practice that means a renewed emphasis on the control of inflation, continuing efforts to uphold the inequitable distribution of private property that is the hallmark of its counterrevolution, and an associated willingness to countenance extremely high unemployment and low investment for the indefinite future.

The reflationary measures of 1984 led to a 5.9 per cent growth in GNP and (according to Escóbar) a fall in unemployment from a 31 per cent peak to 'only' 25 per cent. However, they are also associated with a strong recovery in the demand for imports (one of the reasons for the tariff increase and devaluation of September 1984) and a severe balance of payments problem that alarmed Chile's foreign creditors. Consequently, the economic team in charge since February 1985 has reverted to measures of demand restraint, essentially to regain the confidence of the country's external creditors. The attempt at a more stimulatory policy in 1984 is of some importance as an indicator of how little room the Pinochet regime has for economic manoeuvre, but its macroeconomic significance should not be overstated. Following the severe contraction of 1982–3 there would in any event have been some tendency for the Chilean economy to 'bounce off the bottom' in 1984. Whatever the policy stance of the authorities, the key issue would have been whether the conditions existed for a cumulative recovery. The final point to be made in this chapter is that such conditions are still not present in Chile after twelve years of economic liberalisation. Moreover, it is hard to envisage what further developments or alternative policies might bring them into existence within the near to medium-term future.

Since this judgement runs counter to an influential current of opinion, both sides of the argument should be outlined. International bankers assessing Chile's latest agreement with the IMF (for 750 million SDR phased over the three years 1985–8, linked with a major debt refinancing package and commitments of new money from both private and official banking sources) generally accepted the argument that from 1982 onwards the government had pursued responsible adjustment policies that were beginning to show positive and enduring benefits. Chile's economic performance was said to compare favourably with that of most Latin American neighbours. Indeed, official spokesmen for the economic team went further, claiming that the economic failures of the early 1980s were attributable only to the low price of copper, and not to the policies of the regime. Since those same policies were being pursued with redoubled vigour, and since the price of copper was unlikely to fall further from such a low level, these spokesmen predict an economic 'boom' in the second half of the 1980s. This positive evaluation is very similar to the one made by the same circles in 1978, when my previous chapter on the Chilean economy was in draft. At that time I expressed scepticism, but considered that the verdict was still open. This time the grounds for disbelief are stronger.

Let us assume that the Pinochet dictatorship remains in place for the rest of the decade, and that the prevailing economic strategy is maintained. This model has three key components: (i) a competitive exchange rate; (ii) trade liberalisation; and (iii) rehabilitation of the private financial sector, which is expected to recover its leading role in the economy. Stated in these terms, the existing model does contain at least a tacit criticism of the earlier period when, of course, the exchange rate was allowed to become grossly overvalued. However, it might be argued that the problem of inflation control was more urgent in 1979 than in 1985, and that therefore it was appropriate to hold the exchange rate in the first case but not the second. In any case, the present model does attach considerable importance to the maintenance of a competitive exchange rate, and there is no longer much fear of the inflationary consequences. In 1983, 1984, and again quite markedly in 1985, the rate of devaluation has considerably exceeded the rate of domestic price inflation. It seems that the old 'cost-push' mechanisms propagating inflation right through the economy no longer play the same role as before. This is crucial to the claim that Chile is performing better than most of its Latin American neighbours, and to the hope that the private financial sector can resume its leading role.

Why has inflation remained relatively modest in Chile, whereas in the rest of Latin American it has greatly accelerated since the debt crisis? Expectations certainly play a significant role here, and after twelve years in power the expectation has become quite entrenched that the existing regime will weather the crisis, and will refuse to validate inflationary responses to it. In many other countries there has been greater uncertainty on these two points. In most other countries there has also been less open unemployment and more effective pressure from those in employment to defend their living standards. This point can be stated more generally as follows. Twice in eight years the Pinochet regime has presided over a 15 per cent fall in GNP, which of course created a large reserve of idle capacity both in terms of plant and of manpower. It would be unwise to rule out the possibility of a third similar episode. The combination of such recently idled excess capacity with the expectation that future deflation is at least as likely as a future return to conditions of excess demand is bound to dampen any 'propagating mechanisms' of inflation. In case of doubt about the strength and resolve of the political authorities, there are also two very powerful economic factors in operation to guarantee the same result. The first of these is the exceptionally large volume of dollar-denominated debt held by the private sector. Although devaluation may cause some acceleration of prices from the import side, it also redoubles competitive pressures between heavily indebted enterprises struggling to avoid bankruptcy, and this limits the transmission of inflation. Secondly, Chile remains an exceptionally open market for imports, in accordance with the trade liberalisation strategy. This also serves to dampen inflationary tendencies. In short, therefore, a continuation of the present model is likely to produce a continuation of *relatively* good inflation performance (e.g. 20–25 per cent p.a.), notwithstanding the exchange rate.

A competitive exchange rate is intended to stimulate exports (particularly of non-traditional goods) and to promote import substitution. It may also, in some circumstances, attract direct foreign investment. However, the Chilean economy looks too depressed and over-indebted to offer much of a magnet for long-term productive investment, taking into account the political climate as well. It takes time and resources to build up an effective import-substituting industry, and here too the prospects for Chile are not especially bright. The drive for trade liberalisation has proceeded so far, and so fast, that many potentially viable import-substituting enterprises have been eliminated, especially during the period of gross currency overvaluation. Only slow and modest progress can be expected on this front. Therefore the main medium-term effect of the exchange-rate policy is likely to be felt in the area of export diversification (traditional exports are discussed separately below). There has been significant progress here since 1975, mainly concentrated in a small range of lightly processed products (paper and wood products, seafoods and fishmeal, etc.). These gains may well be extended, and thus might ease the foreign exchange constraint. However, this is insufficient to justify predictions of a major economic upswing, and will have only a very modest impact on employment.

Trade liberalisation has remained a centrepiece of the strategy for over ten years. The tariff rises of 1983 and 1984 were mainly for revenue purposes and are being reversed. The theory is that a neutral tariff and ready access to world markets will not only dampen inflation but also ensure that resources are allocated efficiently, and in accordance with Chile's international comparative advantage. It is claimed, for example, that profitable opportunities to export and to substitute for imports can more readily be seized when capital goods are freely available from the world market. However, it is not this type of import that has been in strongest demand as a result of the trade liberalisation programme. On the contrary, in practice this policy has favoured the importation of consumer goods, while the level of productive investment has remained modest. Scarce foreign exchange has been insufficient to meet both these consumption demands and the requirements of capital formation in order to achieve a long-term growth in employment and in the country's foreign exchange earnings capability. The brief economic recovery of 1984 confirmed the alarmingly high import propensity for consumer goods that has accompanied trade liberalisation. Unless this propensity can be substantially reduced, future bursts of growth will again be cut short by balance-of-payments crises before a reasonable level of investment can be attained. The 'static efficiency' gains from trade liberalisation have so far been quite insufficient to overcome this structural constraint in the model.

Rehabilitation of the private financial sector is clearly a long, slow task after the traumas of 1982–3. Indeed, for some time it was thought that this key element of the model might have to be abandoned, given the scale on which the authorities were forced to socialise bank losses and to assume private foreign liabilities. However, it now seems clear that the policy is once again to return control over the financial sector to private management, even withdrawing from the policy of 'indicating' officially desired short-term interest rates. Real interest rates will once again be determined by market forces (or market leaders), the public sector will withdraw as far as possible from the credit market, and in this way it is thought that domestic savings can be stimulated to the level where they finance capital formation without resort to excessive foreign borrowing. Despite the shocks and losses of the early 1980s, the notion of 'popular capitalism' is being promulgated once more. Foreign bankers and multilateral institutions endorsing the present model have evidently been persuaded that the excesses and abuses of 1979–81 have been overcome and will not be repeated, and that in a climate of overindebtedness, insecurity over property rights and political tension, the middle classes of Chile can nevertheless be inspired with confidence in a still essentially monopolistic and unaccountable financial system. It may be that this approach will prove sufficiently successful to shield Chile from the worst problems of capital flight affecting other countries in the region. However, it requires a considerable leap of faith to believe that within the next few years this financial system will be capable of servicing the needs of productive investment and export-oriented growth, when hitherto it has at best catered for consumption, speculation and superfluous imports.

For all these reasons it seems most unlikely that the existing economic model can deliver. That leaves open a more difficult question, namely whether there is some practical alternative model that would secure substantially better results in the foreseeable future. The consequences of past decisions bear down very heavily not only on the existing team of policy makers but also on any prospective alternative. In the absence of some highly improbable write-down of Third World debt (a contingency in any case inconsistent with the philosophy of the Chicago school) or an almost equally improbably upsurge in commodity prices, the Chilean economy will be labouring under a very severe external payments constraint for at least the balance of the decade. Recent trade experiences highlight how harsh those constraints can be.

In contrast to most of the other countries dealt with in this volume, Chile was unable to achieve its ambitious trade surplus targets either in 1983 or in 1984, despite exceptionally severe demand contraction. The 1983 target of a US $1.2 billion trade surplus was missed by about $200 million, and a similar target for 1984 was missed by almost $1 billion. Although total investment fell much more severely, and stabilised at a substantially lower share of GDP, in Chile than in any other of the major Latin American countries, Chilean national savings plummeted even more dramatically. As a result, between 1982 and 1984 Chile continued to rely on external savings to finance about three-quarters of its meagre total investment whereas in other countries this proportion never exceeded one-quarter.[20] The IMF, the World Bank and the external creditor banks are taking the view that the Pinochet regime should be well supported (a June 1985 refinancing package was considered to contain relatively generous provisions), but even so the real external debt continues to mount, the domestic economy remains deeply depressed, and the underlying level of investment continues to be well below that required for any future recovery.

The extremely depressed level of world copper prices certainly provides a significant part of the explanation for this dismal situation (see Table 5.10). In January 1980, when the World Bank issued a controversial report on the economic reforms of the 1970s and the prospects for Chile in the 1980s, it predicted that the nominal world copper price would double between 1979 and 1983 'as demand catches up with stagnating world supply and the real cost of expanding mine output continues to rise'. By 1965 the free market price of copper was supposed to reach US $1.60 a pound, and $2.15 by 1990.[21] On this assumption, together with its favourable view of the economic reforms already undertaken, the World Bank mission projected that during the 1980s 'Chile may be able to sustain a real GDP growth rate of the order of 5–6 per cent per year while simultaneously reducing its debt service rates and gradually accumulating international reserves'.[22] In the event the 1985 copper price will be in the region of $0.61 cents a pound, and the current IMF predictions for 1990 do not exceed $1. In fact, the short-term prospects for the Chilean economy still largely revolve around the precise timing and scale of any movement in the dollar price of copper. A near-term recovery to say $0.75 or $0.80 would make a substantial difference to the prospective trade surplus (assuming that domestic demand and investment remained unchanged). If copper prices continued to hover around the 60 cent level, the Chilean economy would continue on the brink of insolvency almost regardless of the severity of the domestic austerity measures that might be adopted. There is almost no prospect that non-copper exports can be expanded at a fast enough pace, at least in the short run, to compensate for low copper revenues. Although the import regime could be radically altered to make it more progressive, under the current regime there is little scope for further import compression without further reducing domestic demand.

What, then, are the prospects for the price of copper for the rest of the 1980s, and where does Chilean policy fit in? As Table 5.10 makes clear, the low dollar price has not resulted in any diminution of Chilean

Table 5.10 A traditional explanation: the copper market

	1974	1975	1976	1977	1978	1979	1980	1981	1982	1983	1984	1985 (plan)
Copper production (000 tons)	902	828	1005	1054	1034	1063	1068	1081	1242	1257	1290	1300+
Copper price (cents per lb)	93	56	64	59	62	90	99	79	67	72	$62\frac{1}{2}$	$62\frac{1}{2}$
Copper price projection of World Bank 1979						70	85	–	–	–	–	160

production. On the contrary, output has steadily increased and seems likely to expand still further virtually regardless of the state of the world market. By 1983 Chile was already supplying over 20 per cent of the 'free world' copper, and this share could soon rise towards 25 or even 30 per cent. Chile is a low-cost producer (certainly so long as strikes remain outlawed and the unions face a determined military regime). The second and third largest producers, the USA and Canada, are being forced to close down their more costly mines, and to operate the remainder at a fraction of capacity. Indeed, American (privately owned) mining companies believe 'that Chilean overproduction ... amounts to a predatory "squeeze play" designed to drive high cost US producers under'.[23] This is probably too machiavellian an interpretation, and overall it seems doubtful whether a Chilean policy of restricting output could on its own substantially raise the world copper price. Chilean scepticism about the capacity of CIPEC nations to enforce a collective output ceiling may be well founded. The alternative strategy of expanding market share in a highly depressed sector of world mining may *eventually* position Chile to benefit from an upturn in demand, but the timescale for this is long and indeterminate.

The only alternative approach to easing Chile's balance of payments constraint in the short to medium term would be through some initiative on the capital account. During 1984 the Chileans took some interest in the idea of a joint Latin American approach to the debt problem, limiting service payments to, say, 25 per cent of external earnings. Using round numbers this would mean that a country with US $20 billion external debt and $4 billion per year in foreign exchange would dedicate just $1 billion, i.e. 5 per cent of the existing debt, to the claims of its creditors. Assuming that world interest rates remained above the 5 per cent level, the outstanding debt would certainly have cut itself off from all 'new' credit or grace periods, as the Peruvians are currently demonstrating. This approach could only be pursued if all the major debtors agreed to stand firm (although their interests are far from uniform). Also, it would only provide an eventual solution if the relevant interest rates stabilised at some reasonable (say single-digit level) and if world trade continued to expand. In practice the Chileans concluded that there was insufficient basis for agreement among the debtors, and that therefore they must seek the best terms available by bilateral negotiation with their creditors. It is not self-evident that any other regime coming to power in Santiago could achieve more on this front. Indeed, there is a danger that a weak and disunited government in Santiago could fare even worse. (The record of Bolivia since the restoration of democracy in La Paz in 1982 is held up as an awful warning.) The present Chilean regime is more likely to volunteer itself as a model of good behaviour to the financial community and therefore a claimant to special assistance under US Secretary of Treasury Baker's September 1985 'Third World debt initiative'.

Finally, there is the question of attracting back flight capital. In other Latin American countries, when post-debt crisis balance of payments appears to be an insoluble constraint on the resumption of development, those who advocate financial orthodoxy often argue that the external account would become manageable once more if only the national economic authorities created appropriate conditions of security, flexibility and profitability to attract back the savings that have fled to safer havens to avoid inflation, exchange controls, punitive taxation or confiscation. (Governor Henry Wallich of the US Federal Reserve Board makes this a centrepiece of his recommendations to Latin American economic policy makers, and the influential Boston banker – and ex-Energy Minister from Peru – Pedro Pablo Kuczynski, has also taken up the same theme.) Perhaps there are countries where this approach might yield good results, but Pinochet's Chile is not one of them. In the first place, the great capital flight from Chile took place in the early 1970s, rather than – as elsewhere – in the early 1980s. Secondly, the financial reform of 1975, and indeed all the economic liberalisation policies pursued since the mid-1970s, can be interpreted as measures to lure back flight capital. The very high real interest rates of 1975–82, the privatisation of the financial system, the maintenance of a unified and liberalised exchange regime, and the removal of import tariffs all constitute the most powerful array of measures calculated to reverse capital flight. It is hard to imagine what more the Chilean authorities could do, in the strictly economic sphere. (In the political realm, as I have argued, they have also taken the most strenuous measures to assure property-holders that their ownership rights will be secure.)[24] Statistics on capital flight are by definition unreliable, but to the extent that one can tell, it seems that, relative to other Latin American countries in 1980–2, Chilean wealth-holders used their opportunities to purchase imports or to take foreign holidays, rather than to hold savings abroad. However that may be, it is now the nature of the Pinochet regime itself that constitutes the major influence on the portfolio preferences of Chilean savers. A severely repressive regime which appears to have learnt nothing from its past failures of economic management, and which forces even the most moderate currents of opposition into clandestinity, may have little scope for initiatives that would reassure savers or alter decisions about capital flight. In the light of the Chilean experience, the Wallich–Kuczynski school might perhaps be urged to specify just how high a price it is worth paying to attract back flight capital. It may be at least as important how the repatriated capital is to be used within the host economy, and what political guarantees can be preserved for those who lacked the means or need to take their money (in some cases illegally) out of the country in the first place.

In conclusion, then, the medium-term prospects for economic adjustment in Chile appear heavily dependent upon the evolution of the external account. It is only in the unlikely event that the severe external constraints on economic growth were to be removed that we would need to assess the very considerable accumulation of internal obstacles to healthy adjustment. Neither the copper market, nor the external debt negotiations, nor any initiative to reverse capital flight, offer much prospect of easing the external constraints on the Chilean economy in the near future. Collapsing oil prices and falling world interest rates are of some help, of course, but under current policies any revival is likely to boost import demand. Nor does it seem likely that the Pinochet regime can significantly vary its established balance of economic priorities, nor that an alternative strategy will be imposed by a resurgent opposition. In consequence, the prospects are that the Chilean economy will continue sluggish, with very high unemployment, grossly inadequate levels of investment, and extremes of social inequality and latent tension. But the model will probably still have its defenders. After all, the rate of inflation has been reduced below 30 per cent.

Notes

1.   Chilean economic statistics are probably more carefully compiled than those of most Latin American countries. Nevertheless, the conceptual and practical problems of macroeconomic measurement are acute in any economy experiencing three-digit inflation or the violent shocks so frequent in Chile. Moreover, the Pinochet regime is subject to no democratic controls, and may sometimes have a powerful interest in presenting the economic record in a misleadingly favourable light. Whatever the reason, there is substantial disagreement about most official macroeconomic data, and this greatly complicates the task of summarising the recent record. The well-regarded but opposition-inclined research institute CIEPLAN has produced its own estimates for inflation, growth, the real exchange rates and other key indicators, which often differ markedly from official series (see Table 5.8). Moreover, since 1982 the Central Bank has begun issuing revised figures on some issues (e.g. the debt-service ratio, in Table 5.3) which are very different from earlier statistics. To quote one example, a study in *Estudios CIEPLAN*, no. 15

(published in March 1985) revises the official growth statistics for the 'miracle' years 1976–81. This concludes that GDP grew at 6.5 per cent p.a. over that period, rather than 8 per cent, and that (taking 1974 = 100) the index of industrial production in 1981 was 92.7, rather than the official 110.1.

2. Alejandro Foxley *et al.* (1984, pp. 106–7) put the unemployment rate at 9.2 per cent in 1974 and an estimated 32.0 per cent in 1983.
3. GDP share rose from 3.5 per cent to 5.1 per cent when imputed bank charges (which count as transfer payments) are deducted.
4. J. P. Arellano (1983) p. 12.
5. Arellano (1983) p. 32. Table 5.2 above gives Central Bank figures for the real rates of interest effectively *paid* by Chilean debtors, which confirm the orders of magnitude. Approximately three-quarters of all debt was incurred in pesos, virtually all the rest in dollars.
6. Arellano (1983) p. 22. A more conventional explanation of the persistent willingness to borrow at penal interest rates is that these were considered transitory. As inflation decelerated and financial liberalisation progressed, the real cost of peso borrowing did indeed fall, at least until 1980, and both real profitability and real asset prices rose several-fold. Official 'triumphalist' propaganda may have reinforced unrealistic expectations of further increases that would validate borrowing on almost any terms. To some extent all these considerations played a part. What seems inadequate to me is any explanation purporting to account for such a rapid and unprecedented rise in indebtedness in terms of some return to 'normal' conditions of stability and market freedom.
7. R. Ffrench-Davis (1983), p. 122.
8. Table 5.8 gives two CIEPLAN estimates. Using the earnings index as a deflator, and taking the 1977 exchange rate as an 'equilibrium' level, the peso was 45 per cent undervalued in 1975 and 80 per cent overvalued in 1981. Deflating by the 'corrected' consumer price index the result would be 33 per cent undervaluation followed by a 27 per cent overvaluation.
9. The ecu fell from $1.44 in December 1979 to 69 cents in June 1982 (and 71 cents by December 1984). Thus an ecu-pegged peso would have gradually slipped from 39 to the dollar to 58 to the dollar in mid-1982 and to about 80 to the dollar by end-1984. Almost half of Chile's exports are sold in Europe, under one-quarter in the USA. Obviously, if the Chileans had not only pegged the peso to the ecu, but also denominated half their foreign borrowings in European currencies rather than in dollars (as standard teachings on the avoidance of unnecessary currency exposure would dictate), the debt crisis of 1982 would have been far more manageable.
10. International comparisons of fiscal deficits are fraught with difficulty, not least in Latin America where the results may be greatly affected by the method of inflation accounting used (or not used) and by the choice of exchange rate for valuing foreign interest payments in terms of domestic currency. In Chile, the government's internal debt is revalued in line with inflation end year – i.e. all domestic debt is effectively indexed and the government expenditure account shows only true interest payments, with no disguised capital repayment element. In 1980–1 the overvalued exchange rate meant that foreign interest payments were expressed in

overvalued pesos. But against this understatement of the 'true' interest cost should be set the disguised repayment element as foreign inflation eroded the 'real' burden of the public external debt.

11. Bela Balassa (1984), pp. 71–2 (retranslated from the Spanish by Laurence Whitehead).

12. T. G. Congdon (1985), p. 96.

13. *Ibid.*, pp. 92–3.

14. *Ibid.*, p. 95. Something like this so-called 'currency board' system was also practised in Bolivia from 1956 to 1972, successfully overcoming the hyperinflation of the early 1950s. But, as I pointed out in Thorp and Whitehead (1979), it was one thing to peg a currency to the dollar under the Bretton Woods system, with low inflation and expanding world trade, but quite another matter to attempt this at a time of world-wide high and variable inflation, and sluggish world trade.

15. Sebastian Edwards (1984), p. 121.

16. *Ibid.*, p. 122.

17. *Ibid.*, pp. 123–4.

18. Congdon (1985), p. 102.

19. In September 1983, *before* his appointment as Economy Minister, Escóbar was quoted as saying: 'With 30 per cent unemployment the country is not viable. With 100 per cent inflation it would be uncomfortable, but viable.' After his dismissal he claimed that when appointing him, Pinochet had told him that his highest priority must be to deal with unemployment. When he began to encounter financing problems he told the Central Bank: 'What we shall do is increase our indebtedness in the short-term, and oblige the foreign banks to finance our growth' (*Mercurio*, Santiago, 7 April 1985).

20. IADB (1985) p. 36.

21. IBRD (1980), p. 258.

22. *Ibid.*, p. 257.

23. 'Copper Industry in the Economic Pits', *Washington Post*, 30 March 1985, p. A6. According to the *Financial Times* (London), 10 April 1985, production costs are only 45 cents a pound (down from 75 cents a pound in 1973) and Chilean mineworkers earn just one-tenth of what their US counterparts can.

24. Arellano argues that the regime's failure to provide a coherent long-term solution to the internal debt crisis leaves many indebted enterprises in a state of limbo. These enterprises are unable to raise new capital and therefore cannot hope to expand production even where favourable opportunities arise. In particular, as the owners of the majority of banks are likely to conclude that they have effectively lost their equity, even though they retain managerial control, Arellano argues that this uncertainty over the eventual ownership of indebted enterprises creates a very undesirable structure of incentives, since entrepreneurs may conclude they have little more to lose, and so perhaps take unacceptable risks (Arellano, 1983, p. 10). Clearly a combination of generalised overindebtedness, Central Bank bail-outs, the reluctance of most creditors to realise their collateral, and severely depressed demand in nearly all markets would leave the pattern of private ownership at least temporarily

insecure and undefined. This occurs despite government policies dedicated above all to guaranteeing the sanctity of free-market outcomes.

References

ARELLANO, J. P., 'Liberalización e Intervención en el Mercado de Capitales', *Estudios CIEPLAN*, no. 11, December 1983.

BANCO CENTRAL DE CHILE, *Boletín Mensual*, Santiago.

BALASSA, B., 'Experimentos de Política Económica en Chile, 1973–83', *Estudios Públicos*, no. 14, Autumn 1984, Santiago.

CONGDON, T. G., *Economic Liberalisation in the Cone of Latin America* (London: Trade Policy Research Centre, 1985).

EDWARDS, S., 'Estabilización con Liberalización: Diez Años del Experimento Chileno con Políticas de Mercado Libre 1973–83', *Estudios Públicos*, no. 14, Autumn 1984, Santiago.

Estudios CIEPLAN, monthly, Santiago.

FFRENCH-DAVIS, R., 'Deuda Externa y Apertura Financiera en Chile', *Estudios CIEPLAN*, no. 11, December 1983.

GALVEZ, J. and TYBOUT, J., 'Micro-economic Adjustments in Chile during 1977–81: The Importance of being a *Grupo*', *World Development*, vol. 13, no. 8, August 1985.

FOXLEY, A. *et al.*, *Reconstrucción Económica para la Democracia* (Santiago: 1984).

INTER-AMERICAN DEVELOPMENT BANK, *Economic and Social Progress in Latin America: 1985*, Washington DC, 1985.

IBRD, *Chile: an Economy in Transition*, World Bank country study, Washington DC, 1980.

KLEIN, E. and WURGAFT, J., 'La Creación de Empleo en Períodos de Crisis' (Santiago: PREALC, 1985).

LARROULET, C., 'El Estado Empresario en Chile', *Estudios Públicos*, no. 14, Autumn 1984, Santiago.

THORP, R. and WHITEHEAD, L. (eds) *Inflation and Stabilisation in Latin America* (London: Macmillan, and New York: Holmes & Meier, 1979).

6 Argentina's Most Recent Inflationary Cycle, 1975–85

Guido di Tella

Argentina's present problems are the result of the combination of major external shocks and 'weak', 'wrong' or 'delayed' internal responses. The basic external factors were the two oil shocks of 1973 and 1979, the abrupt increase in interest rates and the reversal of international capital flows that took place in 1982. The main internal responses were persistent deficit financing and the (deliberate) overvaluation of the peso – seen as a painless way of controlling inflation. Two main consequences of this situation were the huge capital remittances from Argentina to the USA (at subsidised rates) during 1978–82, and the collapse of taxable money (M1) from 1982 onwards, which in themselves seriously complicated the internal and external situation. The measures aimed at the correction of the external imbalance were less delayed and more immediately successful than the measures aimed at the control of the internal disequilibrium. Thus, on the one hand, the external situation was speedily improved in both 1975–6 and 1981–2, as a consequence of a series of devaluations; on the other, it proved impossible to control the high and increasing rate of inflation, a result itself not unconnected with the policy of devaluation. Any analysis of the short-term problem has to take into account the longer-run frailty of both the external sector and the growth process. This phenomenon, as we will see once the chronology has been set out, is closely connected with an economic strategy that for many years has emphasised the internal market, assuming the impossibility of industrial exports. This has meant that even today industry contributes less than 20 per cent of total exports, giving rise to an extreme degree of external vulnerability and an inherent weakness in the growth process. It is the superimposition of short-term shocks and responses on a long-term structural problem that is at the root of Argentina's weak performance over this period.

The chapter title reflects a significant aspect of Argentina's recent development, namely a pronounced tendency to cycles, not in income so much as in prices, each cycle taking the economy to a new and higher

162

level of inflation (di Tella, 1983). The chapter first describes the evolution of the most recent cycle, running from 1975 to the first half of 1985. This section concludes with a preliminary evaluation of the new programme implemented at that point. The second section seeks to analyse the nature of the inflationary process and its interaction with policy, stressing that lax monetary and fiscal policy have generated inflation, but that non-monetary elements, in particular expectations, legal and *de facto* indexation and sectoral conflicts, have worsened the inflationary spiral and considerably complicated its cure. The *modus operandi* of different policies is considered. In the third section the burden of adjustment is discussed, and in the final section the nature of the long-term structural problem.

THE MOST RECENT INFLATIONARY CYCLE

The Background before 1979

The basic reason for the cyclical behaviour of inflation rates has been the inability of various governments to control the fiscal deficit, coupled with the fact that inflation has usually *exceeded* the rate one would expect from the size of the deficit and from the way it has been financed. As a result, governments have opted instead for a policy of 'freezing' some crucial prices, reducing inflation but distorting relative prices. Since such a situation cannot be maintained, we observe an alternation between 'repressed' stages – when some crucial relative prices are distorted, inflation falls and disequilibria appear, particularly in the foreign sector – and 'unloosening' stages, when price distortions are redressed, equilibrium is achieved again and inflation is rekindled. The periods in which the rate of inflation falls are, from a macroeconomic point of view, less efficient than those in which inflation rises, as prices become very bad allocators. As discussed more fully on pp. 188–90, in the periods of price acceleration, relative prices may be much nearer to their 'equilibrium values' and might be considered acceptable allocators of economic activity, were it not for the increased uncertainty and the instability of sectoral prices.

The chronology of the most recent governments is set out in Table 6.1. The 'repressed' stabilisation scheme has been tried, in 1961–2 by Alemann and Coll Benegas, in 1969–70 by Krieger Vasena and Dagnino Pastore, in 1973–4 by Gelbard, and in 1979–81 by Martínez de Hoz. Each of these attempts ended by creating gross

Table 6.1 Chronology of presidencies and the economic cycle, 1975–85

	President	Minister of Economy	Stage of cycle
Peronist			
1975	María Martínez de Perón (June 1974– March 1976)	Celestino Rodrigo, Pedro J. Bonnani, Antonio F. Cafiero, Emilio Mondelli	Unloosening ('Rodrigazo')
Military			
1976	Jorge Videla following military coup (March 1976– March 1981)	José Martínez de Hoz	Continued unloosening
1979		José Martínez de Hoz	Repression of prices
1981	Roberto Viola (March 1981– December 1981)	Lorenzo Sigaut	Unloosening
	Leopoldo Galtieri (December 1981– June 1982)	Roberto Alemann	(Malvinas conflict)
1982	Reynaldo Bignone (June 1982– December 1983)	José Dagnino Pastore, Jorge Whebe	Continued unloosening
Radicals			
1983	(Elections) Raúl Alfonsín (June 1983–)	Bernardo Grinspun	Continued unloosening
1985	(June)	Juan Sourrouille	'Plan Austral'

distortions and serious external disequilibria, which prompted 'unloosening' stages such as those begun by Pinedo in 1962, Ferrer *et al.* in 1971–3, Rodrigo in 1975, and Sigaut *et al.* in 1981–5. (The process is charted in Figure 6.1.)

As this chronology suggests, by December 1978 the country had been undergoing a long 'unloosening' stage, which began with the massive devaluations of mid-1975, producing inflation of 900 per cent in the following twelve months. The extraordinary intensity of the process had to do primarily with the internal squabbling within the governing labour-based party, and secondarily with the expansionary fiscal and monetary policies. The strong nominal devaluations succeeded in

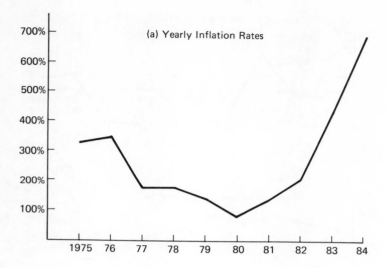

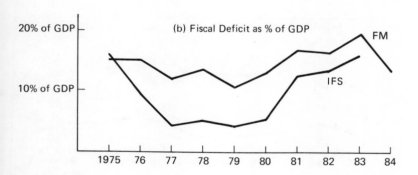

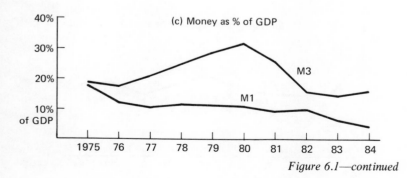

Figure 6.1—continued

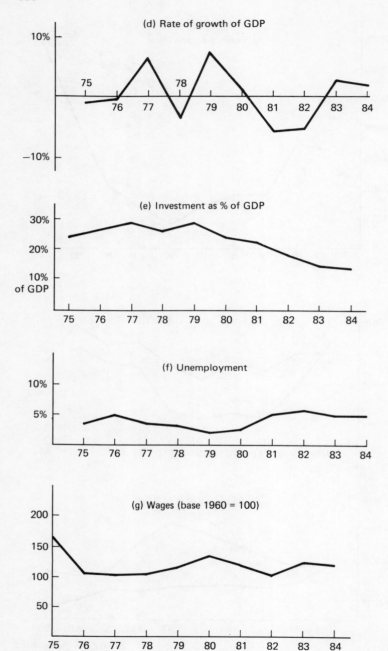

(d) Rate of growth of GDP

(e) Investment as % of GDP

(f) Unemployment

(g) Wages (base 1960 = 100)

167

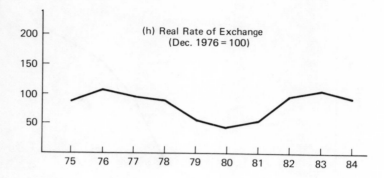

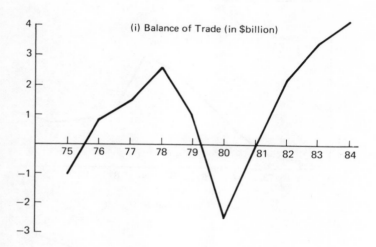

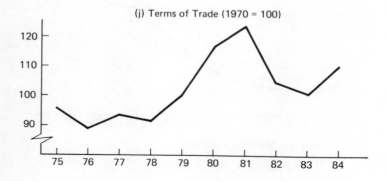

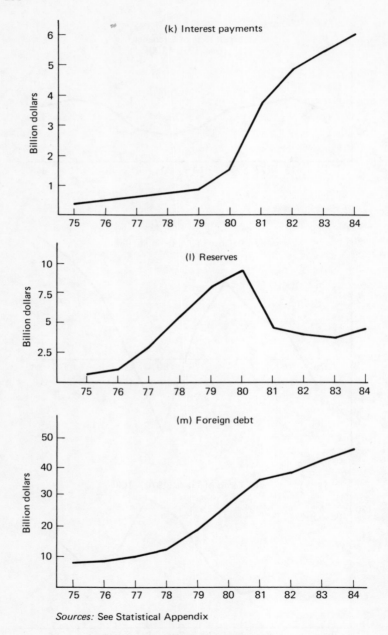

Sources: See Statistical Appendix

Figure 6.1 Argentina: basic series

achieving a fall in the real exchange rate of nearly 30 per cent, which was maintained during the last months of the Peronist administration and during the first two years of the Martínez de Hoz administration. In addition, after 1976, real wages were reduced to about 60 per cent of the previous level, indicating the change in the relative strength of entrepreneurs and workers.

The external sector improved after 1975, basically as a consequence of the devalued rate of exchange, which more than outweighed the 20 per cent fall in the terms of trade caused by the first oil crisis. At the same time import tariffs and export taxes were reduced as part of an opening of the economy, a central tenet of the new policies.

Growth was negative in 1975 and 1976, but positive in 1977 (see Figure 6.1.d), while inflation was brought down to what was a still very high but at least constant level of about 7–8 per cent per month, or 150 per cent per year. Money had come back into existence: not so much M1, which continued at the low level of 10 per cent of GDP, but M3, which increased by more than 40 per cent as a consequence of positive real interest rates (Figure 6.1.c). A financial reform was implemented

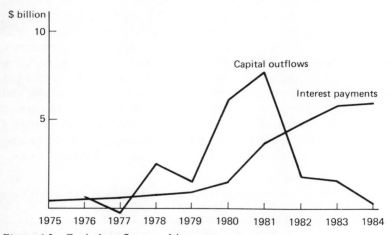

Figure 6.2 Capital outflows and interest payments

Remittances 1976–83 = $19.4 billion
Interest payments 1976–83 = $18.3 billion
Increased debt 1976–83 = $32.1 billion

Sources: the author, based on data from the Central Bank of Argentina and the Bank for International Settlements (BIS), annual reports 1977–84 and Dornbusch (1984).

which allowed for free entry and free rates of interest. A fiscal deficit of 16 per cent of GDP fell to a 'mere' 5 per cent (see Figure 6.1.b and Table 6A.2). This was partly the consequence of the lower incidence of tax evasion; more than half of the deficit was financed through internal and external borrowing. The general favourable context was marred by the still low level of wages, which did not worry the government, and by the still very high level of inflation, much higher than would have been expected from a monetarist perspective. By 1978 inflation was the central and growing concern and was taken as an indication of the failure of government policies. In fact, while the accumulated loss from 1976 to 1978, due to the deterioration in the terms of trade, was about 10 per cent of GDP, workers lost 32 per cent of their share, which allowed more investment in the country (8 percentage points) and in the US (5 percentage points), and more consumption by non-wage earners.

1978 was a year of non-commitment and half-hearted measures. In the early part of the year a politically motivated price-control scheme was attempted in a very half-hearted fashion, but it was soon abandoned. This lack of policy gave rise to restlessness among economic actors: this was the first year when remittances by Argentines to the USA and other countries shot up, reaching $2.5 billion (see Table 6.2 and Figure 6.2), a process that was to become of critical importance in the near future.

During the second half of 1978 a tight monetary policy was attempted. This contributed to a reduction in the level of activity without reducing the level of inflation, which continued at the level of 7–9 per cent per month. Industrial production went down by more than 10 per cent and GDP by more than 3 per cent. Moreover, the policies were criticised as being overdetermined, aimed at both the value of the peso *and* the supply of money. The impression was that the policies were going nowhere, and a new course was demanded by the military and by business circles.

Table 6.2 The balance of payments and external capital movements, 1976–8 ($ billion)

	1976	1977	1978
Non-interest current account	+1.1	+1.8	+2.5
Interest payments	−0.5	−0.6	−0.7
Change in reserves	+1.2	+2.2	+2.0
Increase in external debt	1.2	0.8	2.3
Inflow (+) and outflow (−) of capital	−0.6	+0.2	−2.5

Source: Central Bank of Argentina, *Memoria Anual*.

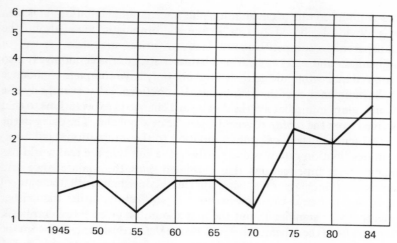

Figure 6.3 Logarithm of yearly inflation rate

Source: Instituto Nacional de Estadística y Censos (INDEC).

One can say that by 1978 the burden of the first oil shock had been absorbed by the Argentine economy, with workers bearing the brunt of the adjustment. The external sector had been redressed but inflation remained untamed. The stage was set for a new stabilisation effort.

By the end of the year the government saw itself faced with two basic alternatives: one traditional, with a free exchange rate and a strict monetary policy, the other a new rational expectations model in which the exchange rate was to be pre-announced, the total money supply was not to be restricted, but the fiscal deficit was to be curtailed. Curiously enough the government, in opting for the latter, thought that the new policies would avoid a recession and that stabilisation could be achieved in a painless way, something that unfortunately proved not to be the case.

Stabilisation, Price Repression, Predetermination of the Exchange Rate and Reliance on Rational Expectations

In December 1978, the government made public the new programme, pre-announcing the value of the exchange rate over the next eight months, the so-called *tablita*. It was clearly indicated that the rate of inflation was *necessarily*[1] supposed to go down to a level equal to the pre-announced rate of devaluation plus international inflation. This idea was obviously based on an extremely optimistic view about the transparency, competitiveness, lack of price stickiness, speed of adjustment and market-clearing characteristics of the economy. It also required that economic actors would not only have complete confidence in the maintenance of the *tablita*, but also confidence that everybody else would adapt immediately: the downward change in expectations to that derived from the *tablita* was central to the new policies. The delay in the convergence of the local rate of inflation to the international inflation-cum-devaluation rate was due partly to the fact that the real world has many more imperfections than assumed, *plus* the maintenance and subsequent increase of a fiscal deficit inconsistent with the rate of devaluation. It was the combination of *both* factors, rather than either one, that was significant, but the first should be given more emphasis. Supporters of the scheme, however, blame the inconsistency between the price target and fiscal management,[2] so as to exculpate the model, forgetting that increased internal borrowing and massive remittances substantially reduced the expansionary effects of the deficit.

The delayed convergence meant a gradual overvaluation of the peso, which soon became the central instrument for the dampening of the inflationary process. For a short while it worked. There is no doubt that 1979 was the 'good year' of this experience, as 1960–1, 1969 and 1973 were the good years of the previous policies. Everything seemed to go well: growth (plus 7.1 per cent), wages (plus 12 per cent), the trade account (positive by $1.1 billion), the fiscal deficit (down by 20 per cent), inflation (down in the second half to a yearly rate of 110 per cent from the previous level of 170 per cent, with tradables going up less than non-tradables). Remittances were still very high, but about 40 per cent below the previous year (Figure 6.2). Tradable goods became cheap, particularly imports, and so did tourism outside the country, while national income and wages increased. Speculation reached an all-time high, everybody had a good time, and stabilisation without sacrifice seemed possible. This spending spree sooner or later had to face the increasingly depressing effects of the policies on production, harmed by the growing difficulty of exporting and, in the case of industry, by the cheapness of imported goods, which forced a large number of local enterprises to close. However, competition also forced improvements in industrial efficiency, despite the increasingly distorted price signals.

The authors of the programme had expected that the internal real rate of interest would be the same as the international one, something that would have happened if convergence had been immediate. Instead, the domestic real interest rate, from the middle of 1979 on, exceeded the international rate by more than 20 yearly percentage points, an unsustainable situation. The existence of real rates of such magnitude attracted foreign capital in increasing quantities. The high real interest rates were required, among other reasons, by the increasingly orthodox financing of the deficit – only 30 per cent of the total in 1977 but nearly 90 per cent in 1979.

During this period one can see a patchy growth record, with two good years, 1977 and 1979, in the midst of a series of negative or low-growth years. Industry fared very badly, while agriculture showed a new strength, growing persistently, a consequence of the beginning of a belated green revolution that was to continue throughout the following period. Despite exchange-rate overvaluation, exports increased from $4 billion in 1974 to $10 billion in 1980, a growth of more than 16 per cent per year. This was the consequence of the dynamism showed by agricultural exports, which more than compensated for the reduction in industrial exports, giving rise to claims that a de-industrialisation strategy was in force. While the export performance was good in absolute terms, and from a short-term point of view, it was very bad from a long-term perspective, as it increased the dependence of the country on primary exports. But we will return to this later.

The economy, which had apparently looked so good in 1979, began to slow down during 1980, and some of the incipient problems of the previous year very quickly became quite serious. The main factor was the increased and by now grotesque overvaluation of more than 30 per cent, and according to some estimates, more than 40 per cent. While in the first stage it had had a stimulating effect, it now began to hinder production and employment. The economy as a whole was stagnant, while growth in industry was negative, the more so as the year drew to a close. Investment, however, was high, promoted by the government, while a massive military re-equipment programme was undertaken at a cost exceeding $10 billion. Wages, like real rates of interest, reached their highest post-1976 levels (Figure 6.1). The fiscal deficit rose by more than 30 per cent, while the proportion financed through borrowing fell from 90 to 60 per cent. The trade deficit exceeded $2.5 billion, while interest payments and remittances by Argentinians increased, the latter to an extraordinary level of more than 8 per cent of GDP, while reserves dwindled (Table 6.3). All the signs of an impending crisis were there.

Of the increase in indebtedness, 52 per cent was used to finance capital remittances by Argentinians, particularly to the USA, while 16 per cent was interest payments, the bulk of them caused by the financing of

Table 6.3 The balance of payments and external capital movements, 1979–80
($ billion)

	1979	1980	Total
Non-interest current account	0.3	−3.3	−2.7
Interest payments	−0.9	−1.5	−2.4
Increase in reserves	4.4	−2.8	1.6
Increase in external indebtedness	6.5	8.1	14.6
Outflow (−) of capital	−1.5	−6.1	−7.6

Source: Central Bank of Argentina, *Memoria Anual.*

capital remittances, past and present. The already precarious situation was worsened by a major financial crisis brought about by the failure of several of the largest private banks. This was due partly to the increasing insolvency of recklessly indebted business firms faced with increasingly high interest rates and diminishing sales. But it was also due to the perverse banking system started in 1977, which combined free interest rates with a government guarantee of deposits, a hybrid system resulting from an incongruous compromise between opposing factions within the government. These bank failures forced the Central Bank to pay depositors and issue the equivalent of $2.5 billion, nearly three per cent of GDP, in the first half of 1980. By the end of the year, the government was relying on the rather improbable hypothesis that the local rate of inflation would eventually fall below the international rate, to such an extent and for such a length of time as to eliminate the overvaluation of the exchange rate. The other more realistic view was that through some kind of subterfuge the government could devalue without destroying public confidence in its policies. A devaluation schedule with an increasingly divergent spread between purchasing and selling values was attempted, with the idea that a flotation of the peso between those upper and lower limits would at some point allow the peso to be devalued more or less 'naturally'.[3]

By the beginning of 1981 the situation was unsustainable, compounded moreover by the serious transition problem between the outgoing and the incoming military administrations. While everybody expected a rather smooth transition, the handover took place in a context of more diffidence and distrust than is usual even among opposing parties.

Realignment of Relative Prices, 1981–2

The lack of confidence that had developed increasingly during 1980 was aggravated to an extreme degree when a 10 per cent nominal devaluation was finally agreed between the outgoing and incoming administrations, thus breaking with the *tablita*. This combined every possible inconvenience: it was not considered large enough, it destroyed confidence not only in any pre-announced devaluation schedule but also in the general policies of the government, and it gave rise to destabilising speculation. During the first quarter of 1981 the country lost more than $3 billion in reserves, nearing $8 billion for the year (see Table 6.4), despite a drastic increase in real local rates of interest.

Table 6.4 The balance of payments and external capital movements, 1981–2 ($ billion)

	1981	1982
Non-interest current account	−1.0	2.3
Interest payments	−3.7	−4.8
Change in reserves	−3.8	−0.7
Increase in foreign indebtedness	8.5	3.1
Outflow (−) of funds	−7.6	−1.3

Source: Central Bank, *Memoria Anual*; Fundación de Investigaciones para el Desarrollo (FIDE), *Coyuntura y Desarrollo*; and Dornbusch (1984).

The repressed stabilisation stage had now come to an end. The situation was similar to, but worse than, the end of the previous stages in early 1962, 1970 and mid-1975. Inflation was low, but overvaluation, external imbalances and price distortions were extreme. The stage was set for the second act, for the 'unloosening' of the economy and the redressing of relative prices: the only doubt was not whether it would take place, but how and when.

The pre-announced change in military presidents in April 1981 gave the signal but, hindered by hectic political developments, it took more time to take shape. The correcting of relative prices went through four distinct stages. The first, introduced by Minister Sigaut, was quite timid and started as though it were still believed that all that was necessary was a small readjustment of the previous policy. The main aims of the new policy were to reverse the external situation, to tackle the problem of internal indebtedness and to reactivate the economy.

Three significant devaluations were made between April and November. This was over and above the daily devaluations, which were no longer pre-announced but made *ad hoc* on the basis of past inflation and on some estimate of future inflation. The first big devaluation (of 23 per cent) was not believed and accelerated destabilising speculation; this forced the opening of a regulated commercial and a free financial exchange market, the latter with no Central Bank intervention. This encouraged underinvoicing of exports and overinvoicing of imports, but stopped *net* capital remittances to foreign countries. Even so, the extraordinary losses of the last three months of the previous administration, plus the delay in implementing the new measures, allowed a final upsurge in remittances. Inflation picked up, reaching a yearly rate of 150 per cent from April to December. However, as nominal interest rates moved upwards, proportionally, the problem of the huge private and government peso indebtedness was not solved, while dollar debts increased not only in nominal but in real terms in domestic prices. This induced the government to grant forward coverage to some of the dollar debts and to attempt a mild subsidy of rates of interest. But in this it was unsuccessful, owing to the opposition of orthodox financial circles which still thought that their credit problem did not require special treatment – a parallel to what is happening today on the international scene.

The problem is that huge fiscal deficits accompanied by orthodox financing is possibly the worst of all possible combinations: through the compounding of interest at a high level it can soon reach an explosively increasing interest bill. From then on, no solution can be found, short of a monetary reform that acknowledges the basic insolvency of the financial system, and this was to come 'Argentine style'. The fiscal deficit went up to about 12 per cent of GDP – again pushed by the erosion of tax receipts – while borrowing was reduced. This was an 'unloosening' without any strings attached. It created a dangerous inflationary situation: only wages, which went down by 16 per cent in real terms, were a dampening factor. But a positive side of the period was the abandonment of the previous incongruous situation for one which was more consistent, even if much more inflationary; the peso was devalued in real terms and the trade balance was reversed, part of the redressment of relative prices typical of the 'unloosening' stage. This can also be seen in the consumer/wholesale price ratio: the consumer price index reflects

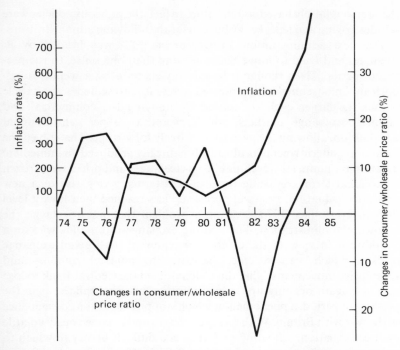

Figure 6.4 Yearly changes in the consumer/wholesale price ratio and inflation rate

Source: INDEC, *Indice de Precios Mayoristas, Indice de Precios Minoristas.*

to a greater extent prices of non-tradables while the wholesale index reflects better the prices of tradables (see Figure 6.4).

The realignment of prices meant that after 1982, the new prices were more in line with their long-term equilibrium value – unfortunately accompanied by a much higher rate of inflation, and by more intense price oscillation, thus nullifying some of the advantages that could have been derived from the 'better' price set.

Of the policies during this period one can say that, despite their shortcomings, they were a step in the inevitable and necessary direction. Devaluation was inevitable, inflation was bound to increase again, and debts had to be reduced. They could have had a different form: in particular there could have been more exercise of restraint in fiscal matters. But the policies were certainly not responsible for destroying the previous falsely based stabilisation. In fact, the previous policies were self-destroying and left a heavy burden for the following administrations. The next administration, in December 1981, was headed by R. Alemann and tried to move back, in more than one sense, to the pre-Sigaut period. Even though it lasted only six months, it went through both an 'unloosening' and 'repressed' stage; it represented a small cycle within the larger cycle. It started by unifying the commercial and financial exchange markets, which meant a 30 per cent nominal devaluation, allowing the peso to float freely for a while. This solved the over- and underinvoicing problems. It naturally produced an immediate inflationary jump. However, public service wages and prices were frozen in nominal terms, reducing them in real terms, giving rise to a new 'repressed' situation. Prices of public services reached their lowest level in real terms since 1973, creating a problem that was to plague the following administration. The floating exchange-rate policy was soon abandoned in view of the erratic behaviour of the foreign exchange market, which was extremely sensitive to political rumours and speculative movements. This 'dirty' float forced the Central Bank to lose reserves, again opening up the possibility of net remittances, as in the pre-Sigaut period, a phenomenon which stopped short as a consequence of the war with Britain. With meagre reserves and a dangerously volatile political situation, a floating exchange is a difficult luxury in which to indulge. It can have perverse effects on inflation due to the ratchet effect of the (under the circumstances) inevitably wide oscillation of the exchange rate. The fiscal deficit was reduced as the lower prices of public services were more than compensated by the reduction in wages of public employees. But the apex of the 'unloosening' stage took place after the war with Britain, when a new president and a new minister took over in July 1982. The new scheme, promoted by the new head of the Central Bank, D. Cavallo, tried to cope explicitly with the problem of domestic indebtedness. The basic idea was to roll it over at a regulated and low rate while prices were encouraged to increase over a short period, reducing the indebtedness in real terms both of the private sector *and* of the government and thus the part of the fiscal deficit resulting from the increasing interest bill. Equally important, money in circulation was to be reduced in real terms (in fact it was nearly halved), helping to put a limit to the inflationary outburst. A small, free interest-rate money market was to be allowed in the future. It amounted to a partial nationalisation of the existing *stock* of credit, although allowing for the development of a new free *flow* of funds. It was in effect a monetary reform, 'Argentine style'; that is, in which cash balances were to be taxed through an inflationary jump rather than through taxes. Exchange rates were devalued and a double market was re-established. Forward coverage of private dollar debts was generously given, subsidising the private sector to the extent of its ability to postpone payments, which was a stronger version of what had been done before. This measure, as in Sigaut's case, was to have a deleterious fiscal effect in the future. The reasoning was that this would be possible as the government was to reduce its peso interest bill, which had reached a significant proportion of the deficit. Prices jumped by more than 50 per cent in the following three months. The idea was that, after such a jump, 'demonetisation' would have been achieved, the initial financial stock would have been reduced in real terms, and a major transfer of income from creditors to debtors would have taken place, benefiting both the private and the public sectors. The problem was that the jump was not instantaneous, and the transfer was from government to debtors rather than from depositors to debtors. While many people in the private business sector were quite happy, there was a general impression that these rather wild policies would not last. The anxiety generated by this new inflationary jump culminated in the removal of the economic team in August.

Just as the 1975 price explosion had moved the expected inflationary level from 3–4 per cent per month to about 7–8 per cent, this outburst moved it to a new and menacing expected level of 10–15 per cent per month.

More Inflation: 1982–5

What was clear as the new team took office was that no more unloosening was necessary: relative prices were basically in equilibrium in the sense discussed above (except for public sector prices, which were reset in the second half of the year) and the imbalance in the external sector had been corrected. The fiscal deficit, however, as in 1975, had jumped to more than 16 per cent of GDP. There had not been such a sudden jump in prices, but inflation picked up and increased persistently. From now on, the problem was to tone down inflation while avoiding major price distortions – exactly the problem the country faced after the 1975–6 jump. This time, however, the military government was on the way out and a civilian administration was coming in: quite understandably, nobody was willing to indulge in a savage cutting of wages as in 1976.

The Whebe administration which took over in August 1982 avoided for a while any major price distortions, and until the second quarter of 1983 was even able to exercise an acceptable control on expenditures, complying with the agreement reached with the IMF over the arrears that had begun to accumulate since the war with Britain in April 1982. Wages were increased initially (rather parsimoniously in real terms), public rates were increased in real terms, and the peso was devalued at approximately the same rate as inflation. The two exchange markets were unified in October (but not freed) at the request of the Fund, with the obvious consequence that a black market reappeared immediately. However, a real devaluation had taken place. Despite the vagaries of the economic policies of the year, a massive trade surplus accrued in 1982, due to the devaluation, coupled with the deepening recession and the reduction of GDP by another 6 per cent, a result of the distributive consequences typical of devaluation, as Díaz Alejandro (1965) has argued.

Due to the control of capital flows, remittances became less important (Table 6.5), although as a consequence of the appearance of a black market, over- and underinvoicing did become important, involving perhaps 20 per cent of trade, which might explain the decrease in exports of more than $1 billion from the 1981 peak.

Table 6.5 The balance of payments and external capital movements, 1983–4 ($ billion)

	1983	1984
Non-interest current account	3.0	3.9
Interest payments	− 5.7	− 5.9
Change in reserves	0.7	+ 0.7
Increase in foreign indebtedness	5.0	3.0
Outflows of funds	− 1.6	− 0.3

Source: Central Bank of Argentina, *Memoria Anual.*

Economic policies began to change from the middle of 1983 as a consequence of the strong political pressures arising from the announcement of October elections. Demand pressures became more significant. Some overvaluation crept in, wages increased in real terms under pressure from the Labour Ministry, adjustments of the prices of public services began to lag, and the deficit increased to more than 16 per cent of GDP – an all-time high, affected by the increased tax erosion. The restrained start of the Whebe administration had an extremely undisciplined finale, very much due to political causes.

The new civilian administration came in at the end of 1983. Great expectations were held of the new policies. President-elect Alfonsín warned that his government had inherited one of the worst economic situations ever known, at least since the 1930s. The big surprise was that there were no new policies; in fact the government tried to continue the last phase of the Whebe administration. Promises were made to increase wages, to reactivate the economy, to increase investment and to start new social programmes. A six-month moratorium on international payments was announced so as to prepare a medium-term programme, and this was accepted by foreign creditors. The government and the Radical Party for a while entertained ideas that came very near defaulting, i.e. unilaterally offering extended terms of repayment at low interest rates. This plan was rejected in May 1984, and negotiations with the IMF started. At that time estimates were made as to the costs of repayment – terribly high in terms of growth, investment and wages – versus the costs of defaulting. These were much more difficult to ascertain. Outright confiscation of international assets, ships and airplanes were part of it, but much more important was the possibility of a trade embargo with the loss of sources of supply and of markets. The possibility of forming a club of debtor nations was aired, but met with no response beyond rhetoric. Despite this unrealistic initial approach, an effort was made to reduce the fiscal deficit, which was quite successful but still insufficient in the new post-1982 conditions. The deficit was reduced from 16 per cent of GDP in 1981 to 12 per cent in 1984. The (operating) deficit, i.e. before interest payments, had gone down from 10 per cent in 1983 to about 6 per cent. But the 'socialisation' of the debt in 1982–3 (an elegant way of saying that it had been dumped on the state) doubled the deficit. Inflation rose, resulting partly from a further reduction in people's willingness to hold cash: M1 now fell below 4 per cent of GDP.

A monthly deficit of about one per cent of GDP and an M1 of four per cent (with a trade surplus equal to the servicing of the debt) and no other capital movements of significant size, was bound, *ceteris paribus*, to produce basic inflation of about 20 per cent per month.[4] Even if one accepts that this situation increased the level of activity to some extent, the impact on inflation would not be very different. During most of 1984 inflation ran at a lower rate because the Central Bank, operating independently of the Ministry of Economy, managed to achieve in the second half of the year a very high rate of interest of 3–4 per cent per month, and some overvaluation of the currency.

During the first half of the year wages were increased above the high inherited level, and a certain revival of the economy took place, led by an increase in consumption of 8 per cent, which pushed GDP up by 2.5 per cent. Inflation moved up to 25–30 per cent per month (nearly 2000 per cent per annum), compared to the 13–20 per cent of the same months in the previous year, while M1 went down still further to less than 3 per cent of GDP. In the meantime the first contract with the IMF, signed in September in 1984, was not fulfilled.

Stabilisation, Fiscal and Monetary Reform, Change in Expectations

From March 1985 on, the first signs of a reversal began: a new technocratic group headed by J. Sourrouille was appointed to the Ministry of Economics. Soon after, the President announced the reversal of the anti-foreign policies in the oil sector and, more importantly, the need for dramatic sacrifices. The scenario was set for the drastic June 1985 stabilisation programme, still in full course at the time of writing (October 1985). The programme was based on three main measures: (i) a drastic cut in the government deficit; (ii) a price and wage freeze; and (iii) a temporary stopping of indexation clauses. *The emphasis on a fiscal target*, as distinct from a monetary goal, was based on the fact that demand for money was bound to increase in an unpredictable way and that a clear fiscal target was necessary to create confidence among the various economic sectors. To reinforce this, a commitment was made not to issue money to finance deficits in the future. This meant that money could only increase as a consequence of increases in reserves, or as a result of an expansionary credit policy that would change the money multiplier. It is important to note that a successful stabilisation policy creates an unusual monetary situation, as the amount of money previously demanded, with high inflation, becomes insufficient after stabilisation, when demand for money jumps, and supply must respond if interest rates are not to go sky high.

The fiscal deficit was to be reduced from more than 10 to 2.5 per cent of GDP as a consequence of three new facts. The first was the increase in public utility rates, particularly in the energy sector, by about 20 per cent, which, however, was not transmitted to prices. The second was a tax on exports, compensating a 15 per cent devaluation made at the same time, and a tax on imports of 10 per cent. The third fact was simply the consequence of stabilisation, which ended the erosion implicit in the delayed collection of taxes which, even if indexed, had a 40-day delay between assessment and collection, a drastic real loss when inflation was running at 0.5 to 1 per cent per day. Stabilisation therefore meant a reduction in the deficit of about 3 to 4 percentage points. That inflation worsens the deficit and stabilisation improves it is an interesting phenomenon seen very clearly in this case, as in those of Brazil and Mexico.

The other main set of measures was *the price and wage freeze*. As with the German hyperinflation of the 1920s, in an economy where all prices are sliding quickly, stabilisation requires the fixing of at least one price, usually the exchange rate (Dornbusch, 1985). In the Argentine case, a complete freeze of the price set was thought necessary, given the terrible and long-standing inflationary experience and the strong relative price oscillations. Given the fact that monetary reasons for inflation were to disappear, the measure was not inconsistent, as other price freezes had been, and was to help achieve a quick reversal in expectations, as no other measure would. The rational expectations approach would predict that fiscal restraint alone would be sufficient[5]: this was thought to be unrealistic. Much more drastic fiscal measures, more than those necessary for monetary reasons, would have been the far more recessive alternative.

The third main problem was *to cut off the inbuilt inflationary inertia* in indexation clauses normally based on past inflation, usually that of the last two or three months. With the halting of inflation, contracts already made would now produce a benefit (in the future) equal to the difference between the past and the future inflation rate. To deal with this, a readjustment schedule, the so-called *desagio*, was established, which readjusted downwards all future prices resulting from indexation clauses – the more the further ahead these contracts were due. This also applied to contracts fixed in nominal terms, which were presumed to have been made assuming an inflationary process that was now not to materialise. This not only eliminated any (unanticipated) windfall gains, but made credible the fact that stabilisation had come. If prices were to continue rising, then the *desagio* would be a tax; if, instead, prices were to be stable, then the *desagio* was neutral, a fact that contributed to the belief in the future stability of prices.

To dramatise the new package, and the *desagio* in particular, a new currency was issued, the *austral*, an exclusively psychological measure.

Besides the three main thrusts, the fiscal crunch, the price and wage freeze and the *desagio*, a policy of very high real interest rates was followed. A nominal rate of 7 per cent per month was established by fiat, a rate which almost turned out to be the real rate in the first month, as inflation from the beginning to the end of July was very low (see Table 6.6).

In a way one can say that the scheme was overdetermined and that there was an excessive number of measures aimed at the same end. However, if one remembers the past, extra safeguards seemed warranted.

The programme was instantly believed, although the degree of conviction varied according to the economic actor. Producers and consumers transacted at fixed prices, complying with the freeze. The black market collapsed, but soon recuperated, giving rise to a 17–20 per cent gap (0.96 australes to the dollar, instead of the official 0.8 to the dollar). A huge inflow of foreign funds – more than $800 million (1.2 per cent of GDP) – took place in the first month. For the most part these funds were constituted by Argentinians bringing back part of their foreign holdings in response to the high real rate of interest. Furthermore, M1 doubled from 2.5 to 5 per cent of GDP. Inflation picked up to about 2–3 per cent per month, which, coupled with a slight downward trend in the nominal interest rate, reduced the real interest rate to 2–3 per cent per month. This, combined with a downward trend in the black market (to 0.92 australes per dollar), gave an appearance of success after 90 days of the programme. But this was only the first stage.

Built into the programme is a series of problems that are bound to affect the second stage. First, there are some explicit negative distributional aspects. Wages were frozen after a 20 per cent real deterioration in the previous few months; moreover, the emphasis on indirect taxation (higher public utility rates) worsened the situation. It is impossible that this will not become a hot issue in the near future, although the drastic reduction in the inflationary tax may compensate in some measure. Although there is no clear evidence, it is believed that as M1 goes down, the last remaining holders will be people on low incomes, that is, those least capable of avoiding the inflation tax; moreover, their monetary holding, compared to their stream of income or to their stock of wealth, was and is far greater than that of middle or upper income people. Therefore it is not absurd to assume that a good proportion of the reduction in this inflationary tax benefits the low-income sector.

The programme also further increases the anti-export bias of the trade structure. Export and import taxes are an emergency measure, adopted for short-term fiscal reasons, but they are very bad for the long term. The reactivation of the economy is not possible except through an upsurge of

Table 6.6 The economy in 1985

	January	February	March	April	May	June	July	August
Rate of growth of GDP[a]			0.5			0.6		
Inflation								
Cost of living	25.1	20.7	26.5	29.5	25.1	30.5	6.2	
Wholesale	20.9	17.6	27.9	31.5	31.2	42.4	-0.9	
Deficit of Treasury as[b] per cent of GDP		6.0			10.8			
M1 as per cent of GDP	3.42	3.23	2.94	2.74	2.63	3.24	3.93	
Real wages (index based 1981 = 100)	143.1	133.7	132.3	132.1	134.9	128.2	120.7	
Black market peso/dollar exchange rate[c]	0.24	0.317	0.402	0.513	0.620	0.803	0.907	0.960
Official[c] peso/dollar	0.201	0.242	0.306	0.396	0.525	0.801	0.801	
Black market[c] official	19.34	30.8	31.53	29.58	18.09	9.16	13.27	19.9
Real rate of interest (monthly and free)	21.9	3.2	-1.0	-1.4	2.6	-14.0[d]	5.8	5.2

Notes:
[a] Compared to the same quarter of 1984.
[b] Does not include public enterprises and other public bodies.
[c] Monthly average.
[d] Average of 1–14 and 14–30 June.

Sources: INDEC, Central Bank of Argentina, *Boletín Estadístico* and *Carta Económica*.

exports, and these measures impede that directly. A further major problem is the need to tackle the end of the price and wage freeze, which was crucial for the initial success, but cannot continue indefinitely without violations and distortions of all kinds appearing. Relative prices were frozen as they were on the day the programme was launched. Some sectors were caught leading, while other were lagging in terms of price adjustments. As a first approach they will have to be brought in line with a measure such as the average price prevailing over the previous period. On top of this, the devaluation and the increase in public tariffs will have to be allowed to affect the prices of other goods.

But, of course, these two sets of price readjustments are bound to produce further reactions among producers who will not only want to avoid the consequences of the new intended real prices (of public services and exchange rates), but will want to improve their own position over and above that implied by their previous average price set. Such 'overshooting' is at the heart of the price oscillations and the price spiralling of the past. Even if the phenomenon takes place this time at a much lower level of inflation, it is bound to reappear.

The final problem is that the Argentine stabilisation has been attempted while the country has to service a huge external debt, which has a tremendous consequence for the fiscal deficit, since a surplus of 5 per cent is turned into a deficit of 2.5 per cent of GDP as a consequence of interest payments on the debt. This is what strains the situation to an impossible point, forcing reductions in wages and investment and increases in taxes with a strong inflationary potential.

One has to remember that the success of the 1923 stabilisation in Germany was associated with the repudiation of war reparations: without that, stabilisation would have failed. In Argentina, success is unlikely if debt repayments are not drastically reduced from their present levels: unfortunately, that is something the country cannot decide alone.

SOME REFLECTIONS

Now that our story has come to an end and we have presented some of the basic facts, we can analyse some of the main characteristics of the external impact and the nature of the Argentine response.

The Short-term Nature of the Problem

As we said at the beginning, there is no doubt that the present problem is the consequence of at least three major shocks, the first and second world oil crisis and the combination from 1981–2 onwards of the rise in interest rates and the interruption of international flows to Latin America. But the particular reactions to these shocks, their timing and nature were as significant. I refer in particular to the systematic postponement of the adjustments, the permanent inability to control the fiscal deficit, and the continuous temptation to relapse into price-distorting strategies. As a consequence of all this, two developments have taken place which have had very serious deleterious effects: the huge remittances to the USA, which explain 85 per cent of the increased indebtedness, and the reduction and final collapse of the level of taxable money (M1). It is the interaction of these factors that explains the bulk of the problem, although other kinds of short-term policies, such as wage policies in 1974 and 1983, have also been important at particular points.

The initial oil crisis was the direct cause of the first adjustment in 1975–6. The two-year period in which the country tried to ignore the need to adjust to the new realities aggravated a situation that was compounded by political squabbling, associated with the distribution of the burden of adjustment. What is interesting to note is that the external situation was quickly reversed, in contrast to the internal situation where fiscal deficits and inflation continued. This is what forced the 1979 predetermination of the exchange-rate strategy, the *tablita*, again an attempt to postpone the harsh measures necessary to bring inflation under control. The *tablita* was chosen because it was regarded as a painless way of controlling inflation. The ensuing overvaluation and the massive inflow of capital did make things easier for everybody. Wages were increased, cheap imports and massive international tourism were enjoyed by the middle groups, massive amounts of military equipment were purchased, and huge remittances of private capital were made, mainly to the USA. But the bulk of the increased indebtedness is explained by the remittances alone, encouraged by the overvaluation of the exchange rate which subsidised these flows.

From 1976 to 1983 Argentina was funded by $53 billion from exports of goods and services and by $35 billion from the increased indebtedness, a total of $88 billion. These funds were used to finance imports of $43 billion, interest payments of $18 billion and remittances of $20 billion (which in turn explain two-thirds of interest payments). Half of the funds Argentina was able to get hold of were used for goods and half for remittances and interest – an appalling picture. The tragic consequence is that the indebtedness was incurred because of the remittances of the rich and will have to be paid for by the abstinence of the poor, which is not necessarily an argument for not paying, but one which should give pause for reflection. The 1979 oil crisis had a relatively smaller impact, but prices of imports and exports increased considerably, improving the terms of trade for a while and making the control of inflation more difficult as import costs rose, contributing to the failure of the *tablita* experiment.[6] Although there is no general agreement among commentators, if one associates the second oil crisis with the jump in interest rates, one can see another stage starting in 1980, not too serious at the beginning as interest payments were refinanced, but very serious when this stopped in 1982. Up to 1981, one can say that the burden of the adjustment had been borne by wage-earners – from 1976 to 1978 – and that a situation (of indebtedness) had been created, transferring part of the burden to the future.

The 1981–3 crisis was brought about not so much by any external event, but by the necessary redressing of the external disequilibrium created by overvaluation. Even if foreign banks had been willing to maintain and increase their loans, production was coming to a standstill; moreover, the extraordinarily high internal real rates of interest had created problems of illiquidity and insolvency in the private sector, compromising the health of the banking system – a scenario not so dissimilar to the present international one. An earlier policy shift would have been less traumatic; this, and the lack of any fiscal restraint, made the inflationary explosion much worse. But again, the external situation was soon reversed, while the internal one was not. By the end of 1982 the redressing of relative prices helped the external reversal at the price of worsening the internal inflationary situation.

The Cyclical Behaviour of Inflation

All this can best be viewed as an instance of the cyclical pattern of inflation in Argentina, i.e. a systematic alternation of periods of high and low inflation (see di Tella, 1983).

The cyclical behaviour of inflation is the consequence of trying to stabilise through the artificial control or repression of some prices, in this particular case the rate of exchange, while expecting all other variables to adjust. The process is depicted in Figure 6.5. The strategy does work for a while: inflation is repressed and the price vector becomes increasingly

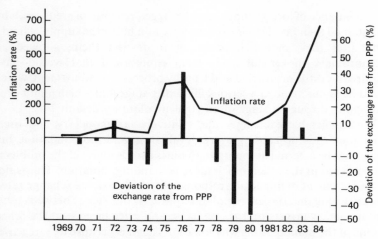

Figure 6.5 Argentina's latest inflationary cycles: inflation rates and deviation of the exchange rate from purchasing power parity (PPP)[a]

Note:
[a] July 1968–June 1969 = 100.

Sources: INDEC and FIDE.

distorted and a very bad allocator of resources. Sooner or later these relative price distortions create disequilibria which have to be redressed. Oddly, when this happens inflation rises, while on the one hand the efficiency of the economy improves as the price vector approaches equilibrium, but on the other hand this greater efficiency is undermined as oscillations creep in. The role of fiscal austerity is to make the repressed stage last longer (if unrealistically extreme, it might even succeed), or in the 'unloosening' stage to tone down the inflationary explosion. The particular case of the exchange rate predetermination scheme was really just a modern version of the gold standard policies of the past. This is not contested and, what is more, it is used as the main argument in the defence of the model:[7] if a fixed exchange rate has worked well in so many countries and for so long, there is no reason why it should not work in Argentina. The problem is that fixed exchange-rate policies have in general been abandoned, basically because once the economy gets off balance, the adjustment process is very costly, if one assumes, as one should, price and wage stickiness, widespread disequilibria, slow adjustments, imperfect and at time strongly oligopolistic markets, and volatile expectations. In the Argentine case, the abundance of foreign funds and the lagged reaction of creditors, who maintained their favourable expectations, and hence the supply of funds, long after they should have begun to restrict them, allowed an extraordinary movement away from equilibrium that would have required a costly, protracted and lengthy process of readjustment, which could have not avoided a serious illiquidity stage and which might even have gone through a stage of outright involuntary default.

With a flexible exchange rate, relatively lax monetary and fiscal behaviour ends up causing more devaluation and more inflation, but adjusting the external accounts at all times avoids many of the problems encountered in the other, much more demanding, situation. This is not an endorsement of financial irresponsibility and flexible exchange rates, but a warning that the least a policy requires is consistency between fiscal and monetary targets on the one hand, and price targets on the other.

One of the main reasons why inflation is bad is because its rate varies in a way that cannot easily be predicted. In Argentina, however, the predictability of the rate of inflation is what keeps the economy going. It has been there for so many years that most people have adjusted and sharpened their perceptions, succeeding quite well, except when drastic measures produce unexpected jumps, as in 1975 and 1982. But what does create a serious problem is the existence of leads and lags in sectoral prices. Doing better than average is the name of the game. It reflects the differing abilities of the various sectors to fight for their share of income. This intersectoral oligopolistic bickering is what creates the oscillation of relative prices, which can be measured as the standard deviation of the rates of change of sectoral prices (in our case, wholesale) compared with the rates of change of the overall index. Moreover, this oscillation gets worse as inflation increases, quite surprisingly more than proportionally[8] (see di Tella, 1979, and Helman *et al.*, 1985; their evidence is shown in Figure 6.6). The price explosion of 1975 marks an increase in the oscillatory behaviour of Argentine inflation, which means that after 1975, one of the most pernicious characteristics of inflation was intensified. This makes inflation more difficult to control, and explains the increased inertia and the greater resilience of inflation to every kind of measure, fiscal or monetary, orthodox or not.

This oscillatory character has given rise to one of the problems of the 1985 stabilisation programme: a particular relative price set was frozen at a certain date, not in line with any previous *average* relative price set, and this created a troublesome discrepancy that will have to be resolved if stabilisation is to stick.

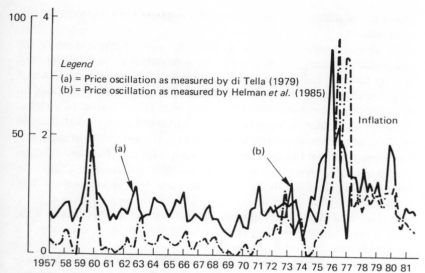

Figure 6.6   The oscillation of relative prices

Legend:
(a) = Price oscillation as measured by di Tella (1979)
(b) = Price oscillation as measured by Helman *et al.* (1985)

Sources: di Tella (1979) and Helman *et al.* (1985).

The Implicit Inflation Model

Throughout this chapter we have assumed that inflation has been 'built in' to the economy and has acquired an 'inertial' character aggravated by a persistently expansionary fiscal and monetary policy, to some extent exacerbated by the increase in the inflation rate.

The idea of a 'built-in', 'inertial' process is associated with expectations, with legal or *de facto* indexation, and with relative price oscillations. Expectations that inflation is a permanent trait have become so ingrained that economic actors are no longer sensitive to any kind of monetary signal, or to assurances about the stability of any set of prices. Indexation, legal or *de facto*, allows the economy to perform under conditions of high inflation, but makes the control of inflation more difficult, and itself feeds more inflation. Indexation cannot be removed unless inflation is removed: hence there is a vicious circle. As explained before, relative price oscillations are partly the cause of the inter- and intrasectoral bickering, and reflect the stubbornness and bellicosity of the infighting. These oscillations in turn aggravate the rate of inflation.

All this is a strong version of the usual cost interpretation of the inflationary process. But monetary causes, mainly fiscal in origin, cannot be ignored. Of course, the deficit itself is also the consequence of incompatible social demands. It is certainly not the consequence of an autonomous government decision, but it is part and parcel of a global picture, and cannot be separated out and thought of as though it could be changed in isolation from the rest. Moreover, part of the deficit is also the consequence of the inflationary process. This is so because inflation erodes tax collections; even in cases where these are indexed, a thirty- to forty-day lag is difficult to avoid between tax determination and collection.

Having said this, the fact remains that no matter for what reason, if the government issues money, a reflection will be seen in prices, even if a simple relation cannot be built.

Traditionally one of the reasons for this lack of proportionality between money and prices has been the possible variations in income. However, in very high inflations, these variations are minor compared to the variation in prices. In other words, when inflation is 10 per cent per year, the argument is very weighty, but when inflation is 10 per cent per month, it loses relevance. Moreover, it is increasingly unnecessary to reach full employment to see prices rising. Previously it was accepted that prices would rise a few percentage points before the 'full employment' point. Now the view is that this happens well before such a point, and instead of an abrupt kink we have a gently upward-sloping curve, which makes unemployment and inflation compatible over a very large range. The combination of this phenomenon with high inflation – high in proportion to the level of unemployed resources – and with a very low level of taxable money causes a given fiscal deficit to have an immediate and rapid effect on prices.

Unfortunately, the converse is not true. That is, an orthodox fiscal and monetary policy is not enough. Even when such a policy has been adopted, inflation has proceeded at a much faster pace than would have been expected from a purely monetary criterion. The view I adopt is that a small and orthodox financing of the deficit is a necessary but not a sufficient condition to bring price stability. If this is the case, two avenues are left. One is that of a more recessionary policy, not warranted in (monetary) theory but required to overcome the structural resistance. The other is to stick solely to the *necessary orthodox* monetary policy, trying to overcome the resistance not by an exaggeration of these policies, but by directly attacking the (non-monetary) causes. An incomes policy, a price and wage control policy, can and should be used *over and above*, and not *instead of*, an orthodox one. This is better than an 'excessively' orthodox policy which mistakes the causes.

The conclusion from this is even more pessimistic than the one we reach with a purely non-monetary or purely monetarist interpretation of inflation. Good monetary behaviour is necessary but it is not sufficient; to *exaggerate* this behaviour is bad, it is not even orthodox, and in such circumstances direct action is necessary.

The Significance of 1982

Before 1982, the inflationary impact of the fiscal deficit was diminished by substantial internal and external borrowing. After 1982, both external and internal financing disappeared, forcing the government to rely for all practical purposes on Central Bank financing. By then, however, the deficit to be financed had nearly doubled, pushed up by the interest bill, which exceeded 7 per cent of GDP – the result of the servicing of a major proportion of the foreign debt that had been taken over by the state during the turmoil of 1981–2.

But the size, structure and financing of the deficit was not the only novelty. Before 1982, taxable money (M1) had been hovering around 10 per cent of GDP. But from 1980 to 1984 it collapsed, falling from 10 to 4 per cent of GDP. The increase in the rate of inflation, from 5–7 per cent per month up to 1982, to 10–15 per cent per month in 1983, rising to 20–30 per cent per month in 1984–5, largely explains this collapse. Moreover, the new inflationary level further aggravated the fiscal deficit, owing to increased erosion of tax collections. Even if indexed, a lag of forty days with inflation running at 1 per cent per day will reduce collections by several percentage points of GDP (in this case about 4 per cent of GDP).

A fiscal deficit twice as large and taxable money one-fourth the previous level, with no external or internal borrowing, would in itself make for a sharp increase in inflation, without regard to the non-monetary elements identified above. But the non-monetary element in the inflationary process also worsened. The oscillation of relative prices increased, aggravating the bitter inter- and intrasectoral bickering, and making an already entrenched inflationary process more resilient.

Moreover, the slow but persistent increase in the rate of inflation began to be expected. Future price rises were thought likely to be more serious than in the past, creating all sorts of perverse reactions. These non-monetary factors meant that inflation worsened even more than one would expect from purely monetary factors. The interaction of 'fiscal', 'monetary' and 'inertial' factors is what created both the spectre of a hyperinflationary outcome and finally the sharp reaction seen in June 1985.

From a longer-term perspective, as can be seen in Table 6.7, it is the jump in the interest bill that is at the root of both the internal and

Table 6.7   The significance of 1982

	1980	1981	1982	1983
Real exchange rate (1974–83 = 100)	60	99	124	110
Balance of trade ($ billion)	− 2.5	0	2.3	3.4
Capital inflow, net interest payments ($ billion)	5.8	9.4	− 0.6	− 0.4
Net indebtedness/exports	2.3	3.4	4.7	5.1
US real rate of interest	1.8%	6.5%	8.5%	5.0%
Interest payments as a percentage of exports	19	40	62	70
Fiscal deficit as percentage of GDP	13.0	16.7	16.4	19.4
M1 (as percentage of GDP)	10.6	9.2	9.9	5.8
Inflation (per cent per year)	88	131	209	433

Source: see Statistical Appendix.

external disequilibria. What can be clearly seen is how the delayed reaction to the 1981 foreign exchange crisis created the present serious situation, but it has to be said that the situation reached in 1981 made the adjustment both painful and difficult.

Fiscal or Monetary Emphasis

The various governments, unable to control the deficit, and unable to finance it in any way except through the Central Bank, have in desperation used the exchange rate and the rate of interest to try to control inflation, and as a result they have pushed both rates well away from any possible equilibrium values. This was the basic reason behind the overvalued exchange rate of 1979–81 and the very high real interest rate, well above the productivity of any conceivable project in the real sector of the economy. But to add to the *fiscal* disequilibria others in the foreign exchange and capital markets is no solution. The recessive rates of interest led initially to a transfer of ownership from producers to creditors, and subsequently to a destruction of production.

The only rationale for such disequilibrium policies would be an expectation of some future development that would reverse the situation – an expected increase in the terms of trade, in the volume of exports, or a change in the international scene. It is a way of buying time, at a price. A strategy that bought time *without* distortions would be preferable, but it must always emphasise fiscal restraint. My own conclusion would be that if the fiscal deficit has to be taken as given, more inflation without distortion is preferable to a lower rate (in the short run) that distorts relative prices, particularly the rate of exchange and the rate of interest.

Another conclusion is that if the deficit is large, financing it by borrowing can be dangerous: beyond a point which depends on the proportion of debt to GDP, the rate of growth of the economy and the rate of interest, it will increase the burden of the debt more than proportionally to GDP. But, one has to be very careful with strategies that increase the burden, even if at times a certain increase may be warranted. Certainly this is not now the case with regard to the external debt, but it might – after the 1981–5 erosion – once again be the case with regard to the internal debt. The inevitable crowding out of the private sector is a phenomenon that might also take place when Central Bank financing is used, as the higher level of inflation ends up having to be checked through the rate of interest: this is an indirect process, but one that still crowds out private investment. Given the vagaries of government behaviour, a strategy of low indebtedness would not be absurd. Obviously this means that an even greater effort to control the deficit has to be made.

Stopping Capital Remittances

The increased outflow of funds from private Argentine investors, in particular to the USA, has become a tragic problem. It is now one of the main forms of investment, taking away 3–4 per cent of GDP per year, i.e. about 20 per cent of total domestic investment. This is done through trade, underinvoicing of imports or through capital flows, particularly when there has been a free capital market *coupled* with a guaranteed rate of exchange.

Free capital movements need not mean capital remittances if the sum of the current account and the capital inflows is equal to the increase in reserves. If reserves fall, they should be being used to finance exclusively current account deficits and international capital repayments. If the Central Bank follows this reserve policy, it need not be concerned about remittances from the private sector. As this rule is not easy to follow and fluctuations interfere, a common alternative to a free floating exchange is one in which the rate is fixed but capital flows are restricted, which will give rise to a black and freely floating market rate. Official capital movements – if any – will be made via the legal market, while the black market clears all other capital transactions, not allowing net remittances.

Another way is a dual system, in which there is a commercial fixed rate (even if with daily changes) and a legal, freely floating financial market where capital movements can be made. This allows remittances equal to *net* capital inflows. If these are zero, the two systems are alike. Moreover, these two systems are more stable and less inflationary than the freely floating system, but at the price of allowing over- and underinvoicing. They make sense when uncertainty is high *and* when both rates are maintained at nearly the same level, allowing for discrepancies only when nervous expectations and speculation creep in. These 'bad' moments create invoicing problems in the dual system, while the unique and freely floating rate system gives rise to general price rises and puts in motion an inflationary ratchet.

Non-market Tools

Price/wage controls and import restrictions are those most generally used. Wages are related to productivity but an important determinant is the changing oligopolistic power of the unions *vis-à-vis* the various governments and the business sectors. Wage increases were instrumental in the problems of 1974–5 and 1983, but not in other years.

Trade unions are not the only actors to behave in an oligopolistic way; industrialists and agriculturalists, for example, behave in a similar way through their producers' associations. In fact, most sectors behave in that way, a phenomenon understandable in the context of inflation. Some sectors, particularly on the right, speak only of wage controls; others, mostly left or centre, speak only of price controls. In fact, both wage and price controls may be warranted at different times, but only if they are measures taken to overcome oligopolistic distortions.

In a perfectly competitive market they would be unnecessary, as their justification lies in the fact that markets are imperfect. But the complementary use of non-market tools may prove to be useful. Equally important is that price targets and their rate of change have to be compatible with the fiscal and monetary targets. But if direct controls are regarded as a substitute for a restrained fiscal and monetary policy, they become worthless and bring into disrepute a modest but at times useful tool. This view is fortunately reflected in the 1985 stabilisation programme, which emphasises both price and fiscal targets – in strong contrast to the 1973 stabilisation effort, where price and fiscal targets were inconsistent.

Import restrictions are used to avoid *excessive* devaluations. This may be justified if foreign trade is assumed to be non-competitive, which is usually the case. Again, if the exchange rate reflects a long-term equilibrium value, a complementary measure might be a non-market restriction on imports sold to the country at marginal prices. But if they are used 'artificially' to overvalue the rate they are quite harmful. In any case, warranted or not, they give rise to quasi-rents and will be a source of sub-optimisation which will have to be measured against the sub-optimisation of a free trade cum imperfect market situation, a matter which is easier to pose than to solve in a numerical way.

THE BURDEN OF THE ADJUSTMENT TO THE DEBT CRISIS

The servicing of the debt requires (as demanded by the creditors) nearly $6 billion a year, or about 7 per cent of GDP. This is the consequence of requiring the payment of nominal interest, which means the capital is repaid to the extent that nominal rates exceed real ones.

At today's high levels of real interest rates, of more than 8 per cent, two-thirds of the payment is interest (real) and a third is repayment of capital. But this is agreed, and for the time being is a fact. The two most likely victims of the debt burden are wage-earners, who were receiving about 35 per cent of GDP before 1981, and investment, which was averaging 25 per cent (over 1979–81). Wages had absorbed the bulk of the cost of the previous stages of the 1976–8 weak stabilisation programme, having fallen to 60 per cent of the previous level. But in the second stage, by 1980, they had risen to about 80 per cent. In this instance they fell only for a brief period in 1981, before the debt crisis, and rose again from 1982 onwards, even exceeding the 1980 level but never reaching that of 1974–5. No figures are available for the distribution of income in very recent years, but the wage share has probably not deteriorated below the 35 per cent level (except in 1981). Investment went down from the level of 25 per cent of GDP for 1979–81 to about 15 per cent for 1981–4, the drop, half private and half public, exceeding the total required for the servicing of the debt.

Remittances by the wealthy to the USA fell from a level of more than 10 per cent of GDP in 1980 and 1981 to a 'mere' 1.5 per cent of GDP in 1982 and 1984. That is, the wealthy 'sacrificed' their local investments, by nearly 5 percentage points, and reduced their remittances elsewhere by 8.5 per cent of GDP, increasing their consumption, while wage-earners maintained theirs (with the exception of 1981). The terms of trade did not deteriorate and have no special bearing on this account. The government sacrificed investment but increased consumption, increasing total expenditures, the fiscal deficit and the inflation rate. As borrowing collapsed, from 70 per cent of the deficit in 1980 to 7 per cent in 1982, the inflationary tax had to be levied on M1 holders. The more M1 went down, the more the holders were those with lower incomes.

Another way to analyse the cost of the adjustment is to express it as the amount that was effectively transferred, expressed in GDP terms, compared with the loss of 'potential' income, i.e. using as a yardstick the potential evolution of the product, assuming no debt crisis. But this is very dubious. The 1981 contraction is not related to the debt problem: it represented the adjustment necessary to deal with the imbalances existing prior to debt repayment.

My main conclusion is that up to 1985 the burden of the adjustment was borne by the rich, who did not forgo consumption and had to forgo investment in Argentina and the USA – a curious 'sacrifice' indeed; by the poor, who saw their cash balances eroded; and by the public sector, which had to sacrifice investment and which, like the private sector, sacrificed the future, but not consumption or the present.

But the future has finally arrived, compromised by the delaying tactics of the past. During 1985 real wages have gone down by nearly 30 per cent, a process deliberately forced by the government, which is eager to make the new stabilisation package stick. The burden of the repayment effort has finally been imposed on the poor and this will be no small effort. The servicing of the nominal debt means the generation and transfer of an economic surplus equivalent to 8 per cent of GDP. This absorbs more than half of Argentina's exports at present levels and makes up more than 50 per cent of the 1983–5 deficits. It also absorbs either 30 per cent of the pre-1982 level of investment, mostly state investment, *or* 20 per cent of wages, *or* a partial combination of both. The debt is equivalent to 20 per cent of the national non-land wealth. Only if wages take the full burden of the adjustment, *and* the resulting surplus is invested, will growth resume its former rate, a most improbable scenario. In any other alternative, growth will suffer still further. On the positive side, a more stable economy free from price distortions will lead to improved allocation and productivity of whatever is invested.

These burdens imply full compliance with the external debt. The continuous renegotiations mean that to an increasing extent forced renegotiation, or what has been more acidly called 'passive default', has been taking place. It has succeeded in reducing yearly payments, but not yet to the level corresponding to real interest payments. It is becoming clear that countries which make a serious effort and at least pay this part will be able to survive in relatively good standing. More is asked, but more is not really expected. If this were to happen, then the economic surplus to be transferred would be reduced by one-third.

But the more significant solution, in the case of Argentina, is to review its long-term, inward-looking strategy, and we turn to this now.

EXTERNAL VULNERABILITY AND THE LONG-TERM STRUCTURAL PROBLEM

One trait that emerges from the experiences described here is the extreme sensitivity of the Argentine economy to external shocks. This may seem surprising if one takes into account the fact that the country is practically self-sufficient in oil and is a substantial exporter of foodstuffs. However, the weakness of the external sector is what complicates stabilisation programmes and makes the burden of the external debt so unbearable. Exports have decreased from their peak of 1981 and have stagnated over the last five years, even allowing for 20 per cent of underinvoicing. This is a reflection of long-term problems, mainly the inward-looking, import-substitution stretagy.

The country has (and has had) a comparative advantage in foodstuffs, but since the 1920s it has been increasing its man/land ratio, and its comparative advantage now includes a range of light industries. A growing part of the industrial spectrum has become as competitive as agriculture and could also export, provided no distortion is allowed in the exchange rate. Many years have elapsed since agriculture could employ the entire population, a clear indication that comparative advantage now has to be broadened to include a substantial part of the industrial sector. A dynamic version of the theory of comparative advantage is what is needed, one that takes into consideration not only shadow prices, but also the learning-by-doing process typical of the new industrial countries.

A view of optimal broad *ranges* of activities, with a good degree of uncertainty as to the optimal activity within the range, is what is needed, which makes a high degree of planning impossible and necessitates a role for market forces. But the main difficulty for an outward-looking strategy has been indiscriminate protection, which has distorted optimal choices and overvalued the peso, making agricultural exports difficult and industrial exports nearly impossible. It has also made the country, and industry in particular, extraordinarily dependent on exports from just one sector: agriculture. It is no wonder, then, that the economy has become so sensitive to the international situation and so prone to external crises, particularly when the structural long-term overvaluation of the peso is compounded by short-term policies of overvaluation for stabilisation purposes.

Export growth in excess of that of imports is now more crucial than ever, as the huge debt requires the generation of a surplus of more than $5 billion in the trade account. Of course, national considerations have to take into account the facts of the international market. The world oligopolistic market structure distorts some advantages and annuls others, but it does not make exports impossible, just more difficult. All this is standard economic doctrine, the violation of which is *one of the main reasons for the stagnation of the industrial sector, the lack of growth of wages, and the worsening distribution of income.* Thus the recurrent external crises, such as those of 1975 and 1981–2, should be seen as short-term crises superimposed on a longer-term structural crisis deriving from the violation of comparative advantage. The comparison between the Brazilian and Argentine export strategy is striking. Brazil has become the first country to abandon the Latin American import-substituting strategy geared to the local market, adopting a version of the new Asian model which is geared to both local and foreign markets, with industrial exports exceeding primary ones. Argentina should follow this example, but as the first industrial country of Latin America, it has had a more enduring inward-looking strategy and requires a more intense and more difficult effort to reverse its former strategy. Table 6.8 shows Argentina with a modest growth of primary exports and an

Table 6.8 Comparative performance of Argentina and Brazil, 1971–84 (US $, yearly growth rates)

	1971–5	*1976–80*	*1981–4*
Argentina			
GDP	2.9	2.1	−1.1
Primary exports	11.7	23.3	3.4
Industrial exports	28.8	14.9	−3.3
Brazil			
GDP	10.4	6.9	1.6
Primary exports	22.3	12.0	0.9
Industrial exports	48.5	27.6	13.9

Sources: Economic Commission for Latin America, *Statistical Yearbook for Latin America* (1983, 1973, 1975 and 1976); *Economic Survey of Latin America* (1973–84).

industrial sector unable to share in the export effort, compared with Brazil, which has been able substantially to increase exports based on industrial goods, giving the impression that it is becoming one of the first Latin American countries to join the Asian countries' new industrial strategy.

CONCLUDING REMARKS

Two remarks must be made before finishing, one referring to the external situation and one to the internal. The first concerns the consequences of the extraordinary external debt. As has already been said, this is the consequence of the delayed reaction to the first oil shock compounded by the delay in reacting to the second, from 1979 onwards; these delays were made possible because of the extraordinary international liquidity. Argentine tried to ignore the need to readjust its economy to the new set of world prices, and was able to obtain financing not only for its complacency, which was reflected in a spree of internal investments, imports of military equipment, tourism and consumer goods, but also for an investment in the USA made at the subsidised exchange rate, resulting in a huge debt.

The beginning of repayment has had an effect not dissimilar to the payment of reparations after the First World War in Europe, particularly in Germany, i.e. it accelerated an already high level of inflation. While this prompted a stabilisation programme, the strain caused by repayment, in terms of negative income distribution and of growth made impossible by the need to remit 7 per cent of GDP (or nearly all of the net investible surplus) looks impossible to sustain.

In the case of Argentina, the main criticism of the IMF is less its economic policy recommendation than the lenient attitude and even encouragement given to the country in the past when it was increasing its debt, and now the lack of will to look at the real possibilities of repayment. This 'ostrich-like' attitude is forcing unrealistically stringent policies, which sooner or later will face non-compliance. 'Muddling through' is not enough and in the end will not suffice. A major political solution is nearing, one that will distribute the loss already incurred but that no one wants to be the first to recognise as such. It is in leading this clarification and in proposing solutions that are also costly to the creditor countries that the IMF possibly has its major future role.

The second comment has to do with the internal stabilisation policies followed in Latin America. They have been the consequence of at least two different approaches, even if at times intermediate policies have been adopted combining elements from both.

One of the positions is based on the assumption that rules that apply in the long term are good in the short term; that the speed of adjustment is high; that there is little, if any, wage and price stickiness; that markets are perfect and the oligopolistic situation plays a minor role; that most markets are stabled and in equilibrium and if altered will settle into a different equilibrium; that economic sectors are rational; that there exists a state that can be defined in an unequivocal way; that first best conditions are usually attainable; that distributive considerations are irrelevant; and that time preferences are very long.

The other, by contrast, thinks that rules, values and conditions that apply in the long run need not apply in the short run; that lags in market adjustments are significant and can mismatch other measures; that there is price and particularly wage stickiness; that fix-price behaviour is not uncommon; that markets are not perfect and oligopolies quite common; that some markets may be unstable and that perverse destabilising behaviour is common; that disequilibria are pervasive in the short and long run (the latter envisaged more as a succession of short runs); that externalities are also important; that futures markets seldom exist; that information is far from perfect; that different economic actors have different information; that rationality cannot always be defined in an unequivocal way; that there exists no such thing as a unique economic model believed in by most actors; that distributional considerations are unavoidable; and that government intervention may be far less risky than no intervention whatsoever.

However, the discussion has narrowed since the 1960s. Fewer people today still think in terms of a non-market approach, or that budget deficits are irrelevant, or that money does not count. Government interference in the private sectors is not seen as necessarily better; governments are not thought to have an unlimited ability to manage any kind of activities; the profit motive and material incentives are not thought of as unnecessary. This shift in the debate has occurred in Argentina probably to a greater degree than in other Latin American countries. Now the discussion is between people who disagree not so much on the model for some distant perfect future, when so many of the abnormalities and imperfections have disappeared, but on the strategies for the shorter term. For the time being, however, the shorter-term imperfect world is the one in which we live and the one in which the longer term is built.

Notes

1. Or so it was put (Fernández and Rodríguez, 1982).
2. Sjaastad (1986).
3. Martínez de Hoz (1986).
4. Congdon (1984).
5. Sargent (1980).
6. Modigliani (1986).
7. Sjaastad (1986).
8. See di Tella (1979) and Helman *et al.* (1985). Their evidence is shown in Figure 6.6.

References

ARIDA, P. and LARA-RESENDE, A., in John Williamson (ed.), *Inflation and Indexation* (Washington: Institute for International Economics, 1985).

CONGDON, T., *The Debt Crisis is Not Over* (London: Messel & Co., 1984).

DIAZ ALEJANDRO, C., *Exchange Rate Devaluation in Semi-industrialised Countries: The Case of Argentina, 1955–1961* (Cambridge, Mass.: MIT Press, 1965).

DI TELLA, G., 'Price Oscillation, Oligopolistic Behaviour and Inflation, the Argentine Case', *World Development*, vol. VII, 1979, pp. 1943–52.

DI TELLA, G., Chapter 7 in di Tella, *Argentina under Peron, 1973–6* (London: Macmillan, 1983).

DORNBUSCH, R., 'The Debt Problem: Argentina, Chile, Brazil and Mexico', mimeo (Cambridge, Mass.: MIT, 1984).

DORNBUSCH, R., 'The German Hyper-inflation', mimeo (Cambridge, Mass.: MIT Press, 1985).

DORNBUSCH, R., Chapter 11 in G. di Tella and R. Dornbusch, *The Political Economy of Argentina, 1946–1983* (London: Macmillan, 1986).

FERNÀNDEZ, R. and RODRÍGUEZ, R., *Inflación y Estabilidad* (Buenos Aires: Ed. Macchi, 1982).

HELMAN, H., ROITER, D. and YOGUEZ, G., 'Inflación, Variabilidad de Precios Relativos e Inflexibilidad de Precios', *Desarrollo Económico*, no. 95, 1985.

MARTÍNEZ DE HOZ, J. A., in G. di Tella and C. Rodríguez Braun, *Testimonios de los Ministros 1946–1983* (Buenos Aires: Sudamericana, 1986).

MODIGLIANI, F., 'Comment on Sjaastad', in G. di Tella and R. Dornbusch, *The Political Economy of Argentina* (London: Macmillan, 1986).

SARGENT, T., 'The End of Four Big Inflations', paper given at the Conference on World Inflation, Fundação Getulio Vargas, Rio de Janeiro, December 1980.

SJAASTAD, L., Chapter 10 in G. di Tella and R. Dornbusch, *The Political Economy of Argentina 1946–1983* (London: Macmillan, 1986).

STATISTICAL APPENDIX

Table 6A.1 Main indicators

	Economic growth			Investment		Inflation (rate of change % from Dec. to Dec.)		Prices of public services (1960 = 100)	Wages (1960 = 100)	Unemployment (%)
	GDP	Agri-culture	Industry	As a % of GDP	Growth (%)	Consumer	Wholesale			
1974	6.2	3.6	5.9	24.4	4.5	40	36	134	170	3.9
1975	-0.8	-3.8	-2.6	24.0	-2.1	323	348	126	166	3.3
1976	-0.5	4.6	-3.0	25.8	5.1	347	386	102	106	4.7
1977	6.4	2.7	7.8	28.0	16.2	175	147	109	102	3.3
1978	-3.4	1.4	-10.5	26.5	-10.4	170	143	112	104	3.0
1979	7.1	4.1	10.2	28.0	135.0	140	129	92	116	2.1
1980	1.1	-6.5	-3.8	24.5	-48.0	88	58	97	134	2.4
1981	-5.9	2.5	-16.0	22.0	-18.9	131	160	112	122	4.8
1982	-5.7	5.5	-4.5	17.4	-16.0	209	311	92	106	5.3
1983	2.5	0.7	10.8	13.9	-8.5	433	491	110	126	4.7
1984	2.0	2.6	4.3	13.4	18.2	688	690	115	120	4.6
1985	-3.0					1532[a] 24[b]	1898[a] 10[b]	130	86	

Notes:
[a] Yearly equivalent of the first six months.
[b] Yearly equivalent of the second six months.

Source: Instituto Nacional de Estadística y Censos; 1985 figures are estimates.

Table 6A.2 Monetary variables

	Money as % of GDP		Government deficit as % of GDP[a]		% of deficit financed by borrowing	Annual real rate of interest	
	M1	M3	IFS	FM		Argentina	US rate
1974	18.7	33.9	8.6	9.3	23		-1.2
1975	17.5	18.8	16.2	15.3	11		1.0
1976	12.0	17.4	9.7	15.1	29		2.3
1977	10.1	20.9	4.2	11.8	55		1.4
1978	11.2	24.4	5.3	13.6	93	22.7	1.3
1979	10.4	27.9	4.2	10.5	88	-4.7	1.8
1980	10.6	30.7	5.6	13.0	68	12.9	8.5
1981	9.2	25.8	12.8	16.7	37	25.7	8.5
1982	9.9	15.2	13.4	16.4	.7	2.5	5.0
1983	5.8	14.9	16.0	19.4	0	44.9	8.1
1984[a]	3.7	15.0		13.0	0.1	14.2	

Note:

[a] Figures for 1984 are estimates. Of the two series for government deficit, one is according to the IFS methodology, which in the case of Argentina adjusts for inflation since 1977. The other series, from Fundación Mediterránea, also adjusts for inflation since 1975, but it is based on the net increase of public debt, including a proportion of government loans and guarantees to the private sector above a certain degree of private indebtedness, above which loans supposedly are not going to be repaid. The surprising differences from 1976–80 are basically due to this.

Sources: Central Bank of Argentina, International Financial Statistics, *Statistical Yearbook* (1983), and Fundación Mediterránea.

Table 6A.3 The external sector

	Real exchange rate		Terms of trade (1970 = 100)	Ex-ports	Im-ports	Balance of trade	In-terest	Remit-tances	Re-serves (3)	Foreign debt (4)	Net debt (3)–(4)	Net debt over expen-diture	Capital out-flows (net of in-terest)
	(1974–83 = 100) (1)	(Dec. 1976 = 100) (2)							*(in billion dollars)*				
1974	93	67.5	113.4	3.9	3.6	0.3	0.3		1.6	6.8	5.2	1.4	
1975	105	88.9	95.2	3.0	3.9	-1.0	0.4		0.7	7.9	7.2	2.4	0.7
1976	153	107.7	89.4	3.9	3.0	0.9	0.5	-0.6	1.0	8.3	8.3	1.8	-0.1
1977	107	96.8	93.6	5.6	1.2	1.5	0.6	0.2	2.6	9.7	5.1	0.9	0.8
1978	94	79.6	91.9	6.4	3.8	2.6	0.7	-2.5	5.5	12.5	7.0	1.1	2.1
1979	67	55.8	100.2	7.8	6.7	1.1	0.9	-1.5	8.3	19.0	10.7	1.4	3.6
1980	60	41.8	117.8	8.0	10.5	-2.5	1.5	-6.1	9.2	27.2	18.0	2.3	6.7
1981	99	51.6	124.6	9.1	9.2	-0.1	3.7	-7.6	4.6	35.7	31.1	3.4	4.8
1982	124	83.8	105.2	7.6	5.3	2.3	4.8	-1.8	3.7	38.7	35.0	4.7	-1.7
1983	110	102.2	101.8	7.8	5.7	3.4	5.7	-1.6	3.5	43.5	40.0	5.1	1.4
1984	105	88.9	110.5	8.5	4.3	4.2	5.9	-0.3	4.2	46.5	4.0	5.0	-2.9

Note: The difference between (1) and (2) is due not only to the base but also to different indices for world prices.

Sources: Central Bank of Argentina; FIDE, and Fundación Mediterránea. The first measure of the real exchange rate comes from FIDE, the second from Fundación Mediterránea.

7 Peruvian Adjustment Policies, 1978–85: the Effects of Prolonged Crisis

Rosemary Thorp

This chapter seeks to compare and contrast the recent (1982–5) adjustment crisis in Peru with the preceding crisis, and attempts to delineate the changing nature of the problem, in regard to both its internal and external components. It is a sequel to a previous work, and seeks to re-evaluate the conclusions and analysis of the earlier study, completed in August 1978, in the light of subsequent changes in the international scene and in the domestic economy.

As explained in Chapter 1, the earlier work, of which the Peru study formed a part, focused on so-called 'orthodox' techniques of adjustment to the disruptions coming from the international economy. The case studies highlighted the problems of 'orthodoxy' (for its definition, see the discussion in the introduction). In the short term the adjustment techniques used appeared to have high costs in both economic and political terms, to the point of non-viability. In the long term, the model was suggested to lack the necessary characteristics for a strategy of capital accumulation or for political viability. In this context, the role of the Peruvian case study was as a rather extreme example of the first: it was argued that the problems of short-term non-viability and inefficiency were so great that there was no opportunity to assess its viability as a long-term model. The Peruvian experience thus served to define characteristics which make orthodox policy peculiarly difficult, with so many negative feedback effects that the policy is ineffective even in terms of its short-term goals. Furthermore, it was argued that the inefficiencies and high costs of the measures were increasing with time, when the policy adjustment efforts of 1959–62 and 1967–8 are contrasted with the period 1975–8.

This chapter will review the period 1982–5 in the light of these conclusions, and gives particular attention to the effects of a prolonged period of stagnation and orthodox policy. This is the background to the unorthodox measures finally adopted by the new government of Alan Garcia which took office on 28 July 1985. The first section reviews briefly the background; the reader is referred to earlier work for greater detail.[1] The second section outlines developments from 1978 to 1985, and attempts to identify the different components of the renewed adjustment crisis 1982 to 1985. The third section explores the causes of inflation, and the fourth examines the growth of defence mechanisms against inflation and recession. The fifth analyses the *modus operandi* of the adjustment measures taken, while the sixth considers the nature of the new policies adopted in August 1985.

THE BACKGROUND: THE UNDERLYING CRISIS

The 1970s and 1980s differ radically from the 1930s, both for Latin America and for Peru, in the sense that external crisis has hit economies with increasingly little room for manoeuvre. The flexibility of the 1930s, as represented by open frontiers and other forms of fairly easy supply expansion, and by ample opportunities for 'easy' import substitution, in industry or agriculture or both, simply did not exist in the 1970s. This was clearly true for Peru, which encountered a problem of export supply at the end of the 1960s, by which time 'easy' expansion of volume by increasing the cultivated area, or by more fishing, say, had ceased to be possible (see Table 7.1). The next route forward lay in mining and irrigation projects of a new level of complexity. What made Peru's problem particularly severe is that the historical pattern of its

Table 7.1   Peru: long-run growth in income and exports, 1950–84 (compound annual growth rates, %)

	GDP	Volume of exports
1950–68	5	12
1969–79	4	−3
1980–84	0	−4

Sources: IMF, *International Financial Statistics*, and BCR, *Memoria 1984* and *Cuentas Nacionales 1950–1974*.

development had endowed the country with a relatively undeveloped state and national bourgeoisie which was ill-equipped to embark on the major investment projects needed to push supply to a new level. Added to this there was beginning to be a breakdown of the political and social preconditions for a model which allowed foreign capital to carry out the task, in a context of unequal distribution of benefits both nationally and internationally. The following twenty years can be seen as years of search for a new 'model' in both political and economic terms.

The military government which took power in 1968 was an innovative but ultimately unsuccessful attempt to solve these problems, an attempt which was vague and poorly based in both its political and economic strategy. In the economic field, the most solid achievement was that some export projects did get off the ground, although after costly delays. The ample supply of bank finance permitted a 'solution' via external debt, while imports rose for defence, food, public investment projects and general consumption. Prospects of oil wealth were one reason for a costly overshooting in 1975, as expansion continued even though external prices did not justify it. The attempts at adjustment in 1976–8 produced a fall in per capita GDP of 9 per cent, and an acceleration of inflation from 17 per cent in 1974 to 58 per cent by 1978. Stagnation plus growing unrest made it impossible for long-term foreign investment to substitute for short-term, which could have been one answer to the finance gap.

My earlier analysis concluded just as a little room for manoeuvre had been secured by debt rescheduling in June 1978. The following section takes up the story at that point.

DEVELOPMENTS, 1978–85

How Room for Manoeuvre Was Used, 1979–82

As Table 7.2 shows, the course of events changed dramatically in 1979 as export proceeds began to exceed earlier projections. Led by copper prices, the export price index rose a remarkable 78 per cent between 1978 and 1980, and the terms of trade swung 43 per cent in favour of Peru. This bonanza led to the apparent disappearance of 'the debt problem', and credits negotiated in 1978 were in part not drawn on or repaid before their due date. The situation was helped by the low level of imports in 1978 and 1979, as the previous policies of demand repression at last 'bit', and by the still-low level of real interest rates. Table 1.1 in the

Table 7.2   Terms of trade, 1974–83 (1981 = 100)

	Export prices[a]	Import prices[b]	Terms of trade[a]
1974	68	53	128
1975	55	62	88
1976	62	63	100
1977	73	69	105
1978	67	80	84
1979	97	89	110
1980	119	99	120
1981	100	100	100
1982	86	100	86
1983	92	102	90
1984	84	104	81

Notes:
[a] Traditional export products only, weighted by structure of exports in each year.
[b] Weighted index of export prices of principal trading partners.

Source: Banco Central, *Memoria*, various years.

introduction shows how the international prime rate, while no longer negative in real terms as it had been in the borrowing boom of the mid-1970s, was still only 2 per cent in real terms in 1980.

What both tables also reveal, however, is how short-lived the room for manoeuvre was to be. As the introduction to this volume makes clear, the conditions of 1979–80 were deceptive. In fact, by the early 1980s world market and finance conditions were extremely unfavourable for all Latin American countries, and Peru was no exception. Peru's terms of trade fell again in 1981, and the dramatic rise in real interest rates in the same year, coupled with the (related) unfavourable trends in primary product prices,[2] led to the Mexican crisis in August 1982, so that the already weakening Peruvian balance of payments was also hit by the general decline in willingness to lend to Latin America as the international crisis of confidence grew.

How was this small room for manoeuvre used, and with what implications for the economy's capacity to deal with renewed external elements of crisis by 1982? The period from June 1978 to July 1980 corresponds to the years of transition from military to civilian government. The transition was effected in two stages, with first the election of a Constituent Assembly, followed in June 1980 by a general election. This produced a large majority for an Acción Popular government with President Belaunde at its head, which duly took office in July 1980. The first part of our period therefore corresponds to a 'caretaker' episode, with a civilian economic team led by Silva Ruete, which was replaced under Belaunde by a team led by Manuel Ulloa, who remained in office until December 1982.

The Silva Ruete period was one of moderate conservatism, pragmatic in style, but making a strong beginning in some lines of policy which were to be taken up in more ideological fashion under Ulloa. In particular, a start was made on lowering tariffs. The expansion of demand coming from rising exports was to be moderated by increased export retentions. The idea was to moderate inflation by expanding imports, reducing tariffs and by continuing the previous policy of limiting exchange-rate changes to less than domestic inflation, a policy made possible by rapidly increasing international export prices. Controlled prices were not raised in line with inflation, and subsidies increased.

With the new government, a stronger pro-market line was adopted. Private foreign investment was seen as a focal point of the development strategy, and obstacles to its entry were to be removed. Contracts were to be negotiated to get the major mining projects moving, under the lively Minister for Energy and Mines, Pedro Pablo Kuczynski. State enterprises were to be sold when possible to the private sector. A stronger programme of liberalisation of imports was to be pursued, starting with the removal of quantitative controls as far as possible. Financial reforms were also to allow the market to operate more efficiently in that sphere. A conservative monetary and fiscal policy was to be pursued. Initially, exchange-rate management was to have deceleration of inflation as its principal goal, since buoyant exports would permit this. In early 1981, the attempt to restrain inflation developed into a British Labour government-style attempt at consensus incomes policy, of which the would-be architects were Richard Webb, President of the Central Bank, and Alfonso Grados, Minister of Labour. The attempt broke down, basically for want of confidence in the government's ability to fulfil its part of the bargain. In August 1981, as inflation did not decelerate and as export receipts weakened, a policy switch occurred: the rate of devaluation was accelerated and the move to full 'market' policies was strengthened by an attempt to end subsidies on critical food products. This policy continued during 1982.

It will be seen, then, that the 'breathing space' allowed by external trends was used basically to attempt to remove distortions and 'set the house in order', the focus being on liberalisation of imports and to a lesser degree on financial reforms. The space was also used to repay debt early, in the hope presumably of improving Peru's creditworthiness, and to push forward major export sector projects.

Of these, the last was undoubtedly of crucial importance, and a number of major projects did make progress or get underway. In particular, the mining projects of Cuajone and Cerro Verde progressed, and Tintaya began. But the efforts made to attract foreign investment were not on the whole successful: terms were liberalised and were initially rather good, but the response was short-lived.[3] Half a dozen foreign oil companies signed exploration and development contracts, but the results they reported were disappointing.[4] Several major state projects, in particular Cobriza and the irrigation schemes, were subsequently harshly criticised.[5]

As to the rest of the strategy, the early repayment of debt was to prove of no avail in the face of the overwhelming influence of rising interest rates and bankers' panic. The financial reforms aimed to simplify and make more logical the structure of interest rates, and to raise rates to stimulate savings; the reforms failed, however, to achieve positive real rates of interest, for reasons we discuss below, and as a result were powerless to slow down the increasing dollarisation of the economy in 1981 and 1982. Holdings of financial assets fell as a percentage of GDP.[6] The policy of privatisation achieved the return of the media to private hands, a new agricultural law facilitating the sale of land and a reduction in the importance of the industrial community, but did far less than was planned or anticipated.[7] The liberalisation of imports was the most radical of the reforms, first attacking non-tariff barriers – in December 1978 only 38 per cent of import categories were unrestricted, by December 1981 virtually all were – then reducing the average level of the tariff from 66 per cent before the reform to 39 per cent by 1980 and 32 per cent by 1981 (Banco Central, 1983). Unfortunately, there is no sign at all that it acted to stimulate in the long run the growth of a healthier and more competitive industrial sector, except in so far as certain very inefficient lines disappeared completely.[8] With regard to inflation, a Banco Central study argues that it did restrain prices, since, although prices accelerated, the price of tradables rose less fast than non-tradables (Banco Central, 1983). However, the much more relevant effect was that with the relative fall in the price of tradables, the resulting increased demand for imports accelerated the depreciation of the exchange rate, which in turn provoked an increase in the rate of inflation.

214 *Peruvian Adjustment Policies*

The Management of Demand, 1979–82

Table 7.3 shows the evolution of the structure of demand, while Table 7.4 sets out the behaviour of the public sector. In Table 7.4 a partial correction is made for the effect of inflation, in accordance with the methodology explained in Chapter 1 (and more fully in Chapter 10). A further distinction is made between the 'internal' and 'external' deficit, for the reasons which we also discuss in Chapter 1. It will be seen that 1979 was a year of very sluggish growth in demand in every component apart from exports, while the rise in tax income and the revenues of state

Table 7.3 GDP by expenditure at constant 1970 prices (indices 1974 = 100)

| | Consumption | | Gross fixed investment | | | | |
	Public	Private	Public	Private	Exports	Imports	GDP
1974	100	100	100	100	100	100	100
1975	113	102	112	129	100	115	102
1976	117	104	106	118	94	89	106
1977	129	103	77	103	109	82	106
1978	109	98	64	93	129	62	104
1979	97	98	73	107	166	65	108
1980	118	102	99	130	154	95	111
1981	118	105	123	155	150	113	114
1982	125	104	130	148	165	110	116
1983	114	92	105	97	144	82	102
1984	99	96	97	90	151	65	107
Percentage share in total							
1974	12	75	8	8	12	−19	100
1984	11	68	8	6	18	−12	100

Source: Banco Central, *Memoria* (1983, 1984).

companies with the export boom was sufficient to reduce the nominal fiscal deficit from 6 per cent of GDP in 1978 to a mere 1 per cent in 1979, with no cut in expenditure. Although the figures for the corrected deficits or surpluses are only suggestive, given the weakness of the data, the fact that they indicate that the deficit became a surplus of nearly 5 per cent of GDP is impressive.

Table 7.4 Peru: public sector operations (as per cent of GDP)

	1978	1979	1980	1981	1982	1983	1984
Central government current revenue	15.8	18.0	20.5	17.9	17.5	14.2	16.3
Central government current expenditure	17.4	14.4	18.1	17.7	17.3	19.2	17.8
Wages and salaries	4.7	4.0	4.8	5.2	5.2	5.2	5.0
Goods and services	0.6	0.6	0.8	0.8	0.7	0.9	1.0
Military outlays	5.5	3.4	4.9	4.4	5.5	5.1	3.5
Interest	4.3	4.4	4.3	4.5	3.9	5.3	5.4
Subsidies and transfers	2.2	1.9	3.3	2.8	2.0	2.7	2.9
Capital expenditure	5.7	6.0	8.4	9.9	10.6	10.4	8.9
of which central government	3.5	4.1	5.2	5.1	4.2	3.9	4.0
Overall nominal public sector deficit (−)	−6.1	−1.1	−4.7	−8.4	−9.3	−12.1	−7.6
Total 'real' deficit or surplus[a]	−0.6	4.7	2.0	−2.4	−3.8	−5.1	−0.6
'Internal' deficit or surplus[b]	(−1.0)	(0.6)	(−1.9)	(−5.7)	−6.0	−7.6	−5.0
'Internal' deficit partially inflation-corrected[a]	(1.9)	(3.6)	(0.9)	(−2.5)	−3.2	−4.5	−3.1

Notes:
[a] This omits interest payments, in accordance with the methodology explained in Chapter 10, to measure the implications for demand. It almost certainly underestimates the deficit – see Chapter 10.
[b] The calculation of the 'internal' deficit or surplus uses the innovative unpublished paper of German Alarco (1984). It makes a correction to his figures by excluding the 'internal income' the sales abroad of state enterprises, on the grounds that this does not correspond to an internal act of saving. However, figures have so far only been obtained for 1982–4; corrections for earlier years have been estimated only and are therefore placed in parentheses. It must be emphasised that all these 'corrections' are extremely fragile, both conceptually and in terms of the data base.

Source: Banco Central (1984) and author's estimates (see notes).

In 1980 and 1981 the growth of demand was led by a boom in investment, both public and private, the latter responding to good export prospects and to a groundswell of confidence in the new government, and rising over 50 per cent above its admittedly very depressed level in 1978. Consumption was far more restrained, real wages rising a little in 1980 to fall again in 1981. There was therefore a stimulus to domestic demand from the expenditure side of the public sector in both years. In 1980, however, the more-than-doubling of fiscal income meant little change in the net effect of the public sector. In 1981 there was strong demand pressure from this source. The inflation-corrected internal surplus of 1980 of 1 per cent of GDP became − 1.5 in 1981. Monetary policy was supposedly restrictive, but even in soles money supply rose relative to GDP (see Table 7.10 below).

In 1982 the rise in investment levelled off as confidence began to weaken and export prospects looked poor; the public sector expansion slowed down considerably as sources of financing looked less promising. Given the acceleration of inflation in 1982, which we discuss below, it is probable that a full inflation correction would show that the real internal deficit did not rise. There was also pressure from the IMF, as a condition for a standby signed in June 1982, 'as a precaution'. The growth in GDP was only 1.8 per cent, negative in per capita terms.

The behaviour of output is shown in Table 7.5. It will be seen that agriculture continued its historically unsatisfactory if uneven performance, while the mining sector stagnated, waiting for new projects to come on stream. The most striking development was in industry, which responded in 1980 to the growth of demand with a 5 per cent growth rate, but thereafter declined in *absolute* terms as the influx of imports undermined its market position. Certain sectors did very badly, the outstanding case being textiles, which was hit by both legal and illegal imports.

Price developments are shown in Table 7.6, which gives 'relative' inflation[9] together with exchange-rate changes, and in Figure 7.1, which presents monthly developments, showing the percentage change each month compared with the same month in the preceding year. It will be seen that overvaluation (and increasing subsidies)[10] led to a disappointingly slight slowdown in inflation in 1980, and that prices were accelerating again by mid-year. This indicates a worrying sensitivity of prices to the rise in demand, despite the prior existence of excess capacity. Once the exchange rate and pricing policy changed, in August 1981, the failure of inflation to slow down becomes no surprise. The liberalisation of imports, the weakening of export prices and the

Table 7.5   GDP by productive sectors 1978–83, constant 1970 prices (indices 1974 = 100)

	GDP	Agriculture	Fishing	Mining	Manu-facturing	Con-struction	Government	Other
1975	102	99	85	87	105	117	104	103
1975	106	102	103	93	109	114	107	106
1977	106	103	97	124	102	105	110	105
1978	104	99	127	143	98	88	109	102
1979	108	102	139	156	102	91	108	107
1980	111	98	132	149	108	108	110	111
1981	114	110	115	142	107	120	113	115
1982	116	113	113	154	105	123	115	116
1983	102	104	68	142	87	97	117	102
1984	107	113	129	151	89	98	117	106
Percentage shares in 1974	100	13	1	7	25	5	8	41

Source: Banco Central, Memoria.

Peruvian Adjustment Policies

Table 7.6   Exchange-rate changes and relative inflation, 1979–84

	Percentage change in nominal exchange rate	Relative inflation[a]	Trends in real exchange rate	Relative inflation equivalent monthly rate
Annual				
Dec. 1979–Dec. 1980	35.8	44.9	Real appreciation	3.7
Dec. 1980–Dec. 1981	47.7	69.0		5.8
Dec. 1981–Dec. 1982	90.7	71.6	Real depreciation	6.0
Quarterly				
1983				
1st quarter	23.6	27.1	Real appreciation	9.0
2nd quarter	30.5	22.1	Real depreciation	7.4
3rd quarter	31.1	25.9		8.6
4th quarter	11.4	14.4		4.8
1984			Real appreciation	
1st quarter	15.9	20.8		6.9
2nd quarter	25.0	19.8		6.6
3rd quarter	22.0	20.8		6.9
4th quarter	31.3	21.4	Real depreciation	7.1
1985				
1st quarter	51.4	36.6		12.2
2nd quarter	36.9	34.2		11.4

Note:

[a] Peruvian cost of living compared with prices in main trading partners.

Source: Banco Central, *Reseña Económica*, several issues, IBRD (1981).

turnaround in financial markets all put pressure on the exchange rate, and the economy entered firmly into the grip of inertial inflation fed from the external sector. We analyse this process more fully in the following two sections.

By the end of 1982 an acceleration in prices was part of the growing lack of confidence in the Ulloa team's approach. A further element in the growing confusion in the second half of 1982 was that as monetary policy became increasingly restrictive, so borrowing abroad increased – in particular short-term borrowing by various public sector enterprises. As this became obvious, the state of chaos in public sector financing became a scandal; as the Central Bank put it, moderately: 'part of the difficulty is that nobody knows how much the state-owned companies have

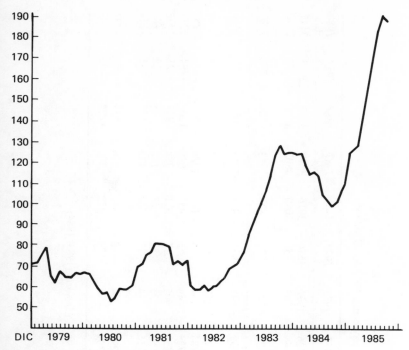

Figure 7.1   Annual inflation, 1979–85[a]

Note:
[a] The month given compared with the same month in the previous year.

Source: Banco Central, *Memoria*.

borrowed'.[11] In October 1982 belated measures were introduced to control public enterprises' short-term foreign borrowing.

The emerging crisis is clearly portrayed in the balance-of-payments statistics of Table 7.7. The more-than-doubling of imports reflects the import liberalisation (consumer goods rose from 6 per cent of the total in 1978 to 15 per cent in 1981) and the investment boom of 1980–1. The fall in exports in 1981 reflects the weakening of mineral prices. The two together generated a remarkable swing of the trade balance from +21 per cent of exports in 1980 to −17 per cent in 1981, a position which carried through to 1982. Still nothing was done even in 1982, in line with the pattern we are observing in country after country. In 1982, although interest rates had risen sharply and terms had shortened, the inflow of public long-term capital did increase, and the basic balance was a mere

Table 7.7 Balance of payments, 1970–83 ($ million)

	1970	1975	1977	1978	1979	1980	1981	1982	1983	1984
Exports	1034	1330	1726	1972	3676	3916	3249	3293	3015	3147
Imports	−700	−2427	−2148	−1668	−1954	−3090	−3802	−3721	−2722	−2140
Visible trade balance	334	−1097	−422	304	1722	826	−553	−428	293	1007
Financial services	−148	−284	−439	−646	−931	−909	−1019	−1034	−1130	−1196
Non-financial services and transfers	−1	−154	78	178	162	−18	−156	−147	−35	−63
Current account balance	185	−1535	−783	−164	953	−101	−1728	−1609	−872	−252
Long-term capital	23	1135	728	444	656	462	648	1200	1384	1233
Public	100	793	659	405	617	371	388	995	1431	1436
Private direct investment	−79	316	54	25	71	27	125	48	38	−89
Private loans	2	26	15	14	−32	64	135	157	−85	−114
Short-term capital, errors and omissions	49	−177	−294	−204	−30	361	576	533	−552	−734
Change in reserves (increase −)	−257	577	349	−76	−1579	−722	504	−124	−40	247

Source: Banco Central, Cuentas Nacionales del Perú 1960–1974, Memoria (1983, 1984).

Table 7.8   Long-term public debt and debt servicing ($ million)

	1978	1979	1980	1981	1982	1983
Part A						
Gross inflow	848	1084	1208	1620	2043	2554
Servicing	702	825	1323	1756	1600	1791
Outstanding debt	5135	5764	6043	6210	6908	8339
Debt service as %						
of exports	35.6	22.4	33.8	54.0	48.6	47.4[a]
						20.5[b]
Part B						
Investment projects	345	342	539	1084	1358	993
Food imports	98	109	171	132	92	172
Refinancing	64	389	8	83	109	1024
Programme loan	0	27	87	1	0	0
Others	341	217	403	320	484	365
Total	848	1084	1208	1620	2043	2554

Notes:
[a] Including debt service, which was in fact refinanced.
[b] Excluding service refinanced.
[c] Includes $195 million of Arlabank to BCRP, refinanced and accepted by the Central Government.

Sources: Banco Central, *Memoria* (1983, 1984); *Reseña Económica* (June 1984).

US $400 million in the red compared with $1.1 billion in 1981. The most ominous symptom was the outflow on account of debt service, shown in Table 7.8: 49 per cent of exports in 1982,[12] compared with 36 per cent in the preceding crisis.

From Crisis to Chaos, 1983–5

On the resignation of Ulloa in December 1982 the issues of confidence and relations with foreign bankers appeared paramount, and precipitated the choice of a banker from Wells Fargo, Carlos Rodríguez Pastor, to lead the new economics team. A new standby was negotiated with the IMF early in 1983, with a World Bank structural adjustment loan (a 'SAL'), on the basis of a sharp increase in the severity of orthodox policies. The IMF programme implied huge cuts in project spending, public sector wage increases were to be well below the rate of inflation, interest rates were to rise, and credit was to be effectively unobtainable either in soles or in dollars. The IMF originally pressed for a reduction in the public sector deficit to 2 per cent of GDP for 1983, but settled for 3.8 per cent (it was still thought to have been nearly 7 per cent in 1982). A 'temporary' tariff increase was accepted, to take the average tariff from 34 per cent to 41 per cent. Tax reform was planned as part of the package, which was conditional on commercial banks maintaining their exposure in Peru. The IMF and IBRD thus joined forces to try to stem the tide of falling confidence. With the agreement came a standby of US $300 million and a SAL of $200 million. Following the signing, by mid-year a substantial (if costly)[13] refinancing was achieved, shown in Table 7.8. The Central Bank's desire to slow down the rate of depreciation of the exchange rate and the increase in controlled prices as a deliberate anti-inflationary policy had to be abandoned for the time being as unacceptable to the Bank and the Fund.

The ensuing months were months of increasing chaos. In January and February 1983 the most severe flooding in living memory hit the North, creating disaster conditions as lives were lost and houses and crops washed away, and also destroying infrastructure and damaging installations, affecting, for example, oil production and delivery. The warm El Niño current reduced the fish catch to zero, and by mid-year drought in the South had also created disaster conditions. Weak administration structures failed to cope with relief work, and the revenue from a special tax imposed on middle and higher income groups, in the form of 'reconstruction bonds', was generally considered not to be arriving at the points of need.

Meanwhile a number of scandals emerged over public accounting, particularly over military spending 'omitted' from the 1982 accounts,[14] and the 1982 deficit was re-estimated as 8.6 per cent of GDP (two points more than the original estimate). Every day saw an increase in the problems of invasion of contraband, dollarisation of the economy, and capital flight.[15] Plans for tax reform and the orderly cutting of public spending were abandoned in favour of day-to-day survival. Bills were paid in the public sector increasingly by 'public investment bonds'. By mid-1983 it was claimed policy was concentrated on restrictive monetary conditions, as the only effective element left; yet with dollars now making up half of liquidity and constantly fed from illegal sources, even that claim was clearly implausible. In May at last the anti-inflationary policy pushed since the end of 1982 by the Central Bank was introduced, and the rate of mini-devaluations slowed down, to the increasing concern of the international bankers. In June Morgan

Guaranty Trust refused to join a rescheduling package on the grounds that it was a 'farce'. At the end of that month the government resorted to the absurd measure of delaying public employees' wage packets for three days in order to scrape inside the IMF target on expenditure. In October the IMF rescinded the standby agreement. A new one was negotiated, as part of which the rate of mini-devaluation was accelerated, but by now the economic team had lost the government's backing and clearly lacked authority. Belaunde announced in December that he was dismissing Rodríguez Pastor, who in fact stayed on till March 1984 in an increasingly untenable and impotent position. The November municipal elections had produced the surprise result of a left-wing mayor in Lima, precipitating panic on the part of Belaunde as to the political consequences of austerity; he was also anxious to spend in order to complete at least some of his projects before the government's term of office ended in July 1985.

There followed much talk of reactivation initiatives, but in reality any possibility of producing a coherent new policy had disappeared. From late in 1983 the general sense was that any new initiative had to await a new government, despite the fact that elections were not due until April 1985 and the new government would not take office until July 1985. A so-called reactivation plan was discarded at the last moment in April 1984 to enable the signing of a new agreement with the IMF, although in Washington it was widely described as the first agreement broken even before it was signed. By August 1984 a decision was taken not to pay interest on the debt (equivalent to two months' exports). Presumably, realising the inability of the present regime to put together a policy initiative, the banks did not push hard for a resolution of the problem. Existing lines of trade credit were not renewed, but what was lost was less than the savings on interest. In December 1984 the new Minister of Economy, Garido Lecca,[16] made a partial payment of $51 million as the critical 180 day limit expired.[17]

Not surprisingly, the room for manoeuvre gained by non-payment was not used to construct a coherent alternative policy – the only real rationale, surely, for risking the wrath of the bankers. The proceeds were used to pay a few public sector bills and wages which would otherwise have gone unpaid. The one sensible measure was a *cut* in taxes which, together with the slight improvement generated by the internal use of money not now needed for debt service, generated an increase in activity and so in tax yield, and hence a small increase in resources available in the later months of 1984. In general, the whole period up to the elections in April 1985 and the entry into office of the new APRA government in July was one of *absence* of policy, where new initiatives were impossible and the bankers, realising this, knew they had to wait.

The Recession, 1983–5: Demand or Supply?

Developments in demand are shown for 1983 in Table 7.3 above. It will be seen that every component of demand fell strongly. The impact of the public sector austerity was very deflationary, with consumption falling 9 per cent and investment 19 per cent, reflecting declining public sector wages, the cuts in investment projects and non-payment of bills.

Exports also fell, by 13 per cent, this reflecting natural disasters since the terms of trade improved somewhat in 1983 (Table 7.2 above). The estimated loss of $10 million in fishmeal and $42 million in sugar and cotton[18] was particularly serious for income levels. The catastrophic fall came in private investment, which fell 34 per cent in real terms as demand fell off, credit restrictions and costs increased and as the crisis of confidence deepened. Wages fell 26 per cent between November 1982 and February 1984, and salaries 16 per cent in the same period.[19] Underemployment grew, and by end 1983 was being estimated at 64 per cent. The fall in labour incomes was reflected in a decline of 12 per cent in personal consumption.

Table 7.5 above shows the evolution of supply. The effect of the natural disasters is seen clearly in the figures for agriculture, fishing and mining for 1983. The fall in manufacturing reflects rather the fall-off in demand, plus the increasingly difficult position of many enterprises with the rise in financial costs, and continuing competition from contraband imports. The 19 per cent of value added in the sector, which represents processing of primary materials, was of course affected by the natural disasters, and fell 17 per cent between the last quarter of 1982 and the first quarter of 1983; it is extremely significant, however, that the output of the rest of the industrial sector fell more heavily over the same period, by 21 per cent, and continued falling in 1984.[21] While the special circumstances of 1983 were clearly of relevance to the disastrous outcome, it is important to note that it was the steep fall in demand which hit industry, plus the fall in investment,[22] itself related in part to loss of confidence, stemming from a sense of the government's inability to cope either with nature or with the growing problem of terrorism.[23]

It is striking that this heavy fall in industrial output and in GDP secured a fall in imports of 'only' 27 per cent – an indication of the low

Table 7.9   Imports, 1982–3 (all figures as percentage of 1982
total = 100)

	1982	1983
Total	100	73
Public	38	36
Private	62	37
Consumer goods	13	10
Public	2	3
Private	11	7
Inputs	35	27
Public	10	11
Private	25	16
Capital goods	38	24
Public	14	12
Private	24	12
'Other' and 'adjustments'	14	12
Public	12	9
Private	2	3

Source: Banco Central, *Memoria* (1983).

'efficiency' of internal recession in producing adjustment. The disaggregation shown in Table 7.9 is revealing: of the fall of 27 percentage points, the private sector fall represented 25, of which capital goods were half.[24] This was enough to lead to a positive trade balance, despite the export fall, due to the supply-side factors described above (see Table 7.7). The overall balance was also positive to the tune of $362 million; reserves, however, fell $40 million, indicating significant capital flight. Without the $1 billion of refinancing shown in Table 7.8 (the largest element in the inflow of new money), the situation would have been impossible.

Inflation worsened during the year, reaching an annual rate of 111 per cent, which slackened only very slightly in 1984. Surely, given the strength of the recession, we are observing not demand pressures so much as stagflationary pressures coming not from the special conditions of these two years, and certainly not from the fiscal deficit, but from cost-push circularities. It is time now to analyse more carefully this inflationary process.

THE CAUSES OF INFLATION

The standard analysis by all recent government teams, as well as by
visiting missions from the IMF and the World Bank, has been to see
inflation as caused by the fiscal deficit and by the expansion of the money
supply. The 1984 Fund report stated:

> The major cause of the internal and external imbalances experienced
> by Peru during the past two years has been the maintenance of a
> public sector deficit at a level averaging 9 per cent of GDP. Public
> financial requirements of this magnitude led to an unsustainably high
> level of net foreign financing, a serious crowding out of the private
> sector in financial markets, and the maintenance of inflationary
> pressures.[25]

The report recommended major adjustments in the areas of fiscal,
monetary and incomes policy.

While it is certainly true that a fiscal deficit of 9 per cent of GDP is
unsustainable because of the implicit level of foreign financing, the two
remaining claims are somewhat exaggerated, to say the least. Referring
back to Table 7.4 above (p. 215), we showed that a significant part of
total public expenditure leaked directly out of the economy on imports
or on debt servicing.[26] Calculating the 'internal deficit or surplus' and
correcting further for the effect of inflation, we argued that on balance
the effect of the public sector, simply via the demand side, was
deflationary in 1979 and 1980, and clearly inflationary only in 1981,
when the deficit rose sharply even in real terms. The continuing deficit of
1983 on, given 'inertial' inflation and the quantity of unused resources,
can hardly have played a direct causal role in inflation. The effect of
devaluation alone in increasing the values in soles of liabilities
denominated in dollars explains part of the increase in the deficit both in
1982 (when the rate of depreciation was particularly strong) and in
1983–4. The large public sector imports and interest payments did, of
course, represent substantial pressure on the exchange rate, which in
turn led to inflation and also directly inflated the deficit – but this is to
enter into a very different causal analysis of inflation from that adopted
by the IMF and the Peruvian authorities.

Turning to monetary policy, the analytical problem here is that, with
accelerating inflation, the demand for money function would in any case
shift, and no estimate of this shift exists for Peru. Thus the clear decline in
real liquidity in soles shown in Table 7.10 cannot be taken as evidence of

Table 7.10   Peru: money and quasi-money as % of GDP

| | Money | Quasi-money | | Total |
		in soles	dollars	
1978	11	6	3	30
1979	10	6	5	21
1980	11	6	8	25
1981	9	9	8	26
1982	8	9	11	28
1983	8	8	13	29
1984	8	9	16	32

Source: Banco Central, Memoria (1983).

a drastically restrictive monetary policy, although there does exist abundant qualitative evidence of the difficulty and high cost of obtaining credit throughout our period,[27] which hardly suggests a causal role running from easy money to demand expansion to inflation.

However, what the table does show clearly is the shift into dollars, which by 1983 represented nearly half of the liquidity in the economy (and by 1985 the proportion was well over half). This suggests the following process. Although real interest rates in soles remained negative throughout the period, there were frequent increases in nominal rates and at times credit in soles became virtually unobtainable. This may actually have had a perverse effect, increasing the demand for dollars and thereby adding to exchange rate pressure and so to the inflation which continually nullified the attempts to achieve a positive real rate of interest. Table 7.10 thus suggests the declining power of monetary policy with dollarisation, and even the possibility of yet another perverse effect.

Our discussion of both monetary and fiscal aspects has brought us back to the exchange rate and to costs. This emerges as the heart of the inflationary process in Peru since 1982. Far from being demand-determined, recent inflation in Peru has derived from costs, and these costs are themselves almost all manipulated by policy. The critical elements in manufacturing costs relevant to pricing decisions are, first, the exchange rate, given the importance of imported inputs. This has been a policy instrument of prime importance. Second, various controlled prices or tariffs of public sector enterprises enter the equation. The crucial one here is petrol, but other transport and energy costs are important. The third element is wage cost, the one element which has not maintained its parity with prices, as we have seen.[28] The fourth element is financial costs. Stagflation models such as those of Lance Taylor place undue weight on this last element. When real interest rates are negative it seems implausible that financial costs can account for such an important part of the process. However, even with negative real rates, there may be a cost-push element operating, if two things are true. First, financial costs must be a significant proportion of total costs. Second, banks must refuse to refinance the inflation-induced rise in interest costs, which they would normally do in a period of inflation. The first point is certainly true for Peru: financial costs represented 31 per cent of total costs in 1981 for the average of the industrial sector, rising to 45 per cent in 1983. An unpublished Banco Central study of the twelve largest firms in the textile sector found a figure of 74 per cent in 1983 (up from 40 per cent in 1979). The lack of refinancing was also occurring by 1983, as banks faced with bad debtors struggled by any means in their power to recoup their losses.

The final factor in the mechanism of stagflation in Peru is the effect of recession itself on unit costs. As the use of installed capacity falls, so unit costs tend to rise, exerting further pressure on prices.

The remarkable aspect of the whole process is the way cost-plus pricing appears to go on raising prices even in the face of strong and growing recession. We suggest that 'expectations' account for this, since instinctively everyone knows that defence mechanisms are well enough developed for the 'privileged' market to continue to exist. The hypothesis of defence mechanisms needs fuller discussion, and it is to this theme that we turn in the following section.

It is this expectations factor which accounts for an aspect of inflation in Peru which makes it exceedingly difficult to handle in policy terms. Table 7.6 above sets out changes in the exchange rate and relative inflation. It will be seen that in the periods where an attempt was made to 'beat' inflation by rapid devaluation and interest rate changes, the policies achieved their goal in small measure only and at the price of accelerating inflation.[30] This was true between the end of 1981 and mid-1983. Unfortunately the reverse policy has, it appears, very small dividends. In 1979–81 the policy was sustained for two years, during which time prices and the exchange rate were deliberately adjusted by less than the rise in prices in the preceding few months. (Pre-announcement was not used, however, which is an important point.) As we saw above (see Figure 7.1) the monthly inflation rate did slow down at first, although hardly enough to build the necessary confidence in the policy. But by mid-1980 the monthly rate was rising again; our analysis of the rise in expenditure suggests that the problem may indeed have been demand pressure. This is serious in its implications, since it suggests that a policy of reactivation risks accelerating inflation, unless careful precautions are taken. In 1983 the problem was that the policy of small and pre-announced changes in the exchange rate was sustained only for six months, and in a context of dwindling confidence. It is again disappointing, however, that the slowdown in prices in the final quarter did not seem to spread beyond controlled prices, except for non-controlled, non-traded foodstuffs, where a recovery in supply following some improvement in climatic conditions was the explanation. The relevant point in the context of late 1983 was probably the general lack of credibility of policy, the known difficulty of reversing expectations, and the continuing fall in levels of activity in industry.

DEFENCE MECHANISMS

It will be our argument here that one effect of prolonged stagnation and painful adjustment policies in an economy like Peru's is that defence mechanisms get developed or more firmly entrenched. This leads, we will argue, to ever less efficiency and higher cost when orthodox adjustment measures continue to be applied.

The first two defence mechanisms we want to consider are strongly interrelated. The first is dollarisation; Table 7.10 above showed how much of liquidity is now comprised by dollars, and how this grew from 10 per cent in 1974 to over 50 per cent ten years later. In part this responds to relative prices – exchange and interest-rate policy – but far more strongly to underlying uncertainty in the face of inflation and loss of confidence in policy. But it also stems from the second defence mechanism: the move into the illegal and/or informal economy. In so far as this involves a move into illegal exporting – namely of coca – and its derivatives, then a steady stream of dollars becomes available. A 1982 estimate put coca as the largest single export item at $800 million;[31] dollars can be either 'laundered' by smuggling in goods which can be sold cheaply, since they perform a double role as well as evading tariffs, or simply used internally with increasing ease, since they are increasingly the lifeblood of the desperate economy. The cancellation in March 1983 of the 1980 law which required dollar deposits to be declared locally for tax purposes was an interesting indicator of the importance of illegal dollars to the Central Bank.[32]

Far more widespread than drugs activity, however, is the practice of shifting into 'informal' and sometimes illegal activity of many kinds. Obviously, as jobs become scarcer, a primary defence mechanism is, as it always has been, the resort to 'make work' self-employment. This is facilitated by contraband imports, which need to be peddled on every street corner. But it is also a route for firms, particularly the smaller ones: under pressure, costs can be cut by retreating out of the formal sector or by increasing the use of subcontracting. As credit becomes scarcer, firms are forced into the informal credit market. All these measures mean that total bankruptcy – the classic 'shake-out' effect – can be more or less avoided by the assiduous taking in of each other's washing.

The larger firms, while they may well use this route, also have other possibilities. First, they may benefit from increasing concentration and so greater market power as the recession grows, if weaker firms disappear;[33] thus their ability to pass on cost increases may stay the same or even grow in a shrinking market. Probably more important than this, however, is the formation of 'economic groups'. Peruvian industrial development has always been characterised by the existence of 'empires', usually centring around a bank: the outstanding and notorious example from the 1940s to the 1960s was the Prado family empire. Where it might be expected that with development and the reforms of the 1970s this characteristic would diminish in importance, in Peru recently it seems to have grown. The best known recent example is the growth of the Romero–Raffo group, centred on the Banco de Crédito and extending into insurance, property, textiles and vegetable oil.[34] (Interestingly, this group is at the heart of the 'modern' sector of the industrial bourgeoisie, taking a leading role in ADEX, for example – the more progressive industrialists' association).[35] Each of a number of bank collapses or near-collapses has also revealed excessive in-house lending within a small group of enterprises.[36] We hypothesise that the effect of years of credit squeeze and economic difficulties is to make firms work to secure links into such groups, as a means of securing working capital and other privileged forms of access (e.g. to insurance). While this can only be hypothesis until it is further studied, we suggest it is one important means by which some firms survive when textbook economics would suggest they would long ago have been 'shaken out'.

Another route to survival for a large or medium-sized firm is division of its activities. Occasionally this is skilfully done so that unprofitable activities and debts can be concentrated in one entity which is then allowed to go bankrupt, while worthwhile assets are saved. A further mechanism which weakens the 'shake-out effect' is that of tying oneself into the public sector by means of a contract. It is fascinating in this respect to compare the 1980s with the 1930s.[37] Whereas in the 1930s public sector projects were abandoned wholesale, in the 1980s the existence of penalty clauses and other protective devices makes it just about impossible to terminate a project. Faced with the need to cut public investment, the ability of the private contractors to defend themselves (by powerful links into Congress) is such that instead of certain projects being completed and others stopped, all projects are cut by a certain amount. Since there are penalties for delay on the government side, absurd situations can begin to develop whereby the remaining funds are eaten up in interest charges and the expenses of 'ticking over'. In the next section we develop the implications of these kinds of developments for the adjustment policies Peru has typically followed.

THE MECHANISMS OF 'ADJUSTMENT' POLICIES

The policies pursued by Peru from 1982 to mid-1985 were broadly similar, as we have seen, to those pursued in earlier adjustment crises. The primary emphasis was put on the reduction of the fiscal deficit via increased revenue and reduced expenditure, while credit restraint was to be followed with regard both to the public and private sectors. The emphasis on making the economy 'healthier', which was predominant in 1979–81, was actually lessened a little, as the invasion of imports resulting from the *apertura* had to be contained: tariffs were raised moderately. But the vision of external advisers from the World Bank and the IMF and of at least some commentators in Peru was still that swallowing the nasty medicine of recession and reducing the size of the state sector would together lead to the emergence of a leaner and more competitive economy able to compete abroad and avoid a resurgence of external disequilibrium. The same medicine would in due course brake expectations, and after the necessary corrective inflation, a conservative monetary and fiscal policy would allow prices to settle down.

In the earlier study we showed how such measures operated extremely inefficiently on both the external and internal disequilibrium in 1975–7. The period we have now described, 1982–5, in no way modifies that analysis; in fact it strengthens it. We argued earlier that relative price shifts could be of little benefit to exports, except non-traditional products; now we see that as the mechanisms of expectations and stagflation became more entrenched, it was difficult even to achieve a relative price change, and that it could only be done by accelerating inflation. The fall in demand as usual was the only instrument that affected the balance of payments in the short term; it required a 34 per cent fall in private investment in real terms and a 21 per cent fall in industrial output to achieve a 25 per cent fall in total imports in real terms (Tables 7.3 and 7.5 above). In 1984, as we have seen, survival was only possible by the precarious procedure of non-payment of interest on the debt. Meanwhile the long-term factors giving rise to the external disequilibrium – the growth in debt and its unhealthy structure, the expansion of defence commitments,[38] the long-run supply problem in exports – were not touched by these measures. Instead of an increase in competitiveness in industry, defence mechanisms were intensified.

On the internal front the more probable effect, as we have seen, was that the fiscal policy followed induced recession; this fed back on tax revenue, which fell disastrously, from 19 per cent of GDP in 190 to 13 per cent in 1983. We therefore have the same circularity that we usually encounter, in which policy, while in fact deflationary, is perceived as not achieving its goal, wrongly defined in terms of the budget deficit, so that further efforts at deflation must constantly be made. These partly take the form of increases in controlled prices, thus feeding the stagflationary mechanism we have described. It is interesting that public investment actually fell less severely in this than in the previous crisis. We have argued that this was due to a greater ability to defend itself on the part of the private sector. While it may have limited the deflation of demand to less than it might have been, it was less effective than ever in terms of the need for public sector projects to be completed and contribute to the removal of bottlenecks.

We have also seen that credit policy became increasingly both ineffective and inflationary, as dollarisation removed more of the economy from internal control and as the rising cost and scarcity of formal sector credit sent enterprises to even more costly informal sources. The private sector therefore suffered increasing costs as a result of every element of the adjustment policies, and, given the growing ability of significant groups to defend themselves, inflation merrily continued. The cost was seen in worsening income distribution and increasing symptoms of distress of every kind: disease rose, infant mortality rose, and real wages fell 20 per cent in the twelve months February 1983–February 1984 (*Reseña*, June 1984, p. 25). We have argued elsewhere that it was only the prevalence of survival techniques in the form of the lower strata of informal sector activity that prevented a more violent and earlier political reaction (Angell and Thorp, 1980).

THE APRA ALTERNATIVE

In April 1985 the political reaction to the above story took the form of a massive electoral swing away from the right and a victory for Alan García and the APRA party, with the left taking a significant per cent of the vote. García took office in July and in August introduced his shock alternative: a set of policies heavily influenced by the 'Plan Austral' introduced in June in Argentina.[37]
After a 12 per cent devaluation, a rise in the price of petrol and a modest wage increase, all prices and wages were frozen for an undefined but limited period. Interest rates on loans were lowered from up to 280 per cent a year to a maximum of 110 per cent. Default was not declared, but service payments on the *public* foreign debt were to be limited to ten per cent of exports. *Unlike* the 'Plan Austral', however, no measures of drastic austerity were taken: deposits in foreign exchange were frozen, leading to an abrupt fall in liquidity and a shortage of soles, but no measures were taken in regard to the fiscal deficit.
The measures thus accepted the analysis we have given here of the inflationary process in recent years: namely, a process operating through costs and where the fiscal deficit enters via its balance of payments effects rather than directly via demand. In October, some modest measures of reactivation followed (small loans to public sector employees, abolition of the payroll tax to encourage employment, increased funds for the state development banks); some import controls were introduced and more promised. The initial programme spoke of an emphasis on agriculture and of using agriculture to stimulate the urban sector; by the time of the reactivation measures it was stated that to operate via agriculture, while desirable, was too slow, so that measures must concentrate on the urban sector in the short term. In fact, rural credit was increased. The radical line on the debt was complemented by the cancelling of oil contracts.
At the time of writing (November 1985) it is obviously premature to assess the effectiveness of this alternative. The immediate effect was a substantial recession, as uncertainty froze spending plans and businessmen destocked. The true behaviour of prices became a matter of great controversy, as the official index registered a fall in the monthly rate from 15 per cent in July 1985 to 3.5 per cent in September–October, but meanwhile it was clear that unofficial food price increases were certainly greater than this. The real test is yet to come. This might appear to be whether a reactivation policy can avoid sharp increases in imports and a renewed acceleration of inflation. In fact the greater test is whether

the long-run strategies so crucial for changing the structure of the
Peruvian economy can be successfully evolved and implemented
without being crushed and destroyed yet again by the exigencies of the
short term.

CONCLUSION

This chapter has argued that the type of adjustment policy practised, or
attempted, in Peru in four sub-periods of the last twenty-five years, and
most recently in 1975–8 and 1982–5, not only failed to achieve its goals
but was also associated with effects over time which made the economy
increasingly less manageable by such tools. So many escape, or defence,
mechanisms developed that the economy became less and less the perfect
market economy that orthodox policy presumes in theory to exist. This
was evident in the growth of economic groups, of the illegal and informal
economies and in the ways the private sector knit itself into the public
sector in order to secure protection for its interests.

Various important conclusions follow from this. The first is that in the
case of Peru, deflation, social cost aside, simply did not solve the
problems which concern the international community. In the Peruvian
case at least, the defence mechanisms, distortions and perverse effects
were such that it is quite simply imperative that Peru be allowed the
breathing space and flexibility that will permit a different approach. In
this spirit the initiative of the García government is therefore to be
warmly welcomed, as a long-overdue attempt to find an alternative,
although in very constrained circumstances.

The second strong conclusion from this chapter is that Peru has paid
too high a cost through the way in which short-term crisis management
has increasingly precluded any long-run policy – and still worse, actually
conflicted with it. There is a need for careful analysis of possible long-run
strategies and ways of maximising complementarity between the short
and long run. (This is important in political terms, since it can make the
immediate sacrifices more tolerable.)

The third conclusion, sadly, is that in the Peruvian situation 'growing
out of crisis' is not an easy option in the short term. While the analysis is
not conclusive, it is possible that demand stimulus in 1980–1 accelerated
inflation and imports. This is the logical result of an extremely distorted
and unintegrated structure, as Peru's has increasingly become. The
prospects in the short term may therefore be for little growth.

Fourthly, the analysis has implications for inflation. When we consider some of the other case studies in this book, it appears that 'old structuralism's' casual attitude towards inflation is now hard to justify. It appears desirable to give some priority to the reversal of these trends, as the new government has done. The analysis of this chapter suggests that the route chosen is the logical one, operating on the manipulated prices which we have shown to be the current central inflationary mechanism. In this, Peru has an advantage over some of the other countries studied in this book: its exports are dominated by minerals and largely traded through state companies. A moderate increase in the degree of overvaluation of the exchange rate therefore represents fewer dangers than elsewhere, especially if subsidies to the still small quantity of manufactured exports are increased.

A major problem with overvaluation of the exchange rate is capital flight. The chapter has identified, as do most of the other case studies, the problem of capital flight, particularly in the last two years. The conclusion has been that the important reason for such flight was total lack of confidence in government policies and the growing sense of 'desgobierno', or lack of government. This focuses attention yet again on the political problem which interacts with the problem of formulating a detailed and coherent alternative strategy. The central argument of this chapter is that the economic crisis and the manner of handling it produced over time major shifts in the character of the economy and a peculiarly unfavourable environment for the application of IMF-style measures. But overlaid on this and interacting with it was the failure to solve the need for a new political model (the contrast with Chile is striking). Various actors entered the stage and retreated in disarray, notably the military and the conservative democratic government of Belaunde. It will therefore be abundantly clear that the limitations on policy have lain acutely in the field of leadership, both at the top and at the local level. But if this be so, then it is particularly important to underline it, since until August 1985 Peru accepted totally the position of the international financial community, that certain *economic* policies, and those alone, bring health and that the 'medicine' therefore had to be accepted – a misdiagnosis that this chapter argues was in danger of killing the patient.

Notes

1. See Thorp and Bertram (1978), and Thorp in Thorp and Whitehead (1979), ch. 4.

2. With higher interest rates, the cost of holding stocks rises, so the demand for primary commodities tends to weaken, *ceteris paribus*.
3. As Table 7.7 below shows, private foreign investment had been $316 million in the previous peak year of 1975. It was $27 million in 1980, $215 million in 1981, and $48 million in 1982.
4. Latin America Bureau (1984), pp. 84–5.
5. On irrigation projects, see *Andean Report*, June 1983, p. 109.
6. Thorne (1985). He argues that the 'simplification' actually made things more complex, by introducing the difficult concept of 'capitalisable', and by treating distinct institutions in the same fashion.
7. See Scott (1985); LARR, *Andean Group Report*, 2 September 1983: 'Velasco's reforms are alive and well'.
8. Such as certain plastics. See Falconi (1983) for measures of the reverse import substitution which occurred from 1979 on.
9. Inflation in Peru compared to its principal trading partners, as calculated by the Central Bank.
10. For example, between December 1979 and December 1980, the 'real' price of rice fell 26 per cent, that of evaporated milk 22 per cent, that of gasoline 25 per cent (data from IMF, 1982, p. 45).
11. *Andean Report*, February 1983.
12. The figure was higher in 1981, but incorporated some early repayment of loans.
13. For example, rolled-over trade credits pay nearly twice the normal rate (*Andean Report*, April 1983, p. 58). But this refinancing was on more advantageous terms than the previous one Peru negotiated.
14. And from the disaggregation of the debt shown in Table 7.8; presumably military items come under 'other'.
15. Using the Dornbusch method of measuring capital flight from Peru (for an explanation see Chapter 4) shows rather surprisingly no capital flight until 1983 – possibly because the method does not allow us to detect compensating inflows of coca dollars. But in 1983 and 1984 the method reveals a substantial outflow.
16. He replaced Benavides, who had taken over from Rodríguez Pastor in March.
17. Critical because after that period the banks must adjust their books and make additional provision against the defaulted amount.
18. Estimated in an unpublished document of the Ministerio de Economía y Finanzas.
19. *Reseña Económica*, June 1984, p. 25.
20. By the Ministry of Labour. Of the 36 per cent 'adequately employed', one-third were estimated to be in the informal sector. See LARR, *Andean Group Report*, 9 November 1984, p. 2. The figure in 1979 was 58 per cent (*Perú Económico*, July 1979).
21. *Reseña Económica*, June 1984, p. 22.
22. Itself a component of demand, of course, but not strongly so given the large import component.
23. The guerrilla movement, Sendero Luminoso, had been operating in the remote and backward department of Ayachucho for some time. Only by

the 1980s was it really beginning to be taken seriously. See Taylor (1983).

24. Implicit in this analysis is the assumption that shortages of imports in themselves did not *cause* the fall in production and investment. Imports were not controlled, so this would seem reasonable. However, it is possible that bureaucratic delays were used as an informal rationing system. Large and well-connected firms probably could obtain imports if they wished to invest, so the emphasis on the fall in demand may be correct.

25. IMF (1984), p. 12.

26. The analysis draws on the stimulating analysis published by Alarco (1984).

27. See, for example, *Andean Report*, September 1984, on the lack of credit in the cotton and textile sectors. The *Andean Report* of January 1983 reports on tight money policy and its effect in increasing enterprises' short-term borrowing from abroad.

28. For wage data see the BCR *Memoria* and *Reseña Económica*. Real wages by 1983 were actually below their level in 1957, and fell 50 per cent from their peak in 1974 to their 1984 level.

29. Conasev (1982–4).

30. It is important to note, however, that in regard to interest rates this was true of the size of increase which the Peruvians attempted – usually 15 or 20 percentage points. Experience in a country like Argentina shows that with far larger increases it is eventually possible to secure positive real rates.

31. *Andean Report*, February 1983, p. 22.

32. *Andean Report*, June 1983.

33. It is hoped to measure concentration in this orthodox sense for 1977 and 1983, once the data become available.

34. See LAB (1984), p. 87.

35. See Ferner (1983) for an interesting discussion of the evolution of different fractions of the industrial bourgeoisie under the military government. The key moment in the group's development was the securing of a controlling interest in the Banco de Crédito in 1979. See LAB (1984), p. 87.

36. See, for instance, LARR, *Andean Group Report*, 20 May 1983, p. 7, on the liquidation in January 1982 of the Banco de la Industria de la Construcción, to be followed by the Banco Comercial, which got into trouble when the Bertello group of companies defaulted massively on repayments to their own bank. Similar situations were revealed as several regional banks hit trouble. See *Andean Report*, February 1983 and May 1983. The June issue reports on CARSA, another example, tied into the Banco del Sur. The fact that these groups did collapse suggests that by 1983 the 'group' strategy was becoming a less successful defence mechanism.

37. This theme will be developed in a work in progress by Portocarrero, Portocarrero and Thorp.

38. See LARR, *Andean Group Report*, 5 October 1983, p. 4 on the Peruvian military's recent purchases. The article is entitled 'Peru Re-equips on a Grand Scale'; in 1983 military spending was 6 per cent of GDP (Scott, 1985, p. 44).

References

ALARCO, G., '¿Es Inflacionario el Déficit Fiscal?', Universidad del Pacífico, Serie Discusiones Programáticas, Document no. 7, Lima 1984.

Andean Report (Lima), monthly.

ANGELL, A. and THORP, R., 'Inflation, Stabilization and Attempted Democratization in Peru, 1975–1979', *World Development* vol. 8, no. 11, November 1980.

BANCO CENTRAL DE LA RESERVA DEL PERÚ, *Cuentas Financieras* (Lima), quarterly.

BANCO CENTRAL DE LA RESERVA DEL PERÚ, *Memoria* (Lima), annual.

BANCO CENTRAL DE LA RESERVA DEL PERÚ, *Cuentas Nacionales* (Lima), annual.

BANCO CENTRAL DE LA RESERVA DEL PERÚ, *Reseña Económica* (Lima), quarterly.

FALCONI, C., 'Efectos de la Apertura al Exterior sobre el Sector Industrial del Perú 1978–81', mimeo (Lima: Universidad del Pacífico, 1983).

FERNER, A., 'The Industrialists and the Peruvian Development Model', in D. Booth and B. Sorj (eds) *Military Reformism and Social Classes: the Peruvian Experience* (London: Macmillan, 1983).

INTERNATIONAL BANK FOR RECONSTRUCTION AND DEVELOPMENT, *Peru: Major Development Policy Issues and Recommendations* (Washington, 1981).

INTERNATIONAL MONETARY FUND, 'Report on the Economy of Peru', mimeo (Washington, 1982).

INTERNATIONAL MONETARY FUND, *International Financial Statistics* (Washington), monthly.

LATIN AMERICA BUREAU, *Peru: Paths to Poverty* (London: LAB, 1984).

LATIN AMERICAN REGIONAL REPORT, *Andean Group Report* (several issues a year).

Perú Económico (Lima), quarterly.

SCOTT, C., 'Cycles, Crises and Classes: the State and Capital Accumulation in Peru, 1963–1983', in C. Anglade and C. Fortin (eds) *The State and Capital Accumulation in Latin America*, vol. II (London: Macmillan, 1986).

TAYLOR, L., 'Maoism in the Andes: Sendero Luminoso and the Contemporary Guerrilla Movement in Peru', working paper no. 2 (University of Liverpool Centre for Latin American Studies).

THORNE, A., 'Savings Determinants in a Developing Economy: the Case of Peru', manuscript (Oxford: University of Oxford, 1985).

THORP, R. and BERTRAM, G., *Peru 1890–1977: Growth and Policy in an Open Economy* (London: Macmillan, and New York: Columbia UP, 1978).

THORP, R. and WHITEHEAD, L., *Inflation and Stabilisation in Latin America* (London: Macmillan, and New York: Holmes & Meier, 1979).

8 Crisis and Economic Policy in Colombia, 1980–5[1]

José Antonio Ocampo

Colombia has been regarded in the international community as an exception to the disequilibria and mismanagement that have characterised the Latin American countries in the last decade. This conception contains an important element of truth. Indeed, Colombia has lower debt ratios, more moderate fiscal deficits and has experienced smaller contractions of real income per capita in the 1980s than most countries in the region. This situation reflects, in turn, both a tradition of prudent economic management – which includes a long experience with the crawling peg, exchange regulations, import controls and export promotion policies – and favourable external conditions in the second half of the 1970s, which allowed the country to face the 1980s with an unquestionably strong net debt position.

Nonetheless, like other Latin American countries, Colombia has experienced a substantial external and internal deterioration in the early 1980s. Moreover, it has undergone in the last few years the typical phases in the Latin American crisis: a period of increasing disadjustment between 1980 and 1982, a phase of domestic corrections of disequilibria with some heterodox elements in 1983 and the first half of 1984, and a period of orthodox policies with increasing external conditionality since mid-1984. In contrast to many other countries, however, the current crisis cannot be viewed as a developmental or structural crisis, but rather as a strong short-term downturn. Indeed, the prospects for recovery in the second half of the decade are quite good, based on the gestation of long-run energy investments.

This chapter is divided into five sections. We first sketch the 'initial conditions' – i.e. the state of the economy in 1980. In the second section, performance in terms of economic growth, inflation and employment in the 1980s is reviewed. In the third and fourth sections, external and fiscal conditions in the first half of the 1980s are analysed. A final section presents the major conclusions of the chapter and the prospects for recovery.

239

THE INITIAL CONDITIONS

As a reflection of the foreign exchange boom which started in 1975, Colombia experienced five years of current account surplus between 1976 and 1980 (see Table 8.1). Coffee prices in the early years and high export volume of the same staple since 1978 were largely responsible for this outcome. The coffee boom was reinforced by the rapid growth of trade with Venezuela, the increasing remittances of Colombian emigrants and the drug trade.[2] The external surpluses of these years were sufficient to induce a radical change in the net debt position of the country. Indeed, by late 1980 the debt of Colombia, net of international reserves, was only $880 million – 21 per cent of the exports of goods and services. This situation was in open contrast to that which prevailed in the early 1970s, when this ratio was close to 250 per cent (Villar, 1983). Very few Latin American countries (in fact, only Venezuela, as a net investor in the rest of the world) faced such favourable conditions at the outset of the 1980s.

The years of foreign exchange boom were also years of satisfactory economic growth (see Table 8.2). Nonetheless, GDP growth between 1975 and 1979 (5.7 per cent in annual terms) was only similar to the average rate of growth of the Colombian economy in the postwar period and lower than that experienced during the previous boom (1970–4). Moreover, the slowdown was quite evident in 1980, particularly in the manufacturing sector. Thus the rate of growth in that year (4.1 per cent) was significantly lower than the postwar average.

Several symptoms of economic deterioration were in fact building up during the boom years. Foremost, for the first time since the 1920s, industrial expansion lagged behind GDP growth, reflecting weak investment ratios, slow productivity improvements and the increasing competition of legal and illegal imports (Echavarría *et al.*, 1983; Chica, 1983; Kalmanovitz, 1984). Food production also lagged behind in the growth process, leading to rising relative foodstuff prices in the 1970s. The diversification of the export base, which had proceeded rapidly in the late 1960s and early 1970s, was reversed, as export subsidies were cut significantly in 1975 and the government revalued the real exchange rate during the boom years. Finally, the bonanza unleashed financial speculation in unprecedented dimensions and led to a rather chaotic proliferation of financial institutions and activities, which enhanced the risks and fragility of the financial system (Montenegro, 1983b).

Although some of these developments reflect the mild 'Dutch disease' experienced during the boom years (Edwards, 1984), macroeconomic

Table 8.1 Colombia: balance of payments, 1975–84 ($ million, net balances)

	1975	1976	1977	1978	1979	1980	1981	1982	1983	1984
Current account	−80	222	455	386	566	104	−1722	−2885	−2826	−1870
Trade balance[a]	322	590	748	706	586	13	−1333	−2076	−1317	−322
Non-financial services and transfers	−139	−54	−21	−19	236	302	38	−22	−591	−344
Financial services	−263	−314	−272	−301	−255	−211	−427	−787	−918	−1204
Capital account[b]	134	188	−15	117	892	872	1923	1967	1127	946
Direct investment	32	14	43	67	104	48	226	330	512	408
Long-term financing	257	89	187	32	618	807	1384	1290	1016	1163
Short-term capital	−155	85	−245	19	170	17	313	347	−401	−625
Other[c]	–	–	–	–	–	–	–	–	–	–
Errors and omissions	38	217	226	131	24	−16	55	−4	−67	18
Global balance	93	626	665	634	1595	1235	242	−701	−1723	−1265

Notes:
[a] Includes non-monetary gold.
[b] Excluding contributions to international organisations.
[c] Contributions to international organisations and counterpart items.

Source: Banco de la República, *National Accounts.*

242

Table 8.2 Gross domestic product, 1970–84 (annual growth rates, %)

	1970–4	1975	1975–9	1980	1981	1982	1983	1984	1980–4
Agriculture	4.1	5.8	4.8	2.2	3.2	−1.9	1.8	0.7	0.9
Mining	−5.0	3.8	−5.1	18.4	5.4	1.8	12.9	14.8	8.6
Manufacturing	9.0	1.2	5.4	1.2	−2.6	−1.4	0.5	6.2	0.6
Public services	12.1	6.9	6.2	7.5	3.3	3.2	4.3	5.3	4.0
Construction	9.0	−9.9	3.3	14.6	7.1	4.0	5.1	4.5	5.2
Trade	8.2	2.2	4.9	2.3	1.2	1.6	−1.9	7.5	0.8
Transport and communications	9.0	1.4	8.4	4.0	2.8	5.2	−1.1	2.0	2.2
Financial services	7.5	6.1	5.8	9.7	9.1	3.1	3.2	2.0	4.3
Government services	7.3	0.5	7.0	10.3	5.8	2.4	3.9	3.7	3.9
Other services	5.4	4.1	5.0	2.8	4.2	4.3	2.8	2.7	3.5
GDP	6.5	2.3	5.7	4.1	2.3	0.9	1.0	3.0	1.8

Source: Departamento Administrativo Nacional de Estadística (DANE), National Accounts.

policies were largely responsible for the outcome. In 1974 the López administration adopted an orthodox stabilisation programme, aimed at reducing the rising rate of inflation of previous years. The programme included a tax reform, strong controls on public expenditure (particularly investment and export subsidies), a liberalisation of interest rates, a reduction of Central Bank credits to the public and private sectors, and a temporary acceleration of the rate of devaluation to compensate for the lower export subsidies. The government's response to the coffee boom was also a massive contractionary programme. Controls on public expenditure were maintained and a harsh monetary policy was adopted – including 100 per cent marginal reserve requirements on current accounts, increased reserve requirements for savings and term deposits, the partial sterilisation of the external surplus through the deferred maturity of foreign exchange certificates, and forced savings of coffee income. Simultaneously, strong controls on capital flows were adopted and devaluation was temporarily suspended in 1977 to reduce the monetary effect of balance-of-payments surpluses. Thus, in open contrast to other Latin American countries, contractionary macroeconomic management was the rule during both the 1974–5 recession *and* the coffee boom years. A significant aversion to inflation was the underlying force in both periods. Although this meant recession first, and reduced multiplier effects of the boom later, it was also reflected in the significant improvement of external accounts.

In 1979 and 1980, the Turbay administration adopted a radically different economic strategy, which was followed up to 1982, regardless of changing external conditions. This policy combined an expansionary fiscal policy with a contractionary monetary policy and a significant liberalisation of import controls. The expansion of public investment was justified on developmental grounds and by the need to reverse the significant reductions of public investment during the López administration, which in some sectors had generated needs which could no longer be postponed (DNP, 1979). The basic assumptions of the new strategy were that the economy was close to full employment and that public investment could only be financed by long-term borrowing abroad. Thus, in the government's conception, import liberalisation and monetary controls prevented the development of an inflationary spiral. Monetary controls were based on massive open market operation in a free capital market. In 1980, this form of intervention replaced the harsh monetary controls of the boom years, which by then had generated all sorts of financial innovations to circumvent existing regulations (Jaramillo, 1982).

As we will see in the following sections of this chapter, the policy mix adopted by the Turbay administration had unsatisfactory results. In fact, as the fiscal deficit increased, the current account of the balance of payments deteriorated rapidly, withouth the expected effects of the former on domestic activity. On the contrary, in the absence of alternative expansionary factors – since coffee had ceased to play that role – economic growth came to a standstill. A policy mix that was conceived for a boom period was thus never adapted to a deteriorating external environment.

ECONOMIC ACTIVITY, INFLATION AND EMPLOYMENT IN THE 1980s

As Table 8.2 shows, economic growth since 1981 has been similar to the rate of population expansion – 1.8 per cent. However, annual data do not provide a precise guide to short-term events in the last few years. Thus, Figure 8.1 includes quarterly data on per capita urban GDP, inflation and 'exogenous demand' (the sum of coffee production, other exports of goods and services and government expenditure, all expressed in terms of their internal purchasing power).

As Figure 8.1 shows, real exogenous demand has been fairly stagnant in the 1980s, indicating that fiscal expansion has not counteracted the contractionary effects of falling coffee and minor export income, particularly in the early years. Demand has experienced three distinct cycles. It peaked in the latter half of 1980, followed by a contraction which bottomed in the third quarter of 1981. Led by public expenditure, demand had recovered by the first quarter of 1982. Shortly thereafter, the strongest contraction took place. After a period of deep recession in late 1982 and early 1983, a rapid recovery was experienced in the second half of the latter year, followed by relative stagnation in 1984. Finally, in the first few months of 1985 there were fresh symptoms of new demand recession, reflecting contractionary fiscal policies.

Economic activity has followed the demand cycle with a lag. Thus, after a peak in the second quarter of 1981, the economy experienced a contraction of per capita urban GDP for the first time in the following quarter. A brief recovery followed, before experiencing deep recession in the second half of 1982 and the first quarter of 1983. The recovery of late 1983 was quite strong, but it was short-lived. By mid-1984, per capita urban GDP was falling again.

Although the 'exogenous demand' cycle has been the basic

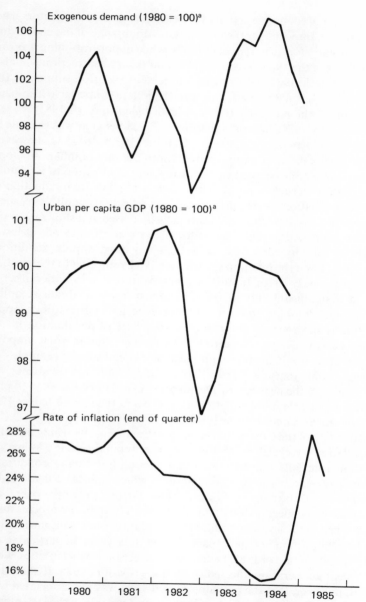

Figure 8.1   Economic activity and inflation: quarterly indicators

Note:
[a] Moving average of three quarters; seasonally adjusted values.

Sources: Fedesarrollo; Bermúdez and Valenzuela, *Memorando Económico*;
DANE.

determinant of economic activity in the last few years, other factors have been present. Import liberalisation was, no doubt, one of the underlying contractionary forces in the early 1980s, while import rationing was one of the bases of the 1983–4 recovery. Real monetary contraction was also important in the early 1980s, while monetary expansion supported the 1983 recovery. Finally, fluctuations in the inflation rate have also been important in the *real* cycle (*Coyuntura Económica*, April 1985).

In the early 1980s, inertial inflation of 25–28 per cent was the rule in Colombia (*Coyuntura Económica*, October 1982). In 1983, however, several events induced a rapid reduction in the rate of inflation. Good harvests were compounded with a change in the direction of foodstuffs trade with Venezuela – particularly cattle – to generate a reduction in food price inflation. On the other hand, as a reflection of policy measures adopted in early 1983, housing rents have increased at a slow rate in the last few years. Although wage contracts were starting to reflect lower inflation rates in 1983 and 1984, changing food supply conditions sharply reversed the inflation cycle in late 1984, returning to the 'inertial' levels of the early 1980s. It must be pointed out that devaluation has not played a significant role in the inflationary process. Reduced dollar prices of Colombian imports and domestic and agricultural supply conditions have amply compensated the effect of devaluation in the recent past, while price controls have forced firms in some import-intensive sectors – transport equipment and chemicals, for example – to reduce profit margins. These favourable conditions will not be maintained in the near future. Devaluation can thus be expected to play a more active role in the inflationary process in the second half of 1985 (*Coyuntura Económica*, June 1985).

Modelling of the Colombian economy (Londoño, 1985) indicates that the inflationary cycle has real effects on economic activity. When the inflation rate falls due to favourable agricultural supply conditions, urban wage-earners have a windfall gain which induces a demand-led expansion of urban activities; this factor prevails over the contractionary effects of lower rural incomes. The opposite process takes place when food shortages induce rising inflation rates. This mechanism has been important in Colombia in the last three years. In particular, the lower inflation rate of 1983 fuelled the recovery of urban activities, while the recent acceleration affected economic growth in 1985. It should be noted, however, that the recession of mid-1984 was not associated with the rising inflation rate, which actually picked up only in the last quarter of that year.

Labour market conditions have reflected the deterioration of

Table 8.3 Employment and average earnings, 1980–4 (four largest cities)

	1980	1981	1982	1983	1984	1985
As percentage of working-age population[a]						
Labour force (activity rate)	54.4	52.4	53.0	54.7	56.2	57.4
Employed	5.3	4.3	4.8	6.5	7.5	8.3
Unemployed	49.1	48.0	48.1	48.2	48.6	49.1
Rate of unemployment[a]						
(% of labour force)	9.7	8.3	9.1	11.8	13.4	14.5
Employment levels (1982 = 100)[b]						
Secondary sector	101.5	100.1	100.0	102.3	107.2	
Tertiary sector	92.3	95.9	100.0	104.5	108.4	
Wage labourers	93.8	98.0	100.0	100.4	101.1	
Self-employed	90.1	93.9	100.0	108.6	111.7	
Average real earnings (1982 = 100)[b,c]						
Private employees	96.1	96.9	100.0	101.8	104.1	99.7
Public employees	94.7	98.8	100.0	102.7	107.2	103.8
Self-employed	88.1	95.8	100.0	91.0	84.2	82.0

Notes:
[a] First two quarters in 1985.
[b] Excludes last quarter in 1984.
[c] First quarter in 1985.

Source: DANE, Household Survey. Average of quarterly rates and levels.

economic activity in the 1980s. In the first years of the decade, however, only secondary employment was clearly affected, while employment in tertiary activities and total wage placements increased at a satisfactory rate (see Table 8.3). Moreover, lower participation rates in 1981 yielded one of the lowest unemployment levels recorded in Colombian history. As the recession deepened, deteriorating labour market conditions spread in 1982. Although the industrial recovery induced a reversal of employment trends in the secondary sector – particularly in 1984 – urban employment stagnated while what growth there was occurred in self-employment, subject to rapidly falling real income levels. Simultaneously, the rate of unemployment increased rapidly, reaching record 1960s levels by 1984.

In the 1980–4 period as a whole, wage employment increased at an annual rate of 1.9 per cent, similar to that of GDP, while self-employment increased at an extraordinarily rapid pace – 5.5 per cent a year. This contrasting trend indicates that one of the most complex legacies of the crisis will be record levels of un- and underemployment and very cautious recruitment practices, particularly by larger firms. The latter have rationalised work processes and have learned to shift the burden of adjustment to the labour force – through the intensive use of subcontracting and temporary workers. New employment practices may actually prove 'structural' so long as confidence in sustained economic growth does not return.

THE EXTERNAL DEFICIT

In the early 1980s, the Colombian economy faced three different external shocks. First, coffee prices collapsed in mid-1980 after a period of growing instability. The fall of coffee prices had two different effects on the economy: on the one hand, it reduced the volumes exported, as the quota agreement was back in effect in the last quarter of 1980; on the other hand, the terms of trade deteriorated by some 18 per cent between 1978–80 and 1981–4. Later on, in August 1982, coinciding with the inauguration of the Betancur administration, the Mexican crisis generated an adverse effect on the supply of capital funds. Finally, the stabilisation programme adopted by the Venezuelan government in February 1983 further reduced legal and illegal exports, border sales, receipts from tourism and the transfers of emigrants.

As we will see in this part of the chapter, the response of the economic authorities to the external crisis changed over time. The Turbay administration did not recognise the rising external disequilibrium. On the other hand, the Betancur administration accepted only gradually and unwillingly the need for external adjustment. For two years, the new administration assumed that economic recovery and the correction of external disequilibria were compatible policy objectives, given the strong reserve position of the country. In mid-1984, this strategy gave way to an orthodox stabilisation programme, in which demand management and rapid devaluation were combined – as a medium-term *desiderata* – with a liberalisation of commercial practices.

Growing Disequilibria

Changing conditions in the coffee market demanded a reversal of external policies, lest balance-of-payments imbalances became unmanageable. The Turbay administration did not recognise, however, the existence of external disequilibria of any sort. On the contrary, economic policy enhanced the growing payments deficit. Import licences reached a peak US $6 billion level, both in 1981 and 1982, while the government linked the peso to the dollar when the latter experienced the first wave of appreciation in the international market. The effect of the latter was a substantial revaluation of the peso between 1980 and the third quarter of 1982, which meant that, by mid-1982, the peso was overvalued by a full 29 per cent in relation to the 1975 'parity' level. Finally, the government consciously encouraged an import-intensive public investment programme. Government imports, excluding oil and foodstuffs, increased from an annual average of $234 million in 1975–8 to $893 million in 1980–2 (*Coyuntura Económica*, October 1984, pp. 66–7).

Accordingly, the deterioration of the current account had three major sources in the early 1980s. First, coffee exports decreased by $700 million, with a simultaneous reduction in other exports by some $300 million. Secondly, imports grew by $1.1 billion. The rising import coefficient did not, however, reflect a sharp expansion of aggregate demand. On the contrary, as we saw in the last section, demand factors became increasingly contractionary during these years. Thus rising imports reflected liberalisation, revaluation and import-intensive public investment policies.[3] In traditional terms, an increasing bias in the *composition* of demand rather than excess expenditure lay behind the higher import level. Finally, as the net debt position of the country deteriorated, with peak interest rates in the world market, net factor payments turned increasingly negative (Table 8.1).

The net result of these developments was a rapid deterioration of the current account. The surplus of $100 million in 1980 had been transformed two years later into a $2.9 billion deficit. Current account disequilibria were financed by extraordinary levels of foreign indebtedness – close to $2 billion in both 1981 and 1982. The economy had definitely entered the Latin American pattern of rapidly rising external debts to finance current account disequilibria and currency overvaluation. By 1982 the extremely solid external position of Colombia had made a radical turn. With current account disequilibria of $2.9 billion and the closing of international capital markets, the threat of a rapid deterioration in the strong reserve position of the country ($5.3 billion in mid-1982) was for the first time quite evident.

Gradual Adjustment

The Betancur administration had a contradictory diagnosis of external conditions. Although it recognised from the outset the need to promote minor exports, to reverse the import liberalisation process and to correct the overvaluation of the peso, balance-of-payments considerations were at first regarded as secondary to the problems raised by the financial crisis, the budget deficit and inertial inflation. In fact, the need for rapid external adjustment was only recognised after the Venezuelan devaluation of February 1983, and even then drastic correction policies were late in coming.

The basic assumption of the administration was that room for manoeuvre was unlimited, given the strong reserve position of the country. Thus, it was possible simultaneously to pursue external and internal policy targets. Balance-of-payments policies focused on traditional instruments: the crawling peg, import rationing, tariff surcharges, export subsidies, exchange controls and prior import deposits. This rather diversified menu, which had been known in the past, implied that external adjustment was rather 'heterodox' in this phase. Nonetheless, it was balanced, since import repression was compounded with exchange depreciation and export promotion policies. However, demand management did not play any role in the process. Rather, fiscal and monetary policies became increasingly expansionary, as the lower trade deficit was not compensated with a similar reduction of the budget deficit, and the falling rate of inflation was not matched by slower monetary expansion.

Although the government did not make an explicit defence of the particular form of external adjustment adopted, it can be justified on several grounds. First of all, the external deficit had little to do with excess demand of any sort. Rather, as we saw in the previous section, the underlying causes were the deterioration of key prices in the international markets (coffee in particular) and policy-induced biases in the *composition* of internal demand. Furthermore, the strong net debt position of the country *and* the favourable export prospects justified recourse to a temporary financing strategy even on very traditional grounds (Londoño and Perry, 1985). Finally, the decision not to use the exchange rate as the major policy instrument reduced the inflationary and contractionary effect of the adjustment process, while maintaining confidence in the crawling peg (Ocampo, 1983).

The first policy measures were adopted in the last months of 1982. The government accelerated the rate of the crawl, raised export subsidies and import tariffs, and transferred some imports from the free to the prior licensing regime. Immediately after the Venezuelan devaluation of early 1983, exchange controls were strengthened. The rate of devaluation was further accelerated in August 1983 as other instruments became increasingly active. The harsher policy decisions had to do with import licensing, where the largest foreign exchange savings could be obtained in a short period. Indecision was paramount in this case. The government did not initially reduce the amount of import registrations. On the contrary, during the first nine months of the Betancur administration (August 1982–April 1983) monthly authorisation reached a level similar to the 1981–2 peak. In April 1983, the government made the first significant move, by massively transferring goods to the prior licensing regime and some to the prohibited list. However, in licensing decisions, the idea continued to prevail that drastic import controls could damage industrial recovery and public investment as a result of the lack of raw materials and imported capital goods. For the first time, the Monetary Board pressed for a strict foreign exchange budget in late 1983, when the rapid fall of reserves was clear. Soon after, in March 1984, harsh import controls were finally established.

Regardless of the lag in the adoption of a strict licensing regime, the gradual adjustment strategy achieved its main objective. Indeed, as Figure 8.2 shows, the trade balance continuously improved from early 1983 and was in equilibrium by the last quarter of 1984. In terms of annual averages, the trade deficit decreased by $1.7 billion between 1982 and 1984. The current account simultaneously improved by $1 billion. Deterioration in the invisible trade (largely due to reduced border sales and tourism from Venezuela) and factor payments account for the difference (Table 8.1). Furthermore, devaluation had been effective in reversing the real appreciation of 1980–2, by late 1984, although it was generally agreed that the peso was still overvalued.

Rapid reversal of the trade account did not impair industrial recovery. On the contrary, import controls were quite effective in improving economic activity, by forcing a substitution of foreign for domestic goods. The stock of imported inputs was reduced, but it created difficulties in only a few industrial sectors, since rationing mechanisms favoured intermediate good imports and there were excess inventories of raw materials and considerable unused capacity at the outset of the recovery. It is even possible that industrial producers and commercial firms massively anticipated import controls, supported by the lax licensing practices of the Turbay and early Betancur administrations. Thus, government precautions in adopting a harsh licensing regime had no empirical support.

While the trade balance improved rapidly a simultaneous deterioration of the capital account led to a significant fall of reserve in

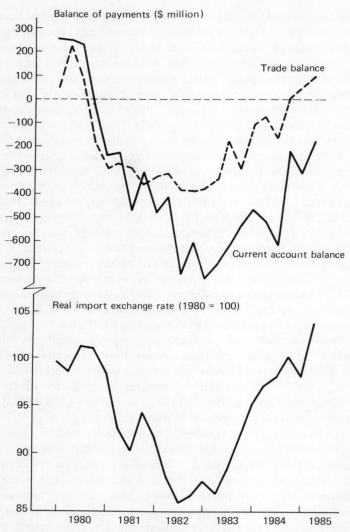

Figure 8.2   Balance of payments and exchange rate: quarterly indicators

Source: Fedesarrollo, *Coyuntura Económica*.

1983 and 1984 (see Table 8.1). This has led some analysts to argue that
capital flight and the Mexican shock were the major sources of external
deterioration during these years.[4] While the evidence of a significant
tightening of the capital market and *some* capital flight is compelling, it

Table 8.4 Determinants of external deterioration, 1981–4 ($ million)

	1981–2	*1983–4*	*1981–4*
Increase in net long-term debt[a]			
Current account deficit	4607	4696	9303
Short-term capital outflow	−706	785	79
Errors and omissions outflow	−207	312	105
	3694	5793	9487
Loss of reserves[b]			
Basic balance deficit	1350	1597	2947
Short-term capital outflow	−706	785	79
Errors and omissions outflow	−207	312	105
	437	2694	3131

Notes:
[a] Net of reserves and short-term assets abroad.
[b] Short-term assets abroad included as part of reserves.

Source: Banco de la República, *National Accounts*.

must be analysed carefully in order to draw accurate conclusions.

Tables 8.4 and 8.5 provide useful complementary evidence on capital flows. As Table 8.4 shows, the current account was the only source of the worsening net debt position of Colombia in the 1981–4 period as a whole. Moreover, the proportion of the current account which was not financed by long-term capital flows was also responsible for the worsening reserve position. Long-term flows did not decrease significantly during these years – the reduction of long-term financing was matched by increasing direct investment in energy projects (see Table 8.1). Short-term capital flows were largely responsible, however, for the different reserve performance of 1981–2 and 1983–4. Indeed, the capital inflows of 1981 and 1982 were quantitatively similar to the capital outflows of the latter years.

Short-term capital flows are partially explained by interest-rate differentials in the two phases.[5] In 1981 and 1982, there were considerable incentives to borrow abroad and to invest in Colombia. As the rate of devaluation accelerated, the contrary was true in 1983 and 1984, particularly when the expectations of massive devaluations are taken into account. However, 'capital flight' is not an adequate description of what took place in the latter years. Under Colombian exchange controls, classical capital flight can only take place through the

Table 8.5   Colombia: foreign debt, 1982–4 ($ million)

	1982	1984	Change
Medium and long term	7270	9527	2257
(i) Public	6078	8090	2012
Multilateral, bilateral agencies and suppliers	3383	4608	1225
Commercial banks	2656	3462	806
Other	39	20	−19
(ii) Private	1192	1437	245
Financial institutions	1090	1142	52
Other	126	186	60
Statistical discrepancy	24	−109	133
Short term	3338	2998	−340
Ecopetrol and Carbocol	470	186	−284
National Coffee Fund	380	468	88
Banco de la República	2	92	90
Other	2486	2252	−234
Total	10 608	12 525	1917

Source: Republic of Colombia, *1985–1986 Financing Plan*, 21 June 1985.

black market for foreign exchange. It only affects the reserve position through the arbitrage between the official and the black markets. The typical measure of this arbitrage – the 'errors and omissions' of the balance of payments – indicates that it was responsible for at most $300 million of reserve losses in 1983–4 and an insignificant $100 million in the period of payments deficit as a whole. More important than capital flight of this sort was the cancelling of short-term debts in 1983 and 1984. It must be clearly borne in mind, however, that this type of capital outflow did not affect the net position of the country, since the reserve loss was matched by an equal reduction in external liabilities. Moreover, these capital flows are largely explained by different trade conditions in 1981–2 and in the latter years. Indeed, since a large proportion of short-term debts are related to import financing, a period of rising imports is accompanied by capital inflows, while a falling import level leads to a capital outflow. The early 1980s were also difficult years for the National Coffee Fund, which was forced to build up large external liabilities to finance stock accumulation and to support domestic prices. However, after reaching $559 million in 1983, the external debt of the Fund was reduced in 1984. Finally, a large proportion of the short-term capital outflows in 1983 and 1984 was related to the debt payments of two government firms – Ecopetrol and Carbocol (see Table 8.5).

In this complex set of developments, policy decisions were partly responsible for the reserve loss of 1983 and 1984. Lack of control over the short-term debt of government institutions (including the National Coffee Fund in 1984) was largely responsible for this outcome, as we have seen. Monetary contraction would certainly have helped to control the private capital outflow. However, it is difficult to defend the point of view that with peak real interest rates in 1983–4 – close to 25 per cent for bank lending – even higher rates were desirable, as some domestic analysts and the IMF missions repeatedly claimed. A more sensible solution was to rely on traditional exchange-control policies to obtain similar results. The obvious proposal was to tie import licences to a matching commercial credit by establishing minimum payment periods for new imports. Alternatively, the government could have reduced the cost of short-term commercial credits – by establishing negative reserve requirements on external liabilities of the banks, for example. It could have gone so far as to force financial institutions to have a minimum ratio of external to internal liabilities, as Brazil had done in the past. The Colombian government finally adopted the first of these recommendations as an emergency policy in late 1984, when private firms had enjoyed a substantial period to adapt to the new situation.

It should be remarked, finally, that the Mexican crisis certainly affected the supply of funds to the country. In particular, it eliminated certain forms of financing – 'clean advances' to domestic banks and general budget financing to the central government, it reduced commercial credit lines for local banks and private bank lending to public institutions, and it resulted in increasingly strict conditions for new lending. Nonetheless, supply conditions were only partially responsible for Colombia's capital inflows in 1983 and 1984.

Even aside from demand considerations – which, as we have seen, affected short-term capital flows – it must be pointed out that the public sector enjoyed considerable room for manoeuvre due to the large stock of undisbursed credits which existed at the outset of the crisis: $3.7 billion in December 1982. Furthermore, from 1982 to 1984 the public debt with commercial banks increased 30 per cent, only slightly less than the growth of debt with multilateral banks, bilateral agencies and suppliers (36 per cent – Table 8.5). The significant fall in new credit commitments in 1983 – $1.4 billion versus $2.4 billion in 1982 – was due in part to the harsher controls on public indebtedness established by the Minister of Finance in late 1982, to reduce the rapid growth of the debt.

Actually, the new credits in 1983 were only slightly lower than the average of the 1979–81 period ($1.5 billion) while the new borrowing programme initiated in mid-1983 led to booming commitments in 1984 of $2.6 million.[6]

The heavy dependence of the Colombian public sector on multilateral, bilateral agencies and suppliers (63 per cent of outstanding loans in 1982) also reduced the impact of the credit squeeze. Indeed, these agencies increased the effective supply of funds to the country, not only in the traditional form of project-financing, but also through balance-of-payments loans under several headings (export promotion, agricultural development, support of the financial and productive sectors and industrial recovery) and through a rollover mechanism managed by the Banco de la República to accelerate disbursements. Finally, new credit commitments from commercial banks in 1984 and the first half of 1985 have been 32 per cent of total new borrowing, slightly less than the share of that type of institution in the outstanding loans in 1982, while they represent 63 per cent of new loans in the final negotiation stages in 1985.[7]

The Orthodox Phase

Some measures adopted by the new Minister of Finance in the second half of 1984 did not constitute a break with the gradual adjustment process that had been taking place since 1982. Minimum payment periods for new imports were established and the magnitude of foreign indebtedness was negotiated with the National Federation of Coffee Growers, to avoid further capital outflows. These measures, together with a balance-of-payments loan from the Andean Reserve Fund, account for the significant slowdown in the fall of reserves which Colombia experienced from late 1984.

The conception of the adjustment process was completely altered, however. This became increasingly clear as negotiations with the IMF, the World Bank and private financial institutions proceeded. The basic element in the new strategy was the emphasis on demand management, which obviously indicated that excess demand was regarded as a basic source of balance-of-payments disequilibria. In 1985 this element was compounded with rapid devaluation to recover the 1975 'parity' level – a real depreciation of some 20 per cent in the year. Finally, following pressures from the World Bank, the government agreed – at least as a medium-term objective – to liberalise the foreign trade regime. This has been reflected in the partial reversal of import controls and tariff policy and in the redesign of the drawback mechanism (Plan Vallejo).

Although orthodox adjustment policies will certainly contribute to the medium-term equilibrium of external accounts, they had minimum effects on the current account of the balance of payments in 1985. Indeed, the government projected a trade balance for the year, an objective which had already been achieved in the last quarter of 1984. This apparent paradox can be explained by recalling that the import level in 1983 and 1984 was not determined by demand but rather by rationing mechanisms, and that most exports (coffee and mineral products) were in the short run independent of exchange-rate policies. Consequently, the significant contribution of the new policy was the confidence it generated. in the international financial community and the corresponding impact on the supply of capital funds. It is therefore unsurprising that orthodox conceptions were so influential in policy design and so disproportional to existing macroeconomic disequilibria in Colombia.

For domestic and international political reasons, the Colombian government followed a negotiation strategy radically different from that of other Latin American countries, with consequences that were not predicted in 1984. In particular, the Betancur administration refused to consider a standby agreement with the IMF, claiming that Colombia had not been subject to economic mismanagement, that it had good export prospects, and that, in any case, self-discipline had been adopted. In the particular strategy followed, the World Bank played a crucial role, both as a supplier of balance-of-payments credits under several headings and as mediator with the private banks. However, the latter did not recognise the World Bank as an adequate interlocutor and demanded IMF support for the adjustment programme. To avoid a standby agreement, IMF monitoring was finally adopted and accepted by the banks. The net result of the negotiation strategy was a proliferation of bargaining tables and increasing conditionality. This element should be emphasised. Indeed, the adjustment programme not only involved an orthodox *macroeconomic* programme under IMF surveillance, but also World Bank interference in *sectoral*, particularly commercial, policies.

THE FISCAL DEFICIT

Origin of Existing Disequilibria

When the Turbay administration was inaugurated in 1978, public finances were in virtual equilibrium. By 1982, however, the central national government and the public sector as a whole were running large deficits – 4.5 per cent and 8.1 per cent of GDP respectively – the highest in the history of Colombia.

Several developments explain this trend. As we saw in the first section above, the Turbay administration adopted from the outset an expansionary public investment programme. However, investment explained only a small proportion of the increasing deficit. Equally important elements were changing conditions in the world coffee market, the slow growth of tax receipts and the rapid increase of government consumption. Changing market conditions forced the National Coffee Fund to accumulate large stocks from late 1980 to late 1983 and to defend internal prices. Falling tax receipts of the central national government (which fell from 9.1 per cent of GDP in 1978 to 8.0 per cent in 1982) were associated with recession, the 1979 tax cut and rising evasion. Finally, the rapid increase in government consumption reflected a less explicit expansionary policy.

Although the budget deficit was matched by rising current account disequilibria, it is very difficult to identify the former as the underlying cause of the latter. Even in accounting terms, the increasing external deficit was associated to a large extent with a falling private surplus (see Table 8.7 below). This indicates, in turn, that domestic aggregate demand was weakening and, therefore, that the expansionary fiscal policy was insufficient to counteract the contractionary pressures coming from falling coffee income and rising imports. Weakening export markets and demand composition policies were, indeed, the fundamental causes of the higher balance of payments deficit, as we saw in the last section.

The concept that the external disequilibria reflected expansionary expenditure policies had few defenders in 1982. Orthodox criticism of the deficit concentrated on the crowding out effects of public on private expenditure. This 'closed-economy orthodoxy', as we will call it, was widely diffused by the pressure groups and differed from the 'open-economy orthodoxy' that spread in 1983 and 1984. It claimed that the deficit pushed up interest rates, inducing a contraction of private activity and recession. The empirical bases for this hypothesis were rather weak, as we will see shortly.

In the alternative conception of fisal policy that was developed in 1982, the deficit was viewed as *compensating* balance-of-payments disequilibria. The basic assumption was that the latter originated in a combination of exogenous forces and import biases generated by foreign trade policies. Under these circumstances, it was necessary to adjust the fiscal to the current account deficit, to avoid either greater recession (if the fiscal deficit was rapidly reduced) or excessive monetary expansion (if it lagged behind). If the former effect was dominant (as was clear in 1982), higher public investment in domestic goods was required, financed by higher taxes, lower import-intensive investment projects, or public debt. If the second effect prevailed (as was clear in late 1984), it was necessary to raise taxes or reduce import-intensive investments, to avoid the greater contractionary effects of lower domestic expenditure. Deficit financing would be provided by external sources or by monetary credits, as long as the external sector generated an autonomous contractionary effect on the money supply. If the latter effect was not present, a rising share of the deficit would be financed by domestic credits – both bonds and 'forced savings'. It was thus possible simultaneously to achieve fiscal targets compatible with external equilibrium and monetary stability.[8]

The Betancur Administration

The fiscal policy of the Betancur administration has had elements of continuity but it has also undergone different policy phases, in which it has alternately supported orthodox and heterodox perspectives. The basic element of continuity has been tax policy. Between 1983 and 1985 the government implemented four reforms. The first of them focused on income and local taxes; it was adopted by Congress in mid-1983 after the failed 'economic emergency' of late 1982 and early 1983. The second transformed the sales tax into a value added tax, extending to industrial, wholesale and retail sales and some services. It was decreed in December and became effective in April of the following year. The third tax reform was adopted by Congress in December 1984. It included an additional 8 per cent tariff on all imports – except foodstuffs and agricultural inputs imported by the government – the elimination of several exemptions to the sales tax, and forced savings in government bonds proportional to the income tax. The last reform, adopted in mid-1985, included a partial redistribution of earmarked revenues within government, a significant extension of the withholding mechanism for the income tax, the partial elimination of income tax exemptions for Ecopetrol and Carbocol, and the abrogation of the declaration form for wage-earners.

Tax reforms have been quite effective. Regardless of the slow growth of taxes on foreign trade (import and coffee taxes), the current income of the national government increased from 8.0 per cent of GDP in 1982 to 8.7 per cent in 1984 and to 9.7 per cent in 1985, one of the highest levels in the history of the country. The erosion of the tax base, which had been taking place since the mid-1970s, has thus been rapidly reversed. The 1983 reform also had significant effects on local taxes (Aghon *et al.*, 1985), whereas the relative price of public services has been increasing for some time.

In relation to public expenditure and deficit financing, the government has undergone three different phases, in which it has shared completely different conceptions of the budget deficit. In the first phase it supported the idea that the deficit was 'crowding out' private activity. In the second, it attempted a short-lived Keynesian recovery. Finally, since mid-1984, it has adopted an orthodox conception of the deficit as the source of external disequilibria.

Closed-economy orthodoxy

The most common criticism of the fiscal deficit in 1982 concentrated on the foreign exchange account, i.e. the profits from the management of foreign exchange reserves. Although these profits were then a current income of the national government, economic analysts regarded them as identical to a Central Bank credit to the government (Jaramillo and Montenegro, 1982; Montenegro, 1983a). Thus, critics of the budget deficit argued that they crowded out private credits. This criticism assumed that there were no autonomous sources of monetary contraction in the external sector, that interest rates were determined by domestic factors, and that high interest rates were the basic source of the recession. On all these grounds the empirical bases for this kind of orthodoxy were weak. In fact, the current account of the balance of payments was already a gigantic force of monetary contraction, interest rates were at least partially related to parity levels (international rates plus devaluation) and there is no significant evidence of private investment sensitivity to interest rates in Colombia (Ocampo, 1984; Ocampo *et al.*, 1985).

The administration's proposal included a complete sterilisation of profits from foreign exchange management, to be replaced by tax receipts and other forms of domestic credit; simultaneously, the larger monetary margin would be used to support private credit. The proposed reform of the foreign exchange account was only partially adopted during the economic emergency of late 1982 and early 1983. In fact, by then it was evident that the budget was considerably underfinanced. As a reflection of this problem, the government adopted a discretionary mechanism by which it could lend or sterilise the foreign exchange profits according to monetary conditions. Since most emergency tax laws were declared unconstitutional by the Supreme Court, the only reform that came out as originally planned was the creation of national savings bonds, which could be used to obtain substantial non-monetary deficit financing on the basis of the experience that the Banco de la República had acquired during the years of massive open market operations.

According to the orthodox conception that prevailed, the government attempted a simultaneous expansionary private credit policy. Major instruments were the creation of large credit lines in the Central Bank for private companies under severe financial strains and the reduction of reserve requirements. The net result of this policy was a fiasco. Banks, which had been facing severe financial difficulties since mid-1982 as a reflection of the impact of recession and the increasing fragility that had been building up during the boom years, used the new credit opportunities very carefully. This process was then called a 'liquidity trap', although it differed significantly from the similar Keynesian concept. Moreover, when the credit expansion was effective, the recovery did not follow, since no company was ready to invest in the bottom of the recession, under fragile financial conditions and record high interest rates (Perry, 1984).

The short-lived Keynesian recovery

In the first half of 1983 two events led the government to change its policy stance. The first was the deep recession experienced by the Colombian economy in the second half of 1982 and the first quarter of 1983 (the second section above). Secondly, monetary contraction generated by the external sector reached peak levels, as credit policy to the private sector proved inadequate. Economic authorities thought that it was necessary to compensate monetary contraction, lest the recession should deepen. Thus, the immediate *cause* of fiscal expansion was reserve contraction. Very soon, however, economic analysts changed their minds over the causal link and claimed that the source of the reserve fall was fiscal expansion.

The basic policy measure was the approval by Congress in mid-1983 of a financing package, which raised the ordinary credit lines of the Treasury in the Central Bank and created a 'reactivation credit line' of Col.$ 60 billion (equivalent to 2 per cent of GDP in that year), of which 60 per cent could be used in that same year. Monetary financing enabled

Table 8.6   Fiscal surplus or deficit, 1980–5 (% of GDP at current prices)

	1980	1981	1982	1983	1984	1985[a]
Central national government (Fedesarrollo)						
Excluding interest payments	−2.3	−3.0	−3.6	−3.5	−3.2	−1.1
Total	−2.8	−3.7	−4.5	−4.1	−4.0	−1.9
Monetary financing	1.3	1.9	3.4	3.8	3.9	1.3
Consolidated public sector (DANE)						
National and local governments[b]	−2.8	−3.8	−4.4	−4.7		
Social security	0.4	0.4	0.2	0.2		
Public enterprises	−2.2	−1.9	−3.4	−3.7		
Total, excluding National Coffee Fund	−4.6	−5.4	−7.5	−8.1		
National Coffee Fund	1.3	−0.9	−0.6	−0.8		
Total	−3.3	−6.3	−8.1	−9.0		
Consolidated public sector (IMF)[c]						
Excluding interest payments				−5.8	−5.4	−2.1
Total				−7.6	−7.7	−4.9

Notes:
[a] Projections, assuming 24 per cent nominal GDP growth.
[b] 1980–2: excluding income tax 'liquidaciones oficiales'.
[c] Excluding National Coffee Fund.

Sources: Fedesarrollo, *Coyuntura Económica*; DANE, *National Accounts*; IMF, *Memoranda*.

government expenditure to recover after the slow execution typical of the first half-year. As Table 8.6 shows, Central Bank funds were almost the sole source of net central government financing in 1983, although they increased only marginally as a share of GDP – indeed, the new funds largely replaced the reduced foreign exchange profits and the exhaustion of the ordinary Treasury credit line in the Central Bank.

The strategy soon encountered difficulties, as the government could not guarantee sufficient funds to maintain fiscal expansion and thought that Congress would not approave a new credit package. Tax receipts were overestimated by some Col.$ 60 billion in the 1984 budget. Later, in early 1984, facing cash difficulties once more, the government used the Banco de la República warranty on the national savings bonds to get monetary financing without congressional approval.

As a reflection of increasing financing difficulties, the rising trend of the budget deficit was partially reversed in 1984. Indeed, excluding the National Coffee Fund, the consolidated public deficit decreased from 8.1

Table 8.7 Colombia: savings and investment balances, 1980–4 (% of GDP at current prices)

	1980	1981	1982	1983	1984
External savings	− 0.3	4.7	7.4	7.3	5.1
Public sector, excluding the National Coffee Fund	− 4.6	− 5.4	− 7.5	− 8.1	− 7.7
National Coffee Fund	1.3	− 0.9	− 0.6	− 0.8	0.6
Private sector	3.6	1.6	0.7	1.6	2.0

Sources: External savings: estimated on the basis of balance-of-payments statistics; public sector and National Coffee Fund: Table 8.6 and estimates for 1984; private sector: calculated as a residual.

per cent to 7.7 per cent of GDP; including the coffee sector, it decreased from 9.0 per cent to 7.1 per cent. The national government deficit had already started to decline in 1983 and continued to do so in 1984. Excluding rising interest payments to serve the foreign debt, the reduction of the deficit was even more noticeable (see Tables 8.6 and 8.7).

The new orthodoxy

For all economic observers, it was evident in late 1984 that current account equilibrium with the rest of the world had proceeded faster than fiscal adjustment. Although this was reflected in a rather significant recovery of economic activity, the threat of a monetary outburst was evident, unless the budget deficit was reduced or a new financing strategy designed. This fact, together with the rapid fall of international reserves in 1983 and 1984, finally strengthened the arm of would-be defenders of the open-economy orthodoxy, according to which excess demand is the *source* of external disequilibria.

This point of view had two variants, which were emphasised at different times. The first, associated with the capital flight controversy, claimed that any Central Bank credit was used to accumulate foreign assets – through the black market – or to cancel external liabilities, thus depressing international reserves. The *monetary* aspects of the budget deficit and the *capital* account of the balance of payments were thus emphasised. According to this argument, to avoid the portfolio reallocation induced by the expectations of devaluation, it was necessary to adopt a contractionary monetary policy, which would adjust the supply of money to the reduced domestic demand. However, under the conditions typical of the last few years, this was only possible if fiscal objectives were simultaneously given up. The second variant emphasised the *real* connections. According to the absorption approach to the balance of payments, excess public expenditure was seen as the source of a *current* account deficit with the rest of the world. Although both points of view tended to be mixed together (since they are by no means contradictory), it should be noted that the first version became popular after 1983, while the second has been used only recently, reflecting the emphasis on excess expenditure as the source of external disequilibria.

Both variants are theoretically and empirically flawed. As we saw in the third section above, the current account deficit was associated with external events and with the demand composition policies of the Turbay administration. Moreover, by late 1984, the non-factor current account deficit had been substantially reduced – i.e. in accounting terms, excess demand was almost non-existent. On the other hand, as we saw in the previous section, the expansionary monetary and fiscal policies of 1983 were initially designed to counteract *autonomous* monetary contractions generated by the external sector. Finally, the short-term capital outflow had many underlying motives, while it was possible, with Colombian exchange controls, to correct many of them without resorting to contractionary monetary policies (see the third section above).

Theoretical problems are related to the role of the budget deficit, import controls and devaluation in the adjustment process. As we saw earlier, import rationing eliminates the traditional link between the current account and aggregate demand. This explains why demand contraction in 1985 had no significant effects on the current account. This apparent paradox can be explained by considering the peculiar macroeconomic adjustment that takes place under import controls. The rationing of foreign goods and services generates a diversion of expenditure to locally produced goods and services. But to the extent that switching is not total, there is also *involuntary disabsorption* (forced savings on the part of consumers and disinvestment by firms), as investment plans cannot materialise, the stock of imported goods is reduced, and consumers face a rationed supply of import-intensive goods (Cuddington *et al.*, 1984; Ocampo, 1985). This form of adjustment is at the root of improvements in the current account, as the traditional absorption approach has argued (Hemming and Corden, 1958). Obviously, many of the underlying processes are only temporary, but while they operate they represent useful adjustment mechanisms since, contrary to devaluation, they have a clearly expansionary effect on domestic economic activity.

From a macroeconomic perspective, this indicates that import controls tend to increase the private surplus – or to reduce the private deficit – as a counterpart of the improving current account (see Table 8.7 on the rising private surplus in Colombia between 1982 and 1984). Under these conditions, cuts in the budget deficit in the recent stabilisation programme spent themselves out in the reduction of the private surplus – through higher taxes and the contractionary effects of expenditure policies – without noticeable effects on the current account.

Simultaneous exchange-rate adjustments reinforced the private-cum-coffee surplus. Indeed, the quasi-rents associated with devaluation generated a substantial improvement in the finances of the National Coffee Fund (Table 8.7) and minor exporters. The wage content of the new rents was minimal, since internal coffee prices were not increased in real terms and minor exports were inelastic to price incentives in the short run, reflecting a very weak employment response. The high tax and profit content of the new income generated in the export sector improved net savings in the economy, with a contractionary effect on internal demand (*Coyuntura Económica*, April 1985).

From the point of view of non-coffee public finances, the effect of fixing a *nominal* fiscal target in an economy experiencing exchange-rate depreciation must also be emphasised. Indeed, factor payments abroad represented the single most important component of the 1985 fiscal deficit (Table 8.6). The rise in the share of interest payments abroad by the public sector – from 1.8 per cent of GDP in 1983 to 2.8 per cent in 1985, according to IMF calculations – reflected the joint impact of the rapid increase in the foreign debt in the late 1970s and early 1980s and devaluation in recent years. In this context, the nominal fiscal target adopted for 1985 generated an additional contractionary effect on domestic expenditure.

There were thus elements of redundancy and overkill in the recent stabilisation programme. In particular, too many instruments were directed towards improving the net savings position of the country, but their joint effect on the current account of the balance of payments was not noticeable. The basic reason was that improvements in the net savings position generated by fiscal adjustment and devaluation largely occurred at the expense of net savings previously generated by import controls. There were, in addition, contractionary effects on domestic economic activity, which were unproductive given the short-run insensitivity of imports to effective demand. It would be quite counterproductive if, in these circumstances, the government were to take seriously the World Bank and IMF recommendation to lift import controls in the near future. This would generate a contractionary effect on internal demand while forcing the government to adopt even harsher demand management policies.

SUMMARY AND PROSPECTS

The recession experienced by the Colombian economy in the first half of the 1980s has been moderate by Latin American standards. In particular, per capita GDP still remains at pre-recession levels and debt ratios do not represent a great obstacle to future development. This reflects the favourable external conditions that the economy experienced in the second half of the 1970s and cautious economic management, which allowed the economy to face the new decade with an unquestionably strong net debt position. Nonetheless, external and internal deterioration has been substantial in the 1980s. The external debt increased rapidly, as the economy faced the worst recession since the 1930s and a substantial aggravation of labour market conditions. Moveover, Colombia underwent the typical phases of the Latin American crisis in the early 1980s: a period of increasing external imbalances, followed by phases of domestic management of existing disequilibria and orthodox policies with increasing external conditionality.

The first of the aforementioned phases came with a substantial lag compared with other countries in the region. Nonetheless, facing a substantial deterioration in the coffee market in 1980, the Turbay administration did not take any steps to reverse worsening payments balances. On the contrary, import liberalisation policies were pushed forward and the exchange rate was further revalued. Large current account deficits were financed by peak borrowing in the international markets. Expansionary fiscal policies adopted for development purposes in the boom years were inadequate to overturn the contractionary effects of falling coffee incomes and rising imports. Thus, growth came to a standstill and the economy faced a deep recession when the new administration was inaugurated in August 1982.

The Betancur administration confronted two additional external shocks: the tightening of the international capital market and the Venezuelan crisis. After initial hesitation, the government adopted a programme of gradual external adjustments and expansionary internal policies. The basic assumptions of this strategy were, on the one hand, that excess demand was not the origin of the external deficit and, on the other, that economic policy enjoyed substantial room for manoeuvre, given the strong reserve position of the country.

External adjustment policies were based on traditional policy instruments: import and exchange controls, the crawling peg, higher tariffs and export promotion policies. Relative emphasis on import controls permitted a rapid improvement in the trade account with favourable substitution effects on domestic economic activity. Furthermore, the strategy did not face supply constraints, as rationing mechanisms favoured raw material imports and firms initially held excess inventories of foreign goods.

The strategy was effective in re-establishing trade balance equilibrium by the last quarter of 1984, while simultaneously experiencing a recovery. However, the loss of reserves was substantial, reflecting the impact of accumulated external shocks and lags in the adoption of harsh import controls and policy measures to prevent short-term capital outflows. The recovery was also short-lived, as the government faced increasing financial constraints. Finally, the recovery was insufficient to reverse deteriorating labour market conditions.

The loss of reserves and the increasing difficulties of ensuring adequate non-monetary budget financing gave way to an orthodox stabilisation programme in mid-1984. In the new strategy, external adjustment and internal economic activity were regarded as incompatible policy objectives. Demand management policies had the predicted effects on domestic economic activity but no substantial impact on the current account, as imports were determined in 1983 and 1984 by rationing mechanisms and most exports were not sensitive to exchange-rate management in the short run.

The most significant effect of the new strategy was the capacity to generate confidence in the international financial community. However, the negotiation process adopted by the government to avoid an IMF standby agreement was rather complex, involving multiple negotiation tables and increasing conditionality. The latter was reflected in IMF surveillance of macroeconomic policies and increasing World Bank influence in sectoral, particularly commercial, policies.

Although orthodox stabilisation will affect economic growth in 1985 and 1986, the prospects for recovery are nevertheless quite favourable in Colombia. Indeed, the gestation of long-term projects in the energy sector – coal and oil – indicates that exports will grow at one of the highest rates in Latin America in the rest of the decade (see, for example, van Ryckeghem, 1985). Prospects for a moderate recovery of the international coffee market are also good (World Bank, 1984), while the new minor export strategy will have at least moderate success, according to current projections.

Economic recovery may, however, prove frustrating if a set of unfavourable conditions are combined. First of all, world energy prices may collapse, reducing Colombian exports and the prospects for a Venezuelan recovery. Secondly, monopolistic behaviour by international banking may continue to spread, backed by IMF and World Bank neo-conservatism. This could force the Colombian government to maintain negotiations and, most important, to push austerity programmes beyond reasonable limits. Similar results may obtain from the pressure of domestic political forces which constitute the domestic counterpart of international banking doctrines. Indeed, as the recent Venezuelan experience with contractionary policies under conditions of fiscal and external *surplus* shows, 'austerity' doctrines tend to have a strong political appeal for certain groups. Thirdly, the new export boom may unleash new forms of the 'Dutch' disease. They might not result, however, from real appreciation, but rather from World Bank and internal pressures for import liberalisation. This situation may be compounded by difficulties in transferring the economic surplus generated in the energy and coffee sectors – the latter due to rapid devaluation in the last few years – to the rest of the economy. In particular, regional pressures and the relative autonomy of public institutions may place considerable constraints on the efficient allocation of rising profits and rents. Finally, 'structural' problems inherited from the 1970s and the recent recession – a weakened industrial sector, lagging foodstuffs supply, a fragile financial system and conservative recruitment practices – may hinder economic recovery, unless special policies are designed to counteract them.

Notes

1. This chapter is part of a larger project on adjustment policies in Latin America, financed by the Ford Foundation. Previous versions were presented at the 45th Congress of Americanists, Universidad de los Andes, July 1985, and the Workshop on Adjustment Policies, Fedesarrollo, September 1985. I am particularly indebted to Rosemary Thorp for detailed comments on previous drafts. I am also grateful to Carlos Caballero, Mauricio Cabrera, Oscar Landerretche, Juan Luis Londoño and Eduardo Lora for useful suggestions.
2. The income from the drug trade must not be overemphasised. During the peak years of the trade, Junguito and Caballero (1978) estimated that only $500 million entered the country – i.e. one-fourth of peak coffee sales and a minuscule part of the real drug trade.

3. Lora (1984) estimated that 53 per cent ($904 million a year) of the trade deficit in 1980–3 could be attributed to a higher import coefficient (due to liberalisation and revaluation) and 15 per cent ($256 million a year) to the deterioration of the terms of trade. Rising interest rates were also an important factor in the worsening current account, representing $375 million a year in the same period. Londoño and Perry (1985), on the other hand, estimated that 88 per cent of the rising import coefficient between 1978–9 and 1982 could be attributed to revaluation (29 per cent), the higher investment coefficient (19 per cent) and liberalisation (40 per cent, estimated as the residual values of the regressions).

4. The capital flight was emphasised by *Estrategia Económica y Financiera* in 1983 and 1984 – see particularly 'Reactivación o crisis cambiaria', May 1983. For further discussion, see *Coyuntura Económica*, June 1983, pp. 95–8, and March 1984, pp. 168–72.

5. If measured by term deposits, Colombian interest rates were above parity levels (US rates plus devaluation) in most of 1980–2, but were significantly below them from the second quarter of 1983 onwards (*Coyuntura Económica*, March 1984, p. 170).

6. All data taken from Banco de la República, *Deuda Externa de Colombia, 1970–1984*, April 1985.

7. See Mauricio Cabrera, 'Situación actual de los cupos de endeudamiento interno y externo', *Memorandum*, Ministerio de Hacienda, 22 July 1985.

8. This paragraph summarises the points of view of Fedesarrollo since 1982 – see particularly Ocampo and Perry (1983), Ocampo (1984) and *Coyuntura Económica*, October 1984. See also Fernández (1982a, 1982b) for a defence of the expansionary fiscal policy of the Turbay administration.

References

AGHON, G., ALVAREZ, B. and CADENA, H., 'Ley 14 de 1983: Primeros Resultados', *Revista de Planeación y Desarrollo*, vol. XVII, no. 1, March 1985.

CHICA, R., 'El Desarrollo Industrial Colombiano, 1958–1980', *Desarrollo y Sociedad*, no. 12, September 1983.

Coyuntura Económica, several issues, quarterly publication of Fedesarrollo.

CUDDINGTON, J. T., JOHANSSON, P-O. and LOFGREN, K-G., *Disequilibrium Macroeconomics in Open Economies* (Oxford: Basil Blackwell, 1984).

DNP (Departamento Nacional de Planeación), *Plan de Integración Nacional* (Bogotá: Biblioteca des Desarrollo – DNP, 1979).

ECHAVARRÍA, J. J., CABALLERO, C. and LONDOÑO, J. L., 'El Proceso de Industrialización: Algunas Ideas sobre un Viejo Debate', *Coyuntura Económica*, vol. XIII, no. 3, September 1983.

EDWARDS, S., 'Coffee, Money and Inflation in Colombia', *World Development*, vol. 12, no. 11–12, 1984.

FERNÁNDEZ, J., 'El Problema Fiscal en Colombia', in *Déficit Fiscal* (Bogotá: Contraloría General de la República – FESCOL, 1982a).

FERNÁNDEZ, J., 'Reactivación, Estabilización y Fortalecimiento Económico', *Coyuntura Económica*, vol. XII, no. 3, October 1982b.

HEMMING, M. F. W. and CORDEN, W. M., 'Import Restrictions as an Instrument of Balance of Payments Policy', *Economic Journal*, September 1958.

JARAMILLO, J. C., 'La Liberación del Mercado Financiero', *Ensayos sobre Política Económica*, no. 1, March 1982.

JARAMILLO, J. C. and MONTENEGRO, A., 'Cuenta Especial de Cambios: Descripción y Análisis de su Evolución Reciente', *Ensayos sobre Política Económica*, no. 2, September 1982.

JUNGUITO, R. and CABALLERO, C., 'La Otra Economía', *Coyuntura Económica*, December 1978.

KALMANOVITZ, S., 'La Rentabilidad Decreciente de la Industria Colombiana', *Controversia*, no. 119, October 1984.

LONDOÑO, J. L., 'Ahorro y Gasto en una Economía Heterogénea: el Rol Macroeconómico del Mercado de Alimentos', *Coyuntura Económica*, vol. XV, no. 4, December 1985.

LONDOÑO, J. L. and PERRY, G., 'El Banco Mundial, el Fondo Monetario y Colombia: Análisis Crítico de sus Relaciones', *Coyuntura Económica*, vol. XV, no. 3, October 1985.

LORA, E., 'Factores Explicativos del Desequilibrio Comercial Externo', *Revista de Planeación y Desarrollo*, vol. XVI, no. 2–3, April–September 1984.

MONTENEGRO, A., 'Aspectos Macroeconómicos de las Utilidades por Compraventa de Divisas de la Cuenta Especial de Cambios', *Ensayos sobre Política Económica*, no. 3, April 1983a.

MONTENEGRO, A., 'La Crisis del Sector Financiero Colombiano', *Ensayos sobre Política Económica*, no. 4, December 1983b.

OCAMPO, J. A., 'En Defensa de la Continuidad del Régimen Cambiario', *Coyuntura Económica*, vol. XIII, no. 1, March 1983.

OCAMPO, J. A., 'El Sector Externo y la Política Macroeconómica', in Ocampo (ed.) *La Política Económica en la Encrucijada* (Bogotá: Banco de la República – CEDE, 1984).

OCAMPO, J. A., 'El Impacto Macroeconómico del Control de Importaciones', *Ensayos sobre Política Económica*, no. 8, December 1985.

OCAMPO, J. A. and PERRY, G., 'La Reforma Fiscal, 1982–1983', *Coyuntura Económica*, vol. XIII, no. 1, March 1983.

OCAMPO, J. A., LONDOÑO, J. L. and VILLAR, L., 'Ahorro e Inversión en Colombia', *Coyuntura Económica*, vol. XV, no. 2, June 1985.

PERRY, G., 'La Política Económica de la Administración Betancur', *Coyuntura Económica*, vol. XIV, no. 3, October 1984.

VAN RYCKEGHEM, W., 'National Responses to the Debt Crisis', mimeo (Inter-American Development Bank, 1985).

VILLAR, L., 'Nuevas Tendencias del Endeudamiento Externo Colombiano', *Coyuntura Económica*, vol. XIII, no. 3, September 1983.

WORLD BANK, *Price Prospects for Major Primary Commodities*, report no. 814, 1984.

9 The Balance-of-Payments Crisis and Adjustment Programmes in Central America

Victor Bulmer-Thomas

INTRODUCTION

Four events of unusual significance for Central America occurred in 1979: oil prices rose sharply, world interest rates started to increase, the Sandinista-led revolution succeeded in overthrowing Somoza's government in Nicaragua, and General Romero was ousted in El Salvador. The first two events had a direct impact on the region's external payments, but the other two (although usually viewed in political or even geopolitical terms) also had a profound influence on the regional balance of payments. In the years after 1979, each republic at one time or another experienced a major problem of external disequilibrium, and it is for this reason that the title of this chapter refers to the balance-of-payments *crisis* in the singular.

The initial response to the crisis was uniform. Each republic tried to surmount the disequilibrium through additional finance, the implicit assumption being that the disequilibrium was temporary;[1] at first, no serious effort at adjustment was made, although El Salvador and Nicaragua could argue with some justification that their economies had already 'adjusted' through the decline in economic activity associated with civil unrest.[2]

The need for adjustment could not be postponed indefinitely, however, and the financing (FN) phase gave way to an adjustment phase beginning in general in 1981. These adjustment programmes varied in content and impact, as each republic adapted the policy mix to its own peculiar socioeconomic and political environment. Thus, we may talk of adjustment *programmes* in the plural.

Unlike many other republics in Latin America, the Central American republics had in general avoided the need for adjustment at the time of the first oil crisis (1973–4). This was due to the sharp improvement in the

271

external terms of trade (TOT) starting in 1975, which by 1976 had pushed TOT above the pre-oil crisis level.[3] Deviations of real GDP from the trend rate of growth during much of the 1970s are therefore more easily explained by natural disasters (hurricanes, earthquakes) than by adjustment programmes.[4]

Consequently, Central America entered its adjustment phase after the second oil crisis with no recent experience of International Monetary Fund (IMF) conditionality. Talks did take place with the Fund and several credits were approved subject to conditionality;[5] all such credits agreed before the second half of 1982 were suspended, however, as a result of the recipients failing to meet IMF-agreed targets.

We may therefore speak of an 'adjustment without conditionality' (AWOC) phase covering in each republic part of the period 1980 to 1982. As we shall see, adjustment certainly occurred, but it did not in general comply with IMF conditions, while two republics (El Salvador and Nicaragua) did not in any case operate under IMF conditionality during this phase.[6]

In 1982, the need for an IMF-agreed programme of adjustment subject to conditionality became more pressing, as the problem of external finance and debt rescheduling became more acute. By 1983, all Central American republics (except Nicaragua) were involved in IMF-inspired adjustment programmes. Thus we may speak of an 'adjustment with conditionality' (AWIC) phase covering part of the period 1982 to 1984, while the performance of the Nicaraguan economy deviates from the general pattern after 1982.

The AWIC phase (excluding Nicaragua) had ended everywhere by early 1984; by the end of the year the beginnings of a very modest recovery were apparent in Central America and it is tempting to speak of a 'post-adjustment recovery' phase. Only Costa Rica reached a new agreement with the Fund,[7] although Guatemala and Honduras may do so in 1986.[8] The recovery since the end of 1983 lacks firm foundations, however, and the underlying external disequilibrium has not been resolved; there is also an inconsistency between short-term policy and the region's long-term needs.

ORIGINS OF THE BALANCE OF PAYMENTS CRISIS

The choice of finance over adjustment is appropriate where the balance-of-payments (BOP) disequilibrium is temporary in nature. A disturbance to BOP equilibrium can be external or internal in origin, but

this should not affect the choice between finance and adjustment.[9] The initial decision in Central America to respond to the BOP crisis with finance therefore hinges on whether the disturbances to BOP equilibrium could be construed as temporary.

The outward and visible sign of the crisis was the massive loss of gross international reserves in the years after 1978, although significantly this decline begins earlier in Nicaragua. The problem is therefore one of determining the causes of this reserve loss. The deterioration in the current account BOP deficit is often taken as an indicator of reserve loss, but this is not appropriate where (as in Central America) the current account is traditionally in deficit and financed 'autonomously' through long-term capital flows.

A more appropriate indicator is the basic balance, i.e. the current account deficit adjusted for long-term capital flows. We may therefore ask what proportion of the reserve loss was due to a deterioration in the basic balance and what proportion was due to changes in short-term capital flows (including net errors and omissions).

The answer is provided by Table 9.1, which shows that during the

Table 9.1 Balance-of-payments contributions to cumulative reserve losses (inclusive of exceptional financing)

	Period (end-year)	(1) %	(2) %	(3) Total loss (million SDR)
Costa Rica	1978–81	+ 72.7	+ 27.3	774.2
El Salvador	1978–81	− 8.5	+ 108.5	399.6
Guatemala	1978–81	+ 21.2	+ 78.8	492.6
Honduras	1979–82	+ 113.6	− 13.6	194.8
Nicaragua	1977–80	− 67.9	+ 167.9	288.7

Notes:
Col. (1) = percentage contribution of current account deficit net of long-term capital flows to cumulative reserve loss.
Col. (2) = percentage contribution of short-term capital flows (inclusive of net errors and omissions, but exclusive of exceptional financing) to cumulative reserve loss.
Col. (3) = reserve loss defined to include exceptional financing, e.g. payments arrears, rescheduling of debt in arrears, loans from Central American Monetary Stabilisation Fund.

Source: IMF, *Balance of Payments Yearbook* (1984).

period of heavy reserve loss the major cause of disequilibrium was changes in short-term capital flows in El Salvador, Guatemala and Nicaragua, while in Costa Rica changes in such flows accounted for nearly 30 per cent of the deterioration.

It may be objected that Table 9.1 is distorted by the inclusion of net errors and omissions in short-term capital flows. This is unlikely to be true; the sign of 'net errors and omissions' in Central America's BOP presentations is not random. On the contrary, 75 per cent of all observations in the IMF *Balance of Payments Yearbook* since 1975 (inclusive) have appeared with a negative sign, suggesting that 'net errors and omissions' is a vehicle for capital flight.

The key element in short-term capital flows has been 'other short-term capital of other sectors'. This includes changes in the US bank accounts of Central American residents, the other important entry being trade credits. The drying-up of trade credits after 1978 is clearly related to developments in the international financial system and could therefore be construed optimistically as 'temporary', but the outflow of private capital to US bank accounts requires a more sophisticated explanation.

The two conventional explanations of such outflows are interest-rate differentials and the expectation of exchange-rate depreciation. Neither carries much weight in an understanding of Central America's capital flight problem. It is true that US interest rates rose sharply in 1979, but this was matched to some extent in Central America. Indeed, Costa Rica launched its ill-fated 'financial liberalisation' programme (with a sharp increase in interest rates) in October 1978,[10] but this could not prevent an increase in 1979 of SDR 62.3 million (US $80.5 million) in claims on US banks.

Expectation of exchange-rate depreciation is also unconvincing as an explanation of private capital flows. It is true that Nicaragua devalued in 1979 shortly before the fall of Somoza, but the outflow of private capital began in 1977; similarly, the Costa Rican currency was floated in December 1980, but the outflow began much earlier. Meanwhile, capital outflows were of great importance from Guatemala and El Salvador, two countries with a very long history of exchange-rate stability.[11]

Both interest-rate differentials and exchange-rate expectations no doubt provide part of the explanation for the private capital outflow. More convincing, however, is the concept of political uncertainty as a cause of capital flight; thus, Nicaraguan investors, aware as early as 1977 that the future of the Somoza government was not secure, began to withdraw capital. By the time of Somoza's fall, Nicaraguan capital flight was more or less complete (at least in its first stage), but the Sandinista victory provoked capital flight elsewhere.[12] This was reinforced by the fall of General Romero in October 1979 in El Salvador and by the sequence of events throughout the region.[13]

Much of this capital flight was clearly not of a temporary nature. In the Nicaraguan case, the capital outflow (much of it belonging to the Somoza family) was lost forever, and the probability of capital repatriation in El Salvador, following the reform programme of early 1980,[14] could only be considered low. Both Guatemala and Costa Rica, on the other hand, could reasonably have expected a reversal of the capital outflow if the regional political environment improved. As the environment steadily deteriorated, however, it became clear that a reversal of capital flight could not be expected in the short term.

Despite the problems created by capital flight, virtually nothing was done to correct it. During 1980, Guatemala and Honduras introduced exchange control, but it was very mild and largely ineffective; El Salvador legalised dollar deposit accounts towards the end of 1980 in an effort to reverse capital outflows, but the result was unimpressive. Nicaragua and El Salvador nationalised their banking systems in 1979 and 1980 respectively, but by then the bulk of the capital outflows had already taken place. In effect, a decision was taken at least tacitly in each republic to finance the outflows by running down reserves accumulated during the years of high coffee prices in the second half of the 1970s.

The other element in the balance-of-payments crisis was the deterioration in some republics of the basic balance (see Table 9.1). In this context, it *is* relevant to ask what happened to the current account deficit, since the cause of the widening basic balance deficit was not a decline in long-term capital outflows, but an increase in the current account deficit not financed by additional long-term flows.

Several factors contributed to the widening of current account deficits in the three republics (Costa Rica, Guatemala, Honduras) where a deterioration of the basic balance was a factor in reserve loss. One was the rise in the price of oil; another was the fall in the price of coffee from its all-time peak in 1977. Between 1978 and 1981, the TOT for the region fell by 29.7 per cent.

The change in the TOT is by no means the whole story, however, as world interest rate rises also added to the cost of servicing external debt. As Table 9.2 shows, this additional interest charge accounts for a substantial part of the deterioration in the current account deficit in the cases of Costa Rica and Honduras.

The table shows that coffee, oil and interest costs are sufficient to account for most of the change in the current account during the period

Table 9.2   Contributions to deterioration in current account deficit

Period	Increase in deficit (million SDR)	(1) %	(2) %	(3) %	(4) %
Costa Rica 1978–80	+219.3	+27.3	+33.4	+39.3	+0.1
Guatemala 1978–81	+281.0	+38.6	+64.9	+19.8	−23.3
Honduras 1978–81	+131.1	+16.7	+59.0	+48.2	−23.9

Notes:
Col. (1) = fall in value of coffee exports as percentage of increase in deficit.
Col. (2) = increase in value of oil imports as percentage of increase in deficit.
Col. (3) = increase in debt service interest payments as percentage of increase in deficit.
Col. (4) = deterioration in current account other than items (a) to (c) as percentage of increase in deficit (a minus sign denotes an improvement).

Source: IMF, *Balance of Payments Yearbook* (1983).

when the deficit was increasing. In addition, Guatemala suffered badly because of a sharp fall in tourist earnings as a result of the adverse publicity surrounding the country during the Lucas García regime (1978–82). One should also note that the contribution of the 'other' column (4) in Table 9.2 to BOP deterioration was negative or zero. This column is roughly equivalent to movements in the non-oil, non-coffee trade account, and a negative sign means an improvement; much of this was due to favourable movements in the prices of traditional exports (e.g. sugar, bananas, cotton, beef) together with a small decline in the volume of imports.[15]

Following the first oil crisis of 1973–4, adjustment was rendered unnecessary through a sharp increase in coffee prices. This time, however, coffee prices could only be expected to fall, so that the deterioration of TOT from 1979 onwards could not be regarded as temporary; in addition, uncertainties about the world economy and the revival of monetarism suggested that the rise in interest rates might not be temporary either. Thus, prudent policy-making would have counselled at least a modest adjustment programme following the balance of payments deterioration in 1979.

El Salvador and Nicaragua did indeed 'adjust', although policy-making played little part in the programme of adjustment. Both countries ran a trade and current account surplus in 1979, as imports fell even in value terms in response to lower levels of economic activity. In

Nicaragua, the value of imports was halved between 1977 and 1979, and the case for financing in response to balance-of-payments pressures after 1979 was very strong; the same could be said for El Salvador, where imports continued to decline in 1980.

Elsewhere, however, the failure to adopt adjustment programmes was a serious error, given that the BOP crisis could not be construed as temporary. The irresponsible resort to finance, particularly in Guatemala and Costa Rica, inevitably increased the burden when adjustment programmes were finally adopted.

THE FINANCING PHASE

Any division between a financing and an adjustment phase in response to a BOP crisis is to some extent arbitrary, because there will usually be elements of both in any policy mix. Central America is no exception, yet in each republic there is a clear contrast between the first response to the crisis, when financing was dominant, and the second, when adjustment prevailed.

As Table 9.3 shows, the financing (FN) phase came to a halt at the end of 1980 in Costa Rica and El Salvador; in Honduras and Nicaragua it ended by the close of 1981, while in Guatemala the adjustment phase was

Table 9.3 Responses to balance-of-payments crisis

	Costa Rica	El Salvador	Guatemala	Honduras	Nicaragua
Financing (FN) phase	Up to September 1980	Up to November 1980	Up to mid-1982	Up to April 1981	Up to September 1981
Adjustment without conditionality (AWOC) phase	Up to December 1982	Up to July 1982	Up to September 1983	Up to November 1982	Up to end 1982
Adjustment with conditionality (AWIC) phase	Up to January 1984	Up to August 1983	Up to July 1984	Up to January 1984	Not applicable
Post-adjustment phase	In progress	In progress	In progress	In progress	Not applicable

delayed until 1982. In each case the transition was marked by a package of emergency measures.

Although the initial response to BOP difficulties in each republic was a resort to finance, this was not sufficient to prevent a slowdown in the rate of growth of real GDP. On the contrary, the massive capital outflow documented in the previous section had as its corollary a collapse of private investment; by 1979, private investment had peaked in all republics except Honduras (where it peaked in 1980) and by 1981 it had fallen to nearly half its peak level in Costa Rica and Guatemala, 38 per cent of its peak level in El Salvador and 91 per cent in Honduras.[16]

Two factors helped to offset the rapid decline in aggregate demand implied by the private investment figures. In turn, this made possible positive growth throughout the region, although at a much lower rate than in 1978 and 1979 (except in Nicaragua, where postwar reconstruction lifted the economy by over 10 per cent in 1980).

The first stimulus to aggregate demand ws provided by the Central American Common Market (CACM) with intraregional trade in 1980 growing by 31 per cent and lifting its value above $1 billion for the first (and only) time in its history. However, nearly 70 per cent of the increase in trade between 1979 and 1980 was accounted for by increased Nicaraguan purchases. This rate of increase could not be sustained, and Nicaragua soon found itself unable to pay its debts arising from the imbalance in intraregional trade. Between 1980 and 1982, Nicaragua's cumulative deficit with Central America on intraregional trade reached some $425 million, and the failure of the Sandinista government to service this debt was one of the factors behind the decline of CACM after 1980.

The second stimulus to real aggregate demand came from public investments. While private investment was falling, public capital expenditure rose rapidly between 1978 and 1980 in Costa Rica and Honduras. Expansion continued until 1981 in Guatemala and Nicaragua[17] (where the increase began after 1979) and even in El Salvador a sharp fall in public investment was prevented until 1982.

The increase in public capital expenditure was much faster than the rise in revenue. Indeed, by 1980 (Costa Rica, El Salvador, Nicaragua) or by 1981 (Guatemala, Honduras), government revenue was not even sufficient to cover *current* expenditure (see Table 9.5 below) and the whole of the capital budget had to be financed by borrowing. The budget deficit as a percentage of GDP rose sharply, reaching over 8 per cent in Costa Rica in 1980 and over 7 per cent elsewhere in 1981.[18]

Between 1978 and 1980 (i.e. during the core of the financing stage), there is a correlation between the size of the budget deficit and the rate of inflation. Only a small part of the variation in the inflation rate, however, can be explained by the budget deficit, as the major factors (as always in Central America)[19] were changes in dollar import prices (including oil) coupled with exchange-rate devaluation (in Nicaragua and Costa Rica). Indeed, as Table 9.4 makes clear, the fall in the inflation rate between 1980 and 1981 in some republics took place against a background of rising budget deficits; the subsequent decline in the budget deficit appears to have had little impact on the inflation rate.

The increase in the size of the budget deficit during the FN phase may not have had much immediate impact on inflation, but it did have an important bearing on domestic credit expansion. Throughout the financing phase the bulk of the deficit was financed internally, with Honduras being the only republic to rely more heavily on external finance (see Table 9.4). As a result, bank credit extended to the public sector rocketed (see Table 9.5) with most of the increase coming from the Central Bank in each republic. This huge increase was not offset by declines in credit outstanding to the private sector (see Table 9.5) and domestic credit expansion (DCE) was substantial during the FN phase, running far ahead of inflation.

During 1978 (i.e. before the BOP crisis), there was very roughly a 1:1 ratio between the stock of bank credit and the flow of imports.[20] After 1978, this ratio (see Table 9.5) rose sharply in all republics, as DCE outpaced the rise in imports even in value terms; this suggests an increase in liquidity, with the public forced to hold unwanted cash balances leading to a rise in inflation. This did not happen, as we have seen; indeed, the money stock expanded in line with nominal GDP after 1978, leaving velocity more or less unchanged (see Table 9.5).[21]

What happened is that the public successfully converted its excess money holdings into foreign currency, draining international reserves out of the banking system and forcing the Central Banks in particular to borrow massively in the international capital market. By the end of the FN phase, net foreign assets had turned or were about to turn negative in each republic, and the inflationary pressures usually accompanying excessive DCE were only avoided by converting the excess into capital flight. This reduced the stock of money of external origin and contributed to a lowering of overall monetary expansion.[22]

The price paid for this largesse on the part of the authorities was a massive rise in external public indebtedness. In the three years after the end of 1978 (see Table 9.6), the disbursed public external debt doubled or more than doubled in all republics; credit from official sources rose most

280

Table 9.4 Budget deficits ($ million) and inflation rates (%)

	1978	1979	1980	1981	1982	1983
Costa Rica						
Budget deficit	151	265	428	61	69	134
Internal (net)	148	235	342	38	40	110
External (net)	24	49	35	18	23	27
Inflation (%)	5.9	9.2	18.2	37.0	90.1	32.6
Food (%)	10.3	12.6	21.7	36.8	113.6	32.2
Housing (%)	4.1	5.6	16.8	35.5	51.7	29.2
El Salvador						
Budget deficit	63	25	199	283	275	98
Internal (net)	26	22	164	226	147	27
External (net)	21	16	50	76	94	105
Inflation (%)	12.9	8.6	17.4	14.8	11.7	13.1
Food (%)	10.6	8.7	19.6	17.9	10.6	13.4
Housing (%)	22.9	8.6	17.1	9.3	11.7	15.1
Guatemala						
Budget deficit	70	179	369	638	410	295
Internal (net)	15	− 50	236	452	441	251
External (net)	94	121	111	96	95	80
Inflation (%)	7.9	11.4	10.7	11.5	0.2	5.8[a]
Food (%)	4.6	10.2	11.3	11.3	− 2.8	7.0[a]
Housing (%)	12.4	16.4	15.9	12.6	0.9	− 1.7[a]
Honduras						
Budget deficit	124	95	198	203	340	282
Internal (net)	37	28	54	92	145	134
External (net)	82	67	127	127	188	125
Inflation (%)	5.7	12.1	18.1	9.4	9.4	8.9
Food (%)	6.2	11.4	17.1	7.3	6.7	5.3
Housing (%)	5.3	14.7	15.5	10.3	6.6	14.0
Nicaragua						
Budget deficit	166	103	143	262	577	958
Internal (net)	85	79	113	91	364	1000
External (net)	9	15	75	58	99	104
Inflation (%)	4.5	48.2	35.3	23.9	24.8	31.0
Food (%)	3.5	63.4	49.1	29.0	29.1	41.5
Housing (%)	6.4	29.9	13.9	20.7	21.2	16.0

Notes: the difference between (i) internal (net) and external (net) finance and (ii) the budget deficit is accounted for by use of cash balances.
[a] obtained by splicing the new index (April 1983 = 100) on to the old series and comparing mid-year figures. See Banco de Guatemala, *Boletín Estadístico*, July–September 1984.

Sources: Consejo Monetario Centroamericano, *Boletín Estadístico 1983* (San José, 1984), unless otherwise stated.

281

Table 9.5 Credit, money and quasi-money ($ million), end-year balances

	1978	1979	1980	1981	1982	1983
Costa Rica						
Credit	1450	2002	2525	691	877	1098
Public	416	760	1119	323	420	458
Private	1034	1242	1406	368	457	641
Credit/imports ratio	1.24	1.43	1.66	0.57	0.98	1.11
Money (M1)	589	649	741	267	374	443
Money/GDP ratio	0.17	0.16	0.17	0.096	0.15	0.15
Quasi-money	674	940	1108	531	701	947
El Salvador						
Credit	1066	1299	1664	1997	2228	2226
Public	178	304	793	1018	1128	1019
Private	888	995	871	979	1100	1207
Credit/imports ratio	1.04	1.27	1.73	2.03	2.6	2.5
Money (M1)	451	543	590	582	603	579
Money/GDP ratio	0.15	0.16	0.165	0.168	0.169	0.15
Quasi-money	494	482	459	583	653	802
Guatemala						
Credit	1262	1385	1831	2431	3076	3469
Public	382	332	542	983	1526	1714
Private	880	1053	1289	1448	1550	1755
Credit/imports ratio	0.91	0.92	1.15	1.45	2.22	3.06
Money (M1)	624	693	709	738	749	787
Money/GDP ratio	0.10	0.10	0.09	0.086	0.086	0.087
Quasi-money	865	915	1074	1253	1540	1473
Honduras						
Credit	771	909	1028	1182	1337	1499
Public	170	230	296	377	451	516
Private	601	680	733	805	886	983
Credit/imports ratio	1.1	1.09	1.01	1.23	1.88	1.98
Money (M1)	267	297	336	353	378	431
Money/GDP ratio	0.15	0.14	0.14	0.13	0.13	0.145
Quasi-money	305	325	347	387	491	585
Nicaragua						
Credit	1146	1012	1521	2020	2612	3544
Public	143	202	498	598	909	1584
Private	1002	810	1023	1422	1703	1959
Credit/import ratio	1.93	2.81	1.71	2.02	3.37	4.44
Money (M1)	245	302	405	523	641	1089
Money/GDP ratio	0.12	0.19	0.19	0.20	0.22	0.30
Quasi-money	347	204	256	307	367	504

Source: IMF, *International Finance Statistics, 1984 Yearbook.*

Table 9.6   Disbursed public external debt, increase from end-1978 to end-1981
($ million)

	Total	%	Official	%	Private	%	% *Increase* *due to* *private* *sources*
Costa Rica	1302.5	137	424.2	82	878.3	203	67.4
El Salvador	329.1	99	339.1	108	−9.9	−47	Negative
Guatemala	505.5	166	444.9	150	60.6	904	12.0
Honduras	639.1	107	381.8	79	257.0	227	40.0
Nicaragua	1126.3	116	713.0	130	413.0	98	37.0

Source: World Bank, *World Debt Tables* (1983–4).

rapidly in the 'war-torn' republics, while elsewhere private credit rose most rapidly. Because of the relatively low starting base for private credit, however, only Costa Rica funded more than 50 per cent of its increase in public external indebtedness from private sources.

The rise in debt during the FN phase was so large that it is not unreasonable to blame much of the current debt problems on the increases incurred in this phase. A considerable share, for example, of the commercial debt (the rescheduling of which has caused such problems for Costa Rica, Honduras and Nicaragua) was contracted during the financing stage. Although adjustment, as we shall see, has its problems, failure to adjust also imposes costs: the increase in the debt burden is one of them.[23]

During the FN phase, several governments paid lip-service to the need for adjustment programmes and some (Costa Rica, Honduras, Guatemala) even reached agreement with the IMF on standby credits (see Table 9.7). In all cases except one these credits were suspended and the exception (Guatemala in November 1981) hardly counts, as the standby was a first credit transfer which is *de facto* free of conditions and is wholly disbursed at the start of the programme; thus it cannot later be suspended if the borrowing country fails to meet the 'conditions'.

Why did the adjustment programmes in Costa Rica, Guatemala and Honduras fail? In the Guatemalan case, there is no mystery; the Fund's conditions included a rise in interest rates and a reduction in the public sector borrowing requirement (PSBR); interest rates were raised in late 1981, but significantly they were lowered immediately the programme expired,[24] and no action was taken to lower the PSBR other than a cut in capital expenditure.

In the Honduran case, the three-year Extended Fund Facility (EFF) of February 1980 was suspended because the authorities failed to meet PSBR targets. During 1980, Honduras introduced new taxes and raised existing ones (mainly direct) and government revenue rose sharply by 20 per cent. Government expenditure, however, rose even more rapidly on both current and capital account and the PSBR doubled over its 1979 level.

The Honduran failure cannot be attributed to the indexed nature of expenditure. Only half the rise in current expenditure was due to wages and salaries, the remainder being due to the increase in purchases of goods and services. The Honduran public sector is highly decentralised, and the armed forces in particular, in anticipation of the return to civilian rule, appear to have increased their share of the government budget and contributed in no small measure to the failure of the agreement with the IMF.

While the outgoing military administration of General Policarpo Paz García faced few problems in raising public revenue in Honduras, the incoming civilian administration of President Carazo in Costa Rica (1978–82) found itself in the opposite position. Carazo and his economic team were committed to a strategy of financial liberalisation on taking office and looked with favour on a reduced public sector and a shrunken PSBR. Minister of Finance Hernán Saenz recognised early in 1980 that an adjustment programme was needed to solve the BOP crisis, and the Carazo administration welcomed the one-year standby credit agreed with the IMF in March 1980.

The relationship with the Fund, therefore, could not have been more cordial, with both sides taking a similar view on policy. By November, however, the credit had been suspended and a year later Carazo expelled an IMF mission from the country.[25] What went wrong?

The Fund's conditions for the March loan were conventional (see Table 9.7), but the stumbling block proved to be raising additional tax revenue. While monetary policy (particularly interest rates) was firmly under the control of the authorities, fiscal policy required the support of a national assembly in which the government enjoyed only a paper majority. Time and again, efforts to introduce tax reform packages failed, so that the government could not meet the end-March, -June, -September quarterly targets set by the Fund for fiscal and credit performance.

The lessons of the Costa Rican and Honduran débâcles are clear. Both

Table 9.7 IMF programmes

Country	Costa Rica	Costa Rica	Costa Rica	Costa Rica	El Salvador	Guatemala	Guatemala	Honduras	Honduras	Honduras
Date approved	March 1980	June 1981	December 1982	March 1985	July 1982	November 1981	September 1983	February 1980	August 1981	November 1982
Date suspended	Nov. 1980 (government failed to meet March/June/Sept. quarterly targets)	Oct. 1981 (government introduced new restrictions on imports, defaulted on debt, etc.)		April 1986, because of budget deficit		All disbursed in 11/81 because it was a first credit tranche	July 1984 because of refusal to restore VAT to 10%	August 1980 because of budget deficit	Early 1982 because of budget deficit	
Type	1-year standby	3-year extended fund facility	1-year standby	13-month standby	1-year standby	1-year standby	16-month standby	3-year extended fund facility	Extended fund facility (re-established)	13-month standby
Budget deficit	Target set for reduction of PSBR in 1980. Government agreed to raise coffee export tax and consumer taxes	Deficit to be limited to 9% in 1981; 7% in 1982 and 5% in 1983. To be achieved through an end of earmarking	Target set at 4.5% of GDP	Target set at 1.5% of GDP. Elimination of subsidies on basic foodstuffs	No target but government spending to be cut by 10%, and taxes raised (new sales taxes and revised taxes on selective consumer items introduced mid-1983)	Reduction in PSBR	3.7% of GDP in 1983; 3% in 1984. Revenue to reach 9.5% of GDP. Reduction in public expenditure (+ wage freeze)	Target stated as cuts in government expenditure programme and reduced number of government agencies	Same as in February 1980	Curb on government expenditure. Increased customs duties, improved tax administration. Wage and spending cuts
Net domestic assets of Central Bank	3-monthly targets set up to 31.12.80 to limit increases	3-monthly targets set up to 30.6.82 (falls targeted for 1982)	Ceilings set to increase flow of credit to private sector		Limited demand management policy		Limits placed on debt to banking system by government. Overall DCE growth to be consistent with targeted improvement in BOP	No details given	No details given	Reduction in growth of DCE from 20% in 1982 to 9% by end 1983
Central Bank credit to non-financial public sector	3-monthly target set up to 31.12.80 to limit increase in net credit extended	3-monthly targets set up to 30.6.82 to limit credit to government	Ceilings set to increase flow of credit to private sector		More balanced distribution of credit between private and public sector			No details given		No details given

Interest rates	The agreement supported the monetary reform of Oct. 1978, i.e. interest rates to be competitive with those abroad		Rationalisation of interest rate and pricing policies	Rise in interest rates	Flexible interest rate policy to be pursued			
Public external debt	Increase in 1981 to be a *min.* of $350m. ($183m. for non-fin. public sector). Increase in 1982 set at $381m.; 1983 $411m.	Agreement reached on rescheduling 1985 and 1986 debts. A 10-yr rescheduling with 3-yr grace. $75m in new money in 1985. None in 1986	No link to external debt	Increase in foreign borrowing to help finance the public investment programme	Commercial arrears must be reduced by $50m. in 1983 and $100m. in 1984. New public debt ≤ $300m.	No link to external debt	No link to external debt	Debt rescheduling linked to IMF programme. Finally achieved in 1985
Exchange rate and trade policies	No exchange-rate commitment	A commitment to a flexible, but stable unitary exchange rate	Adjustment of exchange rate to narrow spread between interbank rates and free market rates to no more than 2% by end 1983. Achieved Nov. 1983. Revamping of export incentives to promote non-trad. products	Devaluation from 45 to 48C. This devaluation, in Oct. 1984, was a precondition	Phased liberalisation of exchange and trade policies. NB: big changes in exchange-rate policy occur *before* and *after* 1-year standby	Exchange restrictions to be relaxed. No new or stricter controls to be imposed on trade or capital transfers. No devaluation and no multiple exchange rate	No exchange-rate commitment	No exchange-rate commitment

the Fund and the borrowing government have to take cognisance of political reality. Although revenue increases in Costa Rica were desirable in 1980, it was clear to all neutral observers that they could not be obtained; similarly, the armed forces' desire in Honduras to protect their position after a decade of military rule was wholly predictable. Other programmes could have achieved the same adjustment, perhaps at a higher (economic) cost, but they were not explored;[26] even a higher cost adjustment programme in 1980, however, would have been preferable to a failed programme, because the discounted cost of the future adjustment programmes almost certainly proved greater.

ADJUSTMENT WITHOUT CONDITIONALITY

The balance-of-payments crisis, with which the FN phase began, did not prove temporary and was reflected in a collapse of net foreign assets. The finance strategy therefore came to a halt when emergency measures were introduced in support of the BOP. This can be dated to September 1980 in Costa Rica, November 1980 in El Salvador, April 1981 in Honduras, September 1981 in Nicaragua and mid-1982 in Guatemala. Each republic then entered an adjustment phase which ended with the approval of a non-suspended IMF credit subject to conditions. This 'adjustment without conditionality' (AWOC) phase therefore runs until July 1982 in El Salvador, November 1982 in Honduras, December 1982 in Costa Rica and September 1983 in Guatemala.[27] In Nicaragua, this stage ended in a different way, as no agreement was reached with the IMF (see the later section on Nicaragua).

As in the FN stage, efforts were made to reach agreement with the IMF; both Costa Rica and Honduras received three-year EFFs in 1981, in June and August respectively, but the Fund suspended both within six months. In the Honduran case the size of the budget deficit proved the stumbling block, while in Costa Rica the Fund took exception to the introduction of new restrictions on imports and the accumulation of debt arrears.

Adjustment programmes were in force, however, despite the problems with the Fund, and we may therefore observe how the five Central American republics approached the adjustment problem when not subject to IMF conditionality. Unfortunately, this cannot be viewed as a 'controlled experiment', because policy making operated under the shadow of conditionality, but one can still observe a difference of emphasis in policy between adjustment with and without IMF conditions.

The preferred method of adjustment in this phase was without doubt the increased use of import controls. Since such an increase is anathema to the Fund, it is not surprising that relations with the IMF were so strained. The increase in import controls consisted of changes in prior deposits, import licences, quotas, increased taxes and outright prohibition. In effect, the authorities graded imports according to their 'importance' and rationed foreign exchange accordingly.

In most republics this rationing was carried out with the help of multiple exchange rates. In El Salvador, a parallel market was authorised in late 1981,[28] and dealings were brought within the purlieu of the nationalised banking system in August 1982. Nicaragua legalised a parallel market in January 1982, also at a substantial discount, and in both republics a black or free market also operated, without government approval, although in El Salvador the black and parallel markets never drifted too far apart.[29] Guatemala and Honduras, the two republics with the oldest history of exchange-rate stability, did not introduce a parallel market in this phase. A black market existed in both republics, however, with the home currency trading at around 25 per cent below the official rate.

The republic which relied most heavily on the exchange rate as an instrument of policy was Costa Rica. In September 1980, 50 per cent of trade was channelled through a free market, and in December the colón was allowed to float freely. By the end of 1981, there were three exchange rates in force, all of which can be compared with the rate of 8.60 colones per US dollar in August 1980: an official rate of C20, which was used for about 1 per cent of transactions, an interbank rate of C36 (which applied to virtually all trade items) and a parallel rate of C39 for tourism in particular. By the end of 1982, when the adjustment without conditionality phase finished, the interbank rate was C40.50 and the parallel rate C45.

While measures to control imports were adopted vigorously and comprehensively, the same enthusiasm was not displayed in promoting exports. Nicaragua introduced new export incentives for agricultural products in the first quarter of 1982, followed by further incentives in the first quarter of 1983, but neither set of measures came close to compensating exporters for an effective *appreciation* of the real exchange rate. Guatemala also adopted an export incentives law in September 1982, and in December 1981 Costa Rica reduced the exchange taxes on export proceeds (introduced to enable the public sector to benefit from the windfall gains associated with devaluation). Nevertheless, the emphasis on export promotion was very slight during the period of adjustment without conditionality.

The combination of import restrictions, coupled with some export incentives, had a devastating effect on taxes on external trade. The revenue from these taxes fell sharply during the AWOC stage, although the decline began during the FN phase. With taxes on trade accounting for roughly one-third of government revenue in 1978, this sharp decline inevitably provoked a fiscal crisis.

During the AWOC phase, little attention was given to replacing lost income from trade taxes with other revenue sources, so that government revenue declined in real terms (except in Nicaragua) and in three cases (El Salvador, Guatemala, Honduras) was stagnant even in money terms. Nicaragua, on the other hand, succeeded in increasing revenue five-fold between 1979 and 1983, partly through the introduction of new taxes (e.g. a levy on the net worth of private assets), partly through increasing existing taxes (e.g. a 10 per cent surcharge on income tax), but above all through improvements in administration, tax evasion having been such a noticeable feature of the pre-revolutionary period.

Fiscal policy therefore tended to focus on expenditure cuts rather than revenue increases. A key element in several republics was wage restraint, with an outright freeze in El Salvador, strict control in Nicaragua and indexing to a basic wage basket in Costa Rica.[30] Some efforts were made to raise the price of public services, but price control continued to be widespread (making an increase in government transfers inevitable) and food subsidies were common. Even these efforts to lower expenditure, however, tended to be dwarfed by the pressure to raise expenditure in support of increased defence spending.

Under these circumstances, it is scarcely surprising that the size of the budget deficit continued to be a severe problem during the AWOC phase. Only Costa Rica and Guatemala managed to lower the deficit as a percentage of GDP in this phase, while in Nicaragua it reached 12.1 per cent in 1982. Even in Costa Rica and Guatemala, the value of bank credit to the public sector increased sharply, as the opportunities for funding the deficit externally became more and more restricted.

With private credit also increasing, although at a slower rate than public credit, the credit–import ratio continued to rise (see Table 9.5). As in the FN phase, however, this excess credit creation was not monetised; velocity remained stable and the inflation rate declined throughout the AWOC phase (except in Costa Rica where the rise to 90 per cent in 1982 was clearly caused by the collapse of the exchange rate).

There are several reasons why excess credit creation did not result in monetary instability during the AWOC phase. First, all republics except Guatemala raised interest rates, thereby increasing the attraction of non-monetary assets; secondly, the use of advanced import deposit schemes encouraged the growth of quasi-money, which was also promoted by interest-rate changes. Thirdly, capital flight continued during the AWOC phase, so that the decline in net foreign assets (and therefore money of external origin) was not reversed. Finally, exchange rate depreciation (whether *de facto* or *de jure*) soaked up a large proportion of any excess liquidity.

Policy during the AWOC phase relied most heavily on import controls, devaluation (often *de facto*) and exchange restrictions. This was reflected in a sharp fall in imports (see Table 9.8) and an improvement in the current account balance-of-payments deficit. This might be seen as a justification for AWOC phase policy, and, indeed, one should not ignore the impact that a direct assault on the balance of payments can have. Nevertheless, several important caveats are in order.

First, the fall in imports was indiscriminate and affected trade within the Central American Common Market (CACM) as much as imports from outside the region.[31] To some extent the fall in the value of CACM trade after 1980 (see Table 9.8) was inevitable, since much of trade consisted of consumer goods, which were the most obvious candidates for import suppression; yet one country's CACM imports are another's exports, so that the effect of import restrictions was to increase the burden of adjustment (see the later section on this) above what was strictly necessary.

Secondly, the improvement in the balance-of-payments position was achieved partly through accumulation of debt service arrears. Costa Rica suspended all service payments in 1981 and resumed interest payments only at a token level in July 1982. By the end of 1982, Guatemalan arrears were estimated at $344 million[32] and Honduras went into arrears in October 1982. Nicaragua, which had reached agreement with its creditors on debt rescheduling in August 1982,[33] narrowly avoided default in December[34] and was again accumulating arrears in 1983. By the close of the AWOC phase, the external debt problem and the difficulty of obtaining new credits had acquired major significance everywhere except El Salvador and, indeed, was the main reason why Costa Rica, Guatemala and Honduras were prepared to try to honour the IMF agreements which marked the end of the AWOC phase.

Thirdly, the weak fiscal position during the AWOC phase was not

Table 9.8   Imports in nominal and real terms ($ million); real imports at 1982
prices (including service imports)

	1978	1979	1980	1981	1982	1983
Costa Rica						
Imports (cif.)	1166	1397	1524	1209	893	989
Imports (CACM)	203	212	220	152	112	120
Imports (ROW)	963	1185	1304	1057	781	869
Service imports	355	425	522	545	672	665
Real imports	1708	1757	1609	1185	806	840
El Salvador						
Imports (cif.)	1027	1022	962	985	857	892
Imports (CACM)	240	257	320	305	261	223
Imports (ROW)	787	765	642	680	596	669
Service imports	346	431	392	383	370	386
Real imports	1514	1320	1031	922	768	721
Guatemala						
Imports (cif.)	1391	1504	1598	1674	1388	1135
Imports (CACM)	208	207	155	186	219	225
Imports (ROW)	1183	1297	1443	1488	1169	910
Service imports	451	483	635	650	490	404
Real imports	1640	1518	1387	1330	1054	838
Honduras						
Imports (cif.)	696	832	1019	960	712	756
Imports (CACM)	92	98	104	118	87	83
Imports (ROW)	604	734	915	842	625	673
Service imports	227	288	352	335	361	320
Real imports	928	1025	1108	972	671	627
Nicaragua						
Imports (cif.)	594	360	887	999	776	799
Imports (CACM)	139	111	301	211	117	110
Imports (ROW)	455	249	586	788	659	689
Service imports	213	206	214	235	254	214
Real imports	581	472	1058	1025	764	710

Sources: service imports: IMF, *International Financial Statistics, 1984
Yearbook*; real imports: Inter-American Development Bank, *Economic and
Social Progress in Latin America, 1984 Report*; others: Consejo Monetario
Centroamericano, *Boletín Estadístico 1983* (San José, 1984).

very satisfactory. The means by which excessive DCE had not been
monetised could only be regarded as temporary, and the rapid growth of
quasi-money posed a potential threat to financial stability. In this
respect, the IMF proved to be more imaginative (and flexible) than is
often realised (see next section).

ADJUSTMENT WITH CONDITIONALITY

The adjustment with conditionality (AWIC) phase begins with the approval by the IMF of standby credits in support of adjustment programmes which were substantially completed. The dates are July 1982 for El Salvador, November 1982 for Honduras, December 1982 for Costa Rica and September 1983 for Guatemala. No agreement was reached with Nicaragua, which has failed to come to any accommodation with the Fund since the revolution; the exact reasons for this have never been stated publicly, but it is assumed to be due to US leverage over the IMF on the one side and Sandinista reluctance to submit to conditionality on the other (see next section). The AWIC phase therefore excludes Nicaragua.

The central policy element in the AWIC phase has been a reduction in the budget deficit. Although the Fund (as we shall see) has proved flexible in other respects, it has clung to orthodoxy as far as the budget deficit is concerned; targets were set for the deficit as a proportion of GDP (except for El Salvador)[35] and each letter of intent committed the signatories to raising revenue as well as cutting expenditure.

The revenue-raising target took place against a background of falling or stagnant trade taxes; thus, any rise in revenue could only be achieved through disproportionately large increases in non-trade taxes. In each republic the executive was able to secure congressional support, but has faced serious public unrest in consequence; in several cases this led to a reversal or partial reversal of the original tax increases.

The most serious case of reversal occurred in Guatemala, the least democratic of the four republics concerned. The Rios Montt government introduced a value added tax (VAT) at 10 per cent in July 1983 as a precondition for IMF support; the new tax, however, is widely conceded to have been one reason for the fall of Rios Montt in August; the new military government, led by General Mejía Victores, agreed a standby credit with the IMF in September, but promptly lowered VAT to 7 per cent in October. The failure by the Fund to secure a reimposition of VAT at 10 per cent finally provoked suspension in July 1984.

The pressure to raise revenue has also affected the price of public services controlled by decentralised public sector agencies. These increases have in several cases been cancelled, but the Fund has been unyielding in its determination to root out loss-making activities in the public sector. The justification for the Fund's concern has been the fact that a large share of the increase in public external indebtedness is accounted for by the operations of these agencies. The latter include investment corporations, which have become holding companies for a number of private sector lame ducks.[37]

The Fund has not demonstrated the same interest in the expenditure side of the public accounts, although in some respects the two are not independent; thus, central government transfers are lowered if public utility prices rise, and so on. Public sector wage freezes and wage control have continued, but this is a reflection of policy in the AWOC phase. Certainly, large numbers of jobs have been lost in the public sector (an estimated 15 000 in Honduras), but this cannot all be blamed on the Fund; in any case, a government which will not raise new taxes, but wishes to meet IMF targets, is bound to cut jobs.

It was argued in the previous section that the growth of quasi-money in the AWOC phase created a potentially dangerous situation for the preservation of financial stability. In El Salvador and Guatemala, the Fund is credited with pioneering the use of dollar-denominated bonds with a medium-term maturity which served a dual purpose: first, they could be used to soak up the quasi-money overhang and, secondly, they could be used to pay for imports without the need for current dollars.[38] It is possible that this unorthodox measure, which has proved moderately successful, was approved by the Fund in El Salvador and Guatemala because of their relatively low levels of public external indebtedness to private creditors. In any case, such bonds were not issued by Costa Rica and Honduras.

More emphasis has been put on export promotion during the AWIC than the AWOC phase. This is partly due to the opportunities created by the Caribbean Basin Initiative (CBI), which was formally launched in January 1984, but whose probable implementation was known about well in advance.[39] It is also due to the Fund's 'export optimism' and preference for export-increasing over import-decreasing measures. A key element in export promotion has been changes in tax credit certificates (CATs),[40] which have been increased particularly for non-traditional exports outside the region. Other measures include reductions in export taxes and the use of free zones.

The Fund has insisted on orthodox credit policies, with targets set for DCE, but has relied merely on exhortation in the case of interest rates. In fact, interest-rate policy has been extremely inactive during the AWIC phase; nominal interest rates have hardly varied at all despite a big fall in inflation, which has left real interest rates positive for most types of non-monetary assets.

The Fund, perhaps surprisingly, has not given much priority to the exchange rate in establishing preconditions for Fund support. In the case of Costa Rica, the Fund insisted on a narrowing of the spread between the interbank rate and the free market rate to no more than 2 per cent; this was achieved in November 1983, one month before the expiry of the agreement. Elsewhere, the Fund called for the phasing out of exchange restrictions, but nothing substantial was done; the best that could be said is that restrictions were not actually increased.

The Fund gave considerable prominence to questions of external indebtedness. In Costa Rica and Honduras, the agreements were explicitly linked to debt reschedulings; the Fund's approval, however, turned out to be a necessary but not sufficient condition for debt rescheduling. Costa Rica, it is true, came to an arrangement with its official creditors quickly (in January 1983), but agreement with private creditors on debt falling due in 1983–4 was only reached in January 1984 (i.e. after the Fund programme had expired). The Honduran debt problem proved even more stubborn; an agreement in principle was reached in late 1983 covering $230 million of arrears, but was not implemented until 1985.

In the case of Guatemala, the IMF agreement was not explicitly linked to debt rescheduling, but the letter of intent stated that commercial arrears should be reduced by $50 million in 1983 and $100 million in 1984; in the agreement with El Salvador, however, the question of external debt does not appear to have arisen at all.

The Fund's programmes were marked by a large increase in the proportion of the current account deficit financed by the IMF's credits. The sums involved, however, were fairly modest, and the increase in the proportion is also a reflection of the improvement in the BOP position; unlike the AWOC phase, the improvement did not depend wholly on a fall in imports; on the contrary, there was a small increase in export earnings (see Table 9.9), while imports increased even in real terms in Costa Rica. The growth of credit was indeed more moderate during the Fund programmes, and the share of DCE going to the private sector rose sharply.

The inflation rate fell sharply during the AWIC phase in Costa Rica (see Table 9.4), but this cannot be attributed to Fund policies. The massive maxi-devaluations of 1981 and 1982 gave way to mini-devaluations in the AWIC phase which produced an appreciation of the real exchange rate; the deceleration in nominal devaluation, coupled with virtually unchanged dollar import prices and nominal wage restraint, reduced the rise in nominal costs, and inflation began to fall back quickly to its pre-devaluation level. By 1984, Costa Rica had achieved a 30 per cent real depreciation compared with 1980 at the cost

294

Table 9.9 Exports in nominal and real terms ($ million); real exports at 1982 prices (including service exports)

	1978	1979	1980	1981	1982	1983
Costa Rica						
Exports (fob)	864	942	1001	1003	869	871
Exports (CACM)	179	175	370	238	167	187
Exports (ROW)	685	767	731	765	702	684
Coffee	314	315	248	240	237	230
Non-traditional	116	161	162	184	167	166
Real exports	1349	1393	1359	1510	1357	1358
El Salvador						
Exports (fob)	848	1129	1075	798	700	736
Exports (CACM)	234	264	296	207	174	168
Exports (ROW)	614	865	779	591	526	568
Coffee	433	675	615	453	403	403
Non-traditional	52	66	61	70	59	67
Real exports	971	1282	983	810	699	770
Guatemala						
Exports (fob)	1092	1221	1520	1305	1170	1092
Exports (CACM)	255	307	441	379	337	321
Exports (ROW)	837	914	1039	926	833	771
Coffee	475	432	464	325	375	309
Non-traditional	141	200	307	260	232	230
Real exports	1769	1946	2047	1769	1641	1429
Honduras						
Exports (fob)	628	757	850	784	677	704
Exports (CACM)	49	60	84	66	52	61
Exports (ROW)	579	697	766	718	625	643
Coffee	211	197	204	173	153	151
Non-traditional	165	215	231	226	191	220
Real exports	687	766	800	830	749	706
Nicaragua						
Exports (fob)	646	616	450	500	406	411
Exports (CACM)	146	90	75	71	52	34
Exports (ROW)	500	526	375	429	354	377
Coffee	200	159	166	136	124	149
Non-traditional	67	112	92	80	65	37
Real exports	622	714	593	681	614	759

Sources: real exports from IDB (see note to Table 9.8); other data from Consejo Monetario Centroamericano, *Boletín Estadístico 1983*, San José, 1984.

of a 466 per cent nominal devaluation, a huge fall in real wages (see next section) and a marked increase in social tensions, but had made no more progress in resolving its external disequilibrium than some other republics which had not devalued and where inflation had been kept to single figures.

Performance gave grounds for cautious optimism during the AWIC phase, and the Fund had shown that it was not as inflexible as its critics have often accused it of being; yet several problems emerged ruring the AWIC phase, which are also of relevance to other countries.

The first problem is one of timing; it is no accident that the AWIC phase begins after the worst of the BOP crisis was over. Given the lagged response of exports to any efforts to promote them, Central American republic are obliged to deal with a severe BOP crisis through import suppression. To achieve this in the short run requires import restrictions, which are forbidden under AWIC because of the Fund's articles of association.

It follows that Central American republics can only enter into IMF-sponsored adjustment programmes when external conditions have begun to improve; in particular, given the Fund's emphasis on export growth, there has to be some prospect for export recovery. Yet if the worst of the BOP crisis has passed and external conditions are improving, why is there any need for conditionality?

The answer is provided by questions of external debt, and finance, which brings us to the second problem associated with the AWIC phase. The main reason for agreeing to IMF conditionality in the AWIC phase was the need for new credits and debt rescheduling, for which Fund approval of the adjustment programme was a necessary condition. This was made explicit in the case of Costa Rica, while it was implicit in the cases of Guatemala, Honduras and El Salvador.[41]

The Central American experience, however, makes it clear that the IMF seal of approval is neither a necessary not sufficient condition for a 'successful' debt rescheduling.[42] It is not sufficient, because the private banks are under no obligation to reschedule, yet alone advance new loans. Only Costa Rica was able to complete a rescheduling programme within the AWIC phase, but even that cannot be regarded as successful because it covered two years only (1983–4) and the amount of new credit involved in the package was very small.[43]

The IMF seal of approval is therefore not sufficient for successful debt rescheduling, but the Nicaraguan example shows that it is not necessary either. Nicaragua rescheduled its commercial debt in 1980 and 1982 without reaching an IMF agreement; subsequently, it fell behind in its debt service payments even on rescheduled terms, and it has the unenviable distinction of being one of only five countries in the world for which US bank supervisory authorities have invented a new category of reserve (Allocated Transfer Risks Reserves) for cases of protracted non-service of country debt.[44] It has also been in arrears on payments to the World Bank, an almost unheard-of phenomenon.

It can be argued that Nicaragua has received few additional private credits since the end of 1981[45] and that, therefore, it has paid a high price for not reaching agreement with the Fund. Nicaragua is not alone in this respect, however, and Guatemala in particular received no substantial additional private credits in the two years before July 1983. Consequently, if governments are to be persuaded of the need for painful IMF-sponsored adjustment programmes, there must be a greater degree of reciprocity by the commercial banks, otherwise the Nicaraguan example of *de facto* default will look increasingly attractive.

The third problem relates to the content of the IMF-sponsored adjustment programmes themselves. While the Fund has proved itself to be not inflexible on many issues, it has proved very rigid on the question of budget deficits; this has provided the main source of tension with the host governments, threatening at times to abort the adjustment programmes.

The Fund's position on budget deficits is as follows:

A rise in the ratio of fiscal deficits to GDP has contributed to the current economic problems requiring adjustment in a good many developing countries. In these countries, excessive deficits have induced accelerated monetary expansion and inflation. The consequences have included impaired capital investment, loss of competitive position, and generally lower rates of growth. Redressing excessive fiscal deficits has thus become an important element of adjustment policy in developing countries.[46]

While it would be foolish to deny that 'excessive fiscal deficits' can produce serious problems, the Fund's analysis does not appear to have much validity in Central America. 'Excessive deficits' are not in general the cause of accelerated inflation; inflation ratios have risen and fallen, as we have seen, to a large extent independently of the size of the budget deficit. Similarly, the Fund lists as *consequences* of 'excessive deficits' what can more properly be described as *causes* of 'excessive deficits'. Thus, capital investment was certainly impaired by capital flight; private investment collapsed and, with it, imports of capital goods; both lowered government revenue and contributed to 'excessive deficits'.

The rise in the PSBR did, however, contribute to a large and potentially destabilising increase in quasi-money, but this can be (and was) dealt with through other measures than a balanced or nearly balanced budget. Furthermore, the Fund appears not to recognise that the fiscal deficit is linked to the trade cycle, so that the 'full-trade' budget deficit is clearly smaller than the actual deficit during a period of trade recession.

The Nicaraguan PSBR experience makes clear that the Fund's concern with excessive deficits is not wholly misplaced. In Nicaragua, the deficit reached 25 per cent of GDP in 1983, and monetary growth was clearly excessive and potentially dangerous (see next section); there is a difference of quality as well as quantity, however, between a deficit of 25 per cent and one of 5 per cent. Outside of Nicaragua, the budget deficit as a proportion of GDP was falling *before* the AWIC phase, but the Fund has still insisted on targets which cannot be justified in terms of Central American macroeconomics.[47]

Let us suppose, however, that the Fund is correct in its choice of targets for the PSBR. The adjustments needed both to public revenue and public expenditure require time for their completion, particularly the former, so that a medium-term framework is needed for the AWIC phase. This suggests that an Extended Fund Facility (EFF) is appropriate, yet in every case the AWIC phase was marked by standby credits, the longest being for sixteen months. Thus the Fund chose unreasonable targets for the PSBR and then allowed too short a period for adjustment.

The final problem associated with the AWIC phase has been its failure to prevent a further deterioration in CACM. It is true that, with one exception,[48] the Fund's conditions did not countenance *additional* restrictions on intraregional trade. The IMF, however, exerted no pressure to remove those actually in existence, and its programme of export promotion made no reference to CACM. Given that the Fund has had agreements running contemporaneously with four of the five members (treating Honduras as a *de facto* member), this failure was a serious waste of an opportunity to reduce the costs of adjustment.

The major obstacle to the recovery of CACM, contrary to popular opinion, has not been political differences among the Central American republics, but the accumulation of unpaid debts between various pairs of states. These debts represent arrears just as much as unserviced debts to international banks; it seems strange, therefore, that the Fund has not insisted on repayment of intra-CACM debt as one of the conditions for standby credits. Such a move would have represented a positive step in favour of CACM's revival, despite the fact that the Fund has had no influence over the largest debtor, Nicaragua.

THE CASE OF NICARAGUA

Although Nicaragua has maintained correct relations with the IMF since the revolution, even settling all its outstanding debts in May 1985 and playing host to a Fund mission the following month, the Sandinista government did not follow the rest of Central America into the AWIC phase; instead, a public-sector boom was engineered from early 1983 (marking the close of the AWOC phase) which lasted until the adjustment programme of February 1985.

Since 1983, therefore, the Nicaraguan case has been *sui generis*; many factors account for this. The most obvious is that it is highly unlikely that the Fund and the Sandinista government could have reached agreement on an adjustment programme, given US influence over the IMF on the one hand and internal Nicaraguan political realities on the other. It was also the case, however, that debt problems (which were forcing other Central American republics into the arms of the Fund) did not have the same significance in Nicaragua; it was clear, for example, by early 1983 that the revolutionary government could not expect any new money from foreign commercial banks or multilateral institutions with strong US participation (above all, the World Bank and the Inter-American Development Bank),[49] while on the other hand its anticipated credits from other sources were not conditional on an agreement with the Fund.

The necessary conditions for avoiding an agreement with the Fund might therefore be said to have existed in 1983, but the external environment deteriorated sharply in that year and the consequent BOP disequilibrium required the continuation and even intensification of adjustment programmes; under these circumstances, the choice of a public-sector boom as the engine of growth of the economy (GDP rose by nearly 5 per cent in 1983) proved to be most unfortunate.[50]

Several factors accounted for the deterioration of the external environment in 1983. Virtually no new loans were forthcoming from multilateral official creditors (although some disbursements continued because of previous commitments) and the increasing intensity of the war against the Contras distorted the allocation of scarce foreign exchange away from the export sector towards the military. The unit value of all major export products (except seafoods) fell in 1983 and gold exports ceased altogether.[51] Finally, Nicaragua lost virtually all its sugar quota to the US market, although this was subsequently picked up by Iran and Algeria at comparable prices.

The public-sector boom in 1983 was the consequence of a 75 per cent rise in central government nominal expenditure unmatched by revenue increases.[52] The central government deficit soared to 24.4 per cent of nominal GDP, with most of it financed internally through the banking system; between the end of 1982 and 1983, the money supply (M1), rose by 67 per cent and the ratio of M1 to nominal GDP rose from about 20 per cent to 30 per cent – a sure sign of short-run, unwanted accumulation of money balances on the part of the public (see Table 9.5).

The huge rise in government expenditure occurred despite a fall in interest payments. Debt repayment problems (see below) led to a virtual 'passive default' and central government interest payments accounted for only 2.5 per cent of expenditure in 1983. By contrast, central government current expenditure on salaries, goods and services rose by around 50 per cent in 1983 compared to 1982, with much of the increase accounted for by additional outlays on defence.

The main reason, however, for the deterioration of the fiscal situation was the 213 per cent rise in 1983 in transfers and subsidies. These reached nearly 20 per cent of total expenditure compared with 7 per cent in 1982; the change is explained by the increasing gap between the producer and consumer prices of controlled goods and services. These included basic foodstuffs (e.g. rice, beans, maize, sugar, milk) as well as the services of public utilities.

The rise in producers' prices for foodstuffs was part of the effort by the state National Foodstuffs Enterprise, ENABAS, to achieve self-sufficiency in food supply.[53] The impact on production of agricultural goods for internal consumption was not unsuccessful,[54] but the state proved incapable of matching supplies through controlled distribution channels to demand (particularly in urban areas). A two-tier market developed for most foodstuffs, with prices in the black market far in excess of official guidelines, although the latter continued to be used in the calculation of the official cost-of-living index.

The Sandinista government denounced speculators and hoarders for the breakdown in the distribution system, but it is clear that the fiscal expansion played a major part in generating an effective demand for foodstuffs which could not be matched by official channels of distribution. Once the two-tier market was in place, moreover, it created a vicious circle: private producers bypassed ENABAS in a search for higher prices, and farmers in the export sector abandoned the production of foodstuffs for their workers since the same commodities could be purchased much more cheaply through official channels. Finally, high prices in the black market attracted migration to urban areas (particularly Managua) and the informal urban sector mushroomed through the expansion of petty commerce.[55]

The scarcity of foreign exchange, coupled with strict import controls, prevented the excess money creation from spilling over into imports, so that financial instability was reflected in domestic inflationary pressures. The rise in inflation (31 per cent in 1983 and 36 per cent in 1984) is not a correct measure of these pressures, because the index relied on official, controlled prices. A proxy for inflationary pressures, however, is provided by the black market exchange rate; this fell from 70 córdobas to the dollar at the end of 1983 to nearly 500 by the end of 1984.

While the black market exchange rate was rapidly depreciating in 1983 and 1984, the official exchange rate was unchanged at 10 córdobas to the dollar. Since foreign trade had been nationalised by the revolutionary government, the exchange rate that mattered for exporters was the one used by the authorities to convert dollar earnings into actual producer receipts; this varied from product to product, and the authorities adjusted the rates for the main export crops to reflect (at least partially) the rise in domestic prices.

As a result of these efforts, the volume of exports of the main products (coffee, cotton, sugar, bananas) rose in 1983, and there was also an increase in the dollar value of export earnings from these crops (except sugar) despite the falls in world prices. Nonetheless, total export earnings were stagnant in 1983, reaching only 63.6 per cent of the pre-revolution level.

The problem of exports continued to be the decline in non-traditional products (including sales to CACM). Only one-third of the fall in the value of exports from 1978 to 1983 could be explained by the performance of traditional exports,[56] although they accounted for 70 per cent of exports in 1978 and nearly 90 per cent in 1983. The non-traditional products came mainly from the industrial sector, where the unrealistic exchange rate and foreign exchange shortages for the purchase of inputs, spare parts, etc. were the major problems rather than demand factors.

The weakness of exports continued in 1984, aggravated by external aggression,[57] and earnings fell below $400 million for the first time since 1975. This was virtually the same as projected service payments on the public external debt, so that the external disequilibrium became unmanageable; the 'passive default' begun in 1983 was continued into 1984, with no payments even of interest on the commercial debt owed to private, external creditors.

By the middle of 1984, it was quite clear that the Sandinista attempt to circumvent the external disequilibrium through internal demand expansion had failed. Not only had the external environment deteriorated, but real GDP also fell in 1984 by 1.4 per cent; the need for a further round of adjustment was recognised, but electoral considerations postponed a decision until early 1985.

The adjustment programme announced in February 1985 was intended to reduce the fiscal deficit, curb inflationary pressures, and at the same time remove some of the worst distortions in the Nicaraguan economy (the authorities correctly noted that all these were linked). The core of the programme has been the raising of official consumer prices in an effort to end transfers and subsidies and reduce the fiscal deficit, while operating under a very tight constraint in which security considerations mean that defence will take 40 per cent of the budget. Government investment and other expenditures have been cut and new taxes have been introduced (particularly on petty commerce in the urban informal sector).[58]

Salaries were reorganised into twenty-eight groups and were increased in nominal, but not real, terms. This inevitable element of the adjustment programme was largely nullified in April, when a further round of salary increases was announced to 'compensate' a further round of consumer price increases;[59] the whole package was therefore in danger of simply creating the same set of problems at a higher level of prices; this was confirmed in June when the authorities announced new producer prices for basic foodstuffs[60] and an 'iron fist' offensive against speculation, hoarding, overcharging and contraband.[61]

The adjustment programme legalised the black market exchange rate (which settled at around 650 córdobas to the dollar) and introduced an official multiple exchange rate; the new rates, however, varied from 10 to 50 córdobas to the dollar, so that the devaluation came nowhere near eliminating the gap between the free and official rates and did not compensate exporters (particularly of industrial goods) for the rise in production costs.

While the adjustment programme was being implemented, the external environment was subject to a number of changes, not all of which were unfavourable. In June 1985, an agreement was reached with the creditor banks to postpone all debt service payments for one year,[62] and the Soviet Union agreed to provide 90 per cent of oil requirements, with Mexico supplying the balance;[63] Nicaragua even received a $44 million loan from the Central American Monetary Council to help its industrial exports to CACM.[64] The most spectacular change, however, was the US embargo on trade with Nicaragua in May, which had been anticipated by the authorities for several years and the damage from which is likely to be less severe than at first was believed.[65]

Several lessons can be drawn from the Nicaraguan experience since the end of the AWOC phase. First, external aggression (however unjustified) is not unlike other external shocks in terms of its macroeconomic impact and should not prevent the adoption of adjustment programmes (however painful). Secondly, revolutionary governments ignore the need for internal as well as external balance at their peril, because the eventual costs of adjustment may be so severe as to rob the revolutionary government of its social and political base. Thirdly, the adjustment package of February 1985 is not unlike an IMF-inspired programme, although its impact has been softened by subsequent, inconsistent policies which threaten to cancel the effectiveness of the original package. Finally, the combination of external aggression and internal policy errors have produced a situation where the external debt cannot be serviced; in the Nicaraguan case, passive default is the only 'solution'.

THE BURDEN OF ADJUSTMENT

Adjustment programmes carry costs, which raises the question of who bears the burden of adjustment. It is a sad comment on the state of economics that the statistics necessary to give a definitive answer to this question are usually unavailable; nonetheless, with the use of some imagination, one can hazard a guess as to the answers.

The period of adjustment (AWOC and AWIC) corresponds roughly to the period 1981 to 1983.[66] Taking 1980 as the base, one can look at the changes in a number of indicators over the period 1980–3 which are relevant to the question of the burden of adjustment (see Table 9.10).

The first indicator refers to the fall in real GDP per head. As the table makes clear, this has been particularly severe in El Salvador (where the decline actually began in 1978); the indequacy of this indicator is shown up, however, by the fact that Nicaragua appears to have experienced an increase. If, for example, we take the change in real wages (see column 2), the position of Nicaragua is seen to be very severe; on the other hand, it now appears that Guatemala experienced an increase in real wages,

Table 9.10   Indicators of the burden of adjustment, 1980–3

	(1)	(2)	(3)	(4)
Costa Rica	−18.2	−37.7	+53	−26
El Salvador	−19.2	−35.1	+85	−39
Guatemala	−12.5	+18.3	+264	−9
Honduras	−11.3	−4.1	+98	−19
Nicaragua[a]	+3.7	−36.9	−4	−39

Notes:
[a] For Nicaragua, the period chosen is 1980–2.
Col. (1) = percentage change in real GDP per head.
Col. (2) = percentage change in real wages.
Col. (3) = percentage increase in unemployment rate (a minus sign indicates a fall). (The unemployment rate in 1980 for the five republics was 5.9%, 16.2%, 2.2%, 10.7% and 18.3% in the order listed above).
Col. (4) = percentage change in real private consumption per head.

Sources: Cols. (1) to (3) from Inforpress, *Centroamericana 1984–6* (Guatemala, 1984); Col. (4) derived from Consejo Monetario Centroamericano (*op. cit.*).

while the unemployment indicator (see column 3) suggests that in this respect Guatemala has been the worst affected.

Data on unemployment and wages (both real and nominal) are notoriously unreliable in Central America; in any case, wage labour only accounts for a part of total labour supply.[67] Consequently, a better indicator of the burden of adjustment (see column 4) is the change in real consumption per head. As Table 9.10 shows, all the republics have been badly affected on this score, with the worst sufferers being El Salvador and Nicaragua.

Real consumption per head is only an average, which implicitly assumes that no group was able to protect its earnings/consumption in real terms. In practice, every country has a 'protected sector', which means that the fall in real consumption per head in the 'unprotected sector' was even greater than implied by Table 9.10. This fall can be simulated on different assumptions about the size of the protected sector (see Table 9.11). The protected sector consists of groups which for one reason or other can manipulate the price of their services to prevent a fall in their real earnings/consumption. They include some (but not all) civil servants, most members of the armed forces, police, etc., some (but not all) employers, members of the professions, politicians, etc. Table 9.11

Table 9.11   Fall in real consumption per head in unprotected sector (%)

Proposition of labour force assumed to be protected (%)	0	10	20	30	40	50
Costa Rica	26	29[a]	33	37	43	52[c,b]
El Salvador	39	43	52[a]	55	65[b]	77[c]
Guatemala	9	10	12	13[a]	16[c]	19[b]
Honduras	19	21	24[a]	27[b]	32	38[c]
Nicaragua	39	43	49[a]	56	65[b]	78[c]

Notes:
[a]   Author's guestimate of protected share.
[b]   Share of full-time workers in total employment (to nearest decile). For source, see note 67.
[c]   Share of modern sector in total employment (to nearest decile). For source, see note 67.

marks the author's guestimate of the size of the protected sector in each republic, which can be compared with what would have happened if the protected sector were the same as (a) the modern sector and (b) full-time employment.

Table 9.11 suggests that in two republics (El Salvador and Nicaragua) the reduction in real consumption has been massive, in two others (Costa Rica and Honduras) it has been severe, while in one (Guatemala) it has been quite modest. This last result is not altogether surprising; Guatemala did not adjust until 1982 and is the least dependent of the Central American republics on external conditions. In addition, the expansion of the oil industry in the period 1980–3 (although far from spectacular) has been a factor contributing towards the relative mildness of adjustment.

The table does not tell us which economic activities have been particularly severely affected by the recent depression. This information is provided by Table 9.12, where it can be seen that the worst affected sectors have been construction, commerce and manufacturing; as these are all predominantly urban activities, it is realistic to assume that it is the urban areas that have carried a disproportionate share of the burden of adjustment.

Agriculture in every case has achieved an above-average performance. This conceals a wide difference, however, between the performance of export agriculture (EXA) and domestic use agriculture (DUA); with the exception of Nicaragua, the performance of EXA has been worse than that of agriculture as a whole, suggesting a relatively strong performance by DUA; this 'defence mechanism' in the Central American context is

Table 9.12 Change (%) in real net output by sector from real GDP peak to trough

Sector	Costa Rica 1980–3	El Salvador 1978–83	Guatemala 1981–3	Honduras 1981–3	Nicaragua 1978–82
Agriculture	+4.3*	−10.8*	−5.1*	+3.7*	−12.7*
Mining	(a)	0*	+5.3*	−5.0	−41.5
Manu- facturing	−16.8	−32.5	−7.2	−2.3*	−14.9
Public utilities	+34.7*	+7.3*	−3.0*	−2.8	−8.8*
Construction	−50.4	−41.6	−37.2	−7.0	−53.8
Commerce	−26.3	−45.0	−9.6	−3.1	−14.3
Public adminis- tration	−0.8*	+16.3*	+8.4*	+3.3*	−2.9*
GDP	−10.5	−22.4	−6.2	−2.4	−13.6

Notes:
* Above average performance.
(a) Included in manufacturing.

familiar to students of the 1930s.[68] The Nicaraguan experience, by contrast, has been of EXA constant in real terms, but a sharp decline in DUA; this has been reversed since 1982, however, as land reform and the removal of price ceilings have begun to take effect.[69]

It would therefore seem that workers and their families in EXA on the one hand and the urban private sector on the other have borne the brunt of the burden of adjustment, while workers and their families in the public sector, together with small-scale agriculture (DUA), have experienced the least hardship. Needless to say, there are exceptions to these generalisations, the most important being EXA in Nicaragua and public employees in Costa Rica and Honduras.

Not all the burden of adjustment can be attributed to the adjustment programmes and even less to the IMF-inspired programmes during the AWIC phase. War-related adjustment has been very important in El Salvador and Nicaragua and is the main reason why those two republics have borne a heavier burden than the others; similarly, once the effects of war are taken into account, it seems safe to assume that most of the burden of adjustment was carried during the AWOC rather than AWIC phase. It would be impossible, however, to quantify the distribution of the burden; in any case it would be inappropriate, as the external environment was much more hostile in the AWOC than AWIC phase.

One final question should be raised, although it cannot be fully answered: what additional costs of adjustment were incurred as a result of delaying adjustment during the FN stage? The answer again cannot be quantitative, but it can be assumed that the additional costs were substantial. Costa Rica in particular would have been able to incur a much smaller burden if adjustment had begun in 1979, while all republics paid a heavy price for their failure to stem capital flight at an earlier stage.

THE POST-ADJUSTMENT PHASE

At the time of writing (August 1985), the four republics which passed through the AWIC phase (all except Nicaragua) can be said to have entered a post-adjustment phase, the hallmark of which has been a modest recovery in real GDP. This recovery as yet lacks solid foundations, however, and may prove to be temporary in nature; furthermore, the continuation of external financial problems forced Costa Rica to sign a new thirteen-month standby agreement with the IMF in March 1985 (for details, see Table 9.7) and both Guatemala and Honduras are expected to do the same in 1986 following presidential elections.

The recovery of real GDP since the end of 1983[70] in all the republics except Nicaragua has had three principal elements. The first has been export growth, the second a revival in private investment, and the third has been a recovery in imports which has helped to unlock various supply-side bottlenecks.

The dominant factor in export growth in 1984 was better prices for the main traditional exports (particularly coffee and bananas), although there was some growth in volumes exported as well. US imports from the four republics grew rapidly (ranging from 25 per cent in the case of Guatemala to 5.5 per cent in the case of El Salvador), but only a small part of this increase could be attributed to the launching of the Caribbean Basin Initiative (CBI) in January 1984; indeed, in the eighteen months to June 1985, new investments under the CBI in the four republics had only reached $29.7 million (50 per cent of which were in Honduras), compared with $44 million in the Dominican Republic alone.[71]

Import demand since the end of 1983 has been stimulated by the recovery in private investment, but the growth of import supply cannot be explained solely in terms of additional earnings from exports. The four republics have benefited from their strategic geopolitical location and have received increased official capital inflows, mainly from the United States, although on a scale below that envisaged in the Kissinger Report.[72]

The sensitivity of imports to even a modest economic recovery[73] has, however, imposed a very serious strain on the balance of payments and the exchange rate, despite the official capital inflows. The strains forced Guatemala to introduce a parallel exchange market in November 1984, in which the quetzal has rapidly depreciated against the dollar.[74] While some of the explanation is due to the failure of the Guatemalan authorities to reduce the budget deficit,[75] the experience of the other republics shows that the problem runs deeper; Costa Rica has been forced to speed up the rate of mini-devaluations despite its fiscal rectitude, and El Salvador has channelled yet more imports through the parallel market, while the black market exchange rate has fallen dramatically.[76]

The four republics, with the possible exception of Honduras,[77] have therefore effectively broken the exchange link with the US dollar and initiated a period of effective real devaluations. Whatever the impact on non-traditional exports, it is certain that inflation will accelerate (as is confirmed by preliminary estimates). This is likely to aggravate the fiscal situation and increase social tensions in republics which can ill afford it.

Exchange-rate instability, and the consequent acceleration of inflation, is one reason for believing that the modest recovery since the end of 1983 may be short-lived. An additional problem is the dependence of exports on markets where growth is problematical (e.g. CACM, USA) and the reliance on traditional primary products for which world prices have been falling (e.g. coffee, cotton, sugar).

A slowdown in the growth of the US economy, coupled with a fall in nominal dollar interest rates, creates pressures on the balance of payments of Latin American countries whose net effects may be uncertain. In Central America, however, the impact is unambiguous, because so much of the external debt is owed to official creditors at subsidised rates.[78] Thus, the current (1985) trends in the US economy can be expected to exert additional strains on the balance of payments of the four republics.

The relatively strong performance of extraregional exports in 1984 contributed to a slowdown in the decline of intraregional (CACM) trade.[79] The subsequent exchange-rate instability, however, coupled with the failure to service debts between the member countries, has produced a further deterioration and a shift to bilateral, balanced trade,[80] which the adoption of a new tariff nomenclature is unlikely to reverse.[81]

It is probable that non-traditional exports outside CACM, stimulated by the CBI and real depreciation, will increase in value. Such exports, however, start from a very low base, and it is not to be expected that they can compensate for the weakness of other exports for many years. There are grounds for believing, therefore, that the export performance of the four republics may deteriorate.

Such a deterioration will bring the servicing of the external public debt back to the forefront of discussion. Both Costa Rica and Honduras in the middle of 1985 rescheduled their debts (and arrears) up to the end of 1986, but this postponement of the debt problem is likely to prove short-lived. Both private and official creditors have shown an unwillingness to reschedule the debts of small countries for more than two years at a time, and in the case of private creditors there has been an even greater reluctance to provide new loans. Thus all four republics will continue to be dependent on new official credits, a dependence which will be increased if export earnings deteriorate.

Although the problem of external debt service is most acute in Costa Rica, it has caused increasing strains in the other three republics; a deterioration of the external environment will increase these strains and short-term policy will concentrate on measures to promote export earnings. This raises the question of whether the evolution of the economies in the short run is likely to be consistent with long-term strategies.

Since the start of the AWOC phase, there has been no long-term strategy in the four republics. Analyses of the Central American crisis, however, have achieved a remarkably broad consensus on the need to emphasise food security and a less import-dependent industrialisation in any long-term solution to the region's problems.[82] These are difficult goals, which depend on a diversification of agriculture (in order to supply the urban economy with the raw materials and foodstuffs needed by industrialists and consumers) and a strengthening of CACM (in order to provide a market for the industrial outputs).

Such a strategy saves foreign exchange in the long run and lowers the trade coefficient, making the region less vulnerable to export instability.[83] In the short run, however, it is likely to cost foreign exchange (through the diversification of agriculture away from exports) and therefore runs counter to the short-term strategy imposed of necessity by the hostile external environment in general and the external debt problem in particular. It would seem, therefore, that in Central

America the long-term and the short-term strategies are indeed in conflict.

CONCLUSIONS

The burden of adjustment has been very severe in Central America, but it cannot all be blamed on external factors. One conclusion that emerges clearly from this chapter is that the failure to adjust in 1979, 1980 and (in some cases) 1981 added significantly to the costs of adjustment; in particular, the debt burden was increased enormously as a result of the FN phase.

The failure to adjust could not be excused on the grounds that the balance-of-payments disequilibrium was perceived as temporary; on the contrary, complex though it was, the BOP crisis in 1979 had all the signs of being a medium-term problem. While the position in El Salvador and Nicaragua was complicated by civil war, the failure to adjust elsewhere was inexcusable on economic grounds. Political constraints help to explain the FN phase, but they do not justify it.

Once the decision was taken to adjust, there was a rapid improvement in the BOP position. This was due to the adoption of import-suppressing policies in the AWOC phase, which would not have been permitted as part of an IMF programme; no other policies, however, could have been expected to achieve such a sharp improvement in the BOP in such a short time-period.

The suppression of imports without a corresponding reduction in nominal demand usually produces financial instability and an increase in inflation; with the exception of Costa Rica (where currency depreciation produced an inflation rate close to 100 per cent in 1982), Central America was fortunate to avoid these consequences during the AWOC phase. The credit–import ratio rose dangerously, but excessive DCE was prevented from spilling over into hyperinflation by the rapid growth of quasi-money; this, in turn, was due in particular to import deposit requirements.

The transition from the AWOC to the AWIC phase cannot, therefore, be blamed on the failure of the former; on the contrary, judged by the improvement in the BOP, the AWOC stage was successful. It could not, however, resolve the external finance and debt problems, and in three of the four relevant countries[84] these problems were a major reason for sticking to IMF conditionality.

Acceptance of IMF conditions has not solved the debt problem, though. The Fund cannot be blamed for this, but it is a major weakness in the case-by-case approach favoured by the creditor nations. A Fund programme, even if successfully completed, is no guarantee of favourable treatment by creditors; private creditors, in particular, are under no obligation to carry out multiyear reschedulings or lend additional funds.

Net lending by official sources, responding to the internationalisation of the Central American crisis, has continued to flow to the region[85] and the sums involved have even increased; this has gone some way towards easing the debt problem, but official largesse cannot dispose of the problem of the public external debt held privately; projected debt service payments to private creditors are equivalent to 50 per cent of current exports until 1991 in Nicaragua and until 1989 in Costa Rica.[86]

Since 1979, many more IMF programmes have failed than succeeded. The high failure rate cannot be blamed entirely on Fund inflexibility; on the contrary, in its different treatment of El Salvador and Nicaragua, the Fund has shown itself to be politically very flexible, although this sensitivity to the international political environment has not carried over to domestic politics, where the internal obstacles to revenue-raising measures have been ignored.

The Fund has also shown itself flexible in the choice of policy instruments. In the matter of exchange-rate policy, orthodoxy appears to have been abandoned (with the possible exception of Costa Rica) and multiple exchange rates have been tolerated, if not approved.[87] The usual rigid credit ceilings appear to have been progressively relaxed and interest-rate policy has not been very active.

It is only on the question of fiscal policy and the budget deficit that the Fund has proved inflexible. This inflexibility appears to be based on the mistaken idea that the causal link between the PSBR on the one hand and inflation and resource misallocation on the other always runs from the former to the latter.

It would be foolish to deny that fiscal reform is important in Central America. The tax level and revenue structure of several republics, notably Guatemala, is very antiquated and in need of overhaul; fiscal reform, however, cannot be achieved in a short period, and the Fund must either pursue it in a medium-term strategy (e.g. Extended Fund Facilities) or settle for a more flexible fiscal policy in a short-term strategy.

The other major criticism of the Fund to emerge from this chapter is its treatment or lack of treatment of the CACM. The IMF has not tried to reverse the collapse of CACM trade and has focused its export promotion programmes exclusively on exports outside the region. In addition, the Fund has tolerated policies discriminating against CACM imports and has not linked standby credits to the settlement of debt arrears within the CACM.

The IMF's articles of association and its voting structure[88] impose certain limits on the Fund's operations. It follows that Fund programmes will not always be the most suitable way of securing adjustment; the success of the AWOC phase in Central America is an example of this situation. Yet, although a sharp (and rapid) adjustment was achieved, a successful AWOC phase is not usually sufficient to secure favourable treatment by creditors.

There is no real need for this inflexibility on the part of creditors (whether private or public); what matters is the degree of adjustment in relation to the scale of the debt. Creditors (represented by steering committees) do not need the intervention of the IMF in order to judge the results. The Fund's seal of approval does not put the creditors under any greater obligation, but it can impose additional burdens on the debtors.

As the global debt problem moves into its 'mature' phase, a dichotomy is emerging in the treatment of small and large debtors. A successful resolution of the latter's problems is essential if world financial stability is to be assured; as a result, the IMF and the creditors have co-operated with some success to ensure sufficient new finance to prevent collapse.

In the case of small debtors, there is no threat to world financial stability. Creditors therefore feel no obligation to lend additional finance, and assistance is often restricted to rescheduling short-term debts (a highly profitable activity). The burden of adjustment is, therefore, borne entirely by the debtor country, unless it defaults; IMF intervention tends to reinforce this unequal distribution of the burden of adjustment, because it ensures that the debtor has the capacity to service its debts (e.g. through a trade surplus) without increasing the obligations of the creditor. It might, therefore, be more equitable if the debt problems of small debtors such as the Central American republics were resolved bilaterally without IMF conditionality.

Notes

1. Costa Rica paid lip-service to the need for adjustment. In August 1980, the Minister of Finance, Hernán Sáenz, said: 'we wanted a programme that would adjust through a policy of demand management. We wanted to control the money supply so that the adjustment would be a real

adjustment and not just a series of patches' (*Euromoney*, Special Supplement on Costa Rica, August 1980, p. 11). In practice, however, there was no adjustment at all in Costa Rica in 1980.

2. Nicaragua's real Gross Domestic Product (GDP) fell by 7.5 per cent in 1978 and 25.5 per cent in 1979. El Salvador's real GDP fell by 1.5 per cent in 1979 and 8.8 per cent in 1980.

3. See Table I in Bulmer-Thomas, V., 'World Recession and Central American Depression – Lessons from the 1930s for the 1980s', in E. Durán, *Latin America in the World Depression* (Cambridge: CUP, 1985).

4. The fall in Honduran GDP in 1974, for example, can be blamed on Hurricane Fifi.

5. Credits subject to conditionality must be distinguished from the compensatory finance and oil facility drawings which are not so subject and of which all Central American countries have taken advantage.

6. Guatemala completed its one-year standby agreement with the Fund signed in November 1981. This was a first credit tranche, however (disbursed fully at the start of the programme) and there can be no doubt that the performance of the Guatemalan economy did not comply with the Fund's conditions as laid down in the agreement.

7. A new IMF loan to Costa Rica was approved in March 1985, and a standby agreement went into force in May.

8. Nicaragua, as we shall see, has had no agreements with the Fund since the revolution. El Salvador has had one agreement, but balance-of-payments pressures (and the debt problem) are resolved through exceptionally high levels of official credits on concessionary terms.

9. This point is made very clearly in Bird, G., 'Balance of Payments Policy', in T. Killick (ed.) *The Quest for Economic Stabilisation* (London: Heinemann, 1984). In practice, of course, the choice of finance may be ruled out by non-availability.

10. The programme is described in Ministerio de Hacienda, 'La Reforma Financiera en Costa Rica', Banco Central de Costa Rica: Serie 'Comentarios Sobre Asuntos Económicos', no. 37, 1980. It is discussed more critically in Rivera Urrutia, E., *El Fondo Monetario Internacional y Costa Rica, 1978–82* (San José: Colección Centroamérica, 1982).

11. The Guatemalan quetzal was at par with the US dollar from 1925 to 1986, and the official rate of exchange in El Salvador did not change from 1934 to 1986.

12. In 1979 the Sandinistas were very successful in convincing North Americans and Western Europeans that they were the representatives of a broad-based government which would not interfere with capitalist relations of production. The capitalist class in Central America was suspicious from the start and capital flight was one way of hedging their bets.

13. Table 9.1 suggests that capital flight was not a problem in Honduras. This contradicts a number of contemporary reports (including those provided by the US embassy) and suggests that capital flight from Honduras was concealed. Perhaps it is no accident that the BOP entry 'net errors and omissions' was strongly negative in 1979 and 1980.

14. This included the nationalisation of banks and much of foreign trade, as well as agrarian reform.

15. This small decline is not enough, however, to justify calling this period one of adjustment.

16. Figures are not available on private investment in Nicaragua after the revolution, but it is generally agreed that it also fell to very low levels.

17. It is assumed that virtually all of the increase in investment in Nicaragua can be attributed to the public sector.

18. See Table III in Bulmer-Thomas, V. (1985), 'World Recession'.

19. This has been demonstrated using both econometric and input–output techniques. For the former, see Siri, G. and Raul Domínguez, L., 'Central American Accommodation to External Disruptions', in W. Cline (ed.) *World Inflation and the Developing Countries* (Washington: Brookings Institution, 1981); for the latter, see Bulmer-Thomas, V., 'A Model of Inflation for Central America', *Bulletin of the Oxford University Institute of Economics and Statistics*, November 1977.

20. In Nicaragua, however, this ratio was nearer 2:1. See Table 9.5.

21. The only sharp changes in velocity are in Costa Rica in 1981 (which can be explained by the conversion of both nominal GDP and the money stock into dollars at the rapidly depreciating exchange rate) and Nicaragua in 1983, when excess money creation was a very serious problem.

22. We should therefore distinguish between the initial capital flight from Central America, which was accommodated by a (passive) financial system, and a later stage of capital flight which was fuelled by the financial system as a result of irresponsible fiscal policies during the FN stage. I am grateful to Jaime Ros (author of the Mexican chapter in this volume) for pointing out this distinction.

23. For a similar argument, see Tseng, W., 'The Effects of Adjustment', *Finance and Development*, December 1984.

24. At the start of the IMF programme, the maximum ceiling for interest rates on commercial bank credits was raised from 11 per cent to 15 per cent; at the end of the programme it was lowered to 12 per cent.

25. See Rivera Urrutia, E., *op. cit.*

26. Import suppression through exchange control and other restrictions is an obvious example.

27. The Guatemalan standby credit of September 1983 was in fact suspended in July 1984 due to the government's failure to meet performance criteria; it is still correct, however, to think of adjustment in Guatemala in two stages: one without and one with conditionality.

28. By December 1981, the parallel market rate was 3.50 colones per US dollar compared with 2.50 in the official market.

29. In Nicaragua, on the other hand, the gap has grown progressively wider. While the parallel market rate remained at 28.50 córdobas per US dollar, the black market rate stood at 70 by the end of 1983.

30. See Rivera Urrutia, E., *op. cit.*

31. Some efforts were made to discriminate in favour of CACM, but they were not sufficient to cancel the forces working in the opposite direction.

32. Between mid-1981 and mid-1983, Guatemala received no major credits from private sources.

33. Agreement had also been reached by Nicaragua with its creditors on part of its debts in the FN phase. See Weinert, R., 'Nicaragua's Debt

Renegotiation', *Cambridge Journal of Economics*, vol. 5, 1981, pp. 187–94.

34. Default on payment of $36 million in interest was only avoided when Nicaragua pledged future export earnings against debt service payments.

35. The Salvadorean programme was extremely flexible, so that the risk of suspension was minimal. The charge that the agreement was politically motivated has been made by several observers; see, for example, Arias Penate, S., *El FMI y la Política Contrainsurgente en El Salvador*, Cuadernos de Pensamiento Propio (Managua: INIES, 1983).

36. Costa Rican electricity price increases, for example, were suspended in July 1983 as a result of public opposition.

37. The most notorious are the Corporación Costarricense de Desarrollo in Costa Rica and the Corporación Nacional de Inversiones in Honduras; the Corporación Financiera Nacional has also been a heavy loss-maker in Guatemala.

38. There is a good description of the scheme in Carlos H. González A., 'Experiencia de Guatemala con el Proceso de Ajuste en 1982–3', in Centro de Estudios Monetarios Latinoamericanos, *Boletín*, vol. XXX, no. 3, May–June 1984, pp. 157–65.

39. The CBI offers duty-free entry to the US markets for almost all commodities for a twelve-year period. The scheme applies to all countries of the Caribbean Basin except Cuba, Nicaragua and Guyana. See Feinberg, R. and Newfarmer, R., 'The CBI: Bold Plan or Empty Promise?', in R. Newfarmer (ed.) *From Gunboats to Diplomacy* (Baltimore: Johns Hopkins, 1984).

40. This has not, however, been important in El Salvador.

41. Although El Salvador cannot be classed as having a major debt problem, it did reschedule its debt with the Dresdner Bank of Germany in June 1983 (i.e. just before the end of the IMF programme).

42. From the point of view of the debtor, 'success' involves multi-year reschedulings together with injections of new credits.

43. In early 1985, Costa Rica rescheduled its debts for 1985–6, but this was outside the AWIC phase (see penultimate section). The partial rescheduling of Honduran debts has already been mentioned (see p. 293).

44. See Crawford, M., 'Third World Debt is Here to Stay', *Lloyds Bank Review*, January 1985.

45. The *World Bank Debt Tables* for 1984–5, however, show that the disbursed debt outstanding to private creditors rose from $832.8 million at the end of 1981 to $1081.7 million at the end of 1983.

46. See IMF, *World Economic Outlook*, 1984.

47. Throughout most of 1984, for example, the Fund was insisting on a PSBR of 1 per cent in Costa Rica. In the final agreement (implemented in May 1985) a compromise of 1.5 per cent was reached; there can be no macroeconomic justification, however, for such a low figure in Costa Rica or any other Central American country. Furthermore, when the PSBR is adjusted for inflation (see the Mexican chapter), it is more than probable that these IMF budget targets would represent a surplus.

48. The exception is Honduras, whose agreement with the Fund in November 1982 allowed for an increase in tariffs on all goods (including those from Central America).

49. Credit from the World Bank was frozen in 1982; the Inter-American Development Bank (IDB) approved its last loan for Nicaragua in 1982, although it was not disbursed until 1984. A $58 million IDB loan was blocked in April 1985, when the USA threatened to reduce its financial commitments to the bank if the loan was approved.

50. In an interview with the *Financial Times* (9 July 1985), the Vice-President of the Central Bank justified the policy as follows: 'At first [1980 and 1981] our expansionist policy brought high levels of growth ... However, from 1982, external finance began to fall sharply and we were faced with the choice of either stopping growth, or trying to continue with internal finance'.

51. See Banco Interamericano de Desarrollo, *Informe Económico – Nicaragua*, October 1974, Table 12.

52. Revenue did rise (by 41.2 per cent) with income tax receipts up by 64.9 per cent, but these efforts were dwarfed by the rise in expenditure. See Banco Interamericano de Desarrollo, *op. cit.*, Table 7.

53. See Austin, J., Fox, J. and Kruger, W., 'The Role of the Revolutionary State in the Nicaraguan Food System', *World Development*, January 1985, pp. 15–40.

54. By the 1983–4 season, production of rice, beans and sorghum had surpassed pre-revolutionary (1978–9) levels. The growth of maize production was disappointing, however, and the expansion of meat and dairy products was very poor. See Banco Interamericano de Desarrollo, *op. cit.*, Table 17, and Austin *et al.*, *op. cit.*, Table 1, p. 25.

55. See Stahler-Sholk, R., 'Debt and Stabilization in Revolutionary Nicaragua', paper presented at XII Conference of the Latin American Studies Association, Albuquerque, New Mexico, April 1985.

56. Defined as coffee, cotton, sugar, beef, bananas, shrimps and gold.

57. The crop most seriously affected was coffee. Earnings plunged by 20 per cent despite a rise of 22.8 per cent in its unit value. See IMF, *International Financial Statistics*, July 1985.

58. Further details on the adjustment programme are provided in Stahler-Sholk, *op. cit.*

59. See Inforpress, *Centroamericana*, no. 643, 6 June 1985, p. 13.

60. See Inforpress, *Centroamericana*, no. 649, 18 July 1985, p. 8.

61. See *Central American Report*, vol. XII, no. 21, 7 June 1985, p. 165.

62. See Inforpress, *Centroamericana*, no. 650, 25 July 1985, p. 3.

63. See Inforpress, *Centroamericana*, no. 647, 4 July 1985, p. 2.

64. See Inforpress, *Centroamericana*, no. 642, 30 May 1985, p. 6.

65. Exports to the USA (mainly bananas, meat and shellfish) had been reduced to $57 million by 1984, and new markets were found fairly quickly. Imports from the USA (almost double the value of exports in 1984) have proved more difficult to replace, because so much Nicaraguan machinery (particularly within the private sector) is dependent on US spare parts.

66. The main exception is Nicaragua, which pursued a policy of expansion in 1983, so that for Nicaragua the years of adjustment are confined to the period 1981–2.

67. See PREALC, *Producción de Alimentos Básicos y Empleo en el Istmo*

Centroamericano, Santiago, August 1983, Table 5.

68. See Bulmer-Thomas, V., 'Central America in the Inter-War Years', in R. Thorp (ed.) *Latin America in the 1930s: the Periphery in World Crisis* (London: Macmillan, 1984).

69. Land reform began in 1981, but the biggest waves of distribution occurred in 1983 and 1984. Price controls were relaxed a little in May 1984 and loosened substantially in February 1985.

70. Preliminary estimates of real GDP growth in 1984 for the four republics (i.e. excluding Nicaragua) vary from 0.2 per cent in Guatemala to 6 per cent in Costa Rica. GDP is not calculated on a quarterly basis, so at the time of writing there are no growth estimates for 1985.

71. See CBI, *Business Bulletin*, June 1985, p. 2.

72. The external financing requirements for Central America and Panama were estimated at $24 billion over the period 1984–90, with $1.5 billion to $1.7 billion in 1984. See *Report of the National Bipartisan Commission on Central America* ('Kissinger Report'), January 1984, pp. 63–7.

73. Guatemalan imports, for example, rose by 13.4 per cent (in value) in 1984, while real GDP rose by 0.2 per cent. This was the most extreme case, but everywhere imports rose much faster than GDP.

74. Guatemala had a three-tier exchange market in 1985. The official rate (at par with the US dollar) was used for essentials (including oil), there were periodic government auctions of foreign exchange for specific goods, and there is also a free market (operated by the banks) where the quetzal had fallen to 3 per US dollar by mid-1985. In 1986, the quetzal was finally devalued.

75. Business pressure groups have consistently and successfully resisted attempts to increase government revenue through tax reform. In April 1985, General Mejía Víctores was forced to reverse a number of revenue-raising measures, and the new measured announced in July (including a 3.5 per cent tax on sales in the parallel exchange market) are not expected to have much impact. Although the ratio of tax revenue to GDP is the lowest in Latin America outside Haiti, cuts in public expenditure have prevented an explosion in the PSBR which fell by 47 per cent between 1981 and 1984 (see Inforpress, *Centroamericana*, no. 646, 27 June 1985, p. 2).

76. The parallel market rate was devalued to 4.50 colones per US dollar in July 1985, but the black market rate had fallen by then to C5.80. The official rate was finally devalued to C5.00 in 1986.

77. Honduras has so far resisted the introduction of a parallel exchange market and the official rate remains pegged to the US dollar at two lempiras (L), unchanged since 1918. The black market rate has been stable at around L2.75.

78. Even in Costa Rica, over half of the debt is owed to official creditors with an average interest rate in 1983 of 5.9 per cent. See World Bank, *World Debt Tables 1984/5*.

79. Preliminary estimates indicate a fall of only 2 per cent in 1984.

80. In the first half of 1985, Costa Rica announced restrictions on exports to CACM until it receives sufficient imports from other countries to cancel their debts. Trade between Honduras and Nicaragua was similarly affected, and commerce between Honduras and Guatemala was

suspended several times before the adoption of new protectionist trade measures by Honduras in July.

81. After years of delay, the Central American ministers of economy agreed in June 1985 to adopt the Brussels customs nomenclature, with all tariffs calculated on an *ad valorem* basis.

82. See, for example, many of the articles in G. Irving and X. Gorostiaga (eds) *Towards an Alternative for Central America and the Caribbean* (London: Allen & Unwin, 1985).

83. See Bulmer-Thomas, V., 'Central American Integration, Trade Diversification and the World Market', in G. Irving and X. Gorostiaga (eds) *op. cit.*

84. Nicaragua did not pass through the AWIC phase and El Salvador's debt was not a major reason for seeking an IMF standby credit.

85. Including Nicaragua; a list of socialist country loans/grants to Nicaragua can be found in Acciaris, R., 'Nicaragua – Pays Socialistes; vers la consolidation des liens économiques?', *Problèmes d'Amérique Latine*, no. 74, 1984. Mexico has also been a very important creditor.

86. See World Bank, *World Debt Tables 1984/5.*

87. This relaxation of exchange-rate orthodoxy has been noted by Killick, in T. Killick (ed.) *op. cit.*, and is explained by the breakdown of the system of fixed exchange rates in the early 1970s.

88. The USA has 19.3 per cent of executive board votes in the IMF; this is three times bigger than the second largest share (the UK with 6.7 per cent), and it is virtually impossible for a country like Nicaragua to secure a favourable vote in the face of US opposition. The Soviet Union is not a member, and the votes of other socialist countries are currently cast by either the Netherlands (Romania, Yugoslavia) or Belgium (Hungary). See *IMF Survey*, September 1984, special supplement on the Fund.

10 Review and Conclusions
Rosemary Thorp and Laurence Whitehead

'Brazil will not pay its foreign debt with recession, nor with unemployment, nor with hunger.' (President Jose Sarney, United Nations, 23 September 1985)

A central preoccupation for any student of the adjustment crisis in Latin America must surely be the prospect for the next few years. In this chapter we move towards an assessment of such prospects in the final section, attempting to integrate what we know of the global scenario with the insights the studies here have offered on the options and constraints in individual situations. With this aim in view we first review the country studies, seeking particularly to define the insights they give as to the consequences of different policy choices faced with the need to adjust, and the interplay between such policy choices and longer-run options and needs. The country experiences with adjustment lead us next to review certain common themes (the role of the IMF, the fiscal deficit and capital flight). Since where the burden of the crisis falls is crucial to understanding the evolution of options, necessities and policy choices, we then discuss distributional issues. The final section comprises our tentative appraisal of the prospects for the late 1980s.

LONG-TERM NEEDS AND SHORT-TERM ADJUSTMENT

In evaluating and comparing the nature of the adjustment, it is important first to define what we count as greater or lesser success. For the purpose of our discussion here, the adjustment to the external shock is the more 'successful', the less the damage to medium-term growth and development prospects. This may or may not involve some reduction in inflation: the gains from any such reduction must be weighed against the damage to development prospects that has frequently accompanied orthodox anti-inflation packages. The comparative data are given in Tables 10.1 and 10.2. We consider separately the distributional aspects of the adjustment process, although they are relevant here too if, for example, their political implications are such that a given policy cannot be sustained.

319

Table 10.1 Percentage change in real GDP

	Change from peak to trough[a]		Change 1980–3
Argentina	−9.1	(1980–2)	−8.1
Brazil	−3.8	(1980–3)	−3.8
Colombia	−	(no fall)	+4.2
Costa Rica	−11.1	(1980–2)	−10.5
Chile	−14.7	(1981–3)	−10.0
El Salvador	−22.8	(1978–83)	−14.0
Guatemala	−3.5	(1981–3)	−2.9
Honduras	−2.2	(1981–3)	−1.1
Mexico	−5.8	(1981–3)	+1.7
Nicaragua	−11.5	(1978–83)	+9.4
Peru	−11.8	(1982–3)	−8.3
Weighted average (*GDP 1982 used to weight*)	−5.7		−3.0

Note:
[a] Considering all years since 1978. Data for 1984 were not available.

Source: country chapters.

Table 10.2 Annual percentage change in consumer prices

	1978	1979	1980	1981	1982	1983	1984	1985
Argentina	170	140	88	131	209	433	688	672.1
Brazil	38.7	52.8	82.8	105.6	98.0	142.0	196.7	227.0
Colombia	17.8	24.6	26.6	27.5	24.5	19.7	16.1	24.0
Costa Rica	5.9	9.2	18.2	37.0	90.1	32.6	11.9	15.1
Chile	40.1	33.3	35.1	19.7	9.9	27.2	19.9	30.7
El Salvador	12.9	8.6	17.4	14.8	11.7	13.1	11.6	22.2
Guatemala	7.9	11.4	10.7	11.5	0.2	8.2	na	na
Honduras	5.7	12.1	18.1	9.4	9.4	8.9	4.6	2.6
Mexico	16.4	17.6	24.8	25.9	59.5	93.8	68.9	57.7
Nicaragua	4.5	48.2	35.3	23.9	24.8	31.0	35.7	219.5
Peru	57.8	66.6	59.2	43.4	33.7	75.4	110.2	163.4

Source: IMF, *International Financial Statistics*.

Of the many themes around which it would have been possible to summarise our case studies, we have chosen to focus on the quality and nature of the response to the external crisis and its interrelationship with long-term needs, believing that this may illuminate not only the comparative response but also the room for manoeuvre and thereby country prospects. In the discussion which follows, we therefore focus on governmental capacity for macro-management, as reflecting the varying relationships between the state and major social forces in the various countries under consideration.

For example, *Brazil* can be singled out as not only the strongest economy under review here, but also as a country in which the central economic authorities have a long record of sophisticated and forward-looking economic management. This is certainly not to say that individual decisions have always been well judged, but that the Brazilian state, compared with other countries discussed in this volume, has displayed a relatively high capacity to formulate and implement reasonably coherent strategies for managing a very complex development process. Even when governments have changed, or there has been a shift in official economic priorities, important elements of continuity have been preserved – in marked contrast to, say, the violent swings of policy that have so long characterised Argentine economic management. The Brazilian state has developed a strong 'technocratic' elite, which has achieved considerable internal legitimacy and authority in relation to the main social forces at play. This structure seems to have survived the switch from military to civilian government in 1985 better than many observers had expected. It is not just characteristics of the state apparatus that have made this possible, but also the patterns of elite co-operation and conciliation in the society at large. These relationships have proved more flexible and durable than is usual in Latin America and have partially insulated the economic managers from short-term pressures. This relatively high degree of underlying social consensus, persisting through military and civilian governments alike, has facilitated forward-looking economic management and helped the Brazilians to preserve the prospect of long-term development even when buffeted by severe short-term adjustment stresses.

It is therefore no coincidence that the nearest to a 'success story' in our earlier volume[1] again appears to do well on this occasion, and particularly in respect to the compatibility between short-term responses necessitated by the crisis and long-term needs. In Brazil, the 1973 shock produced a major policy decision in favour of long-term structural change, as Carneiro's chapter shows. The 1975 Development

Plan embodied large projects in the potential export sector and in import substitution – financed by borrowing from abroad *and* from the Brazilian private sector. The commitment to growth was even then at the expense of inflation – even more so in 1979–80, when policy was very badly mismanaged. These projects were *maintained* throughout the period of restrictive policies, 1981–3, and were yielding dividends as early as 1979, but importantly so by 1984, when several matured just in time to permit a strong response to the US recovery without a rise in the import coefficient. The comparative vigour of Brazil's supply response is shown by examining its share of the rise in US imports between mid-1983 and September 1984, the period of the recovery. Brazil's share in the increment in US imports from the western hemisphere (excluding Canada) was a remarkable 76 per cent compared with its average share of 12 per cent in the preceding five-year period.[2]

One fascinating aspect of Carneiro's story is the extent to which the development effort was financed by state borrowing from the domestic private sector at high interest rates, and lending at lower rates. This, combined with the steep rise in the average level of interest rates, has radically increased the transfers from the state to the private sector. It is the far more desirable Brazilian counterpart to Ros's story of Mexican capital flight and state external borrowing – more desirable because in the Brazilian case the assets are held internally and the yield can be taxed. This gives the always growth-prone Brazilian economy another clear incentive to pursue the option for growth: with growth there is a yield to be taxed; without growth there is a growing fiscal problem.

'Brazilian-style' macroeconomic management was therefore quite heterodox in that many long-term investment projects were preserved throughout the adjustment period. It was also unusual in that import and capital controls were maintained throughout and were effective, both being important elements in preserving growth. As Carneiro stresses, the lack of capital flight was a major asset in the Brazilian case, although the respective roles of capital controls and confidence in Brazilian growth are hard to disentangle. The one way in which the conventional elements of the adjustment policies conflicted with development relates precisely to the consequences for the Brazilian method of financing: orthodox policies increased the financial burden, via increases in interest charges and via domestic recession which affected tax revenues. In common with other case studies, Carneiro concludes that restrictive policies did *not* reduce inflation: in fact, relative price changes worsened it.

The relationship of these relative price changes to the inflationary process is particularly interesting as a contrast to the Argentine experience, which we come to below. There are big shifts in relative prices, benefiting both agriculture and the oil sector. But whereas we shall see how, in the case of Argentina, prices are manipulated as an *anti-inflation* measure, Brazil follows a deliberate policy of using price shifts to induce structural change, *backed* by major investment programmes (not necessarily all good projects, of course, but sufficient to affect supply). As supply begins to respond, because of the back-up measures, prices do not need to be repeatedly raised. It is also significant, of course, with regard to food prices, that the management of wages is 'better'. So although there are strong inflationary consequences, these are nevertheless not as overwhelming as those we see in the Argentine case.

Nevertheless, this statement is only relative. There is an alarming inflationary potential in Brazil, and although so far growth with inflation has yielded dividends, it remains a high-risk strategy. Undoubtedly the restoration of civilian government in 1985, and the further steps towards political democracy that are envisaged for 1986 and beyond, will increase social pressures and thereby add a further constraint on the room for manoeuvre of Brazil's economic managers. However, redemocratisation is by no means always the enemy of realistic economic management. On the contrary, given Brazil's established relationship between the state and society, a more open political system that involves wider sections of the community in decision-making may serve to share responsibility for the difficult choices to be made, without destroying the country's capacity to formulate coherent responses.

Turning to the case of *Mexico*, we find another major and relatively strong economy, with a long tradition of comparatively effective and autonomous economic management by the central authorities. However, there are significant contrasts with Brazil as regards the structural characteristics of the economy and the state–society relationships. As with Brazil, the Mexican authorities have tried to formulate ambitious and forward-looking economic strategies, but beneath the appearance of regime continuity there have been severe erratic and destabilising shifts of policy, at least since the early 1970s. One contributing factor has been the strains derived from a highly centralised presidential system with severe discontinuities around each six-yearly succession crisis. More generally, the Mexican political system seems to have been suffering a prolonged erosion of legitimacy, partly attributable to its longevity. In contrast to Brazil, the Mexicans have not found it possible to broaden social participation in politics substantially as their society becomes more developed. Thus although the technocratic elite in the state apparatus may possess a number of characteristics in common with its counterpart in Brazil, in the society at large there seems progressively less consensus on or trust in the governing authorities. Clearly, bad management and disappointing economic performance have interacted here, but the roots of the trouble go beyond the deficiencies of any one administration.

Turning to Mexico's response to crisis against this background, there was of course no need for response in the 1970s, since the country's oil bonanza carried it right through to 1982. There were big plans for development from oil, under the López Portillo administration from 1977 on, but they did not prevent the industrial sector growing more slowly than GDP, while non-oil exports lost ground substantially. With the crisis of 1982, Ros shows that policy was more than short-term: the implicit long-term model was based, first, on a radical shift in relative prices (towards tradables, towards higher interest and lower wages) and, second, on the elimination of inefficient state intervention (sale of enterprises and import liberalisation). From the government's point of view, its short-term orthodox adjustment plans were perfectly compatible with this long-term model.

In fact, Ros argues, this compatibility is not so obvious in practice. The areas of conflict, in Ros's view, concerned the goal of bringing down inflation while achieving relative price changes. Here conflict showed up even within the government's own framework: the undervalued exchange rate (an important aspect of the desired relative price shift) began to generate a large increase in foreign exchange, and policy-makers anxious about the inflationary effect felt obliged to move more quickly than intended to exchange-rate appreciation from mid-1983 to December 1984. Other conflicts are perceptible from a wider viewpoint, such as that of our study: for example, import liberalisation, by reducing the relative price of tradables, generates pressure on the exchange rate and therefore *in*flation, not the intended beneficial effect on prices (Ros's analysis of this on pp. 92–3 – is particularly interesting). Also, it is clear from every case analysed that relative price changes are only achieved at the price of taking inflation to a new level. Mexico has been no exception, though the new level is lower in relation to the peak than it is elsewhere (see Table 10.2).

However, what is of more concern is that the long-run aspects of the original strategy show no sign of yielding dividends, although a substantial shift in relative prices certainly has occurred (see the data on p. 104). But as of 1985, the behaviour of non-oil exports has ominous implications for the efficiency of the strategy, while there is no sign of a revived dynamic private sector attracting Mexican capital back from abroad. What industrial revival there is, is highly import-intensive. The conclusion is obvious within the terms of our study: it is the lesser efficiency of, and priority given to, concomitant long-run state investments providing the infrastructure and the stimulus that differentiates the Mexican use of relative prices from the Brazilian case.

We do not wish to imply that Brazilian public sector projects have been so much more successful than Mexico's; both countries have, of course, been prone to overambitious and poorly planned projects responding to sectional interests rather than national need. But as in most such cases, a sudden oil bonanza does aggravate pharaonic tendencies; indeed, one good effect of the crisis for Mexico may actually be that some of the wilder projects were curtailed. But whether by luck or judgement, the Brazilian projects were unusually tightly tied in to relieving the balance-of-payments constraint, and an unusually high priority was given to completing the most promising.

What of the short-term adjustment? It *is* remarkable in the Mexican case (a) that the inflationary explosion levelled off as easily as it did (at least until the earthquake), and (b) that the balance of payments turned around so fast. On (b), Ros points out aptly that the short-term success derives from long-term weaknesses: the presence of oil and the lack of a local capital goods industry, allowing a drastic fall in imports when investment falls. On (a) the key factor is wage 'adjustment': the table showing a fall in the adjustment factor from 1 to less than 0.5 is one of the more remarkable in the book (p. 94). Mexico lacks the elements of indexation and defence mechanisms that characterise Brazil (the former), Peru (the latter) and Argentina (both), coming in this respect much closer to the Colombian situation. (But Ros is not optimistic about the resilience of such factors if the Mexican authorities have to persist for much longer with this form of adjustment.)

At the time of writing, Mexico's capacity to manage the economic crisis is quite widely called into question. There are undoubtedly some major risks when the oil price weakens, or if the USA enters a recession, or if tourism falls off because of earthquake fears. Behind these relatively short-term worries, however, lies a deeper malaise: growing lack of confidence in the regime as a whole, and in its capacity to reform itself from within. Fairly or otherwise, there is a widespread perception that political factors contributed substantially to recent economic mismanagement in this case, and that without major changes in the regime such problems will probably recur. Such perceptions are rooted in reality, although they can easily be blown out of perspective. The resilience and adaptability of the regime has been tested through many crises, there is still no easily imaginable, non-catastrophic alternative (in contrast to Brazil) and, however great the malaise, most sectors of Mexican society still have a considerable interest in the preservation of the system. In summary, compared with the past, the Mexican political system may be in serious trouble, but compared with the countries we are about to discuss, the Mexican state still has considerable advantages as an instrument for response to the economic crisis.

The relationship between state and society is obviously quite different in Pinochet's *Chile*, with major consequences for economic management. Since the 1973 coup put an end to Chile's traditional vibrant democratic institution, the state has tried to withdraw from many aspects of economic intervention and regulation. Nevertheless it has acted as a very strong and forceful state in the sense that economic managers have been freed from interest group pressures and restraints, and have been allowed an exceptionally long period to persist with their far-reaching plans for economic and social transformation. These ambitious and internally coherent plans nearly all derive from an integral 'neo-conservative' philosophy, and have been implemented with characteristic method and thoroughness by a well-organised administrative and legal system. Neither flexibility nor participation has in any way characterised the policy-making process, and indeed a major long-term problem for the supporters of this experiment is that it has been passed down from above by a highly authoritarian regime. If that regime were to evolve or collapse, there could well turn out to be rather little underlying social support for the continuance of this particular approach to economic management. On the other hand, so long as the regime endures, the economic experiment can be sustained regardless of its failure to deliver on its promises and its inability to elicit voluntary support.

We see, then, that in Chile's case, the response to crisis is dominated by the goals of the Pinochet regime, which imply, as Whitehead shows, a well-defined long-run model. It is in line with Chilean history, he argues – 'indeed its most distinctive feature' – that the state should undertake a far-reaching project 'intended to reshape Chilean society as a whole'. But this time the attempt was internally contradictory: a society used to this role of the state was now to see the state deliberately trying to write itself out of a number of traditional areas of economic activity. So far the macroeconomic results have proved disastrous – and contrary to the ideological preferences of the authorities.

Whitehead argues that the underlying objective of policy was, as he shows, the restoration of confidence in the 'rules of the game' of a free market economy, so that as the assumptions behind the neoclassical model became more nearly true, so growth would resume and the orthodox response to crisis would yield dividends. The chapter highlights three areas where the assumptions went badly wrong and as a result neither short-term (external) adjustment nor long-term growth was achieved, the one notable success being the inflation rate.

First, the reduced state role was supposed to make way for private investment, stimulated by the new 'rationality' following reduced protection. In fact, the private sector was devastated by reduced demand and import competition, and what potential savings there were went into consumption, imports, etc. The investment needs incorporated many slowly maturing projects which the state traditionally provided and on which the private sector was most unlikely to embark.

Second, the financial liberalisation policies presupposed an order and sophistication in institutions which even after seven years was clearly not there. Instead the result was anarchy and instability: the private sector was led to borrow abroad but not to invest productively, for the reasons just mentioned, and the result in due course was the final irony: state takeover of private debts and, indeed, of part of the financial system.

Third, the reformed economy was meant to be more resilient to shocks. Come 1981–5, however, exports looked no healthier than elsewhere, the debt problem was as bad, and the record on growth and investment was worse than most. The huge fall in imports in 1981–3 was achieved simply via demand compression: with a modest revival in 1984 there was an upsurge in imports. In other words, no change in structure had been achieved after ten years, against the assumptions of the economic philosophy of the long-run model.

Given that the assumptions on which healthy long-run progress was to come about have been proved wrong, on the basis of different assumptions more in line with this book's approach one can see clear and predictable conflict between policies and long-run needs, in particular in areas of needed investment such as industry. What policy has clearly done, by a combination of recession and import competition of unparalleled severity and initially by wage restraint, is brake inflationary expectations and lower inflation dramatically. What is interesting is that this relative 'success' appears to have survived the ending of the fixed exchange rate. This relative 'success', however, must be seen in the context of Chile's exceptionally bad unemployment situation, the very heavy burden of external debt, and the existence of generalised social resistance to an apparently inflexible and immovable regime.

Whereas for Brazil, Mexico and Chile it is at least possible to perceive a long-run strategy, in the case of *Argentina* the preoccupation with the short term appears to be to the exclusion of the long term. Yet there is, of course, a very serious problem of long-run stagnation and failure to restructure the economy so that the dynamics of its foreign trade can keep pace with the international context. As di Tella points out, Argentina is characterised by extreme long-run vulnerability to external shocks *despite* her self-sufficiency in oil and basic foods. This vulnerability results from the discrimination against the export sector, which in practice has been the only obvious way to resolve the sectoral pressures on the division of the 'pie' generated as far back as the 1940s under the first Perón administration.

Thus, whereas in the other major economies relative price adjustments are aimed at the long term, and there is some understanding at least that an inflationary outburst is the necessary price to pay, in Argentina the sole concern of relative price adjustment has seemed to be the short-term management of inflation. As di Tella describes so graphically, price repression (the exchange rate being usually the key price) has been repeatedly used as a relatively painless way of controlling inflation, and *necessitates* readjustment of relative prices once distortions become acute. Thus the 'unloosening' phase is always conceived of as backward-looking and focused on distribution; it is a necessary undoing of sacrifices imposed under the previous policy and a chance to restore income positions. Growth and structural change are no part of the scenario. Thus it is no surprise that what results is a great acceleration of inflation, with few real effects (except externally, to which we return in a moment). The strength of the inflationary pressures has been exaggerated during our period by circumstantial factors, such as the large inflow of capital which permitted the *tablita* to last as long as it did, and by the sheer length of inflationary experience in Argentina. Sensitivity to relative prices goes back at least to the 1950s and Perón's manipulation of the terms of trade; decades of inflation have produced enormous sensitivity, speed of reaction and defence mechanisms. Thus, whereas in Brazil and Mexico the inflationary response could level off – at perhaps twice the previous level – and the new structure of relative prices might be maintained, in Argentina the new level may be five or more times the previous, or the levelling off may only come at the price of introducing controls once again.

Where there *is* apparently some effectiveness of relative prices in the short term seems to be in the external balance: with the change in the exchange rate there *is* a short-term response, particularly in exports. This explains the apparent paradox that although, as di Tella clearly says, the Argentine economy *is* extremely vulnerable to external shocks, as the crises are worked out the external problem appears to be dealt with fairly readily and the general preoccupation with the internal disequilibrium can again become paramount. This, of course, simply aggravates the bias of policy-making against dealing with the fundamental long-run external weakness. Obviously the Argentine record indicates a governmental capacity for macroeconomic management that is far inferior to what we have observed in Brazil, and also worse (at least until very recently) than the performance of the Mexican and Chilean regimes. This cannot be attributed to any lack of ability or specialised skills in Argentine society – quite the contrary. What has been apparent for at least thirty years, if not longer, is an acute inability to co-ordinate these skills and to persist with any effective and forward-looking economic policy until it bears fruit. State policy has been characterised by extremes of instability and incoherence for so long that often the entire society seems to have organised to anticipate and circumvent whatever may be the latest desperate policy initiative. Lack of state authority and credibility has been matched by acute lack of consensus between Argentina's highly structured and relatively autonomous social organisations.

Within this generally discouraging context, how would we assess democratic President Alfonsin's surprisingly ambitious and well-executed *Plan Austral* for economic stabilisation, unveiled in June 1985? With the benefit of only a few months to observe this initiative it would obviously be foolhardy to declare it a watershed. Di Tella's chapter is replete with examples of bold and forceful initiatives producing initially hopeful results before disintegrating into hopeless failure. The basic characteristics of state–society relations outlined above will be slow to change and must meanwhile threaten the long-term viability of the new strategy. Moreover, Argentina remains one of the countries most exposed to any further deterioration of the international debt crisis. Nevertheless, this is one country where a lasting reversal of negative expectations could produce exceptionally strong positive results in the real performance of the economy. The expectations we have in mind refer not only to such narrowly economic variables as the inflation rate, but broader social judgements about the realism, determination, staying power and, in a word, the *trustworthiness* of the national economic authorities. If this could be established on a firm new footing, one of the most deeply entrenched obstacles to good economic performance in Argentina would be removed. If the government of Argentina could achieve a social consensus, permitting a capacity for macroeconomic management comparable with that of its major neighbours, then the country's strong natural resources and human endowments would permit considerable economic progress.

A comparison of *Peru* and Argentina is interesting. Both are clear examples of how the complexity and gravity of the short-run problem prevent attention to the long run, although Peru is a far more extreme example of a grave long-term problem compounded by the short term. Whereas in Argentina the natural resource and skill endowments are rather rich, but conflicting social forces have led to lack of policy coherence, in Peru the poverty is both in the capacity of the state and in natural resources. This was not always true: in fact, Thorp argues that it was in part the very richness and ease of exploitation of natural resources that led elite groups not to look to the state for support but to enjoy a long-run symbiotic and fruitful partnership with foreign capital. *Weak political development* (rather than a proliferation of conflicting interests, as in Argentina), a weak state and weak industrial sector left the country poorly prepared once a more complex stage of resource management was required. The resulting lack of 'policy' competence has been manifest in persistent short-term crises, which, as in Argentina, interact with the long-term problem.

Different levels of conflict between the short and the long term emerge from studying the Peruvian case. The first is an obvious conflict, and one observable in some measure in all cases: investment necessary for long-run growth is reduced – unduly so, if one accepts the argument of this book. The second level emphasises the interaction: the failure to resolve the long-run problem – in the Peruvian case, as Thorp argues, a deep-seated crisis in both the economic and political models – leads to vacillation and poor policy management in the short run, as well as to a particularly severe degree of crisis in terms both of the changes in the variables and the options available. These characteristics of the short term become so serious that they totally preclude any sense of long-term strategy. This in turn is very damaging to morale and to investors' confidence, and is certainly related to the problem of capital flight.

Again, what both countries reveal, but Peru more so, are the pernicious structural consequences of this situation, i.e. continuing recession and accelerating inflation. Both factors, in part interacting with each other, lead to a change in the character of the economy as defence mechanisms develop. These defence mechanisms are described in some detail by Thorp for the Peruvian case. They comprise in part changes in behaviour and expectations, in part changes in institutions (e.g. indexation, formal or informal) and in part the development of 'survival strategies' in the face both of prolonged inflation and recession. In the latter the informal and/or illegal economy plays an increasing role.

There are various problems which result from these developments, as argued for the Peruvian case. The first is that inflation becomes very difficult to control and prone to accelerate. The second is that more and more of the economy moves beyond the reach of standard policy tools, so that conventional adjustment techniques become increasingly ineffective. The third is that as people learn to survive, the political base for alternative policies is weakened.

The 'escape' of the economy from the reach of standard tools means that the classical 'shake-out' mechanism simply does not occur. In a curious way this parallels at the national level what we have pointed to at the international level: there, as Díaz Alejandro argues, neither banks nor countries are ever allowed to 'die', but the rules of the game get changed and survival strategies are invented – in particular, the state takeover of private debts. We now find the process mirrored at the national level: the Peruvian study points, for example, to the way private interests are knitted into public sector projects and effectively prevent their demise.

The Peruvian case also enables us to define the 'limiting conditions' under which conventional adjustment policies work particularly badly: a serious structural crisis, in part responsible for weak institutions and policy management, lack of investors' confidence, deeply embedded inertial inflation, and an external problem extremely unresponsive either to relative price shifts or to demand compression. What is interesting is what is *not* on the list: strong unions. Real wages have fallen heavily and their stickiness has not been to blame either for continued inflation or for lack of external adjustment.

Colombia emerges as such a shining example of growth and pragmatic and successful macro-management (leaving aside for the moment mid-1984 on) that it is tempting to suggest that here is a country that has really managed to mesh short-term adjustment with its long-term development strategy: Brazil, but without the inflation. Ocampo makes it clear, however, that this would be to misdescribe: as he put it in the debate, 'we don't have a long-run policy, but we are remarkable for our prudence'. Even this, however, hardly does justice to the amazing strength of Colombian development, based on coffee but a coffee sector with very special characteristics, and on policy-making that has been not only prudent but often exceptionally undogmatic. This has meant that Ocampo can indeed speak of the 'traditional' elements of Colombian short-term macroeconomic policy as import controls, capital controls and gradual devaluation, so opening up the possibility that the response to an external disequilibrium can quite successfully be import controls plus internal reactivation. This characterised the 1967 crisis as well as policy from 1982 on in response to the present crisis. In a sense, while the coffee sector was as healthy as it was, there was no need for the 'long-term structural adjustment' policies we have seen to be lacking in the case of Argentina – indeed, in most of our studies – although in fact Colombian exchange-rate and other policies *did* promote other exports long before it was fashionable.

Now, however, the situation is changing and beginning to look somewhat more typically Latin American, which will test Colombia's remarkable ability to manage the short term without detriment to long-term growth. It is worth briefly exploring this change. First, coffee will not be the source of dynamism it has been heretofore, owing to international market conditions and the Coffee Agreement. Second, there are hints in Ocampo's chapter that the supply of food may be more of a medium-term bottleneck than it was in the past (he characterises the 1970s as a period of food shortages leading to terms of trade moving against urban areas, leading to falling real urban wages and a limited market for manufactures; his analysis of inflation indicates great sensitivity to food supplies). Third, the new export products which it is universally believed in Colombia will solve the problem presented by the weakening of coffee, are coal and petroleum, both notoriously difficult to handle as a basis for development (requiring large amounts of external financing, and tending to produce a surge of foreign exchange which distorts resource allocation and the political economy of policy-making). Fourth, as early as the Turbay government Colombia was led into very 'Latin' borrowing: although it began to borrow very late, it borrowed at a fast rate once it began (Chapter 8, p. 249). Although comparisons here are very difficult, the extent of criticism levelled in Colombia at the Turbay administration's borrowing does not suggest that it was any more 'prudent' or effectively used than elsewhere in Latin America at the time.

In this context of shifting long-term prospects and types of problems, it is fascinating to note the conclusion of Ocampo's chapter, that the only real reason for the partial abandonment in mid-1984 of Colombian-style adjustment and the move to orthodox policies under the aegis of the World Bank and the International Monetary Fund, is that it will satisfy the latter and yield dividends in the form of the large loans needed for the upcoming export projects (as well as for the Colombian private sector). This conclusion, which follows from Ocampo's assessment of the adjustment already under way before mid-1984 as adequate to Colombian needs, suggests that the very needs and character of the new 'model' may force a style of short-term adjustment which our other cases suggest may have costs for the long run, and will certainly preclude attention to a factor such as a food supply bottleneck, for example. However, there are many signs of Colombian ingenuity, even in the way the present measures are being carried out.

A strong contrast with elsewhere is, of course, that policy has to cope 'only' with 20 to 25 per cent inflation. This does come in part from 'prudence', e.g. the restrianed policies followed during the coffee bonanza (Chapter 8, p. 243). It pays great dividends, since the defence mechanisms and inflationary expectations are weaker and there is more room for manoeuvre. This state of affairs is carefully husbanded: Ocampo describes how the Betancur administration deliberately continued a policy of mini-devaluations even though its slowness would require more controls in the short run, so as not to spark off instability in expectations, such as would be aroused if a sharp devaluation became something typically on the Colombian horizon. So the verdict in favour of the use of controls for short-term efficient adjustment must be qualified by this low level of inflation, which makes *any* policy far easier. But it is striking that the two countries which suffer least from a conflict between short-run adjustment and long-run needs are also the two to make most use of interventionist policies. And note that in the mini-devaluation example just cited, controls were necessary to *permit* prudence.

This rather successful economic management record in Colombia should also be placed in its political context. The democratic Colombian state has not gone in for highly ambitious development policies like those associated with the Brazilian technocrats, but it has displayed a fairly consistent record of careful, inventive and realistic policy-making, quick to anticipate and respond to short-term problems before they become too unmanageable. The function of continual electoral tests has presumably contributed to its record of flexibility and relative responsiveness to social pressures. On the other side, the consociational nature of the system binding the two major parties to the democratic framework has also helped to maintain a rather broad social consensus that has assisted the economic managers and has kept their disagreements within pragmatic and prudential grounds. In this regard there could hardly be a greater contrast than that between Colombia and such strife-torn countries as Guatemala, El Salvador and Nicaragua.

Turning, then, to the *Central American* chapter, we are of course dealing not with one but with five national economies, and with a region dominated by political crisis and by very special types of interaction with the outside world. But as Bulmer-Thomas shows, certain general patterns can nevertheless be observed, though Nicaragua really has to be set apart from the beginning of 1983.

The region makes a salutary case to study following Colombia, where controls plus reactivation appear to work so well. In Central America, too, there is a phase of adjustment policy without Fund conditionality, where the key tools are import controls, multiple exchange rates, devaluation and capital controls. This phase is considered by Bulmer-Thomas to be more efficient than the subsequent orthodox phase, since it operates directly on the trade imbalance, but it is important to note what it does *not* achieve. In such small and import-dependent economies there can be no question of import controls being compatible with domestic growth: the level of activity is depressed and industry in particular suffers badly from supply constraints. Capital controls possibly reduce capital flight below what it might have been, but need to be applied thoroughly at an early stage, which did not happen at first: paradoxically, it is in part capital flight which Bulmer-Thomas argues reduces the inflationary impact of rapid credit expansion, so undermining in part the benefits of import controls. All this is to say that the smaller and more trade-dependent the economy, the more unlikely it is that there can be short-term adjustment that is not very painful.

This theme is pushed further by the author's conclusion on the orthodox adjustment period: the main reason for embarking on Fund programmes is the need to reschedule the debt and seek new funds, yet the countries in question typically do not get the one reward for virtue they can expect: namely, a fresh inflow of private funds. This leads Bulmer-Thomas to stress some important conclusions concerning the asymmetry of large and small (which coincide with Díaz Alejandro's analysis): with a small debtor, 'the world' is quite content with no more than (highly profitable) reschedulings.

Meanwhile, there is a clear conflict between short-run adjustment and long-run development. The lack of promotion of exports and the cuts in investment were severe in both periods, and – a point Bulmer-Thomas stresses – so was the harm inflicted upon the Central American Common Market. This highlights a problem we would do well to consider more amply elsewhere: the extent to which short-term adjustment is often, and futilely, at the expense of other Latin American countries, so worsening their adjustment problem. (The other clear example in this book is the way in which stabilisation in Venezuela crippled Colombia and provided one of three factors precipitating her need for adjustment – see Chapter 8, p. 248.) If we were to sum the cuts in imports which comprised intraregional trade 1981–5, we would achieve a significant percentage of unnecessary adjustment.

But promotion of exports, although crucial for short-term recovery, is not actually at the heart of the long-term strategy for the region, according to Bulmer-Thomas's analysis of the consensus about its future. His analysis reveals yet another level of conflict between short-term adjustment needs and long-term development. The long-run strategy, he argues, must comprise less trade vulnerability and in particular more food security, which implies in the medium term the *diversion* of agriculture from export production – the reverse of the short-term pressure.

THE ROLE OF THE FUND

The Central American study puts sharply a number of criticisms of Fund policy, and in particular of its obsession with budget deficits. Other chapters, notably the Mexico contribution, also take up a dissenting view on the significance of the fiscal deficit. Here we shall briefly discuss the changing role of the IMF since our previous treatment of the subject (Thorp and Whitehead, 1979) and the limitations of its present overall approach, followed by a more specific treatment of the fiscal deficit issue.

During the period of unrestrained commercial bank lending to 'sovereign debtors' that came to such a dramatic halt in 1982, the IMF cannot be said to have exercised much restraint or foresight on the process as a whole. It has, of course, never been in much of a position to constrain the economic decisions of US policy-makers, nor more generally to exert pressure on capital surplus countries or major commercial banks, since these provide the resources that the IMF requires for its operations. When most of Latin America was enjoying easy access to commercial credit and a build-up of official exchange reserves, the Fund's leverage was mostly confined to a fringe of still struggling or uncreditworthy smaller countries. It could be regarded as a 'firefighting institution' that remained largely in the background in the absence of emergencies. It certainly lacked either the authority or the inclination to head off more generalised trouble further down the road. Symptomatic of this general situation was the way the IMF, after one year, effectively acquiesced in major deviations from Mexico's 1976–9 three-year stabilisation plan, once the commercial bankers indicated that they were no longer concerned about the nation's creditworthiness.

With scant advance warning, in 1982 the only available firefighter was suddenly required to be everywhere at once. The Fund necessarily adopted a much higher profile, with substantially changed operating procedures and some major, although not very consciously articulated, changes in underlying assumptions about its role. As an emergency measure, in January 1983 the Group of 10 (rich countries) agreed to an unscheduled and substantial increase in Fund resources, without, however, accepting the need to create international liquidity or still less to earmark liquidity creation so as to assist the most badly affected debtors. Instead it was stressed that Fund assistance would continue to carry with it the strong 'conditionality' clauses that should supposedly serve to reassure commercial bankers of the prospect of an early turnaround in the external finances of their delinquent clients. Although the Fund's own resources were expanded, they remained very small in relation to the magnitude of the financing needs uncovered. It therefore remained essential for the Fund to enforce its conditionality clauses quite severely, and to insist on fairly quick results, in order to maintain a 'revolving fund'.

Probably the major innovation of this period was the fact that, once it secured an agreement with a given debtor nation, the Fund (in collaboration with the world's major central banks) showed itself capable of inducing – in some cases even coercing – commercial bankers to increase their exposure to the debt of that country. This so-called 'involuntary' lending generated much larger commitments of new resources from the private sector that the Fund could inject from its own coffers. In due course emergency involuntary lending was followed by a number of large-scale debt-rescheduling operations, which substantially lengthened the time the commercial banks would have to wait for payment of their outstanding sovereign debt. The IMF's 'seal of approval' was a vital element in bringing about the most important of these agreements (e.g. the 1985 agreement that postponed almost half of

Mexico's official debt into the 1990s, authorised as a reward for Mexico's apparent 'good conduct' under its 1983–5 Extended Fund Agreement). This was certainly a major and constructive new role for the Fund, although to keep its significance in perspective it should be recalled that much of the 'involuntary lending' and rescheduling must be regarded as essentially a book-keeping operation, rather than the provision of new funds. On the one side a debtor country would agree to make interest payments for which the funds were lacking; on the other side the commercial bank would supply the funds needed to pay itself interest. Of course, the IMF and the commercial banks remained adamant that the international market must determine the rate of interest used in these book-keeping transactions and, as disinflation proceeded, the real burden of the outstanding debt continued to mount. As the chapter on Central America makes clear, however, even here the benefits from the Fund's new role tended to flow disproportionately to the larger debtors, whose importance in the portfolios of major banks was such as to necessitate some response. Bulmer-Thomas shows how Honduras, Guatemala and El Salvador reached agreements with the Fund but achieved neither rescheduling nor new bank money; Costa Rica succeeded in rescheduling but with no new money. Peru has received no new money from the banks since 1979.

In view of the essentially short-term, patchwork and anti-developmental content of the IMF-prescribed remedy, it is hardly surprising that the Fund's long-standing difficulties in securing full compliance with its 'conditionality' clauses became far more acute. Time after time, as we have seen in this volume, unrealistic agreements were reached with major debtors (Argentina, Brazil, Chile) only to be breached and suspended within a few months. Other debtors (Nicaragua, Peru) sought to bypass the Fund entirely and to negotiate directly with the commercial creditors. Even Mexico, held up in the 1984 Fund meeting as the 'model of successful adjustment' to be imitated by the others, fell out of compliance with the Fund in the last quarter of its three-year Extended Fund agreement. The underlying rationale of the Fund's approach had been that after a sufficiently rigorous short-term adjustment policy, the typical heavily indebted nation would once again become 'creditworthy', voluntary lending would resume, and further instalments of Fund-administered austerity would become unnecessary. Most experience since 1982 indicates the inadequacy of this approach – not just the failure to apply it in individual cases, but its total inadequacy. Thus, in the international conditions prevailing since 1982 (dominated by Washington's need to attract foreign capital to finance the USA's chronic budget and current account deficits), very little voluntary international lending has been available to any Latin American government, no matter how hard it has striven to satisfy Fund conditionality. In its report on international bank business to mid-1985, the Bank for International Settlements records that lending to Latin America as a whole has ceased to grow even in nominal terms (in real terms there is a contraction underway). For Mexico (the country held up by the IMF until the end of 1984 as a model of good behaviour) there was even a substantial fall in nominal lending. It is in this context that we should judge the resurgence of concern in the autumn of 1985 about the debt crisis, and the so-called Baker plan to direct new lending to some heavily indebted countries and to supplement the role of the IMF.

As past critics of the rigidity with which simplistic Fund prescriptions have formerly been enforced on the more vulnerable countries of the region, we are glad to acknowledge that more flexibility and sensitivity to the economic and political realities of a given country have been in evidence in Fund negotiations since 1982 (perhaps most vividly so in the Fund's acceptance of the Alfonsin programme in Argentina – see Chapter 6). In the last analysis, however, the debtor country must somehow be placed in the position where it can continue to service its contractual obligations without Fund assistance. All other policy objectives are still ultimately required to take second place to this. By its nature the Fund must insist that debtors conform to this hierarchy of priorities, although it is unable to guarantee that creditors will behave in an equally responsible and 'system-maintaining' manner, or that either past or future debtor nations will be sheltered from bearing the entire cost of errors and mismanagement for which the creditor nations may bear major responsibility. The most serious deficiency of all in a supposedly 'technical' institution is that the Fund must, if necessary, insist on a succession of 'downward adjustments' in the productive capacities of 'uncreditworthy' nations, regardless of the long-term consequences for that country's capacity for development (including its long-term capacity productively to absorb and service external credit).

Defenders of the Fund deny that it is such an uncritical agent of the creditor banks and their parent governments as we are here suggesting. They may, for example, point to Fund 'surveillance' of the economic policies of the United States and other leading Western governments, but here the evidence of symmetry is hardly very persuasive. The governments of, say, Washington and Brasilia have never received equality of treatment from the Fund, and it is hard to imagine that they ever will. This reality is now very well understood by increasingly vocal public opinion in Latin America, and helps to account for the Fund's difficulties in exerting influence there. Turning to the commercial banks and the central bankers of individual nations whose collective responsibility it is to protect the Western financial system, the Fund simply lacks much autonomy from this sector. It is dependent on them not only organisationally and for financial backing, but also for personnel and for intellectual support and guidance. It can therefore only act forcefully and effectively when its conduct is congruent with the wishes of the major banks.

THE FISCAL DEFICIT

We have commented on the Fund's increased flexibility and greater willingness to tolerate certain types of infringements of its usual rules on policy, particularly in regard to interest rates and the failure to end various forms of market intervention. But it has remained rigid on two points which have emerged from our case studies as of great significance. It is not permitted to *increase* either import or capital controls, and the substantial reduction of the fiscal deficit continues to be identified as the key policy instrument to reduce both internal and external disequilibrium. In contrast, one conclusion we drew from the survey of case studies presented above is that import and capital controls have been an important ingredient of the relatively more successful adjustment efforts; we here review the verdict on the controversial aspect of the fiscal deficit.

Most of our case studies have quarrelled, implicitly or explicitly, with the Fund's analysis of the fiscal deficit. The line of attack has been twofold. First, it has been demonstrated that current analyses frequently use misleading figures, and that correct inflation-accounting often radically changes the implication for demand of a given nominal deficit (see Table 10.3 for some illustrations). Second, even where a deficit remains in real terms, the causal if not mechanistic role commonly assumed must frequently be questioned.

The logic behind the first point was set out briefly in the introduction, where it was explained that under inflationary conditions 'interest' payments frequently contain an element – sometimes a large element – of repayment of principal, which is not, subject to an important qualification explained below, an addition to demand. The central point is that under inflationary conditions the traditional financial deficit becomes a poor indicator of the fiscal stance, and thus of the effects of fiscal policy on aggregate demand and the current account of the

Table 10.3   Public sector surplus/deficit, % GDP[a]

	1978	1979	1980	1981	1982	1983	1984
Argentina	−13.6	−10.5	−13.0	−16.7	−16.4	−19.6	−13.0
Brazil	−3.0	−2.9	−1.8	−3.1	−2.9	−0.1	−2.2
Colombia (1)	−2.3	−0.8	−3.3	−6.3	−8.1	−9.0	−7.1
(2)						−7.2	−4.8
Costa Rica[b]	−4.3	−6.5	−8.2	−3.6	−3.0	−2.7	na
Chile	−0.8	1.7	3.1	1.7	−2.3	−3.8	−4.8
El Salvador[b]	−2.3	−1.2	−6.6	−8.0	−7.7	−5.8	na
Guatemala[b]	−1.1	−2.6	−4.7	−7.3	−4.0	−3.9	na
Honduras[b]	−6.0	−4.4	−4.7	−6.2	−7.4	−7.1	na
Mexico (1)	−6.8	−7.3	−7.6	−14.5	−17.9	−8.8	−7.1
(2)	−1.9	−1.6	−1.5	−9.2	−2.1	9.0	4.6
Nicaragua[b]	−8.2	−6.7	−9.0	−10.4	−19.5	−26.8	na
Peru (1)	−6.1	−1.1	−4.7	−8.4	−9.3	−12.1	−7.6
(2)	−0.6	4.7	2.0	−2.4	−3.8	−5.1	−0.6

Notes:
[a]   The figure given is that used by the authorities, which is corrected for the effect of inflation via interest payments only in the cases of Argentina, Brazil and Chile. When a corrected figure is available, it is given as number (2). On Chile, see Chapter 5, note 10. On Argentina, see Table 6A.2, footnote (a). On Colombia, see Table 8.6. The figures include the National Coffee Fund; the second line excludes interest payments. On Peru, see Table 7.4.
[b]   Central Government only.

Sources: country chapters; for Central America, Inter American Development Bank, *Economic and Social Progress* (1983 and 1984).

balance of payments, and is itself highly dependent on the rate of inflation rather than vice versa. As an alternative, it has been proposed that we should use the inflation-corrected public sector deficit, the argument being that the proper measure of the public sector deficit (as well as of any deficit) is the change in the real value of the public sector's liabilities. Calculations for the United States, for example, show that such a re-estimate of the effects of inflation turn the US $61 billion deficit for 1980 into a US $7 billion surplus.[3]

It is not certain, however, that the inflation-corrected surplus or deficit is without qualification the right measure of the impact on demand and the level of activity of a given set of public sector actions. As Buiter explains clearly, analysis on the basis of accounts which correctly describe the changes in real net worth over time, and thus permanent

340 *Review and Conclusions*

income, implies perfect internal and external capital markets. In fact,

> cash flow constraints, illiquidity, credit rationing, lack of collateral,
> non-marketability of certain assets and liabilities, and a host of other
> capital market imperfections force the actions of private agents and
> national government to depart from the behaviour that would be
> optimal if comprehensive net worth or permanent income constraints
> alone had to be taken into account (p. 308).

Put very simply, if my real income has fallen and I wish to dissave, but am
prevented from doing so by imperfect capital and credit markets, then, if
I receive (or withhold) an interest payment which is largely capital
repayment, this may, by providing me with the means to dissave,
increase my consumption over what it would have been without the
interest payment. This means that a real surplus corresponding to this
situation would be less deflationary than, say, a simple excess of tax
revenue over expenditure. This might be very pertinent to situations
such as Mexico, where the availability of the capital repayment element
in liquid form might well facilitate capital flight.

It is inconceivable, however, that this could apply to the whole
correction, while the 'inflation tax' element is, as we have said, a tax. We
can safely conclude that conventional accounting *is* highly misleading
on its own, and that 'inflation and changing rates of inflation quite break
whatever links have existed between budget deficits and real income or
changes in net worth of the private sector'.[4] What is needed for a correct
analysis, we stress again, is a careful isolation of each independent source
of demand pressure.

In this volume, Brazil, Chile and Argentina do at least partially correct
public sector accounts. But the case studies of Mexico and Peru, in
particular, argue forcibly that the continuing use both by the IMF and
by national authorities of figures totally uncorrected for inflation[5] leads
to misdirected policy goals, and thus unnecessary deflation, loss of
output and employment.

This conclusion is reinforced and broadened when we turn to our
second line of attack, which questions the *modus operandi* of the fiscal
deficit. The chapter by Ocampo neatly encapsulates most of the various
approaches by describing the shifts in official Colombian thinking in the
period 1982–5 (pp. 260–6). The initial view in 1982 saw the deficit as
'crowding out' the private sector by raising interest rates and so inducing
a contraction of private activity – which was clearly not *in*flationary. By
1984 the 'opposition' version had permeated policy-making: the

balance-of-payments deficit, generated by exogenous forces and by Colombian trade policies, *required* a public sector deficit to offset its deflationary effect. Only in 1984 did the view most common elsewhere take precedence: the fiscal deficit was – must be – generating the external deficit and was imminently about to generate inflationary demand pressure. This latter view is implicit in IMF reports, with more emphasis typically on the inflationary consequences than Colombians would put.

The first view is a quite possible empirical situation, although Ocampo shows it was not an accurate description of Colombia. The third view comes under strong attack in our case studies. In addition to the points already made about the sensitivity of the deficit to inflation, the Central American and Peruvian studies stress the extent to which deficit-financed expansion may have balance-of-payments consequences rather than direct inflation consequences. Depending on the policy response to the balance-of-payments disequilibrium and the sensitivity of inflation to the exchange rate and various policy measures, inflation may result indirectly. The relationship is strong in the Peruvian case.

The second view is accepted by Ocampo, and implicitly in some of the other case studies. Others, however, are unhappy with it: if an economy is very imperfect, an expansion of demand compensating for a fall elsewhere may indeed have inflationary consequences. In the discussion it was clear that some of us considered that demand could influence prices well below full employment, while some claimed almost no sensitivity to demand, at least at the levels of demand experienced in their case studies (Brazil and Mexico).

A further level of analysis, not much developed in our studies, considers the deficit from a 'structural' point of view: although not directly inflationary in the very short term because of the extent of unused resources, nevertheless an inadequate tax base leads constantly to increases in public sector prices and so increased costs and inflation, pressure on the balance of payments and so inflation, and, via both these channels and a more standard crowding-out effect, pressure on the private sector, squeezed by costs, lack of imports and lack of funds.

Where we were in complete accord, however, was in asserting (a) that the nominal deficit is not a reliable guide to the demand implication of the public sector's spending, and (b) that an assumption of unilateral causality flowing *from* the fiscal deficit *to* internal and external disequilibrium simultaneously is dangerous in the extreme, and misguided in most of the cases studied here. Policies based on these two fundamental errors have caused needless recession and social discord, as documented by most of the case studies in this book.

THE POLITICAL ECONOMY OF CAPITAL FLIGHT

As we saw in Chapters 1 and 2, one of the most marked changes in the international economy in the 1970s was the growing internationalisation of financial flows. As the boundaries between national and international capital and markets become increasingly blurred, so the export of capital from Latin America becomes easier and more 'customary'. Our case studies confirm the quantitative significance of the problem for Mexico, Argentina and Central America.[6] In Chile, the major flight took place in response to the Allende government: the phenomenon is certainly not exclusive to the 1980s, as any historian will confirm, although its generality is.

The proximate causes of capital flight as they emerge from the case studies appear to centre rather strongly on the profit motive and rates of return. The chief incentive was typically overvaluation of the exchange rate and expected devaluation (Argentina and Mexico). Political uncertainty and lack of confidence in policy-making is stressed more for Peru and Central America, although, of course, these feed back on rates of return. A separate point emerges from the Central American case, where the increased availability of certain types of liquid assets actively encouraged an increased outflow.

What also emerges clearly, however, is that an asymmetry is at work: while there is great sensitivity to relative price factors in precipitating an outflow, once it has occurred changes in these factors are ineffective in reversing the flow. Or they may at best produce an inflow of unstable short-term speculative capital while the capital for investment stays in the United States. Thus Ros comments that in Mexico the change of policy failed to reverse the flow (p. 106); the same appears true for Argentina and Chile.

The most interesting case of an attempted reversal is Chile. In a sense one of the main objectives of the whole 'reconstruction of capitalism' exercise since 1975 has been to attract back the capital that fled before 1973. In 1979–81 capital *did* flood in – in the form of loans via the international banking system – but *not* for productive investment. It financed imports, luxury consumption, foreign holidays: 'It may be at least as important how the repatriated capital is to be used within the host economy, and what political guarantees can be preserved for those who lacked the means or need illegally to take their money out of the country in the first place' (Whitehead, Chapter 5, p. 158).

This leads us to consider the relative 'successes'. Capital flight was not a problem for Brazil, and not a grave problem for Colombia: we have seen what an asset this was in the adjustment process. Carneiro's study provides four factors for the absence of capital outflows: (1) a 'growth prone' economy, accompanied by (2) very high real domestic interest rates, (3) strict capital controls, and (4) bonds with an exchange-rate guarantee. While it was probably the combination of at least the first three that was so effective, in terms of *reversing* an already occurred flight the first surely becomes central. This is the important background to the interesting proposal from Ros (p. 107); since Latin Americans are holding the Latin American debt via the intermediation of the international banking system, at considerable profit to the latter, could there be room for a 'deal' whereby they are induced to hold it internally and not externally, with the benefits which we have seen the Brazilian system has been able to reap?

DISTRIBUTIVE ISSUES

We have repeatedly stressed the significance of the new element of interest rates as affecting most aspects of the adjustment crisis. High real interest rates are also the crucial new aspect of the distributive dimension: whereas in the 1970s inflation was steadily improving the position of net debtors, in the 1980s the burden has shifted radically, both internationally and nationally. With the increased burden of interest payment has, of course, come heavy curtailment of consumption and falls in investment which imply even more serious losses of growth forgone by future generations.

The data are shown in Table 10.4. The variations in consumption per capita largely coincide with the story we have told: Central America has indeed been severely hit, but the extreme figures for Nicaragua and El Salvador also reflect the costs of war, as Bulmer-Thomas explains. Mexico is not far from the top, reflecting our analysis that its adjustment has been achieved because of structural factors which give rise to concern for future growth, not growth lost today. Ranking by the fall in real wages would put Mexico much lower.

But the information to be gained from such aggregates is limited, as the comment on Mexico already suggests. Bulmer-Thomas estimates the 'protected sectors' and applies the fall in consumption to the remainder: what has almost certainly happened with the rise in interest rates and the increase in capital flight is that certain 'protected' sectors have benefited via these two (related) sources. As Ros comments, a substantial proportion of Mexican debt is held in a sense by Mexicans abroad, so

Table 10.4 Indicators of the burden of adjustment (percentage change 1980–3)

Countries	Change in real consumption per capita	Change in real wages	Change in real GDP per capita
Colombia	−2	−8[a]	+3
Brazil	−8	−3	−10
Mexico	−8	−25	−6
Guatemala	−9	+18	−12
Peru	−14	−13	−15
Argentina	−17	−6	−9
Chile	−17	−3	−14
Honduras	−19	−4	−11
Costa Rica	−26	−38	−18
El Salvador	−39	−35	−19
Nicaragua	−39	−37	+4

Note:
[a] Private sector. The public sector fall is 13 per cent.

Source: country studies.

many of the creditors benefiting from the shift in burden may well be nationals. Consistent with this and expressive of the situation is the fact cited by Carneiro: in Brazil, when interest rates rise, the profits of the 500 largest companies also *rise*.

Di Tella argues that while the rich undoubtedly did much to create the crisis in Argentina by profitable capital export, they now in a sense bear some of the burden of stabilisation because they can no longer export capital. Their remittances to the USA 'declined from over 10 per cent of GDP in 1980–1, to a "mere" 1.5 per cent of GDP in 1982–4' (p. 198). Ros, however, registers an important qualification to this: standard balance-of-payments accounting omits the profits retained on previously exported capital. In Table 4.15 he attempts a calculation of this and reaches a figure which equals some 4 per cent of Mexican national income, or 20 per cent of gross domestic investment. The figure would surely be as high for Argentina.

So the already severe losses shown in Table 10.4 clearly have to be restated to allow for the fact that the burden falls disproportionately on the least protected and poorest sectors. Un- and underemployment have risen everywhere. Rising rates of inflation have meant an increasing 'inflation tax', which falls disproportionately on the poor, who have fewer defence mechanisms. What Table 10.5 shows is that the burden has

Table 10.5 Percentage change in real output by sector, 1980–3

	Agriculture	Industry	Construction	Commerce
Argentina	+9	−11	−35.6	−20.9
Brazil	+6	−12	−18	−5
Colombia	+3	−4	+17	+1
Costa Rica	+4	−17	−50	−26
Chile	+4	−13	−1	na
El Salvador	−11	−32	−42	−45
Guatemala	−5	−7	−37	−10
Honduras	+4	−2	−7	−3
Mexico	+9	−4	na	−4[a]
Nicaragua	−13	−15	−54	−14
Peru	+6	−19	−10	−10

Note:
[a] Commerce and services.

Sources: Inter American Development Bank, *Economic and Social Progress in Latin America*, 1985; and data supplied by country study authors.

also fallen disproportionately on urban areas: export agriculture has been protected by the maintenance of output levels even when prices have been poor. We do not have the data to show whether domestic-use agriculture generally did relatively even better, as it did in Central America.

Our final reflection on the burden of adjustment is induced by placing the figures of Table 10.4 alongside the change in consumption in the industrial countries: while Latin America was experiencing a fall in per capita living standards often near 20 per cent in size in three years, in the USA real per capita consumption *rose* by 4 per cent in the period 1980–3.

PROSPECTS

What, then, are the prospects for development in the heavily indebted and impoverished countries of Latin America in the second half of the 1980s? This conclusion is written three years after the Mexican crisis broke in August 1982, at a point when the immediate shock has passed and longer-term realities can be fairly clearly discerned. Viewed from this perspective there is a clear contrast between the severe crisis and quick recovery that affected Latin American external accounts following the 1975 downturn in the US economy, and the even more severe crisis after the 1982 recession, this time not followed by anything like a return to the *status quo ante*. As we suggested in the introduction, this is due to the quite different characteristics of the 1980s crisis. In particular, the flow of lending broadly continued through the downturn following 1975 and was instrumental in permitting at least some degree of autonomous recovery in Latin America, which in its turn aided recuperation in the United States. Today the net flow has been sharply reversed, as mentioned in the introduction. In fact, between 1975 and 1981 Latin America received a net capital inflow of \$171 billion and paid out \$89.3 billion in profits and remittances. The net external transfer of resources therefore totalled \$81.7 billion, or rather more than 2 per cent of GDP per year. Between 1982 and 1985, however, Latin America received only about \$38 billion in 'new money' from abroad, while the outflow in profits and remittances totalled \$144 billion – a net transfer of resources from the region of \$106 billion, rather more than 4 per cent of GDP per year. The total adverse movement was therefore about 6 per cent of GDP, and not coincidentally gross investment in Latin America fell by rather more than that amount between the two periods. Even on fairly favourable assumptions Latin America faces the prospect of large continuing net transfers of resources to the developed countries for the rest of the decade.

The following reasons can be given for the abrupt reversal of net capital flows in 1982. First, a worldwide trend towards accelerating inflation from the mid-1970s until 1980–1 and a worldwide disinflationary trend for the five years thereafter can be clearly identified. These trends have been particularly visible in dollar-denominated markets and are closely linked with US economic policies – policies that were adopted mainly with US domestic objectives in mind. From 1980–1 to 1985 these policies attracted a large net inflow of foreign capital into the USA, drawn by high real interest rates (as US inflation fell but nominal interest rates remained high), and the perception that US growth prospects compared favourably with elsewhere. The resulting dollar appreciation became an independent factor attracting further inflows. Moreover, the USA was seen as a 'safe haven' for investment capital that no longer seemed so secure in much of the Third World. The 'errors and omissions' item in statistics in international capital flows has recently become so large that it is difficult to determine with much accuracy the precise patterns and sequences involved. In broad terms, however, it seems clear that various forms of registered investment in the USA by foreign nationals rose significantly; in addition, there would probably be a further rise if unrecorded flight capital could be taken into account (we have discussed above the Latin American dimension of this problem). By mid-1985 it was fairly clear that this process had peaked, and the only real debate was between those who feared a sharp decline in foreign willingness to accumulate US-based investments (caused perhaps by expectation of a decline in the dollar, or of a deterioration in US growth prospects, or even fears of renewed US inflation), and those who considered that the existing high levels of capital inflow could be broadly maintained.

A much more clear-cut reason for arguing against further extrapolation of the 1981–5 pattern of capital flows comes from the other side of the 'net inflow' account. That is to say, for many years before 1981 US nationals regularly invested more capital outside the country than foreigners invested in the USA. The component of capital flows that changed most dramatically after 1981 was the willingness of US-based enterprises and individuals to invest abroad. Presumably the high real interest rate, the strengthening dollar and tax incentives to invest at home all combined with a perception fed by the debt crisis and other manifestations of foreign turmoil that external investment had become much more risky than before. By 1985 this part of the process had almost certainly reached a cyclical turning point. That is, US investment overseas had fallen to such a low level, and the anticipated gains of domestic investment had been so fully reflected in exchange-rate movements, that the fall was bound to end. The key questions would be how quickly, how massively and under what conditions US investment abroad would start increasing again.

Authors such as William Cline (who as early as 1983 argued that with patience and sound policies the world economy could essentially grow its way out of the debt crisis) anticipated that most debtors could realistically foresee a fairly prompt reversal of the negative trends experienced from 1981 to 1983. Provided they hastened to 'adjust', their exports would rise rapidly, interest rates would begin to fall, the dollar would weaken, and their debt burdens would again become manageable. Indeed, provided they took no counterproductive measures against their creditors, voluntary lending might resume soon. The events of 1984 were for some time regarded as a vindication of this theory. Although the US dollar continued to rise rather than to fall, and although the real interest burden of dollar debt continued to mount relentlessly, Latin America's exporters achieved very impressive results, and historically unprecedented trade surpluses became the norm. However, this export recovery was very closely associated with an exceptionally rapid deterioration in the US trade account – a process that could not continue, in 1985 or thereafter, at anything like the pace of 1984. With hindsight, it now seems clear that the sharp improvement in external accounts experienced by some major debtors was a once-only gain rather than the first instalment of a cumulative dynamic of recovery.

It is in this context that we would choose to assess Latin America's medium-term prospects. We shall now briefly review the six major developments in the international economy that have been suggested as possible sources of external stimulus to a Latin American recovery, giving our reasons for doubting that these will produce any very major or rapid improvement for the region as a whole.

First, we can quickly set aside the possibility of some massive multilateral assistance programme to enable the region to reactivate, along the lines of 'Marshall Aid' to Western Europe in the late 1940s, or the theory (rather than the practice) of President Kennedy's 'Alliance for Progress', or the prescription of the Brandt Commission. We set this proposal to one side not because we consider it inappropriate to the circumstances, but because we regard it as manifestly excluded from the agenda of the developed countries. We have sympathy with the view that a well-designed and carefully implemented programme of this kind could not only help to meet the urgent development needs of Latin America, but might also strengthen the financial system of the developed capitalist countries and give a healthy, trade-led boost to the world economy as a whole. However that may be, the present intellectual climate in the policy-making circles of the leading rich industrial economies rules out any such prospect for the next few years. The required capacity for international co-ordination would also seem to be absent.

A second source of stimulus would be a large increase in direct foreign investment by multinational corporations. Influential bankers in the developed countries now argue that the fundamental flaw in the region's approach to external finance is that it relied too heavily on debt (where the risks are assumed entirely by the borrower) instead of equity capital (where foreign shareholders take part of the gains in an upswing, but also theoretically accept their share of the losses in a downswing). If this was a practical proposal we would have to consider these arguments with some care, but in the present context we set them aside on the grounds that there is nothing the Latin Americans could offer (certainly not in the realm of practical politics, but also not even if the obvious political constraints were wished away) that would elicit anything like the volume of finance required for the next few years to service debts in the region of $400 billion. A glance at the historical record is sufficient to show that even in far more favourable international circumstances than exist at the present, the strictly *financial* contribution of net direct foreign investment was far too small to make much impact on such servicing requirements. If there is a case for inviting direct foreign investment, it is a long-term one, related to the qualitative advantages deriving from transfer of know-how, etc.; but this is not a serious solution to the debt crisis in either the near or even the medium term.

The third potential development is a resumption of voluntary lending to heavily indebted countries by commercial banks. This is the main solution envisaged by serious analysts of the optimistic school, and it is the proclaimed objective sought by the IMF and by the lead bankers involved in recent debt renegotiation and rescheduling agreements. Two years after Mexico's suspension of payments, that country was presented to the 1984 meeting of the IMF/World Bank as a 'success story' and an example for the other more troubled debtors to emulate. In the enthusiasm of the moment it was claimed that Mexico's agreement with the Fund had worked out so well that either commercial bankers or the bond market would be willing (without compulsion from any external agency) to subscribe to some new issue of Mexican debt. No such thing had happened, however, by the time of the 1985 annual meeting, and indeed the prospect had faded into the distant future as the Mexican economy deteriorated.

It is true that unforeseen shocks (the weakening oil market, the September 1985 earthquake) may help to account for this particular case, but the forces militating against a significant restoration of voluntary lending are system-wide. From the viewpoint of US bankers, for example, five years of disinflation have weakened the asset base of the entire financial system. It is not just sovereign debt that has been 'value-impaired'. A high proportion of outstanding loans to US farmers may also be unrealisable at face value, the domestic mortgage market is plagued with defaults, and so on. In short, high real interest rates sustained over a period of years have left many US banks in a precarious condition, and have created a great sense of 'risk aversion'. In such a climate, further lending to heavily indebted Latin American nations hardly seems a defensible strategy. Whatever they say in public about the prospect of resuming voluntary lending, in practice US bankers are eager to reduce their exposure to this sector. Non-US banks are far from eager to take over from their American counterparts either. In the mid- to late 1970s there was a surplus of international deposits looking for willing borrowers. In the mid- to late 1980s depositors are insisting on security, and the US Treasury is bidding eagerly for any funds that may be available. Large-scale voluntary lending to Latin America is simply

350 *Review and Conclusions*

improbable, as a close reading of the terms of the October 1985 'Baker proposal' to boost lending to the Third World would tend to confirm.

A fourth source of external stimulus has already been discussed. Rising Latin American exports to the USA constituted the main source of economic dynamism for the region in 1984. (The US took only 37 per cent of Latin America's exports in 1981, rising to 44 per cent in 1983 and 47 per cent in 1985.) However, the US trade deficit rose from $31 billion in 1982 to $70 billion in 1983, $123 billion in 1984 and $149 billion in 1985. Henceforth, access to the US market will become more difficult. This can be assumed regardless of whether it is through protectionism, devaluation or recession that the US trade imbalance is reduced.

In theory the other developed economies might be expected to respond to a slowing US economy by expanding their domestic demand. With a strong balance-of-payments position, an undervalued currency and little domestic inflation, a country like Japan or West Germany should be ideally placed to lead a world economic recovery, and in the process to absorb a large increment of imports from Latin America's debt-driven export drive. This would offer a most alluring fifth possibility of external assistance to the region's adjustment efforts. It cannot be ruled out quite so categorically as the first hypothesis (a Marshall Aid-type programme), but it runs into many difficulties of a similar origin. What deters the Japanese authorities, to take an example, from pursuing a more expansionary policy and absorbing a large increase in imports? Whether the explanation is a misguided emphasis on monetary and fiscal caution, or a well-grounded fear of increased exposure to uncontrollable forces in the international economy, the strength of this Japanese resistance can hardly be doubted. If Tokyo is unwilling or unable to respond to current US demands for trade liberalisation and economic expansionism, it seems hardly likely that Japanese policy will be altered to accommodate the interests of the Latin American debtors. Similar arguments apply to Western Europe. In either case, given the nature of their trading links, even were there to be some expansion of trade, it is not Latin America that would feel the benefit.

Beyond these five potential developments we can foresee little else that might occur in the international economy that would substantially improve the prospects of Latin American debtors in the near to medium term. Nominal US interest rates could presumably fall much further, but only if the existing disinflationary trend continued to gather momentum. In that case the gain from lower debt servicing would have to be balanced against the loss from further falls in commodity prices, and the risks of a cumulative downturn in the volume of world trade. None of the various contingencies sketched above should really be assessed in isolation from the rest. It is possible to envisage various forms of interaction, and it must also be recognised that some outcomes could be beneficial to some debtor countries, even if harmful to an equal number of others. However, our general conclusion from this discussion is that, in contrast to the sharp recovery that followed the 1975 recession, and to the typical pattern of recovery mechanisms supposed to characterise self-regulating market systems, we see no very good reason to anticipate that the world economy will offer a more supportive environment to most heavily indebted Latin nations in the second half of the 1980s than in the first half of the decade.

Our final remarks therefore concern some ways in which Latin American policy-makers might on their own try to improve the economic prospects for their countries, without stimulus or support from the international economy. We shall briefly consider four areas: export diversification and non-traditional exports; reviving intraregional trade; attracting back flight capital; and negotiating with creditors under the threat of a moratorium. This is a suggestive, rather than an exhaustive, list of the kind of initiatives we would group under the general heading of 'internal restructuring'. We think Latin American policy-makers would be well advised to concentrate a considerable amount of attention on this type of development for the next few years. Perhaps the international economy will prove more favourable than we suppose, but they would be ill-advised to rely on such an outcome, and even in that event some restructuring would be highly beneficial.

Our relatively pessimistic view about the overall prospects for Latin American exports derives from two assumptions: (a) that most primary commodities are likely to remain oversupplied, so prices will remain weak and new market outlets will be hard to find; and (b) that many of the region's main manufactured exports may face quotas, restrictions or rising tariffs. Moreover, we think it likely that Latin America's 'easiest' export market, the USA, may be the one that closes up the most (relative to the past). However, even on these fairly gloomy assumptions, indiscriminate export pessimism would be unwarranted. Latin America has the potential to develop many new lines of export, and many new markets, simply because so many possibilities have not been seriously tried. Individually, each of the initiatives we have in mind would make only a relatively small contribution to the needs of the economy as a whole. Cumulatively, however, the resulting restructuring could be highly beneficial. Among the countries that have already achieved significant advances along the lines we have in mind, Chile and Colombia may be the most encouraging. There are, of course, problems with this approach (for example, the concentration of capital often required to break into a hitherto undeveloped foreign market), but there are also many benefits to be derived from 'learning by doing'. We do not believe that public sector or small-scale co-operative ventures need necessarily be excluded from participation. However, the approach requires sustained application over a number of years before it can be expected to pay off. In the meantime other measures will also be needed.

During the 1970s intraregional trade grew even more rapidly than the subcontinent's relatively dynamic international exports. But when the debt crisis broke, trade between most Latin American countries contracted even more severely than external trade. It may be that as the foreign exchange constraint tightened, most Latin American trade ministries and private importers gave priority to paying for supplies from outside the region, assuming that their immediate neighbours would be more tolerant of delays in payment. Whatever the reason, there is now a heavy backlog of unpaid bills for intraregional transactions, and in many cases only direct barter exchange deals are now possible. We have made the point above that a severe policy of import compression that might seem rational for one Latin American country viewed in isolation may be less helpful if viewed at the regional level, because it may intensify the balance-of-payment constraint on neighbouring countries and set in motion a dynamic process of retaliation. The reverse is also true. If Latin American governments gave priority to settling outstanding regional trade claims, and offered appropriate liquidity so that barter trade could be superseded, a cumulative process of trade recovery might be achieved. There is scope for substantial 'gains from trade' within the region, even if world trade as a whole remains depressed.

We have already discussed efforts to lure back local flight capital. The limitations on this are all too evident from our analysis of the international economy. Nevertheless, under the heading of 'internal restructuring' it is appropriate to reintroduce the theme, pointing out that there are still a variety of tax, regulatory and institutional initiatives available to individual economic authorities that will to some significant extent affect the decisions of different types of domestic wealth-holders as to whether or not to repatriate at least part of their illicit assets.

Finally, taking the argument in a somewhat different direction, Latin American economic policy-makers undoubtedly have *some* leverage and *some* room for manoeuvre in their negotiations with their foreign creditors. We tend to accept the argument that it would be self-destructive simply to declare an outright moratorium on debt servicing, thereby leaving foreign creditors with nothing to lose from resorting to retaliation. A great deal of uncertainty surrounds the issue of whether or not the physical assets overseas of a defaulting country (its planes, its real estate, etc.) could legally be seized and liquidated for settlement, but the costs of testing this issue are likely in almost all circumstances to outweigh the benefits. It would be a resort of sheer desperation. However, various Latin American governments are in fairly desperate straits and should not hesitate to use that fact as a point of leverage against their creditors. In principle, collective action by a number of debtor governments would seem more productive than isolated confrontations, but it is obvious that at most moments of crisis in debt negotiations the ingredients for international solidarity have so far been lacking. On the whole we expect future debt negotiations to remain essentially country-by-country affairs, although we can envisage some trigger events (e.g. a resort by the USA to a generalised tariff affecting imports from the whole region) that might give rise to an authentic debtors' cartel. Whether the debtor–creditor relationship is national or international in character, we think that the most crucial strategic requirement for the Latin American participants is to formulate a *realistic* strategy that looks capable of restoring some balance to the external accounts within a reasonable timescale. This is far more important than mere resolve to be tough with the bankers. Our assumption here is that hard-pressed creditors who really find the policies of a debtor government to be credible and who are convinced of its determination and solidity, may be persuaded to accept *almost any terms* for repayment rather than publicly to declare a default and take the consequent highly damaging actions. (However, Latin American negotiators must take very carefully into account the views of the bank regulators in the developed countries when formulating a strategy *vis-à-vis* hard-pressed banks.) Thus, in the last analysis, effective and convincing 'internal restructuring' becomes a crucial ingredient of any strategy for reshaping the terms of the international debt relationship.

Quite what such 'internal restructuring' could mean in practice, and how far it would permit a solution not just to survival but also to development in the medium term, is something that can only be answered by returning to the detail of each case study. Clearly this depends vitally on political structure and class relations as much as on economic constraints; hence our attention to policy choices and the interplay between short-term imperative and long-term strategies and needs. For example, given the size of Brazil's capital goods industry, its internal market, its capacity for technological absorption and innovation, its financial bargaining power with a debt which amounts to a substantial percentage of the assets of several lending banks, its relatively consensual political structure, and its comparatively strong and forward-looking state apparatus, its options differ radically from those of, say, Peru, or even more obviously Central America.

At the time of writing, in the autumn of 1985, the need for a drastic reshaping of the international debt relationship is being brought to the front of the policy agenda. As international prospects are seen to darken, the three largest debtors are all concluding that 'good behaviour' has brought no rewards and that very different and more assertive initiatives are imperative. The President of Brazil explained the necessity at the start of this chapter. It will require enormous skill, foresight, patience and good fortune to fulfil his promise.

Notes

1. Thorp and Whitehead (1978).
2. Carneiro neatly deflates the neo-conservative interpretation of the 1982–3 recession by pointing out that in 1984 it was the so-called 'artificial' sector which led the recovery. The recovery was led by metallurgy, chemicals and engineering, responding to export demand. These were some of the most highly protected sectors in the 1970s (see Chapter 3, p. 56).
3. See Buiter (1983) and the bibliography cited there; and Eisner and Pieper (1984). The first exposition for the US case appears to be Siegal (1979). A formal exposition of the methodology is given in Buiter.
4. Eisner and Pieper (1984), p. 17.
5. They are corrected, of course, in the sense that they are presented at constant prices. But the correction to exclude the element of repayment of principal from interest income is not made.
6. There was substantial flight from Peru also, as we know from much qualitative documentation, although the Dornbusch method of calculating it reveals it only in 1984 (possibly because it was balanced in earlier years by inflows of coca dollars!).

References

BUITER, W., 'Measurement of the Public Sector Deficit and Its Implications for Policy Evaluation and Design', IMF Staff Papers, vol. 30, 1983, Washington.
EISNER, R. and PIEPER, P. J., 'A New View of the Federal Debt and Budget Deficits', *American Economic Review*, March 1984.
INTER AMERICAN DEVELOPMENT BANK, *Economic and Social Progress in Latin America*, annual, Washington.
SIEGAL, J. J., 'Inflation-induced Distortions in Government and Private Saving Statistics', *Review of Economics and Statistics*, vol. 61, February 1979, pp. 83–90.
THORP, R. and WHITEHEAD, L. (eds) *Inflation and Stabilisation in Latin America* (London: Macmillan, 1979).

Index